CREATING SOCIALIST WOMEN IN JAPAN

To Anne, Lex, Aaron and Liam

CREATING SOCIALIST WOMEN IN JAPAN

Gender, Labour and Activism, 1900–1937

VERA MACKIE

University of Melbourne

CAMBRIDGE
UNIVERSITY PRESS

PUBLISHED BY THE PRESS SYNDICATE OF THE UNIVERSITY OF CAMBRIDGE
The Pitt Building, Trumpington Street, Cambridge CB2 1RP, United Kingdom

CAMBRIDGE UNIVERSITY PRESS
The Edinburgh Building, Cambridge CB2 2RU, United Kingdom
40 West 20th Street, New York, NY 10011–4211, USA
10 Stamford Road, Oakleigh, Melbourne 3166, Australia

First published 1997

Printed in Hong Kong by Colorcraft

Typeset in Baskerville 10/12 pt

National Library of Australia Cataloguing in Publication data
Mackie, Vera C.
Creating socialist women in Japan : gender, labour and activism, 1900–1937.
Bibliography.
Includes index.
ISBN 0 521 55137 4.
1. Women socialists – Japan – History. 2. Women – Japan –
Social conditions. 3. Feminism – Japan – History. 4. Women
and socialism – Japan – History. I. Title.
335.00820952

Library of Congress Cataloguing in Publication data
Mackie, Vera C.
Creating socialist women in Japan : gender, labour and activism,
1900–1937 / Vera Mackie.
p.   cm.
Includes bibliographical references and index.
ISBN 0 521 55137 4 (alk. paper)
1. Women socialists – Japan – History – 20th century.
2. Feminists – Japan – History – 20th century. I Title.
HX413.M33 1997
305.42'0952–dc21   96–52514

A catalogue record for this book is available from the British Library

ISBN 0 521 55137 4 hardback

Contents

v

Illustrations

Acknowledgments

This book has been completed over a decade in several cities, while working at the University of Adelaide, Swinburne Institute, and the University of Melbourne, with intermittent research trips to Tokyo.

I would like to express my thanks to Stephen Large, whose enthusiasm and encouragement were important in the early stages of this project; Gavan McCormack for his careful comments on successive drafts; and Susan Magarey for her generous advice and support, particularly in discussing questions of feminist theory and the writing of feminist history. More recently, I have benefited from the comments of Gail Lee Bernstein, Janet Hunter, and Tessa Morris-Suzuki.

The staff of the following institutions have provided assistance in locating relevant materials: the Barr Smith Library at the University of Adelaide, Swinburne University of Technology Library, the Baillieu Library at the University of Melbourne, the Fisher Library at the University of Sydney, the National Library of Australia, the National Diet Library, the Meiji Newspaper and Magazine Collection at the University of Tokyo, the Ōhara Social Research Institute at Hōsei University, the Women's Suffrage Centre, Ōya Sōichi Library, and the Women's Research Centre at Ochanomizu University. The staff of the Ōhara Social Research Institute also have my thanks for assistance with locating illustrations and permission to reproduce illustrations.

This research was supported by a University of Adelaide Postgraduate Research Award, and a Japan Foundation Dissertation Fellowship. Thanks to Kano Masanao I was able to be based at Waseda University as a research student for part of 1988. Suzuki Yūko has also generously offered advice, and my debt to her research will be obvious in the frequent citation of her works.

Robin Derricourt (formerly of Cambridge University Press) provided initial encouragement, while Phillipa McGuinness, Jane Farago, and Janet Henderson patiently saw the project to its completion.

The History Department at the University of Melbourne has provided a stimulating and congenial environment for the study of the connections between feminism and socialism. Patricia Grimshaw, Charles Sowerwine, Stuart Macintyre, Antonia Finnane and Maila Stivens have my thanks.

In piecing this work together I have benefited from the support of my family, friends, and colleagues who have provided assistance in many tangible and intangible ways. All my friends in Australia and Japan – too many to mention here – have my gratitude for their support.

CHAPTER 1

Introduction

The Socialist Future. Cover of the socialist women's newspaper *Sekai Fujin* (*Women of the World*) No. 32, January 1909, illustrating the eclectic roots of Japanese socialism. Note the allegorical female figure, drawing on European conventions of socialist iconography, combined with banners bearing the Sino-Japanese characters for 'community' and 'freedom', a scene which is illuminated by the dawn of the socialist future.

In 1885, a young woman was imprisoned on charges of treason. She was one of a group of liberal activists who had planned to take explosives to Korea in support of the independence movement. While she was imprisoned, a fellow member of this movement wrote a pamphlet which eulogized her as a 'martyr to the liberal movement'.[1] It was not until the 1900s that she published her own account of her life, tracing her involvement in the liberal movement and her contact with the fledgling Japanese socialist movement in the early twentieth century.

The woman's name was Fukuda Hideko.[2] Her autobiography, *Warawa no Hanseigai* (*My Life so Far*), was published in 1904. A publisher's advertisement treated the book as a melodramatic account of an exciting life:

> The heroic woman Kageyama Hideko, who participated in the famous Osaka Incident with Ōi Kentarō and others, is the author of this book. How did she become renowned in her youth as a literary woman in her home town? How did she come to be involved in the Ōsaka treason trial? How did she spend her three years in prison? How did she part from her lover and come to know her husband? What kind of life did she lead as a wife in extreme poverty, as a loving mother in grief, and as a widow with many regrets? This book describes the vicissitudes and changes, the complications and entanglements of this great tragedy.[3]

However, I am interested in this book for other reasons. Fukuda's autobiography may be seen as an extended answer to the question of why a young woman from a low-ranking samurai family would rebel, become involved with the extremist elements of the liberal movement, and even after her release from imprisonment identify herself with the socialists – a group whose ideas were beyond the pale of acceptable political discourse in Meiji Japan. While Fukuda's autobiography explains the rebellion of one woman, in quite individualistic terms, the questions raised by her attempt to forge a political identity – to create herself as a socialist woman – are relevant to a succession of individuals and groups in early twentieth-century Japan. One woman's account of her development as an activist thus sets the scene for my discussion of the texts of a whole movement of socialist women, and provides a way of introducing the questions which shape this study.

Warawa no Hanseigai has been referred to as 'the first woman's autobiography' in modern Japan.[4] Although there is room for discussion about the definition of autobiography in early twentieth-century Japan, we can take the point that this was considered to be an important and distinctive text in 1904. Fukuda's writing style reveals her own classical education, and implies a highly literate readership.[5] Her acknowledged reference points, however, do not lie within the

Japanese literary heritage, which includes women's poetic diaries of the Heian period,[6] the autobiographies of such Meiji intellectuals as Fukuzawa Yukichi,[7] or the blurring of autobiography and fiction in modern Japanese novels.[8] Rather she refers to Benjamin Franklin's autobiography,[9] a translated biography of Joan of Arc,[10] and the Russian Nihilists.[11] Fukuda's autobiography may also be placed in the context of other genres of socialist writing. The publications of the early socialist group, the *Heiminsha* (Commoners' Society), with which Fukuda was acquainted by the time she wrote her autobiography, regularly published statements by socialists on their awakening to socialist ideals, under the generic title 'How I Became a Socialist'.[12]

After an introduction which explains her reasons for writing this autobiography, the narrative commences with an account of Fukuda as an exemplary student. Although she was praised by parents and educational authorities for her scholarly achievements, her classmates scorned her because of her tomboyishness. They called her *magai*, or *magaimono*, which has the meaning of 'fake' or 'artificial'. In this situation it refers to a woman pretending to be a man.

> On the way to school, I was always taunted by the naughty brats . . .! Only now can I see how appropriate their taunt was. I really was strange in those days. If we understand *magaimono* to mean something which appears to be what it is not – to make horses' hoof look like tortoiseshell, or to make the new 'rubber'[13] look like ivory – we can see how witty it was to call me by that name. Although it embarrasses me now, at that time I was known as a lively child. It goes without saying that I behaved like a tomboy in everyday life, and while studying I could not even spare the time to put my hair up. I liked reading books so much, that until the age of sixteen I wore my hair short and parted in the middle. Even my clothes were like boys' clothes . . .[14]

In her account of this incident, Fukuda presents the ambivalence of the young woman who found scholarship more important than the conventions of femininity. The autobiography displays a doubled perspective, with the mature author positioned at a distance from her younger self. In the passage quoted above, femininity is portrayed as something natural (but also beautiful and valuable?) through the metaphors of ivory and tortoiseshell. For a woman to appear mannish is fakery – like attempting to replace ivory and tortoiseshell with rubber or horse's hoof. Although the author now appears to identify with the children who are unsettled by the blurring of gender boundaries – 'someone who was not quite male and not quite female' – she also remembers the physical expression of her distress at the children's taunting – 'Whenever I look back on this, I can still feel my back soaked with sweat'.[15]

Further distancing from the young tomboy is achieved in a later passage, when the mature Fukuda is confronted with a young woman, dressed in masculine style, who has come to 'apprentice' herself to Fukuda. Fukuda, however, advises the young woman to wear more conventional dress, and relates the story of her subsequent marriage. This episode suggests that there were other women who shared her ambivalence concerning gender identity. Even before the publication of her autobiography, Fukuda was a well-known figure, because of her involvement in the Ōsaka Incident. Articles about Fukuda had appeared in newspapers, a biographical pamphlet had appeared in 1887, and Fukuda also describes visiting a theatrical performance in Okayama, which portrayed her participation in the Ōsaka Incident.[16]

Despite her ambivalence, Fukuda eventually conforms with the expectations placed on her, and submits to the disciplines of tea ceremony and flower arranging prescribed by her mother.

> Eventually, when I started to grow up, I became embarrassed to wear men's clothes, and it was in the summer of my seventeenth year that I started to grow my hair long, and started to wear my hair up like other women.[17]

Thus, *Warawa no Hanseigai* portrays one woman's ambivalence about accepted notions of gender identity, and how this ambivalence about femininity affected possible forms of political activity.

Fukuda also discusses more conventional political issues. She questions the repressive power of the Meiji State, which she has experienced at first hand, and comments in several places on the arbitrary nature of this power.[18] On the occasion of her release from prison (thanks to an amnesty in celebration of the promulgation of the Meiji Constitution), she comments wryly:

> So, the prison governor informed me that, thanks to the amnesty, my criminal record would be cleared, and I would be free from today. He gave the advice that I should, in future, devote myself even more wholeheartedly to the nation. On hearing this, a strange feeling came over me. Until yesterday – even until earlier today – I had been a traitor, but in the space of an hour I had been transformed into a patriot . . .[19]

Despite her ironic distancing from the concept of patriotism in this passage, until now she has used this concept as justification for her illegal activities. In several places she contrasts her own actions 'for the nation' with those who would act out of selfish or shallow motives.[20] Her criticism is directed both at government which is carried out for the benefit of a few individuals, and at some of her liberal comrades who would betray their cause for shallow motives. Like most other political thinkers of the Meiji period, Fukuda's political discourse is shaped by nationalism, a value which was almost beyond criticism in Meiji Japan.

By the time of the publication of her autobiography, Fukuda identifies herself as a socialist. There is, however, no clear espousal of a socialist political strategy. Rather, the vocabulary and slogans of socialist rhetoric become apparent. In addition to complaints about the repressive power of the Meiji State, she now sees 'capitalists' and 'imperialists' as her enemies:

> Now I intend to oppose the monopoly of capital with all my might, and devote my attention to saving the unfortunate poor . . .[21]

> I was pleased to hear the ideas of the socialists, and eventually came to abhor the words of the imperialists who are bent on their own self interest and personal gain . . .[22]

In 1904, socialist thought was still in its earliest days in Japan, and socialist women had not yet articulated a clear philosophy. Some of the issues of concern to socialist women would later be addressed in the socialist women's paper, *Sekai Fujin* (*Women of the World*, 1907–1909), under Fukuda's editorship; and in other writings by socialist women. But the problem of how to be a woman, and a political activist, was to be addressed in various ways over the next few decades.

Fukuda came to political maturity at a time when discussion of liberalism was flourishing in Japanese society, and the development of capitalist relations was accompanied by the development of modern notions of individualism. Although the Meiji State failed to embrace liberal ideas in any real sense, the discourses of liberalism and individualism held resonance for the intellectuals of early twentieth-century Japan, and these ideas were reflected in the development of new genres of fiction, autobiography, and political writings. Autobiography is a genre which has been linked with modern notions of individualism in the European context, and it is perhaps unsurprising that we should see the development of this genre in Meiji Japan.[23] Fukuda's autobiography may be seen as an attempt to resolve the tension between becoming a woman and aspiring to a modern notion of selfhood which could include participation in public political activity, like many comparable European women's autobiographies.[24] However, such writing must also be understood as being shaped by specific discourses of nationalism and politics, and specific constructions of masculinity and femininity in the context of Meiji Japan. While men and women were addressed in gender-specific ways by nationalist discourse, many resisted their construction as 'imperial subjects', and attempted to explain their situation through the conceptual tools provided by liberal, socialist and feminist thought.

These gendered constructions of subjecthood are explored in more detail in Chapter two of this book.

Many activists attempted to find new ways of imagining relationships between individuals, and theorizing relationships between individuals and the State. In the early socialist movement of the 1900s, people eagerly read and discussed socialist and feminist ideas, and experimented with new forms of social relationships in their everyday lives. This is the milieu where Fukuda's autobiography was written, and her own account of her life reflects the early socialists' experimentation with lifestyles and political practices.

The members of the left-wing movement were intensely interested in the connections between personal relationships and political practices.[25] Fukuda's own life reflects the limitations of such experimentation. Many men and women in the socialist movement were unable to transcend implicit notions of gender identity, and women continued to be constructed as 'wives' and 'helpmates' within the socialist movement. This division of labour was also reflected in the area of political philosophy, with women being addressed in articles on free love, and on socialist forms of marriage and the family, while men were presumed to be interested in more narrowly theoretical discussions of the class struggle. The gendered forms of political participation and political thought in the early socialist movement will be explored in Chapter three.

Fukuda also attempts to come to terms with the experience of a sexed body, and to reconcile the contradictory identities of 'woman' and 'political activist'. Her account of her political development is punctuated by accounts of her first menstruation and other physical developments. She describes 'a certain physiological change', the late onset of menstruation, and links this with her ambivalent gender identity.[26]

In her account of this 'coming of age', Fukuda mixes these physical changes with an account of her tomboyish behaviour as a young woman: 'I was, from birth, rather unrefined like a man, and did not in the least possess any of the feminine graces'. The account of her physical maturation is followed by a discussion of the qualities of her 'ideal husband'. According to the structure of her autobiographical text, physical maturation prefigures an interest in matters romantic. This does not, however, eclipse her political ideals. She had thought that her ideal husband should be 'a great man, with a distinguished reputation', and had first become interested in her fiancé Kobayashi Kusuo, because of shared political ideals.[27] Later, in her account of 'becoming a mother', it is the physical manifestations of her condition that she initially dwells on, before recounting the difficulties of her relationship with her lover Ōi Kentarō.[28]

Fukuda's successors would attempt to bring together an interest in the specificities of women's experiences of the reproductive body, with discussions on the forms of social policy necessary to deal with women's reproductive capacity. A series of parallel, and often contradictory, discourses on motherhood from the 1910s and 1920s will be explored in Chapter four.

At the age of sixteen, when a marriage proposal is made to her family, Fukuda realises the economic vulnerability of women. On her refusal of this proposal her parents explain the state of the family finances to her, and thus the good economic reasons for going through with the marriage. In Fukuda's case, her education means that she can work as a teacher and contribute to the family budget, but this episode prompts Fukuda as narrator to reflect on the situation of women:

> Oh! I thought, how many women are there who, in this way, marry a husband for whom they feel no love, who simply marry ritualistically and mechanically, because of pressure from their families. From this time on, a wish was etched into my mind, the wish to find a way for such unhappy women to live in independence and autonomy.[29]

These thoughts, while attributed to the sixteen-year-old Hideko, are related by the mature narrator who has experienced the economic vulnerability of women. Fukuda bore Ōi Kentarō's son while living in a de facto relationship. She bore three more sons to her husband Fukuda Tomosaku, but was widowed while her children were young.

The young Fukuda is inspired by the message of feminist Kishida Toshiko, a member of the Freedom and Popular Rights Movement, who visits Fukuda's home town in Okayama, and gives speeches on women's rights. Kishida's visit is the impetus for the formation of a women's group which meets regularly, and gives the local women a monthly forum for discussing political issues.[30] Fukuda is shocked at the government's interference in a Liberal Party gathering, and the subsequent closing of her family's school. This is her first experience of government repression, and it is soon after the closure of the school that she decides to travel to Tokyo, to continue her studies and follow her political interests.[31]

The relationship between education, work, and women's independence is a recurrent theme in Fukuda's autobiography, as several other commentators have noted.[32] For Fukuda, work meant primarily intellectual labour as a teacher, writer, and editor, although she had experience of other kinds of work at different junctures in her life. In Tokyo, she survived for a time on the typically 'feminine' jobs of hairdressing, laundry and sewing, proclaiming that all kinds of work were equally sacred and honourable. While joining in preparation for the Ōsaka Incident, she played the part of housewife in the comrades' household which was disguised as a students' boarding house. Her account of this time suggests she was relatively unused to such a role, although she takes credit for thinking of this way of camouflaging their activities. In prison, she joins in sewing with the other prisoners, but is also set apart from the other women in her role as teacher. In this environment, she comes into contact with women who have survived by begging and scavenging, and women for whom the threat of being sold into prostitution is a reality.[33]

While arguing for women's economic independence through productive labour, she speaks from the position of a relatively privileged intellectual. In her plans for teaching women self-sufficiency, she generally focuses on manual labour such as sewing or handcrafts, noting that, while there has been an expansion in education for women, existing forms of women's education generally fail to contribute to women's self-sufficiency. However, while arguing for a change in the economic determinants of relationships between men and women, her view of women's work is shaped by dominant constructions of class and gender in Meiji Japan. Her proposal is to teach women to produce embroidered silk handkerchiefs – a potential export product.[34]

In Fukuda's other relationships with women there is generally some class difference involved, with Fukuda cast as the benevolent provider of charity, knowledge, or educational assistance. An encounter with a female beggar is an opportunity to display Fukuda's benevolence and sensibility, but the beggar also serves as a mirror which reflects Fukuda's own feelings of loneliness and pathos, when she is left alone in an inn while her comrades visit tea houses, using money raised to support their mission:

> Once, when I was alone in the second-floor room of the inn and feeling depressed, I opened the sliding door and gazed down at a boat loaded with trash. On it was a beggar woman, with a child, two or three years old, strapped to her back. She was rummaging through the trash, picking out waste paper and putting it into her basket . . . I was overwhelmed at this sight and thought, 'Alas, I never realised how pitiful life could be. I am poor, but I am certainly better off than this beggar.'
>
> I was overcome with pity for the mother and child and called out to them from the second floor. Taking out a fifty-sen note, a small fortune for me then, I attached a weight to it and threw it down to the mother. She treated it as if it were a gift from heaven. She picked it up timidly, . . . as though she were afraid to take it, and I called out to her and told her to use it for the child . . .[35]

Even a professed socialist was likely to see class differences as 'natural'. While Fukuda feels solidarity with women from a similar class background, in her relationship with the beggar, the barriers between women of different classes are preserved. These barriers are dramatized by the spatial distance between the two women, as the intellectual Fukuda looks down on the working-class woman from the second floor of the inn.

The innkeeper's comment on the suitability of contacts between the respectable lady and the beggar are presented without comment or disclaimer:

> The landlady stopped me and said, 'Was it you who gave some money to a beggar woman?' When I nodded, she said, 'A moment ago the woman with a child on her back came here with tears in her eyes, saying that a woman guest had thrown some money to her and she had come to thank her. She asked me for your name. I didn't think it was wise to let a beggar have your name, so I told her I would convey her message to you, and sent her off . . .'
>
> Charity rewards the giver, and not the receiver. I felt better then than I had for days. Then I forgot about the incident like a haze that passes before one's eyes. Only later – like a scene from a novel – would I again meet this beggar woman where I least expected to.[36]

In these scenes, Fukuda was grappling with the question of class consciousness. Intellectual women faced the question of how to bridge the gap between themselves and working women, and find ways of using their understanding of the mechanisms of class exploitation in order to work for social change. For working-class women, the question was how to forge solidarity when the conditions of work fostered fragmentation and alienation, while constructions of masculinity and femininity worked against the development of a common identity which could bring together working men and women. Questions of class consciousness and workers' identities will be explored in Chapter five, in the context of attempts to organize women workers in groups which addressed their demands to employers in the 1920s and 1930s. The consciousness of an identity as worker was often a necessary stage in socialist women's transformation into activists.

Throughout her autobiography, Fukuda is conscious of the tension involved in being a woman, but also trying to be politically active. She constantly refers to the fact that she is a woman:

> *Even I, a woman*, swore that I would not give up until I had found a way of getting rid of such bad government and evil laws.[37] [emphasis added]

After her arrest, she is sent to remand in Ōsaka, and is conscious that she is the focus of public attention because she is a woman:

> After interrogation by the police, I was to be sent to Osaka. At about eight or nine o'clock at night, we left the police station, tethered together.

Although I may look like I could move briskly, with my woman's gait I tended to get left behind, and was dragged along on the rope until I somehow made it to the wharf, where we were transferred to the ship. Seeing that we were guarded by police, the other passengers stared at us as if thunderstruck, *but it was me – a woman – whom they stared at with rounded eyes* . . .[38] [emphasis added]

At other times it is the supposed weakness of the female body she refers to:

Even though I may have a weak body, when it comes to patriotic fervour, I am second to no man.[39] [emphasis added]

Despite this protestation of physical weakness, however, she can assert women's moral superiority over men who frequent brothels in the midst of a political crisis.[40] This was one of the causes of her disillusion with her Liberal Party comrades, along with her dissatisfaction with the co-optation of many leading liberals by the Meiji government.

Here I would like to make a confession. Not only do I deplore the arrogance of the nobility and the rich merchants, I also abhor the failures and the frivolity of the comrades in the Liberal Party, with whom I shared matters of life and death. *Even I, a woman,* would never as long as I lived, give up the idea that I was acting for the country, and it was this one idea which guided me.[41] [emphasis added]

For any activist in late nineteenth- and early twentieth-century Japan, there was the problem of the lack of suitable models for political activity, particularly oppositional political activity. This was true for both male and female activists. It might have been possible to search for models in the peasant rebellions which had erupted in the latter half of the Tokugawa period and the early Meiji period, for accounts of these rebellions were published in the 1880s. But such accounts provided few examples of heroic women. The women who appear in accounts of peasant rebellions are presented as grieving for lost relatives, or martyring themselves for particularistic family ties rather than acting for the sake of the community as their male counterparts were described as doing.[42]

The most vivid image of a political activist was the *shishi* – a member of the group of samurai who had overthrown the Shogunate and engineered the Restoration of the authority of the Emperor in the 1860s. Although male activists could identify with the bravery and resolution of the *shishi*, the connection with samurai values and the restoration of imperial authority meant that the *shishi* was an ambiguous symbol for male socialist activists.[43] This was even truer for a woman activist of the time.

If Fukuda could not attain complete identification with masculine heroes, then another solution was to find a suitable female model. Although she refers to the intellectual influence of her liberal feminist predecessor Kishida Toshiko, it is the figure of Joan of Arc which is invoked regularly by Fukuda and other commentators. Joan of Arc was a suitably heroic woman, but also a suitably androgynous model for a young woman who had such difficulty in coming to terms with prescriptive notions of femininity.[44]

Fukuda's description of her own political activity and interests makes use of the language of bravery, resolution, and determination, but her identification with the *shishi* can never be complete. Although she refers to her younger self as a *jo-shishi* (female *shishi*), the adult Fukuda's use of this phrase is distanced from the feelings of the young patriot. Although the issue which prompts her political activity is the issue of Korean independence, her consciousness of injustice is also aroused by the lack of political rights for the majority of Japanese people, and the inequalities between men and women in Japanese society.[45]

However, although the adult Fukuda seems to have made some accommodation to the expectations of suitable feminine behaviour, she has not given up her resolve to participate in political activity. Her resolve to 'fight' for various causes is reiterated in several places, and she now has a clearer idea of the enemy she is fighting against:

The [way I have travelled] has been one obstacle after another. I have always been fighting, and have never once been disheartened by setbacks. I have fought in the past; I am fighting in the present; and as long as blood flows in my veins, I intend to keep fighting. My vocation is in fighting, in the struggle against human inequity. On realizing that this is my vocation, I can bear the pain of recollection, and can even look back nostalgically at past sufferings.

The only thing that will relieve the pain of past sufferings is further sufferings. According to my vocation, I will fight against my own sins and the sins of the world.

In the past I became excited by the cries of those calling for popular rights and freedom, those who were enraged by the monopoly over political power. Now I intend to oppose the monopoly of capital with all my might, and devote my attention to saving the unfortunate poor . . .[46]

The text closes with a plan to educate women for self-sufficiency, an ending which may remind the reader of the opening descriptions of Fukuda's own education. We are introduced to Fukuda as a star pupil in the opening, and in the final pages we are told of Fukuda's plans to teach women useful crafts as a means to self-sufficiency. Although there is no simple sense of narrative closure – we see Fukuda embarking on a new venture rather than showing a sense of arrival or completion – there is a sense of symmetry.[47]

In such texts as Fukuda's *Warawa no Hanseigai* we can see the beginnings of a tradition of feminist and socialist activism by women in Japan.[48] Fukuda had been inspired to participate in political activism by the speeches of her liberal predecessor, Kishida Toshiko, and later feminists were able to refer back to Fukuda's writings in their own attempts to construct a political subjectivity.[49] Chapter six focuses on the ways in which women came to construct themselves as activists, and from this position address their demands to the State. In framing strategies to address the State with their demands, activists also came to understand the militarist and imperialist nature of the Japanese State.

I have chosen to introduce this book with an analysis of Fukuda Hideko's autobiography for several reasons. Fukuda was writing at a time when socialist thought was first being articulated in Japan, and discussion of socialist understandings of the 'woman question' was just beginning. Thus, this is a useful entry point for discussion of the relationship between socialism and feminism in early twentieth-century Japan. Her account also traces her participation in the Movement for Freedom and Popular Rights (*Jiyū Minken Undō*), one of the intellectual precursors of Japanese socialism and feminism. In addition, the basic problematic of her text, how to resolve the disjunction between being a woman and aspiring to political activism, was a problem to be addressed implicitly and explicitly by other socialist women in early twentieth-century Japan. Fukuda's autobiography may be seen as a liberal gesture – displaying an implicit faith in individualism. Other writings of socialist women would grapple with similar issues, but would also attempt to address the question of class consciousness with varying degrees of success. Implicit in the writings of Fukuda and others is the search for a 'speaking position' from which to articulate a feminist consciousness. In order to explore this proposition, my narrative of socialist women's writings and activities will be organized around some of these possible 'speaking positions'.

According to the dominant discourses on women in Meiji Japan, women were positioned as imperial subjects, as wives, and as mothers. As I will discuss in Chapter two, women as imperial subjects were explicitly excluded from political participation. Some women, however, attempted to gain a voice by speaking as 'wives' or as 'mothers', as I discuss in Chapters three and four. However, the reality for most women was that they were engaged in various kinds of labour – domestic labour, agricultural labour, factory labour, or sexual labour.

Was it possible for women to speak as 'workers'? In Chapter five I will discuss the disjunction between being a 'woman' and being a 'worker', and the gendered construction of work and class consciousness. The tensions generated by the disjunctions between these positions led many women to political activism, and in Chapter six I discuss socialist women's attempts to engage with State institutions and to speak with a political voice as 'activists'. Finally, in Chapter seven, I close with some reflections on the process of imagining exploitation and liberation, repression and resistance, in socialist women's writings. But first it is necessary to make some further comments on the methodological and theoretical concerns of this study.

The socialist women's writings analysed in this book mainly come from the years 1900 to 1937, but in order to understand the context in which these women were writing, it is necessary to understand the political context of Meiji Japan, for the political institutions, conventions, and practices established in the first half of the Meiji period were to provide the context for political activity in Japan right up to the end of the Second World War. In the years from 1868 to 1898, Japan created all of the machinery of a modern nation-state – a Constitution, a new legal code and policing system, a system of compulsory education, capitalist industry, and an army and navy.

As part of this process, there was extensive discussion of the family, which was to form a crucial link in the chain of loyalty from subject to Emperor. Despite the diversity of marriage and inheritance practices prevalent in pre-Meiji Japan,[50] it was the most conservative form of patriarchal family based on primogeniture which was privileged in the Meiji Civil Code of 1898.[51] This (literally) patriarchal form of the family was dressed up in the ideology of 'good wives and wise mothers' which idealized women's contribution to the family.[52] While intellectuals discussed 'good wives and wise mothers', women came to comprise at least 60 per cent of the industrial labour force,[53] and other women were engaged in agricultural or domestic labour. The major export industries – silk, and later cotton – were dependent on the labour of young women from rural areas.

In Japan, as in many Western countries, economists and social scientists have tended to neglect the importance of women's labour in the early stages of industrialization. Japan's later expansion into heavy industry was largely based on capital built up in the first stages of light industry. Since the conditions of women's industrial labour were extremely exploitative, it is hardly surprising that spontaneous strike activity erupted as early as 1886. (The first textile mill had been established in 1872.[54]) This early strike activity was carried out by female textile workers, without the support of an organized union movement.

The subsequent failure of the organized labour movement to organize female textile workers on a mass basis is one of the continuing controversies of Japanese labour history. The socialist women's writings to be analysed here include discussion of political strategies for mobilizing women workers in union activity.

The Meiji period is often presented as a period of intense interest in 'foreign' ideologies, as both the élites of the new society and their opponents seized on the theories of absolutism and social Darwinism, liberalism and natural rights theory in order to justify a variety of political positions and decisions. It is also true of the early days of socialism in Japan that European socialist works were eagerly read and discussed, interpreted and translated into the Japanese context. However, I am less interested in the 'foreign' origins of Japanese socialist thought, than in the ways in which these sets of ideas were seen to be useful in explaining the situation of workers in the context of an industrializing Japan.

The first socialist groups were established in the late 1890s.[55] The members of these groups would go on to become leaders in the socialist, anarchist, and labour movements. An interest in labour conditions was also promoted by journalists' examination of the situation of the working classes. However, the Peace Regulations of 1887 gave the police powers to ban mass meetings, and the Public Peace Police Law (*Chian Keisatsu Hō*) of 1900 was to give police even more extensive powers. Women, minors, police and members of the armed forces were prohibited from engaging in political activity, and incitement to strike activity was banned.

Women were active in such groups as the *Heiminsha* (Commoners' Society) from its inception in 1903. They attempted to give a socialist critique of their position through these groups, and through separate groups and journals directed at socialist women. The first of the major labour organizations, the *Yūaikai* (Friendly Society), was established in 1912, and developed into the *Sōdōmei* (General Federation of Labour). In the 1920s, socialist women tried to reach working women through the women's departments of unions and the left-wing political parties which were established after the enactment of Universal Manhood Suffrage in 1925. It is difficult to follow the progress of socialist and feminist thought through the political repression of the 1930s, but we can say that there was an active tradition of socialist activity by women until the 1930s, at least. It is the conjunction of socialism and feminism, through the writings of these socialist women, that I will examine in this study.

Several scholars have written about the socialist and labour movements in what is increasingly being referred to as 'imperial

Japan'.[56] These scholars have been interested in the development of liberalism, socialism, and the labour movement. Large,[57] Totten[58] and Gordon[59] have studied labour, anarchist, and social democratic movements while Bowen[60] has directed attention to the early movement for 'Freedom and Popular Rights'. However, until quite recently, in both Japanese- and English-language scholarship on the early socialist and labour movements, the question of the gendering of political participation has been relatively neglected. Many English-language historians of the labour movement have ignored women workers completely, ignoring the nineteenth-century strike activity by women, and dismissing the possibility of organizing women workers.[61] For others, women workers have been seen as figures of pathos. Robins-Mowry, in her history of Japanese women, portrays these women workers as victims, singing 'pathetic little songs to express their unhappiness'.[62] The limitations of Japanese-language writings on women in the socialist and labour movements have been surveyed by Suzuki Yūko.[63]

Other writers, such as Kidd, Sievers, and Tsurumi[64] have re-examined the documents of such pioneers as Hosoi Wakizō, Katayama Sen and Yokoyama Gennosuke[65] in an attempt to understand the failure of the early twentieth-century Japanese union movement to organize women workers.

Until recently, most accounts of women's political activity in early twentieth-century Japan concentrated on the Seitōsha (the Bluestocking Society) and their journal Seitō (Bluestocking) which appeared from 1911 to 1916.[66] There have also been several studies of individual Seitō members.[67] This group was significant, not least for the ability of such writers as Yosano Akiko and Hiratsuka Raichō to call forth an emotional response in their readers. The 'Bluestockings' concentrated on issues of love, sexuality, and personal fulfilment, and paid little attention to issues concerning women's labour. However, in debates on prostitution, and abortion, some writers attempted to link sexuality and reproduction with the State and political structures. Around 1918, several former Seitō members engaged in a debate on State support for single and widowed mothers, which also linked reproduction with political structures. Several former members of the Bluestocking Society went on to engage in feminist activism and labour activism.

Seitō was, however, predated (and postdated) by socialist women's activity. There were at least three socialist women's journals before the appearance of Seitō: Nijūseiki no Fujin (Twentieth Century Woman: 1904), Suiito Hoomu (Sweet Home: 1904), and Sekai Fujin (Women of the World, which appeared between 1907 and 1909). Sekai Fujin only lasted for two years, succumbing to government suppression, like so much progressive journalism of the time, but women continued to be active in the socialist and labour movements, and at times formed separate groups such as the *Sekirankai* (Red Wave Society) and *Yōkakai* (Eighth Day Society). By the late 1920s unions and left-wing political parties all had separate women's divisions or affiliated women's leagues (necessitated by the political regulations restricting women's political activity), and we can trace the development of the political positions of socialist women through the publications of these organizations.[68]

Within Japan, there is a tradition of scholarship on women dating to the 1930s and 1940s. Inoue Kiyoshi's Marxist-influenced history of Japanese women first appeared in 1948.[69] Takamure Itsue's series of works on women's history started to appear in 1938.[70] More recently, feminist scholars within Japan have been engaged in a project of reclaiming Japanese women's history, through oral history projects, and making the writings of early Japanese feminists accessible to researchers through document collections and reprints. There are now several multi-volume studies of Japanese women's history.[71] In general, however, English language scholarship has been slow to catch up with this tradition.[72]

When women's experience was included in some early English language scholarship on Japan, it was often subsumed under the heading of 'the social costs of Japanese development', with 'the status of women' being utilized as a marker of Japanese societal development.[73] However, from the 1970s a series of studies appeared which tended to treat 'women' as a homogeneous category,[74] which could be described in unitary terms.[75] Other studies have been concerned with specific groups of women.[76] An interest in the history of Japanese feminism has been apparent more recently, with several writers adopting a biographical approach to the history of feminism, an approach which has also been favoured by writers on other aspects of Japanese political history.[77] As yet, however, there has been no full-length study of the activities of socialist women in Japan. Sharley Conroy Ushioda's articles on Fukuda Hideko[78] and Sharon Sievers' chapter on early socialist women[79] are useful introductory works, while Mikiso Hane's collection of memoirs by Japanese women makes the words of some activists available in English for the first time.[80] Stephen Large's article on Tanno Setsu and Itō Noe and their partners Watanabe Masanosuke and Ōsugi Sakae examines the links between personal philosophy and political life.[81] E. P. Tsurumi's study of anarchist historian Takamure Itsue touches on Takamure's debates with socialist women in the journals *Nyonin Geijutsu* and *Fujin Sensen*.[82]

Some more recent studies can be situated at the borders of women's history and labour history. E. P. Tsurumi exposes some of the *lacunae* of accepted descriptions of Japanese labour history. Tsurumi challenges the accepted picture of textile workers as 'docile and submissive', using statistics on the transience of the textile labour force to argue that many women in fact ran away, refusing to submit to intolerable conditions.[83] By quoting workers' songs and other sources, Tsurumi shows that these women were far from accepting of their lot, and challenges us to find alternative explanations for the failure to organize women workers.[84]

Similar questions have been raised with respect to European labour history, as explained by Anna Davin:

> We can find women on strike and industrially militant – and when we don't we can look for reasons in the types and conditions and patterns of their work, not in the female character. Still more important, we can extend the conventional definition of political activity (as taking place in parliament and party or even unions and picket lines) and show that it is to be found wherever people combine to resist extortion and exploitation, in the community as well as at the workplace, and that in such struggles women have always been prominent . . .[85]

Davin argues for a feminist history which, in attempting to make sense of women's experience, challenges accepted notions of what constitutes political activity. Politics 'goes beyond mere description of elections and political parties'.[86] In attempting to explain and describe women's political activities we may also be prompted to rethink concepts of domination and subordination, exploitation and resistance, repression and liberation.

Any study of socialism and feminism must also confront the problem of the relationship between systems of domination based on gender and on class. Ever since the first uneasy conjunction of socialism and feminism, there have been debates on the relationship between class oppression and the 'woman question'. Early socialist discussions of the 'woman question' tended to subsume sexual exploitation under class exploitation, and tried to explain the subordination of women by analysing their relationship to the means of production. Socialist revolution, it was argued, would also improve the situation of women. As Sally Alexander has pointed out, anyone familiar with the early literature on socialism and the 'woman question' is used to hearing these questions framed with respect to certain dichotomies:

> The dichotomies – Women and Labour, Sex and Class, Feminism and Socialism have been the intimate inhabitants of both my psyche and my intellectual work (if the two can be separated) as they have been for many women of my political generation.[87]

More recent views of the relationship between class and gender reject any search for origins. While keeping class and gender conceptually distinct, such theorists argue that the two systems are mutually constitutive. These writers are often interested in the ideological and symbolic dimensions of class and gender. Joan Scott, in her work on French labour history, attempts to go beyond the surface meanings of words to consider the structure of texts, and the meanings of masculinity and femininity. 'Historically specific, normative definitions of gender', argues Scott, 'were reproduced and embedded in the culture of the French working class.'[88]

Such a perspective is also relevant to an understanding of the early Japanese labour movement. Implicit in early labour movement rhetoric was the notion that the categories of 'worker' and 'woman' were mutually exclusive. Women were thus denied a consciousness of their class interests as 'workers', and male workers were thus denied solidarity with female workers, as I discuss in Chapter five.

Class and gender also interact with notions of race and ethnicity. 'Japanese' identities were constructed with reference to perceptions of European, American, and other Asian identities, often implying hierarchical notions of national identities. 'Japaneseness' was constructed and experienced in class-specific and gender-specific ways. Japanese workers and intellectuals also considered their relationships with workers of other countries, at times expressing solidarity, at times expressing support for imperialism.

Any consideration of groups or individuals who take an oppositional stance in society must also confront the concept of agency, and the relationship between individual and society.[89] How do we reconcile the recognition that ideology is to some extent structurally determined with the desire to ascribe to human subjects some degree of control over their destiny – the notion of historical *agency*? If agency refers to individuals' actions, their attempts to gain control over their own destinies, then subjectivity refers to the attributes ascribed to these individuals: intentionality, desire, and awareness.[90]

Feminist historians have been particularly interested in the construction of the 'gendered' subject. Sally Alexander, drawing on Lacanian psychoanalysis, has outlined the relationship between the gendered subject and political ideologies:

> Against marxism's claims that the determining social relationship is between wage labour and capital, exploiter and exploited, proletarian and capitalist, feminism insists on the recognition that subjective identity is also constructed as masculine or feminine, placing the individual as husband or wife, mother or father, son or daughter, and so on. And these sub-jectivities travel both into political language and forms of political action, where they may be severed from class or class interests, indeed may be at odds with them.[91]

More recently, some feminist historians writing from a postcolonial or Third World perspective have tried to re-theorize questions of agency and subjectivity.[92] These writers reject any overly deterministic view of the relationship between subjectivity, agency and societal structures. Agency is often seen to reside in a community of people united in a common struggle, rather than the individual of liberal humanist political discourse.[93] Chandra Mohanty, drawing on Foucauldian theories of power and discourse, and the work of feminist sociologist Dorothy Smith, argues for a new conceptualization of power, which attempts to go beyond liberal and Marxist views of political activity.[94] Mohanty brings a new perspective to questions of subjectivity and agency, focusing on the role of writing in constructing a political identity. She argues that:

> ... the very practice of remembering and rewriting leads to the formation of politicized consciousness and self-identity. Writing often becomes the context through which new political identities are forged. It becomes a space for struggle and contestation about reality itself.[95]

In my analysis of the writings of socialist women in early twentieth-century Japan, I will be interested in the role of writing in forging 'new political identities' for these women. Mohanty argues that writing is crucial in 'the redefinition of the very possibilities of political consciousness and action'.[96] However, a concentration on textual analysis need not suggest a neglect of the description of more conventional forms of political struggle. Rather, I would agree with the assertion that:

> Feminist struggles are waged on at least two simultaneous, interconnected levels: an ideological, discursive level which addresses questions of representation (womanhood/femininity), and a material, experiential, daily-life level which focuses on the micropolitics of work, home, family, sexuality, etc.[97]

I will thus be interested in analysing the representations of femininity and masculinity, and the constructions of gender and class to be found in the texts of socialist women, but I will also be interested in linking these representations with the micropolitics of everyday life, and the specific political struggles engaged in by these women. I will also use the terms 'activist' and 'activism' to describe a particular identity achieved by those women who united in group activity in order to attempt to change their situation.[98]

From this perspective I will explore the speaking positions available to socialist women in early twentieth-century Japan, the discursive strategies employed in their writings, and the political strategies they envisaged for changing their society. I argue that the study of social movements must consider not only theories and organizational strategies, but also the process of imagining new political possibilities. My analysis is informed by a methodology which locates representations 'within the contested field of discursive formations'.[99] Discourse may be understood as 'a particular form of language with its own rules and conventions and the institutions within which the discourse is produced and circulated',[100] and I will argue that even oppositional texts were shaped by prevailing discourses of masculinity and femininity, which are revealed through an analysis of metaphor and imagery as well as propositional content. In such an analysis it is also necessary to be sensitive to the possibilities and constraints of particular genres of political writing.[101]

The definition of 'socialist woman' in this study is, by necessity, somewhat pragmatic. Such definitions are essentially relational. The earliest socialist women defined themselves against (bourgeois) feminists – *jokenshugisha*. At this stage socialism could embrace a range of positions from anarchism, through social democracy to a mild left liberalism. However, as the socialist position came to be defined more precisely, and with the development of factionalism within the socialist movement, revolutionary socialism could be defined in opposition to parliamentary socialism, which could both be defined in opposition to anarchism. These factional divisions were relevant to both male and female participants in the socialist movement. Thus, the meaning of such labels as 'socialist' or 'socialist woman' depended on the terms to which they were opposed. I shall thus include in this study the writings of those women who identified themselves as 'socialist', and who chose to publish in socialist journals. The meaning of 'socialism' for these women will be explored in these specific contexts. I will, however, limit my attention to women in urban-based socialist organizations in the Tokyo region. Women in farmers' unions and women in regional socialist organizations deserve independent full-length studies. I will also concentrate my attention on women in the so-called 'legal' left. Anarchist and communist women will be referred to where their activities influenced the socialist movement, and where they contributed to the definition of a 'socialist' position through their debates with members of the 'legal' left.

These questions can only be explored through an examination of socialist women's own writings about their situations. The major sources for this book are the feminist and socialist journals held in several archives in Tokyo,[102] or reissued in facsimile editions. I have also made use of published document collections and collections of interviews with women involved in the labour movement. In addition, several socialist women have written autobiographies. Other materials will also be referred to, in order to show how socialist women's writings were shaped by, or managed to challenge, the dominant discourses concerning women.

In this study I will also be guided by the insights of feminist historians and political scientists who have considered the conjunction of feminism and socialism in other national contexts. Barbara Taylor and others have considered the participation of women in the development of different strands of British socialism.[103] Charles Sowerwine has considered the contradictory position of women in the French socialist movement, as suggested in the title of his monograph, *Sisters or Citizens?*[104] and similar questions have been explored in the context of socialist movements in other countries,[105] including Australia.[106] All of these writers have identified the contradictions involved in the conjunction of feminism and socialism, and the problems involved in trying to bring a gendered perspective to socialism, and a class perspective to feminism. These contradictions, however, are worked out in different ways in each national context, depending on specific historical circumstances and local institutional constraints.

One aspect of this study will be the uncovering of something which has been 'hidden from history',[107] that is, the development of a movement of socialist women in early twentieth-century Japan. I am also, however, interested in what a study of socialist women's writings can teach us about various aspects of political activity in early twentieth-century Japan. Such a study can shed light on the relationship between gender and structures of domination and subordination, and the gendering of political activities and ideologies in this context.

In order to answer these questions, it has been necessary to construct a complex narrative of the activities and writings of socialist women in early twentieth-century Japan. A chronological narrative of events is overlaid with a thematic narrative which explores what I have called the 'speaking positions' available to women in the period from 1900 to 1937: subjects, wives, mothers, workers and activists. Within each chapter, three sets of questions are explored.

- What were the theoretical concerns of socialist women; and how did they understand the relationship between socialism and feminism?
- How were these ideas translated into action; what forms of organization and action were developed?
- What imaginative resources were available for imagining the transformation of society; what rhetorical strategies and metaphorical tropes were employed; and how did these translate into new forms of gendered subjectivity?

CHAPTER 2

Imperial Subjects

Imperial subjects. Frontispiece of Miura Shūsui's book, *Sensō to Fujin* (*Women and War*), Bunmeidō, Tokyo, 1904, which illustrates official constructions of womanhood – as helpmates to a militarist State.

Fukuda and other socialist women faced the contradiction engendered by the disjunction between the discourses of liberalism, socialism and feminism which helped them to make sense of their society, and the official documents of the society which interpellated them as gendered subjects of the Emperor as national patriarch. However, the attention devoted to alternative visions of family and State also paradoxically created a discursive space for the development of the oppositional discourse of feminism.

The period from 1868 to 1898 is crucial for an understanding of the institutional context of gender relations in Japan until well into the twentieth century. The constitutional and legal systems codified in this period were effective until the promulgation of a new Constitution and Civil Code after the Second World War. These years saw the creation of the modern Japanese nation-state, which was based on a constitutional monarchy which denied its subjects – particularly women – basic democratic freedoms. The Meiji State failed to embrace liberal, democratic ideas, and the family was mobilized for the purposes of the autocratic state. In this chapter I will outline the institutional and legal context for women's political activities, and the discursive context whereby women were primarily positioned as subjects of the Emperor – as gendered subjects whose service to the Empire was mainly discussed in terms of service to the home and family.

In the years between 1853 and the Restoration of 1868, there was a reconfiguration of power relations at the élite level, resulting in the end of the military rule of the Shōguns and a reaffirmation of the authority of the Emperor. The creation of a new regime was symbolised by the move of the Imperial court from Kyōto to Edo (renamed Tōkyō), and the designation of a new era name – *Meiji*, or 'enlightened rule'. In the first few years after the Restoration, the feudal domain system was abolished and the feudal class system was dismantled, although former samurai retained some privileges.

The task of the Meiji élite was the creation of a modern nation-state, with all of the political, legal and bureaucratic machinery this entailed. The transition from a semi-feudal economy to industrial capitalism was largely directed from 'above'. The decisions made at this time limited the possibilities for women's full participation in society, and circumscribed the possible forms of a feminist movement. In Europe, the rise of liberal ideology had made possible the first theorization of feminism. In Japan, liberalism held resonance for many Japanese intellectuals and common people, although the ideals of natural rights, equality, and individualism were not espoused as official ideology by the Meiji State, as we shall see. The social conditions of the time also provided the context for the development of socialist and feminist ideas.

Liberalism and Gender

In the first two decades after the opening of the country in 1854, representatives of several domains travelled to Europe and America to study techniques of administration, education, industry, and commercial and military technology. The young men who had travelled and studied overseas became the experts in 'Western learning', and were involved in the establishment of new structures for the dissemination of ideas and knowledge. Newspapers and journals were established on a private basis, but the administration was not slow to institute mechanisms of control in the form of Press Regulations.[1]

In 1873 (the sixth year of the Meiji era), Mori Arinori[2] and others established the *Meirokusha* (Meiji Six Society), a society devoted to the dissemination of 'modern' ideas. The activities of this society contributed to the development of civil society in Meiji Japan, providing a physical space for lecture meetings, and promoting further discussion through the journal *Meiroku Zasshi*. These practices were built on in the creation of other intellectual journals and mass newspapers, and in the liberal movement which deployed 'lectures, debates, demonstrations . . . speaking tours aimed at various villages and their agricultural associations; political party and society newspapers and bulletins; handbills, and even songs and poems'.[3]

In addition to discussion of alternative systems of government, the role of the intellectual, and issues related to education and language planning, the members of the *Meirokusha* used their journal to discuss notions of women's roles, providing a cautious challenge to Confucian notions, and challenging the double standard which allowed such practices as prostitution and concubinage. In the 1870s the new government introduced controversial measures (later rescinded) which gave official legal recognition to concubines, and legitimacy to the children of concubines.[4] To the *Meirokusha* writers, this was seen to be tantamount to official recognition of polygamy.[5]

Although these writers were often promoting radically new ideas of gender relations in the context of Meiji Japan, their arguments were couched in Confucian terms, complete with quotations from Confucius and Mencius.[6] Mori Arinori, for example, who advocated (and attempted to practise) a form of contractual marriage based on mutual consent, used the Confucian language of 'righteousness' to denounce the practice of concubinage:

> When righteousness does not prevail, the strong oppress the weak and the smart deceive the stupid. In extreme cases, immorality becomes an amusement providing a source of livelihood as well as pleasure. Among the

customs common among barbarians, mistreatment of wives by their husbands is especially intolerable to witness . . . [7]

Sakatani Shiroshi quoted Mencius in order to argue for 'separate
spheres' for men and women, but questioned the concept of equal
rights:

> In sum, the word rights includes evil. There is a tendency for the advocacy
> of rights to generate opposing power. This was never the intention of the
> wise men of Europe and America and the translation [of the word 'right' as
> *ken*] is not appropriate. Instead it would be well to speak of preserving the
> spheres of men and women (*danjo shubun*) or of the harmonious bodies of
> husband and wife (*fūfu dōtai*). Further, from the point of view of rights, the
> man should stand slightly above the woman, just as elder brother takes
> precedence over younger brother.[8]

Nakamura Masanao, credited with early usage of the phrase *ryōsai
kenbo* (good wives and wise mothers),[9] argued for purity on the part of
both husbands and wives.[10] Most of these writers argued that education
was necessary in order to instil notions of purity in both sexes. They
advocated monogamy and a single sexual standard for both sexes. The
Meirokusha members limited their discussion of women's role to marriage, however, and even those who referred to 'equal rights' within
marriage were reluctant to grant women equal rights in society at
large.[11] Katō Hiroyuki was actively hostile to the notion of equal rights
for women in any sphere.[12] Fukuzawa Yukichi realised that Meiji men
were not ready to relinquish their privileges, and allowed that they
could 'tacitly' keep concubines, as long as they did not flaunt the fact.[13]
In other writings, Fukuzawa challenged the Confucianist identification
of family and State,[14] and later wrote 'enlightenment' versions of didac-
tic texts for women.[15]

In the previous writings, we should note the gap between theory and
practice – the most liberal of writers were often far from exemplary in
their private conduct. We should also note that this first debate on
gender roles and the connections between family and state was carried
out by male writers only. Although questions of family and gender relations were fundamental to Meiji enlightenment discourse, women were
implicitly excluded from this discussion, and positioned as passive
figures whose fate could be decided by more or less benevolent male
intellectuals and public servants.[16] Some women were, however, able to
participate in the liberal movement of the 1870s and 1880s, before the
enactment of regulations restricting women's political activities. The
prescription that women should aspire to be 'good wives and wise
mothers' was to become the catchcry for those in the bureaucracy and

educational establishments who increasingly devoted attention to the nature of women's support for the imperial State.

From 1874, a series of petitions were presented to the government calling for the establishment of a national assembly,[17] often referring to the relevant section of the Charter Oath of 1868.[18] This was one of the topics which was debated in the pages of almost every issue of the *Meiroku Zasshi*. Although the first of these petitions emanated from disaffected members of the former samurai class, the demand for a popularly elected assembly soon became the focus for other groups, and broadened into a national movement, known as the Movement for Freedom and Popular Rights (*Jiyū Minken Undō*).[19] Although the concept of liberalism promoted by the former samurai may have been somewhat limited, the universalist principles of liberal thought were meaningful to women who had been marginalised under the feudal system, and to those members of the former peasant class who participated in the liberal movement.[20]

In Europe, the development of liberalism and individualism has been identified with the rise of Protestantism, capitalism, and free market ideologies. From these roots came the first bourgeois revolutions, the rise of democratic ideas, and, eventually, feminism. These ideas originated in the writings of Locke and Rousseau, and were developed by Jefferson in the American Revolution, and by Bentham, Mill and Spencer in England. Liberal ideas were particularly congenial with the transition from the subsistence values of feudalism (custom, status, authoritarianism) to the free market ideology of capitalism (mobility, freedom, market values). Ideas of natural rights were employed to justify democratic ideas. Natural rights entailed the notion of equal rights and universal values, and it became logically difficult not to extend these to women. The first major tracts of European feminism were almost contemporaneous with the French Revolution,[21] and some of these writers attempted to use the supposed universalism of liberal theory in order to argue that women were entitled to the same rights as men.[22]

Japan in the nineteenth century was also undergoing the transition from a feudal to a capitalist economy, and market relations were already prevalent in particular sections of the economy. Bowen, drawing on the work of T. C. Smith, links these economic changes with the development of liberal ideologies in rural Japan.[23] Peasants under the feudal relationships of the Tokugawa period had been conscious of the 'right to subsistence', and had been positioned as 'supplicants', who could petition a benevolent government when subsistence was threatened. When their petitions were unsuccessful, their dissatisfaction was at times expressed in riots and uprisings.[24] By the Meiji period they were now participants in a market economy, and many of them wanted to see the freedoms and rights of the market economy extended to the political sphere.[25]

Liberal ideas were debated by intellectuals as the classics of Western liberalism were translated into Japanese.[26] The members of the liberal movement referred to European political thinkers in their demands for a popularly elected assembly.[27] The first petitions for an elected assembly had been submitted to the government in 1874, and the following years saw the establishment of political parties devoted to democratic and liberal principles. From the end of the decade there was a proliferation of popular rights societies, whose members were engaged in discussion of the ideas of parliamentary democracy, and in producing alternative draft constitutions.[28] Discussion of these themes intensified after the announcement (in the name of the Emperor) in October 1881 of a commitment to the establishment of a national assembly by 1890.[29]

The development of a popular press made possible the dissemination of alternative political proposals. In the 1880s the *Minyūsha* (Friends of the Nation) promoted democratic ideas through the journal *Kokumin no Tomo* (*The Nation's Friend*), edited by Tokutomi Sohō.[30] Tokutomi described his political position as *heiminshugi* (commonerism),[31] a phrase which would later be appropriated by the early socialist movement.[32] For a short time in the 1880s a genre of 'political novel' dramatized the new political ideas in circulation.[33] Ueki Emori, like Tokutomi, was influenced by Spencer's ideas.[34] He wrote his own draft constitution – based on popular sovereignty, democratic principles, and equality between men and women, and said to be the most liberal of the thirty-odd drafts around at the time.[35] Ueki also composed a song on the theme of freedom, 'A Country Song of Civil Rights' (*Minken Inaka Uta*), which used the imagery of nature to give metaphorical force to the notion that the rights being demanded were a natural inheritance:

. . . Though the birds have wings they cannot fly;
The caged bird can see the outside.
Though the fish have fins they cannot swim;
The netted fish sees the sea beyond.
Though the horses have hooves they cannot run;
The tethered horse sees the grass out of reach.
[We] are endowed with arms and legs;
We have hearts and minds.
But today we have no liberty or rights.
If we call ourselves [human]
Then each person must . . . stand up and say
'[Humans] have rights.'[36]

Given the currency of notions of 'natural rights', it is unsurprising that many Japanese women also seized on this concept in order to demand 'women's rights' (*joken*). As early as 1878, Kusunose Kita demanded voting rights for the local assembly on the grounds that she held the family property on the death of her husband and was thus liable for taxation (in an argument implicitly based on the logic of 'no taxation without representation').[37] Some women participated in the liberal movement: Kishida Toshiko toured the country making speeches demanding political rights for women and contributed articles to the liberal newspaper *The Torch of Freedom* (*Jiyū no Tomoshibi*); Tomii Tora was inspired by Kishida's example to come to Tokyo and work in the fields of journalism and women's education;[38] Fukuda Hideko also became involved in the liberal movement after hearing a speech by Kishida – as we have seen, Fukuda was involved in the Ōsaka Incident with Ōi Kentarō and others, and embraced socialism after her release from prison.

The early liberal feminist discussion of rights often focused on the family as the site of women's oppression. Given that the family came to be crucial in the structures of authority under the constitutional system, criticism of the family could be said to question the very basis of power under the Meiji system. Discussion of the family was taken so seriously that Kishida Toshiko was imprisoned in 1884 for her attack on the family system.[39] In her writings and speeches, Kishida used the metaphor of imprisonment to describe women's situation. She used the conventional phrase used to describe the upbringing of young ladies, *hakoiri musume* (daughters raised in boxes) but turned it into an image of deprivation.[40] Kishida lamented that daughters raised in this fashion were like cultivated plants whose growth had been stunted, in comparison with flowers growing wild in the mountains and valleys. Like Ueki, Kishida used natural imagery to describe a very unnatural state of subjection. The upbringing of young women was like the cultivation of *bonsai* trees, whose shape is created by the trimming of roots and leaves.[41]

Despite the resonance of liberal ideas for many individuals experiencing the economic and social transformations of Meiji Japan, the legitimacy of liberal ideas could be challenged by the dominance of Confucianist ideas, which emphasised hierarchy and obedience, rather than equality and freedom. Confucianist ideas were particularly dismissive of women's role in society, and revivalist philosophies such as *Kokugaku* (National Learning) and *Mitogaku* (the Mito school) failed to challenge prevailing views of women.[42] Confucianism lacked a liberal conception of individualism and the Confucian emphasis on hierarchy could also be said to be incompatible with notions of equal rights. The

Confucian individual was always placed in social context, and was enmeshed in a series of dyadic relationships (ruler/ruled; father/child; elder/younger; husband/wife; teacher/pupil) where obedience on the part of the inferior was balanced by benevolence on the part of the superior.

After Nakamura Masanao's translation of Samuel Smiles' *Self-Help*, Protestant ideas of individualism and advancement through hard work were understood in Confucian terms.[43] In other cases concepts were reinterpreted or rephrased to fit Confucian principles. Irokawa argues that many of the participants in the Freedom and Popular Rights Movement understood their participation in this movement in terms drawn variously from Confucianism, from the *Kokugaku* (National Learning) School, or from the millenarian *Yonaoshi* movements of the late Tokugawa period.[44] In other words, it was also possible to find, in the Confucian tradition, justification for rebellion against a ruler who did not show the necessary benevolence.[45] The language of Confucianism was not simply a remnant of premodern times, which somehow retarded the development of liberal or democratic ideas. Rather, Confucianism was constantly being reinvented and reconstituted, and Confucianist language could be used to justify the most modern practices and institutions.

While the language of premodern social relations could sometimes be reinterpreted to fit new political realities, in other cases new words were coined. The word for 'rights' (*kenri*) and the compounds formed from this root were all newly coined in the Meiji period.[46] The word used to translate 'rights' – *kenri* – had been discussed since the 1870s. In the early Meiji intellectual journal *Meiroku Zasshi*, Nishimura Shigeki spent several pages explaining the concept of 'rights'. He spent little time, however, on natural rights; most of the article was devoted to describing the limits to rights, and the obligations that go along with rights.[47] Many of the *Meirokusha* intellectuals had expressed anxiety about the 'abuse' of rights – especially if they were extended to women. The word was also to cause trouble in the drafting of the Civil Code in the 1870s.[48]

However, while the concept of people's rights was seen to be problematic by some members of the élite, the concept continued to have resonance for the members of the liberal movement. Rhetorically, people's rights (*minken*) were often contrasted with State rights (*kokken*), or the rights of the ruler (*kunken*). In the political climate of the late nineteenth century, where national sovereignty was perceived to be under threat, and national policy was guided by the slogan *fukoku kyōhei* (a wealthy country and a strong army) the concept of 'state rights' could be used to question the legitimacy of selfish assertions of individual rights by women and commoners.[49]

Another new concept of the nineteenth century was *kokumin* ('the people' – literally: 'nation-person'), whereby Japanese people were seen to have a common identity linked to the construction of the modern nation-state. Implicit in different usages of the word *kokumin* were different possible relationships between individual and state.[50]

Was the individual a citizen with inalienable rights, or a subject whose limited rights were granted by the Emperor? These questions were implicit in the discussions leading up to the promulgation of the Meiji Constitution and the framing of the Meiji Civil Code.

The Constitutional System

It was not only liberal ideas which were made available through translation in the Meiji period. Pittau reminds us that '[A]uthoritarian systems could be very modern and very Western'.[51] The Meiji oligarchy deliberately chose a form of constitutional monarchy where the imperial institution was buttressed against the encroachment of democratic forces.[52] The final form of the Meiji Constitution reflected the desire to pay lip-service to democratic ideals while at the same time ensuring the power of the élite in the name of the Emperor. Although an elected assembly was allowed for, its powers were limited, and the franchise was limited by a qualification depending on the amount of tax paid.[53] 'Preponderant power', explains Andrew Barshay, 'lay with official bureaucracy and a transcendent cabinet rather than with an elected representative body.'[54]

Where other constitutions carried a Bill of Rights, the corresponding section of the Meiji Constitution (Chapter two) outlined the Rights and Duties of Subjects. There was no mention of inalienable human rights – rights were granted to the people as subjects of the Emperor,[55] who was described as 'sacred and inviolable' (Article Three). Freedom of religious belief and freedom of speech and association were only granted 'within the limits of law' and 'within limits not prejudicial to peace and order' (Articles 28 and 29). Any of these provisions were subject to the exercise of the powers of the Emperor 'in times of war or national emergency' (Article 31).[56]

Thus, the Meiji State failed to support democratic or liberal ideas in any real sense. The preamble to the Constitution used Shintō ideas to proclaim the divinity of the Emperor. The 'monarchic principle' of the German Constitutions of the 1850s was adopted to justify the notion that sovereignty resided in the Emperor.[57]

Yet, there were tensions in the establishment of the constitutional system, as Andrew Gordon has outlined:

The promulgation of a constitution and the convening of an elected Diet meant that Japan was a nation of subjects with both obligations to the state and political rights. Obligations included military service, school attendance, and the individual payment of taxes. Rights included suffrage and a voice in deciding the fate of the national budget. The fact that these rights were limited to men of substantial property is well recognized and, of course, important. Clearly the constitution was expected by its authors to contain the opposition. Nonetheless, to stress only the limitations placed on popular rights by the Meiji constitution is to miss its historical significance as a cause of future change: the mere existence of a constitutionally mandated, elected national assembly with more than advisory powers implied the existence of a politically active and potentially expandable body of subjects or citizens. Indeed, the decision of the oligarchs for a constitution was made in acute awareness that such a citizenry was in the process of forming itself and developing its own ideas about the political order.[58]

To overemphasize the repressive potential of the Meiji Constitution would be to deny the efficacy of the popular activism which was one of the catalysts for the creation of constitutional government, and to deny the legitimacy of the oppositional movements which persisted into the twentieth century. Further questions concern the distinction between 'subjects' and 'citizens', and whether the 'potentially expandable body of subjects or citizens' could include women. To what extent was the 'subject' of the Meiji Emperor a gendered subject, and what did this imply for the possibilities for political activity by women? The women who had participated in the Liberal Movement of the 1880s had certainly thought that women should be included in the category of citizen.

Gendered Subjecthood

For Meiji women, the constitutional system meant that they were to live in a state which did not recognise the notion of 'natural rights', let alone extend them to women. Although the language of the Constitution was gender-neutral, women were implicitly excluded in various ways. The duty to perform military service, for example, could be said to imply a male subject. The different duties of male and female subjects were also outlined in various ways in the provisions of the Civil Code. The family and women were not explicitly mentioned in the Constitution itself (except for Article Two which stated that the imperial succession was based on the male line), but the Imperial Rescript on Education of 1890 upheld a Confucian view of a state based on hierarchy and obedience, with the family as the basic unit of society.

There was, perhaps, democratic potential in the institution of a compulsory education system in 1872, but the educational system went through several transformations in the next few decades. The system eventually adopted was based on the assumption that the purpose of education was to train subjects to serve the State more efficiently, rather than the cultivation of talent and learning for its own sake. This suited Confucian conceptions of *seikyō itchi* – unity of government and education.[59] The Education Ordinance (*Gakusei*) of 1872 made education compulsory for both boys and girls,[60] but the actual attendance rates were much lower for girls, who were often expected to carry out home duties or paid work.[61] The Imperial Rescript on Education (*Kyōiku Chokugo*) of 1890 made explicit the principle that education was for the purpose of producing subjects loyal to both family and State, linking the values of loyalty to the Emperor (*chū*) and filial piety (*kō*).[62] Gluck has emphasized the role of the Rescript in defining 'civil morality':

> ... the Rescript itself was raised to the status of a civic creed. What began as an assertion of native values and social ethics became a civil morality: an index of loyalty and patriotism (*chūkun aikoku*) not only for the schools, but for wherever allegiance to the state was at ideological issue.[63]

This emphasis on hierarchy and obedience and the Confucian values of loyalty and filial piety was to provide ideological support for the patriarchal family system codified in the Meiji Civil Code. The Imperial Rescript was supported by commentaries which made explicit the connection between family and State, and linked filial piety with loyalty to the Emperor.[64]

Primary education became compulsory for both boys and girls in the 1870s, but it was some time before women had access to secondary and tertiary education. With respect to women's education, there was a shift from a liberal view of education in the early Meiji period which was seen to be equally relevant to male and female students, to the late Meiji period which saw an emphasis on education specifically directed at women, and based on the ideology of 'good wives and wise mothers'.[65] When higher education was extended to women, it was generally discussed in terms of this doctrine. The gradual extension of education and literacy to women had contradictory implications. Prescriptive images of womanhood could be disseminated to a female reading public, but print media also provided the potential for the dissemination of alternative images and representations.

In broad terms, then, women were granted no basic rights under the Meiji Constitution, and were actively repressed in many ways. But the Constitution was often vague, and many provisions were specifically limited by law. The full implications of this system for women and gender relations can be understood by examining those sections of the

Civil Code which pertain to the family – the sections on marriage, family headship, succession, and divorce.

It was thought vital for the prosperity and stability of the State that the most suitable form of the family be instituted. This reflects the Confucian utilitarianist belief that family, school, and other institutions are inseparable from the functioning of the State.[66] The Meiji Restoration had threatened existing power relations by the abolition of the feudal domains and the modification of the feudal class system. By identifying the State with the family, it was possible to use emotional attachment to the family in the service of the State. Gluck has described this process succinctly:

> ... confronted with increasing individuation and even anomie, ideologues enshrined the family – the hyphenated metaphor of the family-state in effect sanctifying the family at least as much as it domesticated the state.[67]

The principle of loyalty to the Emperor and one's elders described in the Imperial Rescript on Education was carried one step further by ethics textbooks which explicitly linked family to State, and father to Emperor. The father was 'ruler' over his family members and the Emperor 'father' to his childlike subjects.[68] Those sections of the Civil Code which concerned the family were thus seen to be vital to authority relations in the new political system.

The process leading up to the promulgation of the Meiji Civil Code has been described in detail in several sources.[69] The Napoleonic Code was chosen as the first model, and Mitsukuri Rinshō was commissioned in 1870 to translate the French Civil Code into Japanese. In 1879 the French legal scholar Emile Boissonade was requested to compile the new Civil Code. Boissonade's draft, however, encountered opposition; most of the opposition to his draft centred on the family. For example, Boissonade's draft allowed for the sharing of inheritances between siblings, and included the unthinkable proposition that family heads could be deposed.[70] In the final draft of the Civil Code most of the other sections were taken almost literally from French or German sources, but the book on Persons, which contained those provisions relating to marriage, divorce, family headship and inheritance, was completely rewritten by Japanese scholars in line with their vision of a Confucian family-State.[71]

The link between patriarchal authority in the family, and imperial power in the state was made explicit at both ends of the political spectrum, and there was extensive public discussion of the draft Civil Code. On the one hand, liberal Ueki Emori lamented that those who grew up under authoritarian states failed to develop independence and autonomy. Ueki used natural rights theory to argue for equal rights for

men and women, and identified the patriarchal power of the family
head (*koshu*) with the absolute power of the monarch (*kunshu*). He
argued that the country should be made up of individuals rather than
a collection of families, calling for a Civil Code based on the 'new ideas'
of the nineteenth century.[72]

Conservative legal scholar Hozumi Yatsuka criticized Boissonade's
draft, stating that the form of the Japanese State depended on the
Japanese family system, and described an idealized, trans-historical
form of the family system.[73] Hozumi's appeal to antiquity is a common
feature of modern nationalist thought.[74]

Several editorials in *Kokumin no Tomo* (*The Nation's Friend*) were
devoted to reform of the family system, and *Minyūsha* leader, Tokutomi
Sohō, established *Katei Zasshi* (*Family Magazine*) in 1892 for the dissemination of his ideas. Meanwhile, in the pages of the journal *Nihon*
(*Japan*), the nationalist rival to *Kokumin no Tomo*, the desirability of the
'existing' Japanese family system was reaffirmed.[75] Like the members of
the *Meirokusha* in the 1870s, these commentators shared the view that
the family was crucial to the prosperity of the state.

Before the Meiji period there had been no universal, customary form
of marriage and family structure. Until the Edo period there had been
a mixture of matrilocal, patrilocal and duolocal marriage systems, and
inheritance practices were just as diverse. The Tokugawa Shogunate
had failed to unify these practices; laws varied from domain to domain
and actual practice varied according to class and region.[76]

During the Edo period there had been two main conflicting trends
with regard to family form. In agricultural areas, the nuclear family had
become the most efficient unit of production, and feudal relations
based on duty and obligation were being replaced by market relations
whereby labour could be sold on a daily basis.[77] In the samurai class,
increased centralisation of property and authority brought an emphasis
on primogeniture and subordination of all family members to the patriarch. This practice was emulated by the wealthier merchants and artisans, who did not want to see their property (and authority) being
divided up on the marriage of their children.[78]

The writers of the Meiji Civil Code, then, did more than codify a
conservative view of the family. They ignored the diversity of marriage
and inheritance practices in different regions and classes of late Tokugawa society, and imposed a version of the patriarchal samurai family
on all sections of society. The depiction of the patriarchal family form
as unique, immutable, and trans-historical by such writers as Hozumi
was a convenient myth which has persisted to the present day, and the
identification of family with state was a socially constructed ideal, as
described by Gluck:

Family conceptions of the State and folkish views of the nation rested con-
genially with communitarian values that less readily accommodated either
raw individualism or representations of class conflict. On the other hand,
neither State nor nation made the same kind of immediate sense as the
economic and social imperatives of personal success and family survival.
Indeed, the unrelenting efforts of the ideologues to assert the pre-eminence
of public values revealed that it was often the private ones that constituted
stronger personal motivation. The continued tension between the public
and private poles of civic value arose in part because Japan's social meanings
did not readily dispose people ... to make 'the leap to the state'.[79]

Perhaps we can reconsider Gluck's insight with reference to Benedict
Anderson's discussion of nationalism as the construction of an 'imagined community'.[80] In Japan, it seems, the identification of family and
State was to facilitate the imagining of a new community: the nation-
State as family, referred to in the Japanese literature as *kazoku-kokka*
(family-State). This emotional identification with family and state may
have been seen to provide an alternative to other forms of social
grouping based on class or occupation. Barshay's description of the
'family-State' brings together the themes of patriarchalism, national
integration, and the 'exaltation of officialdom':

> The 'family-state' postulated a semi-divine monarch whose family was the
> 'great house' for all his subjects, at once chief priest of the Sun line and a
> modern ruler with enormous prerogatives who 'presided over' (*suberu; tōchi
> suru*) but did not 'involve himself' (*ataru*) in the actual administration of
> the state ... Here let us stress its valorization of organic harmony and patri-
> archal integration over any conflictual notions of the composition of the
> polity. This ties in, of course, with the 'exaltation' of officialdom, which,
> along with the independent military, acted for the first three decades of the
> modern period as the structural expression, so to speak, of the imperial
> will.[81]

The implications for gender relations of this system can be clarified
through an examination of those sections of the Civil Code concerned
with Family Law, and legislation concerned with women's political
activities. The potential for political repression existed in this system,
and this power was directed against women as much as any other
groups in society. The first regulations on public meetings and associations had been passed in the 1870s.[82] New regulations, from 1890
on, added clauses specifically directed at women, similar to regulations
which had existed in Germany from 1851, and in Austria from 1867.[83]
The Law on Political Associations and Assembly of 1890 (*Shūkai oyobi
Seisha Hō*) prevented women from engaging in any political activity,
whether it be attending a political meeting, holding one, or joining
a political party. These bans were reiterated in Article Five of the
Public Peace Police Law of 1900 (*Chian Keisatsu Hō*).[84] Women were

also excluded from the very limited franchise. Thus, there was no scope for Meiji women to demand 'rights' publicly. The repeal of these provisions was necessary before they could even begin to consider other political activity. In the 1880s, as we have seen, it had been possible for women in the liberal movement to make speeches all over the country demanding political rights for women. This would no longer be permissible, and meant that public speaking could no longer be used as a means of promoting feminist ideas. Thus, one of the first activities of both liberal and socialist feminists of the Meiji period involved campaigning for the amendment of Article Five, as I will discuss in Chapter three.

In concrete terms, it was laws concerned with family registration, marriage, divorce and inheritance which restricted women's rights and delimited the role they could expect to play in the Meiji 'family-State'. The basic administrative unit of the State was the family. Each person was registered in the Family Register (*Koseki*) on birth.[85] The head of the family (the father) had authority over each family member, and it was his duty to ensure the loyalty of each family member to the Emperor. The father's permission was necessary for marriage up to the age of thirty for men, twenty-five for women.[86]

On the death of the father, the headship and all property passed to the eldest son. A distinction was made between the headship, which involved 'succession to all the rights and duties of the deceased ancestor', and heirship, which concerned the 'rights and obligations pertaining to the property of the family'.[87] Boissonade's draft Civil Code had made provision for sharing of the inheritance between siblings, and this had been the practice in some regions, but the final draft of the Civil Code affirmed the principle of primogeniture. The practice of adopting a son or son-in-law where there was no male heir continued to be recognized.[88]

Marriage was recognized as legal when the wife was entered in the family register of her husband's family. This sytem was open to abuse, however, and wives were often not registered until they had produced an heir. A married woman lost all control over any property she brought to the marriage, unless it was specifically protected by a marriage contract. Legally, married women were in the same category as minors and other legal 'incompetents'. They could not enter into contracts, or buy or sell property without the consent of their husbands.[89] Under a system where suffrage was dependent on property, this had further implications for the possibility of arguing for women's political rights.

The divorce law alone gave some small improvement in women's position.[90] For the first time, women could sue for divorce, but the grounds were restricted. Women could sue on the grounds of cruelty or desertion, but not adultery. Men could obtain divorce on the grounds of the woman's adultery, but a man could only be prosecuted for adultery by the husband of another married woman. Adultery with a single woman was no offence as it did not threaten the family line. The practice of divorce by mutual consent was often abused, with families coercing an unsatisfactory bride into signing consent for divorce. There were no provisions for alimony or maintenance, so that divorced women were totally unprotected. The father usually retained custody over any children.[91]

At an official level Meiji society was ambivalent towards prostitution and concubinage. Contracts of indenture between prostitutes and brothel owners were officially made invalid in 1872 but the practice continued tacitly.[92] Laws were passed in 1872 and 1873 which included concubines in the family register, and gave their children legitimate status. This legislation was rescinded in 1882.[93]

In sum, the Meiji Constitution outlined a society where the people were constructed as subjects of an Emperor rather than citizens with natural rights. The patriarchal family was the basis of authority relations in this state, and the gendered nature of subjecthood was made explicit through the Civil Code, which was finally promulgated in 1898. This basic structure of Constitutional, Civil, and Commercial Law was effective until after the Second World War. These legal and institutional structures were supported by ideological attention to the duties of subjects and the gendered nature of subjecthood.

Discourses of Family and State

Family structure and family relationships were seen to be crucial to authority relations in the Meiji State. According to Meiji nationalist discourse, the role of women as imperial subjects was seen through the prism of family relationships.[94] Several writers promoted the idea that women should be 'good wives and wise mothers' (ryōsai kenbo), and that they should receive a proper education for this role. Some writers also began to promote monogamous marriage based on love between husband and wife.

By the 1890s, Christian influence had become stronger in certain groups in Meiji society, and the Christian emphasis on social service would become an important influence on the subsequent development of socialist and feminist thought in Japan. Many intellectuals had received their education at Christian mission schools, and this was often the only place where middle-class Meiji women could receive higher education. The Christian influence was apparent in the creation of the Japanese chapters of the Women's Christian Temperance

Union and the Red Cross.[95] The women of the Japanese chapter of the Women's Christian Temperance Union (*Nihon Kirisutokyō Fujin Kyōfūkai*) drew on the Christian tradition of social service and carried out welfare activities among prostitutes and textile workers. The women of the *Kyōfūkai* were involved in campaigns against licensed prostitution, and paid some attention to issues of 'women's rights'.[96] These activities provided women with a positive role, but ultimately women were positioned in the domestic sphere, and any public activities could only be legitimated as extensions of the role of 'good wives and wise mothers'.

Many young writers of the time were influenced by Iwamoto Zenji, principal of the women's school *Meiji Jogakkō*,[97] and editor of the women's education journal *Jogaku Zasshi*.[98] Iwamoto, in addition to being principal of the women's college, was leader of the Bungakukai school of romantic novelists, and many of the school's romantic ideas found their way into the pages of *Jogaku Zasshi*, or the literary magazine *Bungakukai*.[99]

These writers displayed a variety of stances on women's rights and women's education and the emphasis of the journal *Jogaku Zasshi* shifted several times. The journal promoted women's education and women's political rights, but in the context of ideas of romantic love and monogamous marriage.[100] Education for women, indeed, was often promoted for the sake of the women's children. *Jogaku Zasshi*, then, was important in the promotion of a notion of monogamous marriage which supported a form of *ryōsai kenbo* ideology.

Articles by Ueki Emori[101] on women's political rights in this journal sit uneasily with Hatoyama Kazuo's 'Become your husband's closest friend rather than [demanding] equal rights'[102] and Kitamura Tōkoku's 'Misanthropic poets and women'.[103] This publication was, however, one of the places where criticism was voiced against the regulations which prevented women from participating in political activities.[104] Both Shimizu Toyoko and Iwamoto[105] himself criticised the Law on Political Assembly and Association of 1890 – the precursor of the Public Peace Police Law of 1900. Iwamoto was also mildly critical of the Imperial Rescript on Education, recognizing that the Rescript could be used as justification for discriminatory treatment of women.[106]

Domestically oriented women's magazines started to appear in the Meiji period, with such titles as *Meiji no Katei* (*The Meiji Family*). Although the more progressive of these magazines supported women's education and political rights, they generally placed women firmly in the family, and took a patriotic tone.[107]

The popular culture of the Edo period had dramatized the conflict

between societal obligation (*giri*) and emotional ties (*ninjō*). This conflict was dramatized along class lines, or in economic terms. Sometimes
the conflict was between the merchant's duty to his wife and his emotional ties to his mistress. Or perhaps a poor clerk did not have enough
money to redeem his lover from her rich patron. These dramas invari-
ably ended in suicide, reinforcing the idea that sexual passion was a
dangerous force. Although the new discourses on women and family
continued to see sexuality as a dangerous force, there was a new linkage
of romantic love with monogamous marriage.

Meiji popular culture dramatized conflicting notions of romantic
love. Such writers as Nagai Kafū, Izumi Kyōka and Sato Ryokū continued in their romanticized (and often misogynistic) portrayal of the
licensed quarters. The *Bungakukai* writers dramatized the problems of
romantic love in the mission schools – an idealized version of love in
marriage, which they were often unable to achieve in their private
lives.[108] One writer to demystify notions of romantic love was Higuchi
Ichiyō – a member of *Bungakukai* – in her portrayal of young people
on the fringes of the licensed quarters.[109]

With the popularity of Nakamura Masanao's translation of Smiles'
Self-Help, young people became interested in worldly success – *risshin*.
The feudal debate on *giri* versus *ninjō* was reframed in terms of *risshin*
versus *ren'ai* (romantic love).[110] This conflict was dramatized in the
novels of Mori Ōgai and Tsubouchi Shōyō, and in the debate on
romantic love between Tokutomi Sohō and Kitamura Tōkoku.[111] The
ideology of *risshin shusse* was, however, implicitly masculine. Tachi
Kaoru has argued that, while the young men of the Meiji period aspired
to worldly success, *risshin shusse*, young women were being educated
according to the ideology of *ryōsai kenbo*, 'good wives and wise
mothers'.[112]

When linked with *ryōsai kenbo* ideology, ideas of romantic love and
companionate marriage provided a justification for the restriction of
women's role to the domestic sphere. Takamure has traced *ryōsai kenbo*
ideology as an amalgam of European and Confucian ideas.[113] This has
become a common theme in Meiji political history. Useful 'Confucian'
ideas were retained or revived and combined with only those 'Western'
ideas congenial to the type of state envisaged by the Meiji power élite.[114]
Tachi Kaoru has traced in more detail the transformations of *ryōsai*
kenbo ideology, from an initial emphasis on the relationships between
husband and wife and mother and child, to a later version of *ryōsai*
kenbo ideology which linked these relationships to nationalist goals.
Tachi is also sensitive to the class basis of this ideology, arguing that
the development of higher education for women in Japan was linked
to the perceived necessity to provide partners for men who were already

finding social location in suitable class positions through an increasingly stratified education system. The growth of the higher schools for women (*kōtō jogakkō*) was spectacular, and these schools were the site for the promotion of *ryōsai kenbo* ideology among middle and upper class women.[115] Although the increased demand for women's labour in the industrial sector could be seen to threaten the stability of the patriarchal family system, Tachi argues that familial ideology was also promoted among the working classes, in order to counter any perceived threat to the family system.[116]

The Japanese Ministries of Education and Home Affairs built on *ryōsai kenbo* ideology in campaigns aimed at mobilizing women through the educational system and semi-official patriotic organizations in the early twentieth century. This corresponds to Tachi's discussion of a 'nationalist' phase of *ryōsai kenbo* ideology. Nolte and Hastings quote official statements on the exclusion of women from participation in parliamentary politics. The head of the Police Bureau, Kiyoura Keigo 'argued that women's political participation would undercut home management and education', while the architect of the Public Peace Police Law, Arimatsu Hideyori, 'commented . . . that political meetings were disreputable affairs that might compromise women's virtue'.[117]

Nolte and Hastings argue that women's exclusion from political activity reflected their role as semi-public servants whose sphere of activity was the home.[118] Women's activities were explicitly politicized, and the state (in Nolte and Hastings' succinct phrase) 'claimed the home as a public place'. There were also, however, contemporary criticisms of these activities. As we shall discuss later, the socialist women who campaigned against Article Five were sceptical about women's co-optation as servants of a state which denied them political rights.

We should, however, be careful about aligning *ryōsai kenbo* ideology too closely with European ideas of 'separate spheres'. In Europe, bourgeois marriage developed as the site of production moved out of the home, and middle-class men engaged in paid labour outside while their wives looked after the management of the domestic sphere.[119] The ideological construction of the private sphere rendered aspects of gender relations 'invisible' in political terms, and naturalized the gendered hierarchy in the family.

In Japan, however, there were different configurations of 'public' and 'private'.[120] According to Confucian ideology, power relations in the family were articulated directly into the power relations of the state. In Europe, the concept of 'separate spheres' could be used by some feminists to argue for equal political rights for women, on the grounds that women made an equally significant contribution to society. In

Japan, under the Constitutional system, notions of a gendered hierarchy within the family were made explicit, and the family itself was politicized, rather than being seen as a private haven.

Mainstream political ideology in the Meiji period was antithetical to feminist ideas in several major ways. The Meiji Constitution described an autocratic State, based on divine right rather than popular sovereignty and natural rights. The Civil Code encoded a patriarchal family system, which was an essential part of the authority structures of the new State. Ideals of monogamy, and a new emphasis on the importance of women in rearing and educating children, persuaded women that they could achieve emotional satisfaction within marriage, and compensated them for their lack of political rights. However, these official discourses were counterbalanced by the development of oppositional discourses on women and gender relations. Indeed, it could almost be said that the official and semi-official pronouncements on family and state opened up a discursive space for the articulation of oppositional points of view on these matters.

While the élite discussed 'good wives and wise mothers', women soon made up the majority of workers in the textile industry, Japan's major export product. Such ideologies may even have allowed the more efficient exploitation of such women; if they thought that their primary loyalty was to the family and future husband, this may have hampered the development of class consciousness. In this context, one task of feminists in the late nineteenth and early twentieth century was to bring discussion of women's labour into the mainstream of political discussion. As long as women themselves confined their discussions and demands to the role of women within the family, there could be little challenge to the dominant political discourse.

Socialism developed as an oppositional discourse which provided a critique of industrial capitalism as it developed in Japan. In Chapter three, I will consider how socialism in early twentieth-century Japan was conjoined with another oppositional discourse – that of feminism. Within socialist and feminist discourse, women attempted to speak in ways which challenged their construction as gendered subjects of the Emperor. In their attempts to speak as wives and as mothers, they could be seen to be attempting to appropriate official constructions of womanhood to their own purposes. Attempts to speak as workers and as activists, however, provided a challenge to these discourses. In the following chapters I discuss the writings of socialist women, structured around these possible speaking positions: as wives, as mothers, as workers, and as activists.

CHAPTER 3

Wives

Wives. This anti-war graphic by Takehisa Yumeji from the socialist press illustrates the construction of woman as helpmate which was common to both mainstream and oppositional discourses. The inclusion of the skeletal soldier figure signals pacifism, while the grieving feminine figure is a conventional trope of pacifist art. *Chokugen,* 18/6/1905.

WIVES

43

In the 1900s, a group known as *Heiminsha* (the Commoners' Society) brought together men and women who were attempting to apply the new ideas of feminism and socialism to their situation as Imperial subjects in Meiji Japan, against a backdrop of industrialization. One of their activities was a seminar series directed at women.

At one of these meetings a young woman – Matsuoka [Nishikawa] Fumiko – gave a speech on her understanding of socialism. Her speech demonstrates the humanistic tenor of early Japanese socialism, and the gendered forms of political participation and understanding to be found in the first socialist groups:

> When you mention socialism, there are many people who understand it as something violent, but socialism is in fact a set of ideas deep in mercy. Thus, I believe that women, who are naturally gentle and full of sympathy must agree with socialism, and women's (voices) will be heard on certain points. I think that the power of women is stronger than has been supposed, and women should give up being shy and reticent, and devote all their energies to socialism.[1]

This chapter focuses on the development of early Japanese socialism from the roots of the liberal movement, the conjunction of feminism and socialism in the 1900s, and the ways in which the political philosophy and activities of the early socialists were shaped by gender ideologies. While women in mainstream society were constructed as helpmates to the militarist state, women in the socialist movement were constructed as 'wives', as supporters of male activists, who were addressed in gender-specific ways in socialist writings.

The Conjunction of Feminism and Socialism

While feminists attempted to use the universalist principles of liberalism and see them extended to women, socialists sought to point out some of the limitations of liberal ideology and to provide a critique of the capitalist system. The context of the early development of Japanese feminist thought has been traced in the previous chapter, where we noted the participation of women in the liberal movement, and the influence of Christianity through the mission schools and philanthropic organizations. The intellectual antecedents of socialist thought in Japan can be found in the left wing of the liberal movement, in the Christian emphasis on social service, and in the study of American labour activism and British socialism.[2] The male and female workers who had withdrawn their labour in strike activity in the 1880s and 1890s (albeit without the support of an organized union movement)[3] had also made an important step towards recognition of the basic contradiction between the interests of capital and labour, although the history of this early strike activity was not always available to later generations of workers. The growth of factory labour and the concomitant development of labour disputes has been traced by Stephen Large:

> The dimensions of the labor question, while not great by recent standards, were nonetheless considerable in the context of the period. As the number of factories multiplied, from 778 with a combined capitalization of 44,590,000 yen in 1894 to 1,881 factories with a combined capitalization of 105,380,000 yen by 1897, so too did the industrial work force begin to assume large proportions. For instance, in 1892, there were 294,425 factory workers in Japan; by 1897, this number had reached 439,549. In the last six months of 1897, the year in which the first unions arose, there were thirty-two strikes encompassing 3,517 workers; in 1898, forty-three strikes occurred, involving 6,293 participants.[4]

Within the bureaucracy, socialist thought was seen to be beyond the pale of acceptable political discourse, but the German school of social policy (*Sozialpolitik*) became influential as a way of dealing with social problems without resorting to socialist solutions. The formation of the Society for the Study of Social Policy (*Shakai Seisaku Gakkai*) in 1896 reflected this influence. Indeed, some of the more progressive social policy decisions of the early twentieth century could be seen as ways of containing the spread of the oppositional discourse of socialism.[5] The modestly reformist position of the Society was laid out in a prospectus issued on its formation:

> Since the spirit of extreme self-interest and of free and unrestricted competition gives rise to widening gulfs between rich and poor, we reject the principles of *laisser-faire*. We are also opposed to socialism because its plans for the destruction of capitalists and for the overthrow of the existing economic system would be detrimental to the fortunes of the nation. We believe that, if the present system of private property is maintained and if, within its limits, class friction is prevented by the exercise of state power and by exertions of individual citizens, we may look forward to the continuation of social harmony.[6]

Socialist ideas were first introduced through the publications of the *Minyūsha*. The *Minyūsha* journal *Kokumin no Tomo* (*The Nation's Friend*) included articles on aspects of socialism, and reports on socialist movements in Europe.[7] Some Japanese monographs on socialism appeared in the 1890s[8] and the first sustained socialist organizations were established in the late 1890s.[9] The *Shokkō Giyūkai* (Knights of Labour) laid the groundwork for the formation of the Society for the Promotion of Labour (*Rōdō Kumiai Kiseikai*, established in 1897). The Society for the Study of Socialism (*Shakai Shugi Kenkyūkai*, established in 1898) re-formed as the Socialist Association (*Shakai Shugi Kyōkai*) in 1900.

Members of these pioneering organizations were to become leaders in the socialist, anarchist, and labour movements. Katayama and others published the journal *Rōdō Sekai* (*Labour World*) from December 1897,[10] and an interest in labour conditions was also promoted by such journalistic works as Yokoyama Gennosuke's *Nihon no Kasō Shakai* (*The Lower Social Strata of Japan*) which appeared in 1899.[11] At the same time, former liberal activist Ōi Kentarō was involved in founding the Greater Japan Labour Association (*Dai Nihon Rōdō Kyōkai*), an organization devoted to research on labour issues. After an initial focus on the amelioration of working conditions, these early socialists started to campaign for the removal of property qualifications for suffrage, and worked for the creation of socialist political parties.

Although women formed the majority of the still small industrial labour force, the earliest labour reformers spoke to an implicitly masculine group of workers. The writers of 'A Summons to the Workers', issued in 1897, refer to workers' desire to support their wives and children, and lament that industrialization has taken women out of the home and into the factories, describing this as 'unnatural', and displaying a protective attitude to women workers. Although the workers are referred to in ostensibly gender-neutral terms, gender bias is revealed by the references to the workers' 'wives and children'.[12] While the journal *Rōdō Sekai* (*Labour World*) included reports on the conditions of women workers, these women were constructed either as competitors for men's jobs, or as objects of pity. Suzuki Yūko also notes the journal's portrayal of women's participation in waged labour as a threat to the family, and describes this attitude as 'the labour movement's [version of] the ideology of good wives and wise mothers'.[13] Women workers were an object of description and analysis, rather than being addressed as potential unionists.

The development of the socialist and labour movements was restricted by State actions. The Peace Regulations of 1887 had given the police powers to ban mass meetings, and the Public Peace Police Law of 1900 was to give even more extensive powers. Women, minors, police and members of the armed forces were prohibited from engaging in political activity. Article 17 of the Public Peace Police Law banned the promotion of labour organizations and it was illegal to incite workers to strike.[14] This legislation was used in May 1901 to ban the newly-founded Social Democratic Party (*Shakai Minshutō*).[15] From this time on, 'people intending to hold a meeting involving political speeches or discussion were required to report this to the police, giving information about the site, time, and names and addresses of the chief participants.'[16]

Several books devoted to an exposition of socialism appeared around the turn of the century.[17] The philosophy espoused by the early social-ists was somewhat eclectic: Saint-Simon and Fourier, Marx and Lassalle, Proudhon and Bakunin, Henry George, and Tolstoy, represented strands of thought which could all be included under the broad banner of socialism in the early 1900s in Japan. It was not until after the Russo–Japanese War that socialism came to be synonymous with Marxism in Japan.[18]

The first conjunction of feminism and socialism became apparent in the Commoners' Society (*Heiminsha*), through the participation of some women in this organization, and through socialist attempts to address the 'woman question'. The society was established in 1903 by Sakai Toshihiko and Kōtoku Shūsui, and continued its activities in one form or another through the first decade of the twentieth century. The name *Heiminsha* may remind us of one of the antecedents of the social-ist movement – the left wing of the nineteenth-century liberal move-ment, where Tokutomi Sohō espoused his philosophy of *Heiminshugi* ('commonerism') in the pages of the journal *Kokumin no Tomo* (*The Nation's Friend*); a lineage which was acknowledged by the founders of the Commoners' Society:

> The Japanese Socialist Party is indebted to the Minyūsha . . . He [Sohō] became an instigator of strikes . . . The Minyūsha was a second Meirokusha, it became a well-spring for new thought. The currents of socialism in Japan can truly be said to have emerged from this source.[19]

The founders of the *Heiminsha*, Sakai Toshihiko and Kōtoku Shūsui, were employed as journalists by the *Yorozu Chōhō* (*Complete Morning Report*) until they resigned over their criticism of the newspaper's edi-torial support for war with Russia. They then started publishing the weekly *Heimin Shinbun* (*Commoners' News*).[20] Pacifism was to be a major theme of writings in the newspaper, and the Russo–Japanese War pro-vided the socialists with an opportunity for public statement of the principles of internationalism.[21] Despite the internationalist sentiments of the socialists, Japan's first military victory over a European power also became a focus for nationalist sentiment, in the form of the Hibiya Riots of 1905, where people protested against the terms of the Ports-mouth Peace Treaty.[22]

The weekly *Heimin Shinbun* appeared until January 1905. After its closure *Chokugen* (*Plain Talk*) moved from a monthly to a weekly sched-ule, and became the main publication of the socialist movement.[23] The background of the *Heiminsha* members is revealed in a series of short articles where individual male socialists explain 'How I Became a Social-ist'. Several mention a background in Confucianism and contact with the liberal movement, followed by flirtation with the religious doctrines of Christianity or the scientific doctrine of Darwinism. Influential texts include Bellamy's *Looking Backward*, Ely's *French and German Socialism*, Schäffle's *The Quintessence of Socialism*, the writings of Henry George, and the publications of the *Minyūsha*.[24] Few of these books would be included in any modern canon of socialist texts.

Most of the contributors to this series see socialism as the answer to poverty and other social problems, problems which are made concrete in Yamaguchi Koken's description of walking through a Tokyo slum. He considers religion, science and virtue as possible solutions to the problem of poverty, rejecting each in turn until he hears about socialism. According to socialist thought, society should be made to resemble 'a big family' where work and the necessities of life are guaranteed. Yamaguchi also includes mention of sexual equality in his vision of an ideal society, where there would be 'no difference between ranks, or between rich and poor, male and female', and all would be given equal access 'to benefits and to happiness'.[25]

Sakai Toshihiko employs the language of enlightenment in his account of his conversion to socialism, and this semi-religious attitude to socialism appears in several of the accounts.[26] Sakai had suffered great confusion after trying to reconcile Mencius, Confucius and French philosophy; liberalism and patriotism; Christianity, the theory of evolution, and Utilitarianism. But socialism provided him with a 'ray of light' which he could use to shed light on all of these philosophies. Finally, he felt relief when he was able to put all of these ideas in order, until there were 'no shadows and no darkness'.[27]

After this initial eclecticism, the socialist movement split into Christian socialist and materialist socialist factions in October 1905. The Christian socialist faction, including Ishikawa Sanshirō, Kinoshita Naoe and Abe Isoo, produced the journal *Shin Kigen* (*New Era*),[28] while the materialists, including Nishikawa Kōjirō and Yamaguchi Koken produced the journal *Hikari* (*Light*).[29] A second attempt to form a socialist party was made in February 1906 by members of both the Christian and materialist factions. The Japan Socialist Party (*Nihon Shakai Tō*) declared its intention to pursue legal, parliamentary means to social change, and survived until 1907. Later splits involved a conflict between the espousal of direct action and parliamentary tactics, precipitated by Kōtoku's speech on direct action at the congress of the Japan Socialist Party, just before its dissolution in 1907. The *Commoners' News* was revived as a daily newspaper from 1907.[30]

What has been relatively neglected in scholarship about these developments is that a consideration of women's issues was one element of the writings of these male socialist journalists, albeit a small element in some cases. Sakai, Kōtoku,[31] Kinoshita Naoe[32] and others wrote and gave lectures on such topics as 'Women and War' and 'Women and Politics'. Sakai in particular showed an early interest in issues related to the 'woman question'. His earliest writings on these issues appeared in the *Yorozu Chōhō*, and these articles laid the groundwork for his six-volume work: *Katei no Shinfūmi* (*A New Style of Family*), published from 1901–2.[33] Sakai's early writings carried on the liberal tradition of Ueki Emori and Fukuzawa Yukichi.[34] He would, however, go on to bring a socialist perspective to issues related to women, marriage and the family in the journal *Katei Zasshi*.[35] Of the socialist newspapers *Chokugen* had a better record than the *Heimin Shinbun* on the inclusion of women's issues. A special women's edition of *Chokugen* appeared on 23 April 1905, bearing the slogan 'The ideals of socialism develop from the gentle hearts of women'. This edition carried articles by Kinoshita Naoe and Sakai Toshihiko, and several statements by women on 'How I Became a Socialist'. The speeches from the Socialist Women's Seminar were reported regularly in the pages of *Chokugen*. Stories about women workers appear sporadically in the pages of the Commoners' publications, particularly in the weekly digest of news from Japanese newspapers.[36] Songs and poems about factory workers also appear occasionally.[37] The *Heiminsha* was also responsible for the publication of several pamphlets on Socialism and the 'Woman Question', under the *Heimin Bunkō* (Commoners' Library) imprint.[38]

Women were active in the *Heiminsha* from the earliest days.[39] The journal *Katei Zasshi* had been established by Sakai Toshihiko in order to promote socialist ideas among women, but socialist women soon established their own journals. There were at least three socialist women's journals in the first decade of the twentieth century, *Nijū Seiki no Fujin* (*Twentieth Century Woman*: 1904),[40] *Suiito Hōmu* (*Sweet Home*: 1904), and *Sekai Fujin* (*Women of the World*). Some issues of *Nijū Seiki no Fujin* have survived, but I have found no extant issues of *Sweet Home* (although we can see advertisements for *Sweet Home* in other socialist publications). The most prominent of the early socialist women's publications, *Sekai Fujin* (*Women of the World*), appeared between 1907 and 1909.[41]

Women in the Socialist Movement

Accounts of women in the early socialist movement often describe these women's activities as having been shaped by the influence of familial, marital, or romantic relationships with male socialists. In many cases, the women in such groups as the *Heiminsha* were indeed involved with male socialists. However, this emphasis on familial connections tends to obscure the independent political commitment of many of these

women. Fukuda Hideko, for example, already had a 'career' in oppositional politics before her contact with the socialists in the early
1900s.[42] She was well known for her involvement in the liberal movement, and was often described as 'the heroic woman of the Ōsaka Incident' (Ōsaka Jiken no joketsu). Her fame spread with the publication of
her autobiography Warawa no Hanseigai (My Life so Far) in 1904, and
the semi-autobiographical novel Warawa no Omoide (My Recollections) in
1905.[43]

Such a stereotypical presentation of women's political commitment
as inevitably being a result of the influence of male relatives can
ultimately tell us little about the motivations of women in the socialist
movement. What is worth exploring, however, is the use of familial
metaphors and gendered metaphors of political philosophy within
such groups as the Commoners' Society. Even women who were not
actually married to one of the male socialists were metaphorically
constructed as 'wives',[44] while the senior woman of the group, Fukuda
Hideko, was referred to as shūtome, 'mother-in-law'.[45] The use of such
fictive kinship terms implicitly constructed the organization as an
extended family, a metaphor which was made explicit by Matsuoka
[Nishikawa] Fumiko in an account published in the Heimin Shinbun.
Matsuoka identifies herself as being responsible for the Heiminsha
kitchen, and describes the Heiminsha as an extended family (daika-
zoku), complete with a pet dog called Maru (short for 'Marx'), which
performs the function of bringing out the human side of the Heiminsha members.[46]

However, within the metaphorical Heiminsha family, women performed the very real labour of providing meals and supporting the
activities of their male comrades.[47] Matsuoka makes this explicit as she
closes her reflection on the Heiminsha family: 'I still have various things
to write about, but it is time to start preparing dinner, so I will leave
them for another occasion.'[48]

Matsuoka's advertisement for a kitchen helper, which appeared in
the Heimin Shinbun of January 1905, reveals an unselfconscious accep-
tance of a sexual division of labour within the socialist movement. The
members of the Heiminsha are reluctant to employ a maid in the conventional sense, for they 'hate class differences between people'.
However, it is taken for granted that it will be a woman who assists
Matsuoka in the kitchen. On behalf of the Heiminsha 'family', Matsuoka
states that she wishes to hear from a woman who 'knows our ideas;
wishes to work for our ideals; wishes to help our happy family; and is
willing to do any kind of work'. It will be possible, she adds, to arrange
flexible hours, and time to study.[49]

The woman who answered Matsuoka's advertisement was Nobuoka

[Sakai] Tameko.[50] Accounts of such women as Nobuoka provide evidence that many young women in fact made an independent decision to leave country towns and come to Tokyo to participate in the socialist movement, without the influence of a male partner. Kanno Suga also contacted the socialist movement independently after hearing speeches by Kinoshita Naoe, and reading Sakai Toshihiko's journalistic writings.[51]

Some sense of the motivations of women who became involved in the socialist movement can be gained from a group of short articles in the women's edition of *Chokugen* (*Plain Talk*) in April 1905. Each takes the form of a statement by a woman on 'How I Became a Socialist'.[52] Nishikawa Fumiko identifies the inheritance of private property as the cause of inequality in society, and refers to having read the journal *Rōdō Sekai* (*Labour World*).[53] Nobuoka Tameko was influenced by such publications as Sakai Toshihiko's *Katei Zasshi* (*Family Magazine*). Nobuoka states that she was influenced by Sakai's views on the family, and started reading the *Commoners' News* when Sakai left the *Yorozu Chōhō*. The Russo–Japanese War was another major turning point in Nobuoka's politicization.[54] Sugaya Iwako refers to reading a Russian novel which portrayed a woman who sacrificed herself to the socialist cause, and states that this stimulated her curiosity about socialism. A 'kind Professor of Economics' spent several hours explaining socialism to her.[55] Kamikawa Matsuko gives an almost visionary account of meditating on the injustices of the world, and realizing the futility of religion, education, and virtue in rectifying such problems. Like Sakai Toshihiko and Yamaguchi Koken before her, she concludes that it is better to trust in socialism than religion in cleaning up 'the muddy stream' of society.[56]

Several of the women relate heart-wrenching scenes of poverty and hardship which prompted feelings of compassion. For Matsuoka, it was those who had to eke out a living while studying hard; for Nobuoka it was the wounded in the Russo–Japanese War; for Sugaya, it was the sight of a beggar woman suckling her baby.[57] Few of the women profess any philosophical knowledge. Rather they emphasize feelings of compassion which led them to the socialist movement.

In the case of Matsuoka [Nishikawa] Fumiko, the link between compassion and socialism is explained in gendered terms. This 'gendering' of socialist philosophy is explained in the text of the aforementioned speech from the Socialist Women's Seminar.[58] According to Matsuoka [Nishikawa]'s account, socialism as a humane and caring philosophy is implicitly contrasted with the masculine and aggressive values of capitalism. Such a linking of socialist philosophy and 'feminine' values could also be found in the writings of the British Utopian socialists,[59] and contrasts with the language of 'class war' to be found in Marxist socialism.[60] Thus, while the women of the *Heiminsha* challenged expectations of suitable feminine behaviour by their decision to participate in oppositional political activity, the form of their participation was often understood in gendered terms.

The Socialist Women's Seminar

One of the *Heiminsha* activities specifically directed at women was the Socialist Women's Seminar (*Shakai Shugi Fujin Kōen Kai*).[61] These lectures were held at either the *Heiminsha* premises or at a public hall in Kanda. The commencement of the new lecture series was announced in the *Commoners' News* in January 1901. The participants intended to 'investigate the woman question', focusing on such issues as 'professions for women, the reform of the family, free marriage (*jiyū kekkon*), and education for women'. The author of the report is confident, however, that 'the basic solution to these issues is none other than socialism'.[62]

The first Socialist Women's Seminar was held 23 January 1904, and meetings took place roughly once a month after that. Only a short report of the first meeting appears in the *Heimin Shinbun*,[63] but later sessions are reported in more detail in *Heimin Shinbun, Chokugen* or *Katei Zasshi*. At the first few sessions, not only the speakers, but most of the audience were men. Speeches included Sakai Toshihiko on 'The Class System within the Family', 'Relations Between Parents and Children', and 'What is Femininity?;[64] Nishikawa Kōjirō on 'The Main Points of the Woman Question';[65] Ishikawa Sanshirō on 'Woman's Vocation';[66] and Abe Isoo on 'Women and Revolutionary Movements'.[67] Some of the speeches are prescriptive statements by men on their expectations of women in the socialist movement. In other cases, however, the occasion provided an opportunity to introduce the ideas of Bebel and others.[68]

The first occasion at which women spoke was 6 November 1904. The speakers were Sugaya Iwako, Teramoto [Oguchi] Michiko, and Matsuoka [Nishikawa] Fumiko. A summary of Nishikawa's speech was published in the *Heimin Shinbun* under the title 'Socialism and Women's Nature'.[69] Gradually the women in the audience expanded beyond the immediate Commoners' circle to include various women with an interest in socialism.[70]

Matsuoka [Nishikawa] Fumiko contributed several speeches to the series. In one contribution she tells the story of Shizuka Gozen, the mistress of Yoshitsune, and uses Shizuka as an example of a woman who stuck to her ideals without wavering. This historical figure is presented as an example for modern women to emulate.[71] An interest in literary and historical figures is also apparent in Sugaya Iwako's speech on 'Women in the Tale of Genji'. Sugaya categorizes the women in Murasaki's novel according to the particular form of exploitation suffered: some are sacrificed in political alliances, some are trapped in loveless marriages, some are sacrificed to men's 'animal passions', while others are unhappy because of the practice of polygyny. Sugaya uses Genji as a starting point for a critique of the sexual double standard.[72]

Socialist Views of Marriage and the Family

A constant topic of discussion at the Socialist Women's Seminar and in the socialist press was marriage and the family. Issues related to marriage and *jiyū ren'ai* (free love) were aired repeatedly in the mainstream socialist press and in socialist women's journals. Many of the male speakers and writers on socialism assumed a natural connection between socialism and 'free love', and seemed to assume that their female listeners and readers were primarily interested in romantic matters. While Matsuoka [Nishikawa] Fumiko had linked socialism with the 'feminine' values of nurturance and compassion, Murai Tomoyoshi invited women to 'fall in love' with socialism.[73]

Views on love and marriage ranged from descriptions of the European bourgeois ideal of companionate marriage, to an espousal of 'democratic' family arrangements reminiscent of the early Meiji debate on women, to an affirmation of 'free love' which accompanied a complete rejection of marriage and the family system. Women's role within marriage was occasionally likened to slavery,[74] and the condition of wives could be linked with the situation of other women, such as prostitutes, who laboured under unfree conditions.[75] Sakai Toshihiko attempted to develop a socialist perspective on marriage and the family in his writings in *Katei Zasshi* and in several monographs and translations. The socialist women's newspaper *Sekai Fujin* also included extended debates on issues related to marriage, the family system, 'free love', and women's economic independence.[76] Nishikawa [Matsuoka] Fumiko contributed articles on marriage and the family to all of the early socialist publications, and would continue her critique of marriage in the journal *Shin Shin Fujin* (*The True New Woman*) which she edited from 1913 to 1923.[77]

In an article on 'Women as Wives' in *Nijū Seiki no Fujin*, Imai Utako presents a view of marriage almost indistinguishable from European ideals of bourgeois companionate marriage. Indeed, most of the examples she chooses to illustrate her discussion of women's provision of 'assistance', 'solace', and 'entertainment' to their husbands come from Europe: they are the wives of Bismarck, Gladstone, Madison, and Fawcett. She does, however, mention some Japanese examples of notable wives, including Hatoyama Haruko.[78]

In another article, however, Imai criticizes the ideology of 'good wives and wise mothers' and considers the possibility of women engaging in public activities, and working for 'the happiness of society and peace for all' on the model of American women. For Imai, it seems, the role of woman as helpmate in the home could be compatible with some kinds of public activities, although these were likely to be gender-typed activities: nursing, education, the arts, and voluntary activities.[79] In another article, she valorizes the role of women as having perfect qualifications to act as 'conciliators' for society (*shakaiteki chōwasha*).[80] Other socialist women, such as Nishikawa [Matsuoka] Fumiko and Kanno Suga, attempted to expand the notion of suitable activities for women. Kanno's initial proposal was somewhat modest – that women should set aside half-an-hour each day for reading, and thus take an interest in political matters.[81]

In an editorial in the *Heimin Shinbun* on the topic of 'free love', Ishikawa Sanshirō quotes British Socialist writer Robert Blatchford, who advocated that men and women should be able to enter into relationships freely and break off relationships just as freely without the structures of marriage and divorce. Ishikawa concedes that there are some dangers in the practice of 'free love'. In response to fears that such practices would result in an increase in separations, however, he asserts that this is better than existing marriages, which are entered into under false pretences.[82]

Faults in the existing marriage system could also be linked with the issue of prostitution. In 1905, Matsuoka [Nishikawa] Fumiko reported on a walk through the Yoshiwara licensed district with two other women. The title of the report 'Record of Sightseeing in Yoshiwara' suggests a somewhat voyeuristic attitude to the women of the Yoshiwara, an attitude which would be replicated in the more famous incident involving members of the Bluestocking Society.[83] Matsuoka's account focuses on the conditions of the prostitutes – their confinement behind wooden gratings is compared with that of caged animals in the zoo. Matsuoka laments that the women are treated like 'non-human commodities', and that they have 'lost the freedom [to express] human emotions'. Matsuoka understands that they are probably doing this work for the sake of aged parents or invalid relatives, and 'in thinking about their fate', she hated 'the society which placed our comrades in such pitiful circumstances'. The issue was also raised by Ibara Hanako, in *Women of the World*, who contrasted women who sought individual liberation in calling for women's rights with the situation of prostitutes who were in a condition of slavery.[84] For some later socialist writers, prosititution would be used as a symbol for the exploitation of women in a capitalist society.[85]

Not all socialist writers, however, advocated a complete rejection of the family system. An editorial in *Women of the World* in December 1908, considers 'The Family in Communal Society'. The writer considers the view that socialism necessarily means a rejection of the family in favour of communal solutions to problems of childcare and care for the aged, and concludes that people may be reluctant to resort to solutions which may conflict with the ideal of *ninjō* (human feeling and compassion). The writer refers to the transformations which the family has undergone through history and suggests that, while the family will continue to exist in a communal society, it will undergo further transformation.

The writer goes on to argue that, once the wealth of society is communalized, the family will no longer be held together simply by economic necessity. This will allow the emergence of relationships within the family where the motive power is that of the pure human feelings of love between husband and wife and between parents and children. In response to the view that love within the family is based on selfish individualism, and should thus be abolished, the writer argues that it is the present social system which sets up this conflict between the needs of the family and society, and that under a communal society, love will be able to emerge in a purer, more beautiful form. This is presented as only a provisional view, for socialist thought, it is argued, will undoubtedly undergo further transformations.[86] Although the names of Morgan and Engels are not mentioned, it seems likely that the writer is drawing on this strand of thought on the family. By this time Sakai Toshihiko had published at least two works which drew on Engels' ideas on the family.[87]

Abe Isoo tackles the subject of 'Women and Genetics', in an article published in *Sekai Fujin* in January 1909. Abe uses quasi-scientific arguments to challenge some accepted notions about women and marriage. He challenges the view that a woman's body is only a vessel for the unborn child (encapsulated in the Japanese saying '*onna no hara wa karimono*'), arguing that this view displays a superstition that the child only inherits its father's genetic makeup. Abe points out that a child receives its genetic inheritance equally from its father and mother: thus, the mother's body is more than a 'borrowed womb'.[88]

In the 1900s there was also some discussion of the roles of fathers, with several writers mentioning the necessity of 'good husbands and wise fathers' (*ryōfu kenfu*) as companions for the 'good wives and wise mothers'.[89] Some writers challenged the sexual divisions in the labour market, and argued that more occupations and professions should be opened to women. Few of these writers, however, addressed the division of labour in the home whereby women have the major responsibility for childcare and domestic labour.

The search for a socialist view of marriage and the family involved, first of all, a questioning of the relationship between husband and wife. This concern could be extended to an interest in relationships in society at large. As in the early Meiji period, the family could be seen as paradigmatic of social relations in general. The deficiencies of the present family system were seen to be symptomatic of problems with the existing economic system, and the family was a site for imagining the forms and practices of an ideal communal society.

In Japan, as in other socialist movements, the family could be used as a metaphor for any organization run on communal principles. The familial metaphor was employed by Sakai Toshihiko, who described the *Heiminsha* as a refuge from the restrictions of society.[90] Here, it is the *Heiminsha* that is described as a family. In socialist rhetoric on the ideal society, however, the whole of society was sometimes described as a family where all members of society would be looked after. Yamaguchi Koken, for example, had described the ideal socialist society as a 'big family'.[91]

Imagining New Relationships

Socialists also turned to fictional genres in order to facilitate the imagining of a new society, with new relationships between individuals, and between individuals and the State. Fiction also provided a forum for the dramatization of social issues: the experience of the families and friends of young men conscripted to fight against China and Russia, or the conditions of workers under industrialization.

In Kinoshita Naoe's novels, *Hi no Hashira* (*Pillar of Fire*)[92] and *Ryōjin no Jihaku* (*A Husband's Confession, 1904–1906*), descriptions of social issues and the activities of socialist groups are overlaid with melodramatic and romantic plot structures.[93] The protagonist of *Hi no Hashira* is a Christian socialist journalist with some similarities to Kinoshita himself, who comes in contact with an early socialist group, is instrumental in helping a *geisha* leave her tea house, and witnesses a coal miners' strike in Kyūshū. *Ryōjin no Jihaku* centres on a lawyer, and social issues are depicted through 'such characters as tenant farmers, a prostitute, a *geisha*, the hostess at a hot springs hotel, and a noble representing the Red Cross', and textile factory workers.[94]

An interesting example of such writing is Fukuda Hideko's *Warawa no Omoide* (*My Memories*). Fukuda, as we have seen, was an important member of the liberal and socialist movements, who had dramatized the experiences of a female activist in her autobiography *Warawa no*

Hanseigai (My Life So Far). While the autobiography had crossed boundaries of public and private, displayed anxieties and ambivalences about gender identity, and included discussion of the experience of embodiment, the novel is much more conventional in form, in particular being bound by the plot structures of romantic fiction. In its choice of a woman as main character, it contrasts with Kinoshita's novels.

The main character, Yamamoto Setsuko, seems at first quite similar to Fukuda herself, in her move from Okayama to Tokyo, and her philosophical trajectory from liberalism, through an interest in Christianity, to an embrace of socialism. The main character also undergoes similar educational experiences, and shares Fukuda's aspirations to help educate women for self-sufficiency, in ventures carried out with female comrades. However, rather than focusing on these biographical details, I am interested in the author's attempt to come to terms with the complexities of personal relationships in intellectual circles of the 1900s. As in Kinoshita's novels, the Russo–Japanese War and the development of the early socialist movement provide the backdrop for a romantic plot.[95]

The characters in the novel all experience various restrictions on their freedom: men are conscripted, both men and women are promised to unacceptable marriage partners, and women are unable to achieve economic independence through their lack of education. It takes several years for Yamamoto to be united with her partner, but they are finally married in a resolution which evades the contradictions between the 'old philosophy' and the 'new philosophy' of marriage. The narrator explains that while old-fashioned marriages were based on considerations of property, status, and bloodline, modern marriages are based on mutual compatibility of partners.[96] Yamamoto Setsuko marries the partner of her choice, on his return from studying in America, but he is adopted into the family of the uncle who has acted *in loco parentis* for Yamamoto. The uncle/father allows them to continue their work and studies in Tokyo, and even the patriarchal naming system is blurred slightly as *both* partners take the surname of the uncle's household 'Kobayashi'. While Fukuda's autobiography had depicted a subject-in-process, ending with a woman widowed but determined to continue her activities in pursuit of socialism and women's emancipation, in the novel all contradictions are resolved. The main character marries the object of her romantic interest, and they resolve to work together, free of the contradictions between activism and domestic expectations which dogged the lives of actual women activists.[97] Fukuda's novel is thus utopian in imagining a comradely form of marriage, where activism and romantic love come together, but also demonstrates that, in imagining ideal forms of society and personal relationships, even oppositional thinkers were often constrained by conventional plots.

Socialists and the Patriotic Women's Association

The search for more equitable relationships and a more democratic family form was linked to a questioning of the role of woman as 'helpmate' within marriage. This led to a questioning of the role of woman as 'helpmate' to the State, and a revaluation of the possibilities for women's political activities. The dominant construction of women as 'wives and mothers' of the State had become explicit with the formation of the Patriotic Women's Association (*Aikoku Fujin Kai*) on 24 February 1901.[98] In 1902, the organization started publishing its own journal *Aikoku Fujin* (*Patriotic Woman*). By the end of the Russo–Japanese War, the membership of the Patriotic Women's Association had leapt from an initial 45 000 to 463 000. By 1912 the organization had 816 609 members, making it the largest women's organization in the Meiji period.

Although initially formed as a private organization, the activities of the Patriotic Women's Association were congruent with bureaucratic definitions of the role of 'good wives and wise mothers', and the organization came to take on a semi-official character. The Russo–Japanese War saw an expansion of the membership of the Patriotic Women's Association, and several other women's organizations also became involved in activities which supported the war effort, including fundraising activities and the preparation of packages to send to soldiers serving overseas.[99]

The activities of this association provided an opportunity for comment by several socialist writers on the issue of women's political participation. In a sense, the Patriotic Women's Association provided a living example of the implications of subjecthood for women under the Meiji regime which emphasized 'a wealthy country and a strong army' supported by 'good wives and wise mothers'. While women were politically confined to the domestic sphere by Article Five of the Peace Police Law of 1900 which prevented them from attending or holding political meetings or joining political parties, their support for militarism could be sought where necessary. By contrast, several of the male and female socialist writers argued for a view of women and politics whereby women could become citizens with rights which matched their obligations. In addition to direct criticism of the notion of good wives and wise mothers,[100] they also criticized the activities of the Patriotic Women's Association.

Several of the male socialist journalists wrote and gave lectures on 'Women and War' and 'Women and Politics'. Although sometimes demonstrating an essentialist position on women's peace-loving nature, they were universally critical of the Patriotic Women's Association's support for militarism. Such criticism was voiced by both Kinoshita Naoe and Kōtoku Shūsui.[101] In a speech to the Socialist Women's Seminar (*Shakai Shugi Fujin Kōen*), Kōtoku pointed out the contradictions of a state which expected women to devote their energies to the war effort, but denied them basic political rights.

> In Japan, the relationship between women and politics is a very strange one. When there is a war, suddenly women are told to devote their energies to the state because they are Japanese subjects. But, up till now women have been said to have no connection with politics, and have even been prohibited from listening to political speeches! It is strange that no women lament the fact that they are manipulated at the whim of man and the state, and are told to sacrifice their own needs by a society and laws based on masculine principles. So this is the state of women in this twentieth century civilized nation, this first-rate nation, this Imperial Japan![102]

Kōtoku stated that women would be better off working for world peace than supporting the war effort, and suggested that helping the hundreds of thousands of female factory workers might be a more lasting occupation than short-term work as a war nurse. Kōtoku even blamed war – with its emphasis on masculine physical strength (*wanryoku*) – for the low position of women in society, and predicted that women's position would only improve with the eradication of war, and the advent of a society which did not value physical strength.[103] Kōtoku also attempted to extend the definition of politics to include what goes on in the home. The following passage displays a cautious challenge to existing stereotypes. Kōtoku wavers between trying to take women out of the kitchen, and trying to bring politics into the home:

> The aim of politics is [the achievement of] a comfortable life for all people. If the basis of a good life is a good kitchen, then there must be a relationship between politics and the kitchen, therefore women also have a connection with politics. While women have ignored politics and followed the words of men, they have had their needs and rights trampled on. If they can't protect their own rights and needs, how can they promote those of their husbands and children? In order to become a 'good wife and wise mother' first of all learn about politics and participate in politics. Don't say 'I could do it if I were a man', rather say 'I must do it because I am a woman'. You should demand political rights without feeling inferior to Western women, and without being scared of being labelled as 'impudent'. Strike out into the world of politics and demand the return of the rights which have been snatched away from you.[104]

What is interesting about this extract is Kōtoku's use of the language of rights. According to Kōtoku's rhetoric women are potential citizens who should 'demand' the 'rights' which have been taken away from them. In a common rhetorical move of the time, he also employs the conventional language of 'good wives and wise mothers', but redefines the phrase to include an interest in politics, and a new definition of suitable feminine behaviour. Kōtoku's women are still identified with the kitchen, but this space is redefined.

Nijū Seiki no Fujin (Women of the Twentieth Century), was established in 1904. Its founders, Imai Utako and Kawamura Haruko,[105] were connected with the *Heiminsha* and also founded a women's organization known as the Hokkaidō Women Comrades Society (*Hokkaidō Fujin Dōshi Kai*).[106] Although the journal does not display a clearly articulated socialist philosophy, there was a willingness to consider women as workers, and in roles which could not fit easily into the framework of 'good wives and wise mothers'.[107]

As this was at the height of the Russo–Japanese War, several articles were devoted to a consideration of the theme of Women and War.[108] Imai Utako – the journal's editor – pointed to the dangers of excessive excitement about Japan's military engagements on the mainland.[109] She warned that Japan must also take responsibility for what happened *after* the war with Russia, and her discussion of this issue reveals an implicit support for Japanese imperialism. This passage supports Suzuki Yūko's view of Imai as a proponent of women's rights (*jokenshugisha*) and nationalism (*kokkenshugisha*), rather than of socialism.[110]

Unlike most other writers in the socialist press, Imai saw the charitable activities of the Patriotic Women's Association in a positive light. In other words, she did not go very far in challenging the notion of woman as helpmate.[111] Unlike Kōtoku, Imai valorized the activities of nurses,[112] and displayed an emotional attitude towards bereaved families. Imai and other women also pointed out one of the consequences of women's role as passive supporters of militarism. They were likely to become war widows, with little hope of receiving State support.[113]

While Imai was relatively cautious in her criticism of women's support for the militarist state, the issue of the relationship between individual and state was highlighted in a graphic way from another quarter. There were several anti-war poems written at the time of the Russo–Japanese War, the most prominent of which was '*Kimi shini tamau koto nakare*' (*Do not give up your life for the Emperor*) by Yosano Akiko.[114] Yosano was castigated for the publication of this poem, which was described by a literary columnist as 'an expression of dangerous thoughts which disparage the idea of the national family'. Yosano was described as 'a traitorous subject, a rebel, a criminal who deserves the nation's

punishment'.[115] It seems that Yosano's placing of personal loyalty above
loyalty to the Emperor was what made the poem treasonable:

> Do not offer your life.
> The Emperor himself does not go to battle.
> The Imperial Heart is deep;
> How could he ever wish
> That men shed their blood,
> That men die like beasts,
> That men's glory be in death?

> Dearest brother,
> Do not offer your life in battle.
> Mother, whom father left behind
> This past autumn,
> Suffered when
> In the midst of her grief
> Her son was called away.

Other women's anti-war poems at the time of the Russo–Japanese
War were similar in their focus on private experiences of grief at odds
with the prevailing mood of patriotism.[116] The female narrators of these
poems were constructed as passive observers of militarism.[117] Although
their private suffering was not linked to a political critique, there was
radical potential in the mere suggestion of private interests at odds with
public interests. Since the earliest years of the Meiji period, the words
family and state had always appeared in conjunction, with the implication that family interests and State interests were identical. Women,
in these poetic representations, were asserting particularistic claims
based on family and community, in opposition to State interests.[118]
These anti-war poems provided an imaginative space for questioning
the relationship between individual, family and state. Further questioning of this relationship was carried out in socialist writings on women's
political participation, in their attempts to conceptualize a relationship
between individual and state which was not mediated by the family.

In 1907 Fukuda Hideko established the fortnightly socialist women's
newspaper *Sekai Fujin* (*Women of the World*). The author of *Warawa no
Hanseigai* and *Warawa no Omoide* had already explored the problems of
female political activism from an individual point of view through the
genres of the autobiography and the novel. In *Women of the World* she
was able to place questions of women's political participation in a
broader societal context, and work towards the articulation of a socialist
position on these issues. An early issue carried an editorial on 'Women
and Political Freedom', including a scathing attack on the Patriotic
Women's Association, in terms which echoed Kōtoku's speech of 1904:

. . . We have seen the activities of the Patriotic Women's Association from the time of the recent Russo–Japanese War. All of the tens of thousands of members of this organization, from the president down, are women without political rights under Japanese law. Yet everyone, from members of political parties to the general public praises the success of this organization.

Recently, we often see press reports of the interesting fact that women have been described as 'servants of the state' (*hanninkan no ninmei*), but I feel that people should look critically at [such statements]. After all, the law of Japan which designates women as 'incompetents' (*munōryokusha*) is the same law which appoints women to the role of serving the state.

In the midst of the 'success of the Patriotic Women's Association' and 'the appointment of women as servants of the state' – of all this glory and recognition for women – it should be said that women are not free. The 'success' of women who are not free is the success of slaves . . .'[119]

The issue of women's political participation was followed closely in the pages of *Sekai Fujin*. Although *Sekai Fujin* also carried columns on cookery and sewing, the title of the journal (*Women of the World*) signalled that women's interests went far beyond the confines of the home – indeed to the whole world. In addition to articles on women's issues, fiction and poetry, and articles on sewing and cooking, each issue carried columns of domestic and overseas news. There is coverage of the conditions of women workers, and reportage of strikes by woman factory workers (Nos 3, 11, 23, 28 and 30). The problems of professional women are also considered (Nos 1 and 5), and at least one article reports on *Karayuki-san* – the women sent to Southeast Asia to work as prostitutes (No. 30). Struggles by other workers were also reported, such as the actions of the mine workers at Ashio (Nos 4, 11 and 12), an early site of labour activism in Japan. Thus, the journal emphasized the fact that women were *workers* as well as carrying out a domestic and mothering role. International news included coverage of suffragist and women's labour movements. Almost every issue carried reports on women's political activities, not only in Australasia, America and the United Kingdom, but in such places as Iceland, Finland, Hungary, Turkey and India. There were articles on labour conditions and political activities of women in these countries (Nos 4, 11, 14 and 16), and reportage on suffrage conferences, international socialist conferences, and peace conferences (Nos 6, 13, 16, 28 and 30). The front page often carried a profile of some famous woman, such as Madame de Stael (No. 2), Madame Roland (No. 3), Florence Nightingale (No. 5), Sappho (No. 6), Jenny Lind (No. 7), Harriet Beecher Stow (No. 4) or Joan of Arc (No. 24). A concern with the working conditions of Japanese women was thus linked to a consciousness of the existence of an international feminist movement and an interest in the history and conditions of women in other countries. This consciousness also extended to socialism, pacifism and unionism as international movements.

Many of the contributors to *Sekai Fujin* were male members of the socialist movement. In addition to articles by Kōtoku Shūsui, Sakai Toshihiko, Yamaguchi Koken, and Abe Isoo on socialism and the woman question, Ishikawa Sanshirō translated Kropotkin's thoughts on anarchism, Stendhal's attack on the family, and introduced the works of Marx in issues 26 to 29. Other contributors included Tanaka Shōzō, the leader of the people's struggles at the Ashio copper mine, and Futabatei Shimei, a well-known literary figure, who contributed articles and translated literary works from Russian.

The eclectic roots of early Japanese socialism are apparent in the cover illustration of *Sekai Fujin*, No. 32, January 1909 (see p.1). An image of 'the dawn of socialism' has been adapted to the Japanese context with the addition of vertical banners bearing the words 'liberty' (*jiyū*) and 'community' (*kyōsan*) in Chinese characters. The torch-bearing female figure in the illustration is reminiscent of Joan of Arc, a figure idolised by Fukuda herself, and often employed in European socialist and feminist iconography.[120] The illustration is bordered by quotes from William Morris, Robert Blatchford and Kropotkin.

The producers of *Sekai Fujin*, in common with other left-wing journalists of the time, were subject to constant police harassment. Several issues were banned, and the writers and publisher were fined or imprisoned several times. Finally, in 1909, the journal was forced to close. Unfortunately, Fukuda was not backed by a strong organization, so that the journal's fate depended on the energy and endurance of Fukuda and a few of her socialist comrades. However, in addition to the role of this journal in attempting to bring together two strands of oppositional thought – socialism and feminism – *Sekai Fujin* provided a focus for the latter stages of a campaign for the repeal of Article Five of the Public Peace Police Law.

The Campaign for the Repeal of Article Five

Criticism of the activities of the 'patriotic women' in the socialist press challenged the construction of woman as 'helpmate' to the state. A logical conclusion of this criticism of women's position was a campaign for the modification of Article Five of the Public Peace Police Law: the regulation which prevented women from attending public political meetings or joining political parties. This campaign, carried out by women connected with the socialist movement between 1904 and 1909, has been described as the first group action by Japanese women for the purpose of the attainment of political rights.[121]

Imai Utako, Kawamura Haruko and Matsuoka [Nishikawa] Fumiko

led the first stage of the campaign for the revision of Article Five. Their petition of 460 signatures was presented to the Lower House by two sympathetic Diet members (Ebara Soroku and Shimada Saburō) on 24 January 1905.[122] A second petition of 227 signatures was presented on 1 February 1906. A further petition of 233 signatures, collected by Sakai Tameko, Kōtoku Chiyoko, and Fukuda Hideko was presented on 13 March 1907. At this stage a proposal for an amendment to the law was presented to the Lower House. A further attempt was made on 24 March 1908 when Endō Kiyoko was able to collect 64 signatures. Each petition was discussed in the Diet and an amendment to allow women to attend political meetings actually passed the Lower House, but failed to pass the House of Peers.[123]

Justification for the amendment of Article Five in the socialist press generally used the logic of liberalism and the rhetoric of progress. Writers emphasized the similarities between men and women, pointing to the illogicality of a system which denied women political rights but required certain obligations of them.[124] It was pointed out that women, like men, were subject to the obligation to pay taxes, women were liable for punishment by the criminal system, and women were subject to the effects of government legislation. The demand for such rights was described as 'natural' and 'reasonable', and comparisons were made with other countries, in particular Australia, which not only allowed women to engage in public political activities, but also to vote and stand for office.[125]

In one article, this law is presented as anachronistic, a hangover from former customs of 'seclusion of women'. This writer points to improvements in women's education, and the increased interest shown in politics by women as justifications for extending women's political rights. These arguments were reproduced in petitions and statements on the issue. Petitions and articles on this issue also reproduced the list of categories of people prevented from engaging in political activities: military and naval personnel, police, Shintō and Buddhist priests, students and teachers of public and private schools, women, minors, and those whose 'rights had been removed or suspended'.[126]

While some members of the bureaucracy had apparently attempted to use the example of police, teachers and other public servants to suggest that women were excluded because of the important public implications of the service they performed in the home, the socialist women concentrated on the category of 'minors', and pointed out the insulting implications for women. The aforementioned editorial on 'Women and Political Freedom' in *Sekai Fujin* brings together all of these themes. In an attack on the hypocrisy of a state which denies women political rights while expecting them to perform state functions,

the writer questions the fashion for describing women as 'servants of
the state':

> Recently, we often see press reports of the interesting fact that women have
> been described as 'servants of the state' (*hanninkan no ninmei*), but I feel
> that people should look critically at [such statements]. After all, the law of
> Japan which designates women as 'incompetents' (*munōryokusha*) is the same
> law which appoints women to the role of serving the state.[127]

This editorial presents one of the few attempts at this stage to go
beyond liberal arguments for women's political rights. If this editorial
was authored by Fukuda, as has been assumed, she has obviously had
access to some of the European socialist writings on the 'woman question' in the three years since the publication of her autobiography. The
editorial refers to the work of Morgan on 'primitive' societies where
men and women participate equally in the political life of the group,
and uses the argument that women's decline in status is linked to the
defeat of matriarchy and the development of patriarchy.[128] Modern
Japanese society is contrasted with 'barbarian' societies (*yabanjidai*)
where women had political rights. However, she sarcastically attempts
to reassure her readers that what she and her fellow campaigners are
asking for is much more modest than what women had in these 'primitive' societies. They are only asking for the freedom to attend political
meetings and form political organizations.[129] Like many socialist and
feminist writers since Engels, we can see anthropological evidence of
radically different forms of social organization being used to argue for
the possibility of transforming present-day society for the better.[130]

An editorial in *Sekai Fujin* entitled 'The Dual Struggle' provides
another perspective on the issue of women and politics.[131] Here, it is
argued that women have two enemies – the class of men (*otoko no
kaikyū*) and the class of 'aristocrats and the rich' (*kizoku-fugō no kaikyū*).
It is argued that 'the class structure of society' (*shakai no kaikyūteki
soshiki*) is responsible for women's need to fight against the two
enemies. However, because the same word 'class' (*kaikyū*) is used to
describe the two sets of relationships (man/woman and propertied/
propertyless), it is at first glance difficult to distinguish this 'double
struggle' from an argument which simply gives primacy to the class
struggle.[132] Socialists in Japan were still searching for suitable language
in which to describe the issues and struggles specific to women, and
were still trying to formulate specific strategies for the resolution of the
'woman question'.

The progress of the petitions and proposals for reform of Article Five
was followed in the socialist press. When the reform proposal was
rejected by the House of Peers, the *Heimin Shinbun* reported to its

readers (in an unsigned article called 'The Women and the Peers') that women had been dealt a grave public insult by 'an organization made up from members of the male class (*danshi kaikyū no ichi dantai*), an organization called the House of Peers (*Kizokuin*)'.[133] The whole article explains the defeat of the Bill in terms of a distinctive interpretation of class politics similar to the aforementioned editorial in *Sekai Fujin*. The members of the ruling class

> do not see women as human individuals (*ikko no jinrui*) or as citizens of the nation (*ikko no kokumin*). They treat their wives and [other] women as slaves and concubines, and turn them into ornaments and playthings.

They can do this because 'it is men who hold economic power'. The solution to these issues is, of course, socialism. Although socialism is seen to be relevant to both men and women, a specific appeal is made to women. In addition to 'collectivization of the land and capital', women will benefit from 'independence and freedom in romantic matters'.

> While socialism prevents the exploitation of workers by the capitalist class, it also stops the arrogance of the male class against women. It gets rid of the rich and poor classes, and removes sexual discrimination. We will collectivise the land and capital, and we will also guarantee women independence and freedom in romantic matters.[134]

In socialist writing on the 'woman question', the analogy of man/woman and worker/capitalist appeared quite regularly, and this analogy is made quite explicit in the previous extract. What is striking in these articles, however, is that men are described as a 'class'. However, a clear distinction is not really being made between ruling class power and what we would now call patriarchal power. It is difficult to separate patriarchal power from class power in the case of members of the House of Peers, who are described as *kizoku-fugō* (aristocrats and wealthy [men]).

Several features of the participation of women in the early socialist movement can be understood from an analysis of this campaign for the repeal of Article Five. We can perhaps detect a middle-class bias in this campaign, and a blindness to the class differences between women. We can see that, with a few exceptions, women within the socialist movement at this stage tended to see the 'woman question' in terms of liberal discourse, in terms of rights which should be extended equally to males and females. In criticizing the activities of the Patriotic Women's Association, and campaigning for the repeal of Article Five, socialist women were attempting to reconstruct women as citizens.

The conduct of the campaign also followed liberal political practice.

The women wrote articles, collected signatures, lobbied,[135] and (with the help of sympathetic parliamentarians) presented their demands to the Diet. The activities and demands of these socialist women may seem quite moderate when compared with the militant activities of the British suffragettes – roughly contemporaneous with this campaign.[136] The Japanese women's proposal was defeated, however, by the unelected Upper House, proof that Japan was a long way from the liberal democratic society whose ideals these women espoused.[137]

Some socialist writers could, and did, argue that a focus on parliamentary politics was a distraction from the main goal of transforming society according to socialist ideals, while for others the women's campaign was congruent with the earliest socialists' emphasis on social democracy. Katayama Sen and his colleagues in the *Rōdō Kumiai Kiseikai* had formed the League for the Attainment of Universal Suffrage (*Futsū Senkyo Kisei Dōmeikai*) in 1900,[138] and several socialist men were involved in collecting signatures for petitions for Universal Suffrage at around the same time as the socialist women's campaign for the repeal of Article Five.[139]

In the early 1900s, Kōtoku Shūsui had had no objection to using the language of rights and citizenship with respect to women's political activity.[140] By 1907, Kōtoku's own position had shifted from social democracy to anarcho-syndicalism. This was reflected in his criticism of the Article Five campaign, in an article on 'Women's Liberation and Socialism':

> Kōtoku indicated that for women to use parliamentary tactics, as they were doing in the Article 5 campaign, was useless: working men in Europe and America had the vote, but were still treated like draft animals and slaves in the capitalist system, moreover, women had the vote in some parts of the United States, but that had certainly not freed them from bondage.[141]

Others, however, realized that, under present conditions, the repeal of those regulations which limited women's political activities was necessary for women to participate fully in the socialist movement.

Two Incidents

The government, far from modifying the provisions of Article Five of the Peace Police Law, invoked Article 16 of this same law in 1908 to prosecute several male and female socialists for the crime of carrying red flags bearing the slogans 'Anarchism' (*Museifushugi*) and 'Anarcho-communism' (*Museifu Kyōsanshugi*). This incident is referred to as the Red Flag Incident (*Akahata Jiken*).[142] The incident took place on 22 June, 1908. After a gathering to celebrate a comrade's release from jail, participants sang socialist songs and carried red flags bearing the slogans 'Anarchism' and 'Anarcho-communism' into the street at the end of the meeting. Ten men and four women were arrested in the incident. Two of the women, Kanno Suga and Kamikawa Matsuko, were not involved when the incident broke out, but were arrested when they went to the police station to enquire after their comrades. Ōsuka Satoko and Ogure Reiko had already been arrested.[143] The first response to the incident in *Sekai Fujin* was an article explaining the significance of the red flags. The writer explains that the red flag is used to signify socialism and a black flag for anarchism. Later editions included reports on the imprisoned comrades and their associates.[144]

The defendants were placed on remand until the trial, and the verdicts were handed down on 15 August of the same year. Ōsugi Sakae, Sakai Toshihiko, Yamakawa Hitoshi and Arahata Kanson received sentences of between eighteen months and two and a half years. Two of the women, Ogure Reiko and Ōsuka Satoko, received suspended sentences of one year, and the other two women, Kanno Suga and Kamikawa Matsuko, were found not guilty. Although Kanno was found not guilty, it is said that at the time of her arrest she was subject to brutal interrogation, and this was the turning point where she renounced peaceful parliamentary tactics for reform, and came closer to the philosophy of 'direct action' espoused by her partner Kōtoku Shūsui.[145]

Kanno would go on to become one of the martyrs to the oppositional political cause through her involvement in the Great Treason Incident.[146] Kōtoku and Kanno were executed with ten others in January 1911 for their alleged involvement in a plot to assassinate the Emperor. The combination of the Red Flag Incident and the Great Treason Incident showed the lengths to which the State would go in the suppression of socialism.

Kanno Suga is one figure who, in her writings and in her actions, transcended the role of woman as helpmate in the socialist movement.[147] Descriptions of Kanno, however, have too often focused on her relationships with her male comrades, at the expense of a serious consideration of her writings and ideas. This picture of Kanno has recently been challenged by Sharon Sievers and Hélène Bowen [Raddeker], who have been critical of the portrayal of Kanno in writings on the socialist movement and on the Great Treason Incident.[148]

Beyond the *Heiminsha* Family

Within the socialist movement, the publication of separate socialist women's journals in the early 1900s, and the campaign for the repeal of Article Five, marked a transition. In many ways, women were still seen as helpmates to male activists within the socialist movement (a role which unfortunately duplicated dominant constructions of womanhood in mainstream society). However, when it came to what were seen as specific women's issues, socialist women conducted their own campaigns. They now had their own publications, their own political agenda, and their own experiences of organizing a political campaign. Although we may criticize the lack of class consciousness, and the lack of a clearly articulated socialist feminist philosophy, we can see this as an important stage in the development of a movement of socialist women.

Socialist women challenged the dominant construction of woman as helpmate to the state at a conceptual level, but also provided a visible challenge to this construction, as they took their activities into public space. Women in the socialist movement engaged in such activities as selling socialist newspapers and distributing leaflets in public places.[149] In the campaign for the repeal of Article Five, they were also involved in the collection of signatures for a petition, in lobbying, and in having this petition presented to the Imperial Diet.[150] The activities of the women of the *Heiminsha* were thus important, not only for the development of a feminist and socialist critique, but also in building up experience of political practice.[151] Writing, distributing leaflets and selling newspapers, collecting signatures and petitioning the Diet were activities which would be repeated in future campaigns.

Women could also be subject to repression in the form of censorship, through the experience of police surveillance, or through arrest and imprisonment. Even those women who escaped imprisonment themselves were likely to have the experience of visiting friends and partners in prison, or observing court proceedings.[152] Many of the extant photographs of men and women in the socialist movement commemorate the ritual of farewelling comrades entering prison and welcoming comrades on their release.[153] Women were still supporters within the *Heiminsha*; and men were still able to pontificate on women's issues; but women also produced their own publications, an implicit recognition that women's struggles could not simply be subsumed under the class struggle.

It should also be remembered that the legal restrictions on women's political activities prevented them from full participation in the activities of the socialist movement, and necessitated the creation of separate quasi-political organizations for socialist women. These organizations may have been seen as placing women's issues in a 'ghetto', but it could also be said that they created a space for the discussion of women's issues. Although socialist women engaged in activities which involved the use of public space for such activities as distributing leaflets, collecting signatures for petitions and selling publications, the restrictions on participation in public meetings meant that writing was the major means for the communication of feminist and socialist ideas to other women. In all of the aforementioned activities, socialist women challenged the dominant discourse of women as 'good wives and wise mothers'.

The second decade of the twentieth century is often presented as the winter years (*fuyu no jidai*) for socialism in Japan, as socialist activities were restrained by the consciousness of the repressive power of the State after the Great Treason Incident. Many of the social policy issues which had been discussed by the government since the late nineteenth century were also acted upon in this decade, in the form of Factory Legislation and policies on trade union activity. From within the socialist movement, there were some important developments in the refinement of socialist views of the 'woman question' in this decade, as we shall see in Chapter four. The second decade of the twentieth century also saw the beginnings of women's involvement in the organized labour movement.

CHAPTER 4

Mothers

女工さんに贈る

― 岩内善作著 ―

Mothers. Motherhood could refer to physical reproduction, a social role, or to abstract qualities of nurturance and compassion. The figure on the cover of a pamphlet addressed to factory women embodies these contradictory meanings. Iwauchi Zensaku, *Jokōsan ni Okuru*, Tokyo: Nihon Rōdō Sōdōmei Kantō Bōshoku Rōdō Kumiai, 1926.

In the second decade of the twentieth century, the latter part of the slogan 'good wives and wise mothers' became the focus of attention in official discourse, popular culture, and public debate. A series of parallel discussions of motherhood were carried out in this decade, and motherhood had different meanings for each of the groups involved. Some of these disparate meanings and associations are suggested in 'new woman' Hiratsuka Raichō's contribution to the debate:

> The mother is the source of life, and when a woman becomes a mother, she moves from the realm of private existence to an existence which is part of society, the nation, and humanity. For this reason, the protection of the mother is not just a matter of individual happiness. Rather, because it ensures the livelihood of the child, it is necessary for the whole of society and all of humanity.[1]

Until the turn of the century, as we have seen, official policies on women had concentrated on the family – an implicitly middle-class family where women were not expected to engage in waged labour, and could devote attention to the fulfilment of the role of 'good wife'. Official policy 'exhorted women to contribute to the nation through their hard work, their frugality, their efficient management, their care of the old, young, and ill, and their responsible upbringing of children'.[2] By the time of the Russo–Japanese War, it had become apparent that the only public role afforded to these women was as helpmate to the militarist State through patriotic women's organizations, a role which was criticized by socialist writers. The other side of the slogan 'good wives and wise mothers' involved constructions of women as mothers. Nolte and Hastings suggest that, until around 1910, official interest was focused mainly on women as wives rather than as mothers. This seems to be broadly true for middle-class women, although anxiety about working-class women's role as mothers commenced well before the promulgation of the Factory Law in 1911.[3]

In the second decade of the twentieth century, the development of labour policy on the part of the bureaucracy and the development of an organized labour movement were accompanied by further discussion of the relationship between individual and State in several spheres. As far as women were concerned, they became the objects of State concern in the form of protective legislation specifically directed at women workers. The official construction of women as 'mothers' tended to position women as passive recipients of the protection of the State, and as more or less passive supporters of militarism.

The progress of industrialization meant that questions of the management and protection of labour became harder to ignore. From the latter half of the Meiji period 'social problems' (*shakai mondai*) had become an increasingly important part of public discourse.[4] However, the enactment of the Public Peace Police Law of 1900 and the trial and subsequent execution of activists in the Great Treason Incident at the end of the Meiji period had demonstrated that there were limits to acceptable public discourse on political issues. Writers could also be subject to harassment for unsuitable criticism of the family system, suggesting that the family was still seen to be basic to the political structures of the society.[5] With respect to labour, official attention was focused first on the supply of labour, and only later on working conditions and trade unionism.[6] The promulgation of factory legislation in 1911, however, was a sign of the government's recognition that it could no longer be seen to be ignoring social problems.

The Meiji Emperor died in 1912, after forty-five years of rule, during which Japan's status as an imperial power in Asia was consolidated.[7] The new era was called *Taishō* (Great Rectification) and is remembered as the time of 'Taishō democracy'.[8] The applicability of this term has been debated in recent years. A narrow interpretation of Taishō democracy refers to the alternation of party governments in the years from 1918 to 1932. A broader interpretation refers to the development of mass political activity in the years after the Russo–Japanese War, including the development of labour organizations and the public discussion of feminist issues. This period saw the development of political interest groups representing 'previously unorganized sections of Japanese society', such as the outcaste class, farm labour, students, and business groups.[9] Several historians have, however, rejected the use of the term 'Taishō democracy' altogether.[10]

A new kind of labour organization appeared with the formation of the *Yūaikai* (Workers' Friendly Society) on 1 August 1912.[11] The organization was modelled on the early British friendly societies, and took a non-confrontational approach based on 'harmony between capital and labour'.[12]

In the background to many of the developments of the Taishō period was the First World War, Japan's participation in the international economy, and the effects of the war on the domestic economy. The economic effects of the war included expansion in industry, trade, and shipping, accompanied by inflation. Worker dissatisfaction at the gap between price rises and wage rises resulted in industrial unrest. The Russian Revolution of 1917 also provided inspiration to socialists who had survived the 'winter years' after the

Great Treason Incident.[13] In the context of the post-war inflation, demonstrations against the rising price of rice erupted all over the country in 1918. For the socialist movement, the rice riots were evidence of a growing class consciousness. For the government and bureaucracy, the rice riots were a harbinger of just the kind of working-class militancy they wished to discourage.[14] By 1919, the *Yūaikai* had been transformed into the *Sōdōmei*, a rather more militant labour organization with affiliated unions organized along industrial rather than regional lines.[15]

In parallel with these developments in the labour movement there were further developments in feminist thought. The year 1911 saw the establishment of the Bluestocking Society (*Seitōsha*) and the beginnings of discussion of the 'new women' (*atarashii onna, atarashiki onna*). Although the 'new women', as we shall see later, burst on to the public stage in a rather more flamboyant way than the socialist women whose activities were discussed in Chapter three, we can see a continuity in their concerns with questions of marriage, free love and women's financial independence. Their concern with freedom for sexual expression for women also led to a concern with such issues as contraception and abortion.

The discussion of the 'new women' showed that there was a public eager for discussion of 'women's issues', and several intellectual journals, including *Taiyō* (*The Sun*) and *Chūō Kōron* (*Central Review*) ran special editions on women's issues. A new intellectual journal for women, *Fujin Kōron* (*Women's Review*), was established in 1916. These publications provided a public space for the discussion of issues related to women's financial independence and the care and financial maintenance of children, particularly in the 'motherhood protection debate' (*bosei hogo ronsō*) at the close of the decade. This debate would provide an opportunity for the discussion of alternative visions for social change. The discussion of women's economic independence, in the context of motherhood and the desirability of State financial support for mothers and children, would inevitably lead to a consciousness of the class differences between women.

Women's reproductive capacity thus became the subject of discussion in several different spheres. The identity of 'mother', however, received different interpretations, whether in the context of official discourses of 'good wives and wise mothers', or the oppositional discourses of socialism and feminism. In this context, some feminist writers tried to transform 'motherhood' into an image of power and creativity. The second decade of the twentieth century, then, saw major developments in both socialist and feminist thought. But before surveying these developments in the socialist and feminist movements in this decade, it is necessary to consider official discourses on women as workers and as mothers. State policies provided the context for the feminist and socialist discussions of the relationship between individual and State.

Factory Legislation

The first group of workers to be the object of State policy were the mining workers. Regulations concerning miners were issued as early as 1872, and a Mining Law (*Kōgyō Jōrei*) was promulgated in 1890. The first regulations were devoted to ensuring employers' control over workers, through the use of 'mine police'; but also included several articles on the 'protection' of workers, including the power to limit the working hours of women and children under the age of fourteen.[16] Discussion of the need for protective legislation in factories began in the 1880s, when surveys of factory production were carried out by the Ministry of Agriculture and Trade, and draft Factory Operatives Legislation was drawn up.[17] Successive drafts were submitted to the Higher Council on Agriculture, Commerce and Industry in the 1890s.[18] However, employers' representatives opposed the proposed legislation, at times arguing that the profitability of industry would be affected by restrictions on working hours, and at times denying the need for State regulation of employment practices on the grounds that 'a Factory Law would destroy the relations between worker and employer which are based on the good customs and ways of our history'.[19] The draft which was approved by the Higher Council on Agriculture, Commerce and Industry in October 1898[20] referred to safety measures, restrictions on child labour, factory inspection, and apprenticeship systems, but had little to say about women workers.[21] In Chapter Five of the legislation, on inspection, Article 27 stated that the Ministry would have power to prohibit or restrict the use of women and minors in dangerous industries.

Katayama Sen and the *Rōdō Kumiai Kiseikai* carried out a campaign to expose the limitations of this draft, which was only applicable to factories employing more than fifty workers, and was selective in the problems it chose to address.[22] This draft was also criticized from within the bureaucracy. Saitō Kashiro, who published a book on Japan's attempts at regulation of labour, commented that he had never seen in practice those 'familial and affectionate relations' which were often spoken of, and reiterated the need for protection of women workers.[23]

This draft was not presented to the Diet.[24] However, with an increase in labour disputes (by workers who presumably were not so attached to 'traditional' relations between worker and employer) and increased attention being paid to the conditions of factory workers, the need for a Factory Law was added to the list of social problems. Several works appeared which exposed the conditions suffered by factory workers – women and children in particular. *Shokkō Jijō* (*The Conditions of Factory Workers*) was a five-volume report commissioned by the Department of Agriculture and Industry in preparation for the drafting of factory regulations. The journalism of Yokoyama Gennosuke, and his book, *Nihon no Kasō Shakai* (*The Lower Classes of Japan*), brought the conditions of factory workers to a wider audience.[25]

The conditions of factory workers were also mentioned in the progressive women's newspaper *Fujo Shinbun*.[26] In an editorial on the mistreatment of factory workers it was said to be scandalous that such violation of the human rights of women workers could take place under a constitutional system, and the women readers of *Fujo Shinbun* were enjoined to show compassion and listen to the complaints of the factory women. It is interesting to note how the appeal made in this editorial is addressed specifically to women. First, a link is made between the clothing worn by the (presumably middle-class) readers of *Fujo Shinbun* and the labour of the factory workers who have produced the fabric for this clothing. Second, women are enjoined to show the compassion which is a specifically feminine vocation. Finally, women are enjoined to show compassion to the factory workers because they are of the same sex. In other words, compassion is seen to override the class differences which divide women.[27] This editorial is quite distinctive in its discussion of the human rights of women workers rather than competing notions of the 'national interest'.

A new draft Factory Bill was prepared in 1902, but was not presented to the Diet immediately. The passage of the law was further postponed by the Russo–Japanese War of 1904–5. At this very time, several British writers were promoting Japan as an imperialist power which promoted 'motherhood' and realized the importance of children for the strength of the Empire. In fact, the Japanese 'national interest', in the form of increased exports and increased military power, was used as justification for the delay in the introduction of protective legislation for women and child workers.[28] The next attempt to present a Bill to the Diet was in 1909, but this Bill was soon withdrawn. Business representatives were critical of the proposal to phase out night work by women and children.[29]

A Ministry pamphlet on the 'Explanation of the Factory Bill' was distributed in 1909. Among comments on the issue of night work by women, the Central Hygiene Institute proposed that night work for women be prohibited within five years of the institution of the law.[30]

In other discussion of the issue, reports on the health of factory
workers appeared which linked factory work with the spread of tuberculosis in the villages, and the infection of potential military recruits.[31]
With respect to the prohibition of night work by women and children,
both sides referred to the national interest.[32] Employers argued that
the national interest would be served by postponing the introduction
of restrictions on working hours in the interest of the profitability of
export industries. Reformers argued that the national interest would
be served by protecting the health of the mothers of future recruits.[33]

Finally, after thirty-odd years of discussion, and opposition by industrialists, the Factory Law (*Kōjō hō*) was promulgated in 1911. The law,
however, would not become effective until 1916,[34] and there was
extensive provision for the granting of exemptions. In August 1916
an Imperial Ordinance for the Administration of the Factory Act was
promulgated, and the Act came into force in September 1916.[35]

Protective provisions of the Factory Law prevented women and children under the age of fifteen from working more than twelve hours
a day, prevented them from working between the hours of 10 p.m.
and 4 a.m., and allowed for at least two days leave per month. The
minimum age for workers was set at twelve years, except in light
industry, where the minimum age of workers was ten.[36] However, there
was provision for particular industries to apply for exemption, and
some provisions were further postponed after the law became effective
in 1916. With respect to night work, these provisions could be waived
where a factory worked on a shift system, meaning that night work
for women workers continued until it was prohibited completely in
1929.[37]

In justification of the protective provisions of the Factory Law,
women workers are described as the 'women who will be the mothers
of the nation' (*kokumin no haha naru beki fujo*), and protection of
women and children is linked to Japan's status as a military power
(*gunkoku*).[38] Article Nine of the Law concerned maternity provisions.
Employers were prevented from allowing pregnant women to work
for five weeks after parturition (or three weeks with a doctor's
approval), and women were entitled to nursing leave on their return
to work.[39] However, this was not framed in terms of women's rights
to maternity leave. Rather, the State was preventing employers from
the exploitation of pregnant women. In other words, the paternalistic
State was 'protecting' women as a labour force from excessive exploitation by industrialists. The Factory Law only covered workers in factories of a certain size, and regulation of working conditions in other
industries could only be achieved on an industry-by-industry basis.[40]

Women were seen as the objects of State protection, rather than as workers with rights. This attitude appears explicitly and implicitly in writings on the Factory Law. In one commentary, the numbers of workers are enumerated, and divided into two categories, those who need protection, and those who do not. Adult male workers are not seen as needing protection, while women and children belong to the category of workers 'needing protection' (*hogo o yōsuru shokkō*).[41] The duty of the State to protect women workers was, however, counterbalanced by the desire to protect the profitability of industries employing women workers, as evidenced by the delay in enacting many provisions of the Factory Law.

Women were not seen as potential unionists or strikers. In contemporaneous commentary on the Factory Law, it is asserted that in Japan, it has been mining and shipbuilding, rather than the textile industry, that have seen the most strikes, and this is attributed to the high number of women workers in textiles. This perceived lack of militancy on the part of women workers is given as further justification for the necessity of factory legislation. It is necessary for the State to protect these less assertive workers. This highlights the differing views of male and female workers from within the bureaucracy. While male workers were seen as potentially militant, and in need of social control in the form of restrictions on union activity, women were seen as needing protection. Despite the extreme exploitation under which these women worked, and some history of strike activity, they were constructed as harmless, passive, and in need of protection.[42] In the earliest days of the labour movement, such attitudes were shared by labour organizers. The gendering of relationships between individual and State affected the kinds of political demands which could be made by men and women in early twentieth-century Japan.[43]

It has been pointed out that the Factory Law was formulated with little input from organized labour. Indeed, it was suggested at the time that the Factory Law was granted by the Emperor from 'above', in the same manner as the Meiji Constitution.[44] Although the members of the League for the Promotion of Labour Unions (*Rōdō Kumiai Kiseikai*) did attempt to influence the bureaucracy, there appears to have been little attempt on the part of the bureaucracy to engage in formal consultation with labour representatives.[45]

The *Yūaikai* (Workers' Friendly Society) was not established until after the promulgation of the Factory Law. Although the *Yūaikai* could have no input into the creation of the Factory Law, the organization took a great interest in campaigning for its proper implementation, particularly with respect to the abolition of night work by women, which had been postponed because of pressure from business.

The *Yūaikai* Women's Division

The *Yūaikai* was founded on 1 August 1912 by Suzuki Bunji,[46] a member of the Social Policy Association (*Shakai Seisaku Gakkai*), an organization which provided several advisers to the union. The name of the organization referred to the British 'friendly societies', after which it was modelled. The union's members were kept informed through the journal, *Yūai Shinpō* (*Yūai News*).[47] The society's activities were based on 'harmony between labour and capital'. The platform of the organization stated:

1 We will harmonize with one another and endeavour to attain the objective of mutual aid through unity and co-operation.
2 We will abide by the ideals of the public and endeavour to develop intelligent opinion, cultivate virtue, and make progress in technical arts.
3 We will depend on the power of co-operation and endeavour to improve our status through sound means.[48]

The growth of the *Yūaikai* was impressive when compared with earlier attempts to form union organizations.[49] A women's division was created in 1916, with Inaba Aiko as secretary.[50] Until 1917, however, women could only be associate members of the association.[51] The activities of the women's division included the publication of the journal *Yūai Fujin* (*Yūai Woman*), the holding of public lectures for the education of workers, the awarding of prizes to model union members, and the provision of advice on home-based work to the wives of male workers.[52]

The women's journal, with a print run of around 3000, appeared monthly between August 1916 and June 1918. There was a gap between February and July 1917, when the women's journal was replaced by a supplement in the union journal *Rōdō oyobi Sangyō* (*Labour and Industry*).[53]

In the second edition of *Yūai Fujin*, union adviser Soeda Juichi advised that women who had some spare time could engage in home-based work, and he suggested spinning, weaving, artwork, sewing or other crafts. This suggests a recognition that most families could not survive on one wage. However, the advice that women engage in '*naishoku*' (casual, home-based work) rather than more permanent employment, also implies that women's work was seen to be secondary to the work of the male breadwinner.[54]

The creation of the women's division at this time has been linked with impending enactment of the Factory Law.[55] One of the important activities of the women's division was providing women workers with information about their rights under the new legislation. Both women workers and wives of male *Yūaikai* members could join the women's division. The reasons for setting up the women's division were set out as follows:

> The world is not made up of men only, and is not supported by men only. Half of humanity are women, and the world can be made light or made dark according to the work of women and the attitude of women. The *Yūaikai* is an organization which has been formed in order to raise the dignity of work, and improve the conditions of workers. But, up till now, [the *Yūaikai*] has mainly worked for men. Recently, however, it has also become apparent that we should also do something for the women who are working alongside men in factories and other workplaces, and for the women who support men by their work in the home. For this reason we have established the *Yūaikai* women's division, and wish to carry out various activities from now on.[56]

While the women's division did play a role in advising and informing women workers of their rights, female workers were still seen primarily as women: as wives, daughters and sisters. This emphasis on femininity over class consciousness was given visual expression on the cover of the journal: like more mainstream women's magazines, the covers of early editions of *Yūai Fujin* were decorated with flowers.

Suzuki Bunji in particular addressed the readers of *Yūai Fujin* as wives and as mothers. Suzuki's editorial in the founding issue of *Yūai Fujin* made much of women's support activities for husbands and children.[57] Thus, even within the labour movement women were initially contained within the role of 'good wives and wise mothers', a phrase which was used approvingly by Suzuki Bunji. Suzuki's support for *ryōsai kenbo* ideology contrasts with the men and women of the *Heiminsha*, who had been critical of attempts to contain women's activities in the ideology of 'good wives and wise mothers', and critical of the mobilization of women for nationalist purposes without the granting of rights to match their obligations.

The *Yūaikai* policy of non-confrontation with capital was also linked with a support for nationalist goals. A message from the editor in the first edition combined the conventional seasonal greetings about the weather with a homily about the pleasures of working for the country:

> The rainy season has come to an end, and it will gradually get hotter from now on. It might be hard for all of you to keep working [in this heat], but if you remember that the wealth of the country will be increased thanks to your efforts, then work will be a pleasure, don't you think?[58]

Both the union journal *Rōdō oyobi Sangyō* (*Labour and Industry*)[59] and the women's division journal *Yūai Fujin* carried commentary on the enactment of the Factory Law. The second edition of *Yūai Fujin* reported that the provisions of the Factory Law would soon become effective, and explained these provisions for the benefit of women workers. The article explains the restrictions on working hours for women and children and the provisions for two days holiday per month. The exceptions to the applicability of the law are explained in relentless detail, as if to emphasize the inadequacy of the protection offered by the law.[60] Compensation provisions are also explained in some detail, and women are enjoined to register any irregular relationships, as a de facto spouse may not be able to receive compensation on the death or injury of her partner. It is also explained that a worker may receive compensation if unable to continue work, and that a woman whose looks have been spoilt by facial injury may claim the equivalent of one hundred days' pay.[61]

Thus, in early labour movement publications, women were construed either as wives of workers or as women workers in need of protection. This attitude towards women was common to the official discourse which underpinned the protection of women workers by the Factory Law, and the discourse of labour organizers who cast the union in the role of 'protector' of weak women workers. In the following parts of this chapter, I shall consider how some feminist writers in the second decade of the twentieth century theorized the relationship between individual and State, and consider whether feminist writers shared the view of women as needing the protection of a strong State.

The New Women

In 1911, the women's literary journal Seitō (Bluestocking) was established by a group of women led by Hiratsuka Raichō.[62] The first editor of Seitō, Hiratsuka Raichō, was a woman who had links with literary circles. Hiratsuka's father came from a samurai family and was a member of the Meiji bureaucracy. Hiratsuka's mother allowed Raichō to use the money set aside for her trousseau to set up the journal.[63] Hiratsuka had already created a scandal in 1908 by her attempted double suicide with a married literary figure, Morita Sōhei.[64] This contrasts with Fukuda Hideko's appearance on the public stage as the heroine of the Ōsaka Incident. Fukuda was already a well-known figure in oppositional political circles when she established the journal Sekai Fujin.

The title of the journal Seitō was a direct translation of 'Bluestockings', the name given to women who attended Elizabeth Montague's literary salon of the 1750s. As the choice of this name might suggest, this journal had an international emphasis, but the focus was, at first, literary rather than political in the narrow sense. In particular, the Blue-stockings had links with the Naturalist school of writers.[65] The first issue was almost entirely devoted to short stories and poetry, often with a romantic theme. Although some of the early contributions to *Seitō* may seem naïve in their emphasis on individual liberation, it is also possible to interpret these discussions in terms of what we would now call 'consciousness raising'.[66]

Two contributions to the first edition of *Seitō* made a great impression on the women of the time and continue to provide inspiration for modern Japanese feminists. The first was a series of linked verse by Yosano Akiko, already an established poet. The first section, *Yama no Ugoku Hi Kitaru*, uses the metaphor of the volcano to describe the hidden power of women which will burst forth one day. This poem has been translated as 'Mountain Moving Day', or 'The Day the Mountains Move':

> The day the mountains move has come.
> I speak but no one believes me.
> For a time the mountains have been asleep,
> But long ago they all danced with fire.
> It doesn't matter if you believe this,
> My friends, as long as you believe:
> All the sleeping women
> Are now awake and moving.[67]

The evocative natural imagery in this section of the poem has been much quoted, but other verses include an evocation of the difficulties of Yosano's life, references to Nietzsche's 'Thus Spake Zarathustra', and a passionate assertion of individual identity. Yosano claimed the right of women to speak:

> I would like to write only in the first person
> I am a woman!
> I would like to write only in the first person
> I am! I am![68]

The first edition of *Seitō* also carried Hiratsuka Raichō's poetic essay *Genshi Josei wa Taiyō de atta* ('In the beginning woman was the Sun . . .'). Hiratsuka also uses evocative poetic language to lament the hidden power of women and call for a retrieval of this power. Here, women's former powerful status is represented by the sun which shines from its own energy, while her present condition is evoked by the moon, which can only shine by reflected light:

In the beginning woman was the Sun.
An authentic person.
Today, she is the moon.
Living through others.
Reflecting the brilliance of others . . .[69]

Once again, women are exhorted to retrieve their former power, their 'genius'.[70] The metaphor of the sun has particular resonance in the Japanese context, with its echoes of Amaterasu, the sun goddess in Japanese mythology.[71] The other striking element of this manifesto is the use of maternal imagery. *Seitō*'s emergence is described as the cry of a newborn baby (*ubugoe*), and this metaphor is elaborated upon, as Hiratsuka wonders how her child will develop.[72]

Both of these texts portray an assertion of individual creativity, using the genre of the poetic essay to imagine the meaning of liberation. Hiratsuka, in particular, is interested in meditation as a way of focusing the attention for the purpose of engaging in creative activities. She complains that women's responsibility for housework affects their ability to concentrate.[73] Liberation is initially seen as an individual matter. While Hiratsuka recognizes the importance of social issues such as higher education for women, she asserts that such matters as education and the suffrage are simply means to an end. For Hiratsuka, the words 'freedom' and 'liberation' are primarily understood in terms of individual genius and creativity.[74]

Seitō appeared around the time that Ibsen's plays were being performed in Tokyo, and the image of such women as Ibsen's Nora was soon connected with the Bluestockings.[75] The scandal surrounding the first production of *A Doll's House* became connected, in newspapers and magazines, with images of the 'new women' of the Bluestocking Society. Examples of the scandalous behaviour of the 'Bluestockings' included such activities as the women's visit to the Yoshiwara licensed district, or their sampling of exotic Western liqueurs.[76]

The appellation 'New Woman' gained currency after Tsubouchi Shōyō lectured on 'The New Woman in Western Theatre' using as his examples Ibsen's Nora, Sudermann's Magda, and Shaw's Vivie.[77] In January 1912 the Bluestockings ran a special edition devoted to discussion of Ibsen's *A Doll's House*, and several mainstream publications produced special issues on the 'new women'. Hiratsuka defiantly adopted this label in her 1913 manifesto, *Yo no Fujintachi ni* ('To the Women of the World'), in which she defended women's choice not to marry, stressed the importance of women's economic independence, attacked the existing family system, and declared proudly that she was a 'new woman':

I am a New Woman. I am the Sun!
I am a unique human being.
At least, day after day I desire to be so.
The New Women not only desire the destruction of the old morality
and old laws built on men's selfishness,
they also try day after day to build a new world where there will be
a new religion, a new morality, and new laws . . .[78]

Successive issues of the journal carried translations of stories by Edgar
Allen Poe (Volume 2, Nos 3, 5, 6, 7, 11, 12), Maupassant (Vol. 2, No.
7; Vol. 2, No. 12), Chekhov and Alfred de Musset (Vol. 2, No. 10; Vol.
3, No. 1). In later issues Ibsen's *Hedda Gabler* and *A Doll's House*[79] and
Shaw's *Mrs Warren's Profession*[80] stimulated discussion of marriage,
divorce and prostitution. There was a gradual shift in emphasis in the
journal, from an interest in individualism to an engagement with social
issues. In generic terms, essays and debates appeared alongside fictional
and poetic writings. Unlike the early socialist women's journals,
however, little attention was paid to the situation of working women in
Japan.[81] When *Sekai Fujin* looked overseas, attention had been directed
to international feminist, pacifist and socialist movements, while translations in the pages of the early editions of *Seitō* were more likely to be
from literary or intellectual figures.

The Bluestockings and the Socialists

In 1913, Fukuda Hideko contributed an article to *Seitō* on 'The Solution
to the Women's Question' in which she emphasized the importance of
socialism for women's emancipation, and reiterated some of the themes
addressed in her writings in *Sekai Fujin*. In this article, Fukuda casts
herself as an elder of the women's movement, reflecting on her time
with the liberal movement. The liberals, she explains, had identified
women's liberation with simple equality between men and women, a
limitation on which she elaborates. Fukuda refers to Hiratsuka's
manifesto, agreeing that it would be fine if everyone could feel that
Jibun wa Taiyō de aru ('I am the sun'). Liberation, Fukuda points out,
must be for both men and women, and she believes that the establishment of a 'communal system' (*kyōsansei*) will bring liberation for both
men and women. Implicit in Fukuda's criticism is a recognition that
individual liberation cannot be achieved without social transformation.
In Fukuda's case this implies transformation along socialist lines.

Unlike many other socialist and communist writers, however, Fukuda
is not committed to the destruction of the existing family system. She
is confident that the destruction of the private property system will
modify the economic relationships implicit in marriages under the

existing system, and believes that science and technology may be used to relieve the burden of domestic labour.[82]

Itō Noe took over the editorship of *Seitō* in 1915.[83] Two strands of feminist thought were represented by the two editors. Hiratsuka was influenced by the maternalism of Ellen Key, while Itō identified with the anarchism of Emma Goldman. The journal now carried translations of the writings of Emma Goldman,[84] Olive Schreiner[85] and Havelock Ellis.[86] Itō also engaged in debates with other writers, including socialist Aoyama [Yamakawa] Kikue on the issues of prostitution and abortion.[87] Yamakawa also participated in the 'motherhood protection debate' to be discussed later.

In the pages of *Seitō*, women were initially presented as 'new women', as single women free from the ties of a repressive family system. Such criticism of the family system was obviously seen as potentially subversive, for several issues were banned.[88] However, an interest in sexual freedom led the women of *Seitō* to deal with issues related to women's reproductive capacity, including contraception and abortion. Motherhood, for contributors to *Seitō*, could be a metaphor for individual creativity, as in Hiratsuka's poetic essay, 'In the beginning woman was the Sun'. For other women, the capacity for motherhood represented feminine qualities of compassion and nurturance, which could be opposed to the masculine qualities of militarism. This is apparent in Saika Kotoko's comment on the First World War, which otherwise received little attention in the pages of the journal:[89]

> Who was it who said that if it were women who stood on the battlefield, then war would surely stop – no woman could bear to watch the cruelty of war. That is absolutely true! How could women, who live for love and mercy, be able to kill? I believe that women, who have the ability to be mothers, would never be able to line up on the battlefield and witness the spilling of blood.[90]

Saika, like several other *Seitō* writers, links maternity with an essentialist view of women's compassionate nature. The social meaning of motherhood was also explored, however, and it was in this context that the Bluestockings drew on the writings of Ellen Key, a theme to be explored in more detail below.

'The True New Woman'

Some themes of the early socialist women's journals were continued by former *Heiminsha* member Nishikawa Fumiko in the journal *Shinshin Fujin* (*The True New Woman*).[91] In the popular press of the time, *Shinshin Fujin* was presented as a rival to *Seitō*. Although Nishikawa no longer called herself a socialist (after her husband's renunciation of socialism), her writings show a continuity with the writings of some of the early socialist women discussed previously.

Nishikawa explicitly linked family and State, calling for a 'democratization' of the family, and a 'maternalization' (*boseika*) of society. Unfortunately she did not elaborate on what this 'maternalization' would involve.[92] Nishikawa extended the definition of politics to include what went on in the home, and linked reform of the family with reform of society at large:

> We think it most important to raise the consciousness of women, and we will study all things from the standpoint of women, for the purpose of (on a large scale) bringing peace to the world, and (on a small scale) improving everyday life. We will devote our energies to this purpose, for the sake of the home, for society, and for the peace and happiness of mankind.[93]

While the Bluestockings had used motherhood as a metaphor for women's individual creativity, Nishikawa used the maternal as a metaphor for a caring society. Since her earliest writings, Nishikawa had identified socialism as a compassionate philosophy which was particularly congenial to women. Nishikawa's vision of a compassionate society was linked with pacifism. In later writings, Nishikawa praised the contribution of European feminists who had 'humanised' (*jindōka*) politics,[94] and lamented that Japan had not yet produced a great feminist pacifist leader.

Nishikawa questioned the sexual division of labour in society,[95] and predicted an end to the 'male-centred' ideologies which limit women's activities:

> I believe, without doubt, that men have a thoroughly male-centred philosophy. This philosophy will, of course, follow the same fate as such ideas as 'humans are the centre of the universe' and 'the earth is the centre of the universe' – such a philosophy will certainly fall apart. At this stage, however, such ideas still lurk in the hearts of men.[96]

She saw the necessity of changing masculine as well as feminine behaviour, and criticized 'old-fashioned men' who had failed to change as women were changing. Men were said to be 'ignorant' in emotional matters, and education for good husbands and wise fathers (*ryōfu kenfu*) was just as necessary as education for good wives and wise mothers.[97] Nishikawa, in her advocacy of the 'maternalization' of society and the 'democratization' of the family, tried to reconceptualize the relationship between family and State and tried to rethink the sexual division of labour.

The Motherhood Protection Debate

Seitō ceased publication in 1916, but several contributors to the Blue-stocking journal went on to engage in various kinds of feminist activism. The new intellectual journals such as *Taiyō* (*The Sun*), *Chūō Kōron* (*Central Review*) and *Fujin Kōron* (*Women's Review*) also provided a forum for further discussion of issues related to women's independence. The so-called *bosei hogo ronsō* (motherhood protection debate) in Taishō Japan centred on the issue of State financial assistance for working mothers, rather than the maternity or protective provisions encoded in the Factory Law.[98] The first reference to the possibility of such State support that I have found is in the women's newspaper *Fujo Shinbun*[99] at the time of the Russo–Japanese War (1904–5). Here the issue is the support of war widows and their families. The debate between Yosano Akiko, Hiratsuka Raichō and others discussed State assistance for supporting mothers in more general terms. Articles related to this issue appeared in several journals from 1915 to 1919, but I will focus on several contributions around the end of the decade in which the different feminist positions on this issue are crystallized.[100]

The issue of 'motherhood protection' was also alluded to in two editorials in the progressive women's newspaper *Fujo Shinbun* as early as 1917.[101] In the first, editor Fukushima Shirō refers to a recent incident where a widow had committed suicide with her children on being unable to support her family. This incident is used to argue for the necessity of legislation to look after such families.[102] Fukushima notes that in Europe two movements had developed: a women's civil rights movement (*fujin sanseiken undō*) and a mother's rights movement (*boken yōgo undō*). In Japan, argues Fukushima, the more pressing need is a movement for the protection of motherhood (*bosei hogo undō*).[103]

In March 1918 Yosano Akiko published a short article in the progressive women's journal *Fujin Kōron* criticizing calls for State protection (i.e. financial assistance) for mothers on the grounds that this displayed a 'dependence mentality' (*irai shugi*).[104] Yosano continued the theme in a series of articles in the journal *Taiyō*, where she stated that no woman should marry or bear children until she was capable of financial independence. Yosano placed women who asked for State support in the same category as the 'aged or disabled who require institutional care'. Yosano's view has resonance for more recent feminist discussions of gender and the welfare state: she recognized the dilemma of women who must choose between dependence on an individual male or dependence on a patriarchal State, but believed that it was possible for women to reject both alternatives.[105]

Hiratsuka Raichō, in the next issue of *Fujin Kōron*, accused Yosano

of simplifying complex social problems, and jumping to subjective con-
clusions on the basis of her own – rather atypical – experience. Yosano,
she said, talked as if 'she knew nothing about the physical and mental
situation of women, or the economic life of women under the present
system'.[106] Hiratsuka pointed out the difficulty of women achieving
financial independence in the present labour market, where their job
opportunities are restricted, and wages low. In such a situation, the
State has a responsibility to provide assistance. Hiratsuka also included
discussion of illegitimate children, showing that she recognized that
some women raised children outside the conventional family system.

Hiratsuka tried to explore the social context of decisions concerning
reproduction and childcare, rejecting the extreme individualism
espoused by Yosano:

> The mother is the source of life, and when a woman becomes a mother, she
> moves from the realm of private existence to an existence which is part of
> society, the nation, and humanity. For this reason, the protection of the
> mother is not just a matter of individual happiness. Rather, because it
> ensures the livelihood of the child, it is necessary for the whole of society
> and all of humanity.
>
> Because the maternal function has such a social meaning, I think it is
> mistaken to equate the demand for State protection for a mother who,
> through childbirth, has lost the ability to work, with 'the care of the aged
> and disabled in institutions'. Even if there is such a similarity, this is no
> reason for denying protection to such women.[107]

Hiratsuka's emphasis on the social meaning of motherhood showed
that her thought had progressed from the individualist emphasis of her
earlier writings to include a recognition of the social context of individual decisions on the care and maintenance of children. While official ideology articulated the family and State, and expected women's
support for State policies, there had been little suggestion that the State
should intervene in the financial maintenance of mothers and children.
Rather, this was seen to be the responsibility of the family unit.

A different perspective on the relationship between women and the
State appeared in an editorial in *Fujo Shinbun* in 1918. In this editorial,
Fukushima Shirō makes an argument sometimes found in European
and Australian discussions of the necessity for State support for motherhood. He argues that bearing children is analogous to military
service.[108] While men risk their lives in combat, so that enemy forces
will be reduced by one, women risk their lives in childbirth, so that our
own forces will be increased by one. Therefore, one could argue that
women who die in childbirth should be honoured in the same way as
war dead, and women who survive childbirth should be treated like war

heroes. In European and American magazines, according to Fukushima, such proposals were already being put forward quite seriously.
Fukushima calls for the creation of a system of 'mothers' insurance' on
the model of Italy, which treats pregnancy as a form of disability.
However, he realizes the difficulty of arguing for such a system in Japan,
which still does not have a proper workers' insurance system. This does
not, however, decrease the urgency of the need for a mothers' insurance system.[109] There is little evidence that this particular argument was
influential in the Japanese context, although the participants in the
motherhood protection debate were keenly interested in theorizing the
relationship between women and the State.

Hiratsuka's call for State assistance for supporting mothers highlighted the contradictions of the official discourse on the relationship
between family and State. Similar discussions in other national contexts
often led women to demand political rights commensurate with their
responsibility in rearing children for the support of State policies.
Hiratsuka, too, became involved in the demand for women's political
rights in her subsequent activities in the New Women's Association.[110]

The July issue of Taiyō carried Yosano's detailed rebuttal of
Hiratsuka's criticisms.[111] Yosano could not agree with Hiratsuka's faith
in the State, and reiterated her faith in individualism. Change at the
national level could only be brought about by first achieving change at
the individual level. Hiratsuka, according to Yosano, was guilty of
glorifying motherhood. Yosano was perceptive in pointing to the
dangers of an excessive glorification of motherhood, and emphasized
that motherhood was only one part of women's lives:

> Hiratsuka gives motherhood 'absolute respect'. I do not think that being a
> father or mother is the most highly valued part of human life. For this
> reason, I am opposed to kenbo ryōsai shugi. Of course I do recognise that
> being a mother or father is one aspect of human life which has its relative
> value. But I do not think that becoming a mother is the means for a woman
> to achieve supreme happiness.[112]

Yamada Waka, another former contributor to the Bluestocking
journal,[113] entered the debate by emphasizing the family as the basic
unit of society, and emphasizing the different contributions made by
men and women. Yamada affirmed the principle of the family wage,
assuming that if men received a wage which would support a wife and
family, then the problem of 'motherhood protection' would be
obviated.[114]

Although Yamada's emphasis on the the positive evaluation of
women's capacity for motherhood had something in common with

Hiratsuka, her emphasis on an idealized form of the family was incompatible with Hiratsuka's rejection of the family system. The rejection of the family system and conventional marriage meant facing the question of how to reconcile the desire of the 'new women' for independence and autonomy with the realities of reproduction and childcare. Hiratsuka had also recognized that not all women bear children within the 'protection' of the family system.

The debate on 'motherhood protection' raised several issues which were to recur over the next few years.[115] What is the social significance of procreation – is it an individual matter, or a social, public matter? Who should bear financial responsibility for the support of children – the individual or the State? What is the relationship between State and individual? Yosano represented a form of bourgeois individualism, where each person's situation depended on individual effort. Hiratsuka recognized the inequities of capitalism, but relied on welfare provisions to redress these inequities. Yamada relied on an idealized family system supported by a family wage. Socialist Yamakawa Kikue's contribution to the debate brought out the competing visions of political change implicit in the views of Hiratsuka and Yosano, and placed the other writers in historical context.[116]

Yamakawa identified Yosano with the 'women's rights' (*joken*) movement espoused by Wollstonecraft and others in eighteenth-century Europe. Such ideas as individual rights, educational freedom, equal employment opportunities, financial independence, and suffrage were congenial in capitalist society. Hiratsuka, on the other hand, represented the 'mother's rights' (*boken*) theory of Swedish feminist Ellen Key.[117] Maternalist feminists recognized the sacrifices made by women under waged labour in the capitalist system, and attempted to compensate for these sacrifices. Key and her followers have, said Yamakawa:

> gone beyond the [women's rights campaigners] in recognising the problems brought about by capitalism, but [have] no program for basic political change – rather they rely on policies of financial assistance which only provide partial solutions.[118]

Yamakawa recognised the strengths of both arguments, while cautioning on the dangers of maternalism. She admitted, however, that striving for financial independence or asking for State assistance were necessary short-term measures. Yamakawa noted that neither Yosano nor Hiratsuka challenged the capitalist system, and stated that only the destruction of existing economic relations would solve these problems:

As someone who does not expect, or even believe in, the continuation of the present economic system, I do not give economic independence the same absolute value as Yosano, but I recognise that economic independence is necessary in the present situation. And I realise that the sacrifices made in the name of financial independence must be recognised as the price we have to pay – as a stage we must go through – in the process of creating a higher society – a better society. At the same time, I recognise that there is some truth in the insistence of Key and her followers on motherhood protection as a way of lessening the burden of mothers and children – the ones most likely to have their needs sacrificed in the introduction of such measures . . .

Unlike Yosano, I have little faith in suffrage as a way of bringing about an ideal society, and unlike Hiratsuka, I do not believe in waiting on the benevolence of the State – on these points I should state that I differ from both writers.[119]

What these women were debating involved competing visions for social change. Yosano Akiko had faith in liberal individualism and rejected dependence on men or on a patriarchal State. Hiratsuka Raichō valorized motherhood but emphasized the social meaning of motherhood and expected the support of a welfare State. Neither Yosano nor Hiratsuka challenged the capitalist system. Yamakawa Kikue saw the measures proposed by Hiratsuka as basically reformist – useful in the short term but failing to contribute to the long-term transformation of society according to socialist principles. Yamakawa also identified the class basis of these debates, accusing Yosano of being bourgeois through and through.[120]

In contrast with the previous writers, Yamada Waka provided little challenge to existing gender relations. She emphasized an idealized family system and a gendered division of labour. In Yamada's later writings, she would make explicit links between maternalist values and nationalist values. In an article on women's liberation in the journal *Fujin to Shinshakai* (*Women and the New Society*), which she edited from 1920, Yamada eulogized a mother's love as 'the fount of all that is good, the seedbed of human compassion, the source of patriotism – the source of social order'.[121]

What brings together the Meiji discussion of protective legislation for women workers, and the Taishō debate on State assistance for supporting mothers is a view of women as needing the protection of a strong State. Both of these aspects of social policy are referred to as *bosei hogo* (protection of motherhood) in the Japanese literature. However, there are in fact several distinct areas of social policy involved here. It would perhaps be possible to summarize these debates in terms of recent feminist discussion of 'equality versus difference', but what is at stake is more than the issue of biological differences between men and women. Rather, these debates involve several features of the social organization of waged labour, domestic labour, childcare, and the financial support of children. These discussions also highlight the fact that the relationship between individual and State is a gendered relationship, and that this recognition must form part of strategies for social change.[122] As other writers have pointed out, discussions of the relationship between family and State inevitably highlight the intersection of class and gender politics.[123]

Discourses of Protection

What is normally referred to in the Japanese literature as *bosei hogo* 'motherhood protection' actually refers to several distinct areas of social policy, each of which implies a different definition of motherhood. I have isolated four separate areas: maternity provisions, protective provisions, financial assistance for supporting mothers, and childcare.

Maternity provisions refers to maternity leave and nursing leave provided by employers during pregnancy and breastfeeding. *Maternity provisions* are directed at the biological mother – the woman who faces the physical conditions of pregnancy, parturition, and feeding, and as such are relatively uncontroversial. Such provisions were encoded in the Factory Law of 1911, although it is questionable how many women were actually able to take advantage of these provisions.

Other regulations prevent women workers (whether or not they are mothers) from working late at night, from working overtime, or from working in dangerous industries such as mining. I shall reserve the phrase *protective provisions* for these regulations, which are at least partly concerned with protecting the safety of women workers. *Protective provisions* are directed at *all* women workers, on the premise that they are *potential* mothers. This is revealed by the fact that legislation does not distinguish between women who do and do not have children. *All* women are protected from shift work or late night work on the grounds that they potentially have responsibility for childcare. The health of young women is protected for future childbearing. *Protective provisions*, then, are directed not at the physical conditions of pregnancy for any individual woman, but rather at an abstract potential.

There was also discussion of the issue of the provision of financial assistance by the State for mothers without the financial means to support their children because of such reasons as widowhood or desertion. *Financial assistance for supporting mothers* is directed at the person who has financial responsibility for the day-to-day care and upkeep of children. This woman is theoretically distinct from the biological mother, and the person who actually carries out the labour of *childcare*. Social policy should also consider the problem of *childcare*, but this problem was not addressed explicitly in the initial stages of the motherhood protection debate.

There are several reasons for trying to disentangle the disparate meanings subsumed under the phrase *bosei hogo*. Each of the above policies implies a different definition of the word *bosei* 'motherhood'.[124] Where the biological facts of pregnancy are involved, it is necessary to implement policies directed solely at women. Protective provisions are directed not at an individual woman, or mother, but rather at an abstract potential for 'motherhood'. This is revealed by the fact that protective legislation is directed at *all* women, not just pregnant women or those with children. Where childcare and financial support are concerned, however, several approaches are possible, including individual responsibility, communal solutions, partial State assistance, or full State responsibility.

The use of the word *hogo* (protection) for such provisions as maternity leave implies that pregnancy is a handicap suffered by women, rather than a socially useful function which should be supported by society as a whole. In the case of what I have called *protective provisions*, the implication is that women are physically weaker than men, and therefore need protection. This impression is reinforced by the fact that factory legislation groups women and minors together. Where financial assistance is concerned, it seems that women *and children* are the target of legislation; presumably it is the effects of poverty from which they are being protected. Once again, there are several possible solutions to this issue, including individualist solutions, communal solutions, State solutions, or reliance on the attainment of a 'family wage'.

By conducting this debate according to the language of *bosei hogo*, the feminists of the Taishō period unwittingly reinforced the notion that the normal relationship between the State and individual women is one of 'protector' and 'protected'. Thus, a common ideology lay behind the discussion of the 'protection' of women workers and the discussion of State financial assistance in the 'motherhood protection' debate. As we have seen, labour organizers shared this view of women as the objects of protection. The use of the language of protection places women in the position of seeking protection from a strong State, rather than as citizens who can demand rights from the State.

Other writers have referred to such a view of the relationship between women and the State as the 'discourse of protection'.[125] While men are positioned as workers or as citizens with rights, women, according to the discourse of protection, are positioned as weak, and as supplicants, in need of the protection of the State.[126] The implication is that the category of 'woman', and the categories of 'worker' or 'citizen' are mutually exclusive. Only men are constructed as citizens, while only women are constructed as supplicants in need of protection.

Another feature of these discussions concerned different views of social transformation. Yosano Akiko espoused an individualist view of the relationship between individual and State. She resisted State intervention and saw individual independence as the solution to problems related to the care and maintenance of children. Hiratsuka Raichō, while valorizing 'motherhood' as an image of women's creativity and power, also discussed the social meaning of motherhood, and was led to seek State support for the resolution of women's problems. At this stage, however, Hiratsuka did not seek the transformation of the capitalist system. She would go on to found the New Women's Association (*Shin Fujin Kyōkai*) with Ichikawa Fusae in 1920.

Yamakawa Kikue brought a socialist perspective to discussion of the relationship between individual and State, rejecting individualist solutions, and rejecting solutions which failed to challenge the capitalist system. For Yamakawa, this meant an engagement with socialist and labour politics. This debate highlighted the issue of class differences between women, an issue which would become important in socialist discussions of women as workers. The debate also allowed Yamakawa to continue the process of defining the differences between socialist and liberal feminist positions on women's issues. This process would continue into the 1920s and 1930s, with further refinement of the socialist position in debates with anarchist women.

Speaking as a Mother

According to official ideology, women were positioned as wives and as mothers. For middle-class women, this involved promotion of their activities as educators of their children and as supporters of the militarist State through semi-official patriotic organizations. For working-class women, the focus of official policies on motherhood became the production of healthy recruits. When the reproductive needs of the State conflicted with the needs of industry for women workers, the working conditions of female factory workers became a social issue, and this was linked to the enactment of factory legislation. For labour organizers, too, women were primarily seen in familial terms, as wives, mothers, and daughters rather than as workers. Unions, like the bureaucracy, took a protective attitude to women workers.

For feminist writers, however, the capacity for motherhood was what made women distinctive, and there were attempts to link women's reproductive capacity with creativity, power, and genius. While such imagery was powerful, there were limitations in a view of women's creative power which was not linked to a consciousness of the social. Others used the maternal as a metaphor for a caring society and attempted to give legitimacy to what were seen as 'feminine' values.

Hiratsuka argued for the importance of the social meaning of motherhood, and attempted to use this position in order to make demands on the State. However, while motherhood was linked to the concept of protection, women were inevitably constructed as supplicants, rather than as citizens who could make demands. Given this view of women, it was necessary for women to reposition themselves as workers and as citizens, in order to gain legitimacy to approach the State with demands rather than as supplicants. In socialist discourse, while women were primarily seen as wives and as mothers, discussion of the 'woman question' could be restricted to issues of marriage, the family, and reproduction. If women could be seen as workers, then all aspects of socialist theory and strategy could be seen to be relevant to women.

The Taishō debates on motherhood and related issues were important in clarifying the differences between liberal feminist, maternalist feminist and socialist views of social change. These debates highlighted the relationship between State policies and the supposedly individual matters of reproduction and childrearing. For someone like Yamakawa Kikue, this was an important stage in the definition of a socialist position on the 'woman question', a quest she would continue throughout her life. For a woman such as Hiratsuka Raichō, these debates brought a realization that writing alone was not enough to effect changes in women's situation.[127] It was time for organized group action by women, although this was by necessity carried out within the limitations of Article Five of the Peace Police Law. Article Five was modified in February 1922, and this made possible the formation of organizations devoted to the cause of women's suffrage.[128] Meanwhile, socialist women attempted a closer engagement with working women.

In Chapters five and six, I will explore women's attempts to go beyond polemic and attempt to implement social change in various ways. Chapter five will focus on women as workers. The contradictions involved in the disjunction between the identities of 'woman' and 'worker' led many women to participate in labour activism, a path which brought women as workers into conflict with capital. Other women's activism, however, led them to attempt to engage more directly with State institutions, a theme which will be explored in more detail in Chapter six, on women as activists.

CHAPTER 5

WORKERS

Workers. In labour movement publications in the 1920s, women started to be represented as workers. Once they were represented as workers, questions of solidarity and class consciousness were also seen to be relevant to women. Note the group of women workers in Japanese dress, leaving the factory after dark. Detail of the cover of the textile workers' journal *Seigi no Hikari* (*The Light of Justice*), No. 3, 1926.

In February 1919, Yamakawa Kikue contributed an article on 'The Present and Future Situation of Working Women' to an intellectual journal.[1] Yamakawa would become one of the major theorists of women's position within the socialist movement in the 1920s, and had attempted to bring a socialist perspective to the 'woman question' in her debates with the 'Bluestockings'. Yamakawa now contributed to various intellectual journals and socialist publications. In this article, Yamakawa describes two encounters with working women. Recently, she had been woken early in the morning by her baby, and took him out so as not to disturb the other members of her household. On walking outside, she observed a group of factory workers, dressed inadequately for the cold weather, going from the dormitory to the factory at the change of shifts. Yamakawa does not enter the factory, but describes the incessant noise of the machines which emanates from the factory at all times of the day. One young girl whom Yamakawa glimpses snatching a bite to eat on the way to work is described as being like 'a cross between human, machine, and animal'.[2] Yamakawa's distance from the young women is intensified when she describes the songs sung by the factory women. The songs 'have the same monotonous, detached tone as soldiers' songs'. She only catches the phrase, 'I was left at Ōmori Station, and sold to the factory'. For Yamakawa, this phrase 'seems to tell the whole story of their lives'.[3]

Some years earlier, she had accompanied a group of Salvation Army members on a factory visit. They taught the factory workers hymns, which preached that work was sacred, and that those who worked hard would be blessed by God. Yamakawa was angered by the inefficacy of religion in helping these women. But she, too, felt helpless. Sitting on a platform with the representatives of the Salvation Army, she was unable to bridge the gap between the evangelists and the workers. The spatial distance between Yamakawa and the factory workers dramatizes the gulf of class which separates them. Yamakawa is also, however, aware of her own position as a middle-class beneficiary of the exploitation of the working class:[4]

> I wanted to leave the platform where I sat with the other visitors and join the factory girls. I wanted to apologise to these women. I wanted to prostrate myself before them. I wanted to do this because I was tormented by the guilty feeling that I – we – are the ones who have corrupted them, who have cheated them, who have trampled on them. So, I wanted to apologise to them, to tell them that I was their friend. Instead, I sat on the platform with their enemies. From the heated platform, I looked down on them, as they knelt, barefoot, in the unheated hall. I have never forgotten those feelings of guilt and distress.[5]

Yamakawa then attempts to link the plight of the young women, who told her how much they hated night work, and how they wanted to go back to their home towns, with the broader question of organizing women in the labour movement. Yamakawa mentions the opinion that the large number of women workers had hindered the development of the labour movement in Japan. Yamakawa recognizes the problems involved in organizing workers who are always under strict supervision and control, but affirms the possibility of making the slogan 'Workers of the world unite' mean something for Japan's women workers.[6]

This article encapsulates the dilemma of the intellectual who cannot share the experiences of working women, but who wishes to use her intellectual understanding of the mechanisms of exploitation in the service of the working class. In the 1920s, the socialist movement employed several strategies to organize proletarian women. These included the formation of socialist women's organizations such as the *Sekirankai* (Red Wave Society) and the *Yōkakai* (Eighth Day Society), the creation of women's divisions in union federations, and the formation of women's leagues affiliated to the socialist parties which were formed after the enactment of Universal Manhood Suffrage in 1925. For Yamakawa, attempts to bridge the gulf between intellectuals and working women included support for these socialist women's organizations and fighting for space for the inclusion of women's issues in the platforms of the proletarian parties and left-wing union federations.[7] Such activities were carried out in the context of a labour movement subject to constant repression and surveillance, and fragmented by factional disputes.

Socialist thought underwent further refinement in this decade, as socialists and anarchists discussed political strategies and political theories, in debates known as the anarchist-bolshevist debates (*ana-boru ronsō*).[8] Debates on socialist strategy intensified in the 1920s, as more of the works of Marx, Engels, and Lenin were translated into Japanese.[9] In the 1930s, further debates, known as the *Rōnō-Kōza* controversy, centred on the correct interpretation of the Meiji Restoration, and the implications for the implementation of socialist revolution in Japan. If the Meiji Restoration was seen as a bourgeois revolution, then Japan was ready for a proletarian revolution. If the Meiji Restoration was simply seen as an élite coup d'état, then a two-stage revolutionary strategy would be necessary. With respect to women's issues, these different perspectives affected the emphasis given to 'feudal remnants' as an explanation for women's present-day situation.[10]

The Japan Socialist League (*Nihon Shakai Shugi Dōmei*), a broad-based left-wing organization, was formed in December 1920, but an official opening could not be held due to the provisions of the Public Peace

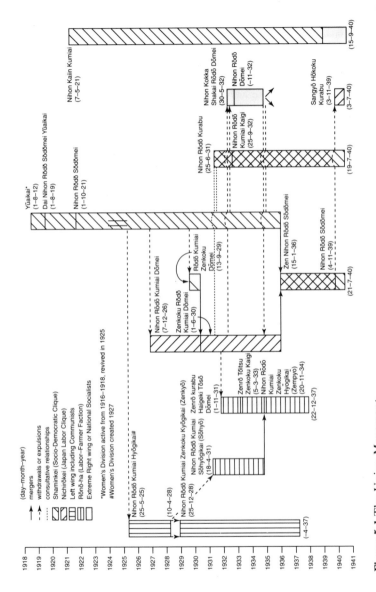

Figure 5.1 The Union Movement
Adapted from Stephen S. Large. *Organized Workers and Socialist Politics in Interwar Japan*, Cambridge: Cambridge University Press, 1982, p.261. For translations, see Glossary.

Police Law. The League was disbanded within six months. Other activities connected with the proletarian movement included the formation of a Birth Control Institute.[11] The *Suiheisha* (Levellers' Society), an organization devoted to the liberation of the former outcast class, was also formed in 1922,[12] as was the Japan Farmers' Union (*Nihon Nōmin Kumiai*), an organization of tenant farmers, and the Proletarian Youth League (*Musan Seinen Dōmei*).

The Japan Communist Party was formed in July 1922.[13] Figures associated with the party included Sakai Toshihiko, Yamakawa Hitoshi, Yamakawa Kikue, Nakasone Sadayo and Sakai [Kondō] Magara.[14] The party was disbanded in 1924 after government crackdowns in the summer of 1923, and was not reformed until December 1926. Even though the party itself disbanded and re-formed several times, and largely operated as an underground organization, communists continued their activities in the union federations. The extension of communist influence in the *Sōdōmei* union federation culminated in a split in 1925. Communist elements were expelled from the *Sōdōmei* and formed the *Nihon Rōdō Kumiai Hyōgikai* (Japan Labour Unions Council, abbreviated as *Hyōgikai*) on 25 May 1925. A second split occurred in December 1926, resulting in the formation of the centrist *Nihon Rōdō Kumiai Dōmei* (Japan Labour Union League) and leaving the *Sōdōmei* in the hands of the most moderate elements of the labour movement.[15]

Left-wing political activity in the 1920s, then, was characterized by acrimonious intellectual debates, accompanied by increased factionalism in the unions, proletarian parties, farmers' organizations, tenants' unions, and the women's divisions and women's leagues which followed the factionalism of the 'malestream' organizations. To simplify an immensely complicated picture, there were three major 'cliques' involved: the Social Democratic clique, the centrist *Nichirō* clique, and the left-wing Labour–Farmer clique.[16] Each one of these cliques was involved with one of the major union federations, which in turn formed the support base for an affiliated political party. While some communists continued to operate underground in the illegal Japan Communist Party after it was reformed, others operated in the left wing of the legal proletarian party movement.

For women within the socialist movement, the 1920s brought attempts to theorize the class position of women workers, and discussion of the best ways to mobilize these women. Debates on the most appropriate ways to organize women were carried on in the union federations, and continued with the formation of proletarian political parties after the enactment of Universal Manhood Suffrage in 1925.

State policy on labour was carried out in the context of Japan's participation in the Paris Peace Conference at the end of the First World War, and the government's stated commitment to supporting the aims of the International Labour Organization (ILO) as part of the terms of the Treaty of Versailles. Union federations attempted to use the government's official support of the ILO to put pressure on the government for the official recognition of unions and the improvement of working conditions.[17]

Modifications to the Factory Law were carried out in 1923 to become effective in 1926.[18] The abolition of night work for women and minors was postponed a further three years, eventually being abolished in 1929.[19] In other aspects of social policy related to labour, there were unsuccessful attempts in 1926 to pass a union bill which would have legalised union activity. A conciliation bill was passed, however, and Article 17 of the Public Peace Police Law was repealed. The Health Insurance Law which had been passed in 1922 did not become effective until 1926.[20]

The enactment of Universal Manhood Suffrage in 1925 was counterbalanced by the enactment of the repressive Peace Preservation Law (*Chian Iji Hō*) of 1925. Communists and other leftists operated in a context of surveillance, censorship, and regular purges in the 1920s. Workers came into direct conflict with capital and State in strikes, and this activity intensified at the end of the decade. From 1929 to 1931, depression resulted in layoffs in the textile industry, and women workers were in the vanguard of some of the most militant labour disputes. Before considering in detail socialist views of women as workers, and women's participation in the socialist movement as workers, it is necessary to make some comments on the kinds of work performed by women in the first decades of the twentieth century.

Women in Industry

In the period for which we have reliable statistics, roughly a third of women were classified as being engaged in gainful employment. The figures are 36.7 per cent in 1920, and 32.69 per cent in 1930.[21] These figures do not, however, include women engaged in unpaid farm or domestic labour. Until at least 1936, the majority of gainfully employed women were in agriculture, although this proportion declined between 1906 (65.5 per cent) and 1936 (57.4 per cent). The high proportion of the population employed in the agricultural sector posed problems for the articulation of a form of socialist theory relevant to early twentieth-century Japan, while the proportion of women engaged in agricultural labour presented particular problems for the conjunction of socialism and feminism.[22] Mining workers were less than 1 per cent of gainfully employed women between 1906 and 1936.[23]

The next highest proportions of women gainfully employed were those working in factories or as domestic servants. Although women consistently formed a high proportion of the total number of workers in factories, there was a significant degree of gender segmentation according to industry. In 1909, for example, women comprised 85.2 per cent of workers in textiles, but only 2.0 per cent in machinery and metal manufacturing. In food, chemicals, and other industries, women were around one-third of total employees.[24] By 1930, 40 per cent of women in manufacturing were married, suggesting that the stereotype of the young farmgirl filling in time before marriage was no longer applicable.[25] Home-based piece work was an important source of income for married women in urban areas. One survey in Tokyo in 1926 found that 90 per cent of piece-workers were or had been married.[26]

Although the labour movement concentrated on factory labour (after belatedly recognizing the importance of the high proportion of women workers), domestic servants formed a significant proportion of women engaged in waged work from the turn of the century. From 1906 to 1936, between 5 per cent and 8 per cent of gainfully employed women were engaged in domestic work, fewer than the number of women engaged in manufacturing as a whole, but roughly comparable with the proportion of women engaged in textile work. It was not until 1916 that the proportion of domestic servants was overtaken by textile workers. Given that domestic service is a gender-typed occupation, which does not fit the model of waged labour addressed in Marxist theory, it is perhaps unsurprising that the labour movement initially paid little systematic attention to the possibility of mobilizing domestic workers. We can, however, see demands for 'improvement in maids' working conditions' in the policy statements and newsletters of the women's leagues formed in the early Shōwa period.

Other categories of work engaged in by women included various kinds of service work: in retailing, restaurants, and entertainment. These industries, too, were initially neglected by the labour movement, but we can see attempts to organize waitresses in the early Shōwa period. Prostitution, in socialist writing, served as a metaphor for the exploitation and degradation suffered by workers under the capitalist system, but these workers did not become obvious targets for the attention of labour organizations.[27]

It is difficult to quantify the numbers of 'professional women' (*shoku-gyō fujin*), as the methods of categorizing white-collar occupations changed from survey to survey. However, the category of *shokugyō fujin* was a recognizable one in the popular and academic discourse of the Taishō and early Shōwa periods. For women, growth was particularly conspicuous in the categories of nursing and teaching; and the number of white-collar women employed in government offices almost doubled between 1920 and 1930.[28] The visibility of these new categories of women workers in urban areas can perhaps be connected with the developing public discourse on the 'modern girl', the successor to the 'new woman' of the Taishō period.[29]

Much of the theorization of the class position of women workers and the most effective ways of mobilizing women workers was initially carried out by educated, middle-class leaders of the socialist movement. However, it soon became necessary to use the union movement to nurture labour leaders – both men and women – from within the ranks of working people.

May Day and International Women's Day

Workers in Japan celebrated May Day publicly for the first time in 1920, and thousands of workers gathered in Ueno Park in Tokyo. Women participated in May Day activities from the second May Day in 1921, when an estimated 10 000 workers marched.[30] Preparation for May Day was one of the first activities of the socialist women's group, the *Sekirankai* (Red Wave Society), established in April 1921.[31] It has often been pointed out that many of the members of the *Sekirankai* had connections with male activists in the socialist movement. Even Yamakawa herself has described the *Sekirankai* as being like 'the Women's Division of the Socialist League'.[32] However, this does not seem to be any reason to belittle the contributions of Yamakawa Kikue, Sakai Magara and others to the socialist movement.

In preparation for May Day, the *Sekirankai* manifesto was written by Yamakawa Kikue, and this was distributed as a leaflet enjoining women to participate in May Day and join the socialist movement. The manifesto employs the language of class struggle, in a very different tone from the gentle version of socialism espoused by the Commoners' Society in the 1900s:

> The *Sekirankai* is a women's organisation that plans to participate in the enterprise to destroy the capitalist society and build a socialist society. The capitalist society turns us into slaves at home and oppresses us as wage slaves outside the home. This is a society which has driven many of our sisters into prostitution, and for the sake of its own aggressive ambitions has taken away

our beloved fathers, lovers, children and brothers – a society which for the
sake of its own greedy profiteers, greets the proletariat of other countries
with artillery and slaughter . . .
    The *Sekirankai* declares all-out war on this cruel, shameless society. Women
who wish to be liberated, join the *Sekirankai*. Socialism offers the only way
to save humankind from the oppressions and abuses of capitalism. Sisters,
who love justice and humanity, join the socialist movement![33]

The stated enemy is 'capitalist society' rather than individual males,
patriarchy, individual capitalists, or the State as an autonomous entity.
Exploitation under capitalist society is seen in gendered terms. Women
are not only 'wage slaves', but are also exploited as 'slaves at home'. In
addition, exploitation takes on a corporeal dimension, as women are
forced into prostitution, while men are forced into military service.
Official discourse drew analogies between textile work and military
service: different ways in which women and men could work for the
nation. Socialists, on the other hand, saw prostitution and military
service as analogous: these were different ways in which working-class
women and men were exploited in the interests of the ruling class.[34]
    Although there is some recognition that exploitation takes gendered
forms, it is also possible to argue that feminist struggle has here been
assimilated into the class struggle, with 'women and workers' united in
a common struggle. Similarly, the evocation of class consciousness may
be seen as being somewhat ritualistic: a matter of intellectual belief,
rather than a keenly felt identity with the needs of male and female
workers.
    About twenty women marched under the red and black flags of the
Sekirankai on this second May Day in 1921, and all of them were
arrested. The flags were made by Hashiura Haruko, enrolled in a dress-
making school at the time. A photograph of Hashiura Haruko's arrest
appeared in the next day's newspaper, and this photograph resulted in
her harassment, and eventual withdrawal from the school.[35] Two
women were charged with violation of press regulations for the distribution of the pamphlet bearing Yamakawa's manifesto, and the next
major activity of the organization was fundraising for their fines of
20 yen each.[36]
    At a fundraising meeting held on 12 June, Kutsumi Fusako introduced
veteran speakers Ishikawa Sanshirō and Akita Ujaku, who were joined by
Itō Noe, Fujimori Seikichi, and Sakai Magara. Sakai Magara's first speech
in public was a great success, as she entertained her audience with a
lighthearted account of her arrest.[37]
    In July of the same year, a series of lectures was held over five eve-
nings. The list of speakers in this series tells us something about the
genealogy of the *Sekirankai*. In addition to the women of the *Sekirankai*,

several male socialist activists contributed lectures to the series. Several of these speakers, including Sakai Toshihiko and Ishikawa Sanshirō, had contributed to the *Heiminsha* lectures on the 'woman question' in the 1900s, and their topics show a continuity. Sakai Toshihiko now continued his exposition of the thought of Friedrich Engels, Lewis Henry Morgan, Lester Ward, and Edward Carpenter. Itō Noe was a former editor of the Bluestocking journal, *Seitō*, and had been responsible for translations of the work of anarchist feminist Emma Goldmann. She now, however, distanced herself from the 'Bluestockings' with her criticism of the 'mother's rights' theorists. Yamakawa Kikue contributed a discussion of the First International and the Third International.[38] The new generation of activists was represented by Sakai Magara, nineteen-year-old daughter of Sakai Toshihiko.[39] A consciousness of the *Sekirankai's* place in history is evident in the themes of two of Sakai Toshihiko's lectures. On the first night he discussed the ideas of Lester Ward, and added reflections on the women's movement in the days of the *Heiminsha*. On the final evening, he spoke on 'The history of the women's movement in the Meiji and Taishō periods, and the function of the *Sekirankai*'.[40]

These years offered further opportunities to clarify the differences between the socialist and liberal feminist positions on the 'woman question'. Both Yamakawa Kikue and Itō Noe were critical of the activities of the New Women's Association (*Shin Fujin Kyōkai*) formed by some of the former Bluestockings. Yamakawa, as part of her efforts to delineate a socialist position on the 'woman question', was scathing about the activities of the New Women.[41] Yamakawa was critical about the reformist emphasis of the Association, stating that the New Women wanted 'equal opportunity to enjoy themselves'. However, instead of presenting a viable socialist alternative, much of the article is taken up with personal criticism of Hiratsuka. The article also displays the tendency of Yamakawa and other socialists of the time to idealize post-revolutionary Russia.[42] Oku Mumeo, by contrast, showed her consciousness of the problems of working women, and refrained from personal criticism of Yamakawa.[43]

The activities of the *Sekirankai* were, however, relatively short-lived, for several members suffered arrest and imprisonment. In addition to those who suffered imprisonment in various incidents, Hashiura Riku died suddenly in 1923, while Hashiura Haruko and Nakasone Sadayo withdrew from the socialist movement for personal reasons. Takatsu Tayoko and her husband were charged with *lèse majesté* for allegedly producing a publication which included threats against the imperial household.[44] Sakai Magara and Nakasone Sadayo were among a group of socialists placed on remand for some forty days in an incident which involved the distribution of subversive material to soldiers billeted in Tokyo for manoeuvres.[45] Sakai and Nakasone were among the seventeen found guilty. They were sentenced to four months imprisonment, the first women to be imprisoned for offences related to dangerous thought since Kanno Suga's involvement in the Great Treason Incident in 1910.

In 1922, socialist women in Japan prepared for the celebration of International Women's Day, and the *Yōkakai* (Eighth Day Society) was formed for this purpose. International Women's Day is celebrated on 8 March, hence the name 'Eighth Day Society'. International Women's Day was celebrated for the first time on 8 March 1923, and marked with a lecture meeting, where 'Kaneko Hiroko' spoke on 'The Possibilities of Professional Life for Women'. Her speech was interrupted by anti-communist agitators as soon as she mentioned Russia; the meeting became disordered, and was broken up by the police. Other speakers were to have been Yamakawa Kikue, Tanno Setsu, Tajima Hide and Nakasone Sadayo.[46] International Women's Day was also marked by a special women's edition of the proletarian arts journal *Tane Maku Hito* (*The Sower*), one of the sponsors of the meeting.[47]

The *Sekirankai* and the *Yōkakai* were important as relatively autonomous socialist women's organizations, devoted to exploring the possibilities of a socialist answer to the 'woman question'. Although these organizations had intellectual importance, their existence was too brief for them to work for building a mass base among proletarian women; they could not successfully bridge the gap between intellectuals and working women.[48]

Women's Special Demands

After the dissolution of the Japan Socialist League in May 1921, the splits between anarchists and bolshevists resurfaced. Many of the leaders of the Japan Communist Party, formed in 1922, were former anarchists, and the next few years were marked by conflict between the anarchists and the communists. Yamakawa Hitoshi published his article in support of the Bolshevist position, 'A Change of Direction in the Proletarian Movement', in the summer of 1922.[49] For many socialists, this also marked a shift from the hitherto intellectual and theoretical emphasis of the socialist movement. Under the slogan 'to the masses', many individuals moved to a closer engagement with the labour movement, including such women as Kutsumi Fusako and Tanno Setsu.[50] Members of the *Yōkakai* also briefly participated in the Tokyo Federation of Women's Organizations (*Tōkyō Fujin Rengōkai*), a broad-based federation, initially formed to co-ordinate women's relief activities in the aftermath of the Great Kantō Earthquake of 1923.[51] The context for women's political activities had improved slightly in 1922 with the modification of Article Five of the Public Peace Police Law. Women could now attend and speak at political meetings, but could not vote or become full members of political parties.

The Communist Party was disbanded in 1924, the result of severe police repression before and after the earthquake of September 1923, and was not reformed until 1926.[52] In addition to mass arrests of communists in the summer of 1923, several labour leaders were murdered by police in the aftermath of the earthquake. Anarchists Ōsugi Sakae and Itō Noe also became martyrs to the left-wing cause after their murder at the hands of a police officer.

Other members of the proletarian movement worked towards the creation of legal proletarian political parties, in anticipation of the enactment of Universal Manhood Suffrage. The *Seiji Mondai Kenkyūkai* (Political Issues Research Association, later shortened to *Seiji Kenkyūkai*, Political Research Association) was formed in December 1923. The members of the organization were preparing for the formation of a proletarian political party which would represent both workers and tenant farmers. Initially, the only part of the *Seiji Kenkyūkai* platform which specifically mentioned women, however, was the call for suffrage for both men and women.[53] Yamakawa Kikue and other women connected with the Kōbe branch worked to ensure that women's demands would be included in the platform of the organization. These demands included:

• the abolition of the household head system;
• the abolition of all laws which treat women as incompetents; and equality in grounds for divorce for both sexes;
• the granting to women and colonized peoples the same rights to education and employment as mainland males;
• a standard living wage regardless of sex or race;
• equal wages and equal treatment for all regardless of sex or race;
• nursing time (30 minutes per 3 hours worked) and nursing room for working women;
• sacking of women on grounds of marriage or pregnancy should be prohibited;
• the abolition of the public prostitution system.

These demands were criticized as 'petit-bourgeois' by the men of the *Seiji Kenkyūkai*, but they were supported by Yamakawa in an article on 'women's special demands'.[54] Yamakawa argued that women's so-called 'special demands' (*tokushu yōkyū*) were in fact basic to the interests of both men and women. The removal of laws which discriminate against women and uphold feudal ideology is seen to be necessary for the political awakening of the whole proletarian class. One of the things which prevents women from full participation in the proletarian movement, argues Yamakawa, is the feudal ideology which sees women subject to the vigilance of supervisors in factory dormitories, and the control of parents in the home.[55]

In her discussion of the treatment of working mothers, Yamakawa was able to build on the insights gained through her debates with the Bluestockings in the previous decade. With respect to working mothers, Yamakawa argued for:

- the necessity of eight weeks *paid* leave before and after parturition;
- the creation of nursing rooms in workplaces;
- the provision of thirty minutes nursing time for every three hours work;
- State responsibility for expenses related to childbirth; and
- State provision of living expenses for the mother.

The proposal for State provision of living expenses was aimed at putting working women and other women on an equal footing, and was justified with reference to British health insurance.[56]

Yamakawa links the situation of women workers with workers in Japan's colonies.[57] She argues that both women and non-Japanese workers should have equality of opportunity with Japanese male workers. In answer to the 'craft unionist' anxiety that such workers will undercut the wages of male workers, she argues for equality of pay, and equality of education so that these workers may compete equally as skilled workers.[58] While Yamakawa has already devoted some attention to the 'feudal ideology' which helps determine women's subordinate place in the labour market, she does not, in this article, attempt to tease out the specificities of sexist and racist ideologies. Rather, she sees the position of women workers and colonized workers as analogous, and as requiring similar political strategies.

Much of Yamakawa's criticism in this article is directed at representatives of the new *Hyōgikai* union federation, which until now had failed to address women's issues seriously. In response to the criticism that it is not necessary to add 'regardless of race or sex' to demands for minimum wages, Yamakawa counters that, although this may go without saying in a society run on 'proletarian principles', the present society is run on 'bourgeois principles' which take discrimination against women for granted. Thus it is necessary to add this phrase to demands for equal pay, or suffrage. Her critique of universalist language has relevance to late twentieth-century debates on this issue:

> Even in a proletarian country, it is necessary to make explicit [the principle of equality regardless of sex, race or religion], because, in a society with

deep-rooted customs of discrimination, if we simply say 'the people' [*minshū*], there is a danger that this will be taken to mean only people of the ruling race [*shihaitekina minzoku*], and people of the dominant sex [*shihaitekina sei*].[59]

Many of the policies now espoused by Yamakawa were similar to those she had previously criticized as 'bourgeois'.[60] Yamakawa, however, distinguishes demands which will benefit the whole proletarian class by allowing the full participation of proletarian women from those of 'bourgeois feminists', 'shallow maternalists', and 'sentimental humanists'. In her criticism of the public prostitution system, for example, Yamakawa is keen to dissociate herself from the 'sentimental humanists' of the Japan Women's Christian Temperance Union.[61]

Yamakawa sees prostitution first of all as a labour issue, seeing the sexual labour of indentured prostitutes as a particular kind of unfree labour. She also points out the violation of human rights under enforced medical inspections.[62] Another feature of this article is Yamakawa's consciousness of the imperialist context of Japanese politics, a significant advance from the discussions of the previous decade.

Organizing Women in the *Yūaikai/Sōdōmei*

The next task of socialist women involved creating the organizational structures for the participation of women in the labour movement. While the *Yūaikai/Sōdōmei* had had a women's division since 1916, women connected with the *Hyōgikai* had to argue afresh for the necessity for special organizations for women.[63]

The first labour organizations had tended to pay most attention to workers in heavy industry. In early labour movement writings, as we have seen, the worker was implicitly constructed as masculine, while the convention of writing about women workers as objects of pity and compassion continued into the 1920s, particularly with the publication of Hosoi Wakizō's book *Jōkō Aishi* (*The Pitiful History of the Female Factory Workers*) in 1925.

In the pages of *Yūai Fujin*, the journal of the *Yūaikai*, the first labour organization to create a women's division, women were primarily portrayed as wives and mothers. Articles often focused on cooking and housekeeping, and women were encouraged to be supporters for their husbands. Union leader Suzuki Bunji, in particular, unashamedly addressed working women in the language of 'good wives and wise mothers'. When women's work was considered in the women's division journal, it was often in the context of casual, home-based work, and advice was given on suitable home-based work for housewives. The Friendly Society also, however, acknowledged that some women were working alongside menfolk in factories, and the union attitude to these workers was initially a protective one, as we have seen previously.

It was not until 1917 that women could become full members of the organization, and in the time after the 1917 annual conference, some attempts were made to mobilize working women. The Women's Division held meetings and lectures in local areas, and after contacts had been built up among the working women, leaders would be chosen from among them. These local leaders would then be responsible for broadening the contacts of the union, and ensuring communication between local factories and the union branches.[64]

The Friendly Society was extensively reorganized at the 1919 Conference, held from 30 August to 1 September. The organization was renamed the *Dai Nihon Rōdō Sōdōmei-Yūaikai* (Greater Japan General Federation of Labour-Friendly Society), and transformed into something closer to a union federation. Two women, Yamanouchi Mina and Nomura Tsuchino, were elected to the Executive Committee.[65] The twenty stated objectives of the revamped organization included several which were directly relevant to working women:

- equal pay for equal work;
- the prohibition of night work;
- the appointment of inspectors for women's work; and
- the abolition of indentured work.[66]

The Women's Division now employed Ichikawa Fusae as Secretary, and allocated a separate budget. The name of the women's journal was to be changed from *Yūai Fujin* (*Friendly Society Woman*) to *Rōdō Fujin* (*Labour Woman*), and it seemed at first that this new title might signify a changed attitude towards the women members of the *Sōdōmei-Yūaikai*.[67]

One of Ichikawa's first activities was to chair a public meeting on 5 October 1919 about issues of importance to working women. Around 1000 attended, mainly workers involved in the textile industry. The distinguished guests, including Tanaka Takako,[68] Hiratsuka Raichō, Kaneko Shigeri, and Itō Noe, heard testimonies from several women currently working as factory operatives. For most of the factory women it was their first time to speak in public. Kikuchi Hatsu spoke of the problems of working mothers, while cradling her baby. Kikuchi and several other speakers called for a reduction of the working day to eight hours, and the abolition of night work for women.[69]

Ichikawa's tenure as Secretary of the Women's Division was to be short-lived, however, for she resigned in November 1919 over conflict with the union leadership about who would be the women's advisor for

the Japanese delegation to the International Labour Conference. Ichikawa's resignation meant that the journal *Rōdō Fujin* did not appear as
planned.[70] The Women's Division was further weakened after the defeat
of the *Sōdōmei-Yūaikai* affiliated spinning workers' union in the Fuji Gas
Spinning Factory Dispute at Oshiage in July 1920. The strike leaders
were sacked from the factory as a result of this dispute. This was an
important strike which involved demands for the recognition of the
union by management. It also involved dormitory workers, but their
action was suppressed by the management's preventing workers from
leaving the dormitory, and preventing organizers from entering the
dormitory. Although this particular dispute was unsuccessful, its importance was in developing a more assertive attitude in the women workers,
and training them for future activities.[71]

Other women would attempt to carry on the activities of the
Women's Division, but they were initially faced with the incomprehen-
sion of the male leaders of the union. Yamanouchi remembers that the
attitude of *Sōdōmei-Yūaikai* leader, Suzuki Bunji, and his colleagues was
that what most women involved with the union really needed was to
find a good husband, and they would attempt to find suitable partners
for such women as Yamanouchi.[72]

In April 1923 the issue of the now moribund Women's Division was
raised at the Kantō (Eastern Japan) and Kansai (Western Japan)
regional conferences of the *Sōdōmei* by Nozaka Ryō and Kutsumi
Fusako. The decision was delegated to a committee by the Kansai conference, but passed at the Kantō conference.[73] The proposal for the
revival of a central Women's Division was taken to the *Sōdōmei* annual
general conference in 1924, but the decision was postponed until 1925.
The Kantō Women's Division continued its activities, and Nozaka Ryō
was responsible for producing a women's supplement to the union
journal *Rōdō* (*Labour*) from April 1924.

Just when the Women's Division seemed to be on a firm footing once
again, the first of two major splits occurred. In April 1925, the first split
resulted in the establishment of the *Hyōgikai*. In May 1926, the second
split resulted in the establishment of the *Nihon Rōdō Kumiai Dōmei*. With
the breakaway first of communist-influenced elements to the *Hyōgikai*,
and then of centrist elements to the *Nihon Rōdō Kumiai Dōmei*, the
Sōdōmei was left in the hands of the most conservative elements of the
labour movement, who continued their activities under the slogan of
'realism'. The first split also resulted in the loss of many of the major
women leaders from the *Sōdōmei*. Kutsumi Fusako, Komiyama Tomie,[74]
Yamanouchi Mina, Nozaka Ryō, and Tanno Setsu left to join the new
Hyōgikai Federation.[75] Within the *Sōdōmei*, the activities of the Women's
Division were first carried on by Matsuoka Komakichi, and then by

Iwauchi Zensaku, leader of the newly created *Kantō Bōshoku Rōdō Kumiai* (Kantō Textile Workers' Union). In 1926, the *Sōdōmei* and the Kantō Textile Workers' Union were active in a campaign for the immediate banning of night work for women. A petition of 50 000 signatures was presented to the Diet in March 1926. Petitions were supported by the distribution of pamphlets in the streets of Tokyo.[76] Iwauchi and the textile workers, however, left the *Sōdōmei* to join the centrist *Nichirō* federation at the time of the second split.

While the *Sōdōmei* had a Women's Division which had operated sporadically from 1916, within the new *Hyōgikai* federation the necessity for a women's division had to be debated again from first principles, this time under the influence of Comintern pronouncements.[77]

The *Hyōgikai* Debates on the Women's Division

In September 1925, a two-day meeting of representatives of local women's divisions of the *Hyōgikai* union produced the 'Women's Division Thesis'. This sets out the relative numbers of male and female workers, and demonstrates that because women are the majority of factory workers, it is they who 'hold the key to the labour movement in Japan'. The development of class consciousness in women, however, has been hampered by their place in the feudalistic family system, and by the feudal attitudes of both men and women. It is stated that women are bound by the twin shackles of sex and class; that they are exploited as women and as workers; and thus women must promote their own special demands.[78] This document owes an obvious debt to Yamakawa's paper on women's 'special demands', and the whole debate can be seen as an attempt by socialists to address the question of 'equality versus difference'.[79]

The demands listed in the thesis are:

- a six-hour working day for women;
- the prohibition of night work, overtime, and dangerous work for women;
- the abolition of the dormitory system, with existing dormitories to be managed by unions;
- the abolition of enforced savings;
- the abolition of wage differences according to sex; and
- nursing leave for working mothers of 30 minutes for three hours work.[80]

These specific demands were a great advance on previously vague union policies on working women.[81] Many of the practical proposals for organizing women, however, were quite similar to the activities of the *Sōdōmei-Yūaikai*: the holding of tea parties and lecture meetings, the publication of pamphlets directed at women, the inclusion of a women's section in union publications, the training of women organizers, and the creation of a central women's division.[82]

However, there was immediate criticism of the proposal for a separate women's division to address these issues. Opponents of this proposal included some of the major male socialist activists of the time – Yamamoto Kenzō, Sugiura Keiichi, Mitamura Shirō, and Nabeyama Sadachika – with Yamakawa Hitoshi and Watanabe Masanosuke being distinguished by their continued support for the women's division.[83] Opponents argued that:

- the creation of a women's division would engender a consciousness of division between men and women which would militate against the development of class consciousness;
- women's issues were problems that should be solved outside the union movement;
- the functions of a women's division could be met simply by having more women organizers; and
- the creation of a women's division would make the organization itself more complicated.[84]

Watanabe Masanosuke responded to these criticisms in an article published under the pen-name 'Itō Manabu'. He argued that men and women must work together against the common enemy – capitalists. Because women have been disadvantaged by years of feudal strictures, they need education and training. It is awakened women who are best able to carry out this work, and they can best do this work with the support of the proper organizational structures, that is, with the support of a women's division. The women's division will have the function of facilitating communication between women members and the other specialist divisions: the education division, the political division, the recruitment division. Yamakawa Hitoshi also published a defence of the Women's Division proposal.[85]

The proposal was also defended by the *Hyōgikai* Printers' Union, who argued that the failure to support the women's division demonstrated a failure to recognize the special situation of women. Features of women's social situation included: the short-term nature of much women's work, which made them harder to organize; the extra commitments of women which made it harder for them to take part in union activities; and the fact that women were in unskilled positions meant that they tended to work longer hours for lower wages. Because unions have not taken these conditions into account, they have been unable to organize women effectively (for example, union meetings tend to be held at times which only suit men who have free time after work). Thus, a special women's division is necessary to reflect the particular needs of women workers and to carry out propaganda and education among women.[86]

The draft proposal for the setting up of a women's division in *Hyōgikai* headquarters was presented to the second annual conference, held in April 1926.[87] Tanno Setsu, who had been involved in the setting up of women's divisions in local branches of *Hyōgikai*-affiliated unions, led this discussion. She pointed out that on its founding the *Hyōgikai* had recognized the importance of organizing women, who were the majority of factory workers in Japan. Most local unions and regional branches had responded by setting up women's divisions. In the general headquarters, however, activities related to women were carried out under the auspices of the Recruitment Division (*soshikibu*), and this had not been satisfactory. Tanno called for clarification of the functions of the women's division, and for national co-ordination of the activities of women's divisions. Tanno's proposal clearly set out the functions of each level of the organization. The proposed central women's division would be responsible for formulating strategies for organizing and training women workers; for guidance and co-ordination of regional women's divisions; and for collating information. The regional women's divisions would be responsible for maintaining contact with local unions; for relaying information from the general headquarters; and for the gathering of information. Women's divisions in local unions would be responsible for contact with women members; education and training of women members; promotion of the union, and recruitment of non-unionized workers.[88] The 1926 Conference was unable to make a decision on the proposal, and the discussion was delegated to affiliated unions. The proposal was finally passed at the third annual conference in May 1927.

Although the creation of the Women's Division may be seen as a victory for women in the *Hyōgikai*, the actual implementation of the proposal was somewhat different from what the women had demanded. A new Women's League (*Fujin Dōmei*) was to be created, which would work in parallel with the union Women's Division. Rather than directing the union federation's policies on women, the Women's Division's main task was to be liaison with the Women's League which would organize working women and farming women outside the union movement.[89]

In Yamakawa Kikue's comments on this issue, she argues directly with Yamamoto Kenzō, who had argued that women's issues should be handled outside the union organization: that is, through a separate 'Women's League'. Yamakawa, however, is firmly opposed to the idea of a separate women's league, arguing instead that all proletarian organizations should strive to increase the membership of women, and increase educational activities directed at women.[90] While Yamakawa had been pleased to argue for the creation of a women's division within the union federation, in order that the organization could mobilize women more effectively, she is not willing to argue for autonomous women's organizations outside the union movement. It is interesting that she uses the *Sekirankai* (with which she was involved at the beginning of the decade) as a negative example of an autonomous women's organization.[91]

Yamakawa also cites the example of women's organizations in the United States which organized solely on the basis of sex, but she sees such organizations as basically bourgeois. For bourgeois women, she argues, the basic conflict is between men and women. For proletarian women, however, sex cannot take primacy over the class struggle. Even though we may talk of the 'proletarian women's movement' (*musan fujin undō*), what we really mean is 'the activities of women in the general proletarian class movement' (*ippantekina musan kaikyū undō ni okeru fujin no katsudō*). Yamakawa then goes on to explain the phrase 'work among women', which was the standard Comintern position on organizing women.[92]

Behind these debates on how to organize women were implicit theories of the relationship between class politics and feminist politics. Until the mid-1920s, most of those involved in unions had almost unconsciously given primacy to the class struggle. Male union organizers had either ignored women workers or assumed that the liberation of the working class would automatically mean the liberation of women, too. The debates over women's divisions in unions introduced the possibility that women may have different needs from men. Although women within the socialist movement were willing to argue for women's 'special demands', or to argue that women's 'special situation' meant that different strategies were necessary to mobilize women effectively, these demands were always presented in terms of allowing men and women to co-operate more effectively in fighting for the liberation of the proletariat.[93]

Yamakawa's thought on these issues had gained in subtlety since her earlier, rather ritualistic dismissal of the demands of bourgeois women. She was thus able to argue cogently for the creation of women's divisions within unions, in order to strive for some of the objectives she had previously criticized as 'bourgeois'. Yamakawa still, however, gave primacy to the class struggle and did not stray far from the Comintern line on 'work among women'. There were, however, problems with this position, as Yamakawa herself realized. Women were still prevented by Article Five of the Public Peace Police Law from becoming full members of political parties. Thus, Yamakawa could argue for the full integration of women into labour unions, farmers' unions, youth groups, and other proletarian organizations, but women's integration into political parties was impossible without the complete repeal of Article Five.[94]

In effect, what happened in the 1920s and the 1930s was that each of the major union federations had a women's division, while each of the proletarian political parties (which roughly corresponded with the structure of the union federations) had an affiliated women's league. Thus, women's activities within the proletarian movement were divided between these different organizations, and generally followed the splits and alliances of the 'malestream' organizations. A further layer of organization involved the mobilization of rural workers.[95]

After the ratification of the women's division proposal in 1927, the women's division acted to support women engaged in disputes. A statement issued in June 1927 listed the kinds of demands already being pursued, and a new demand for the 'protection of women during menstruation'.[96] In September 1926, the *Hyōgikai* and the Labour–Farmer party held a meeting which called for the enactment of five pieces of legislation:

- an Unemployment Benefits Law;
- a Minimum Wage Law;
- an Eight Hour Day Law;
- a Health Insurance Law; and
- a Working Women's Protection Law.[97]

A national movement for the institution of such legislation was started, but the *Hyōgikai* eventually succumbed to government suppression, and was dissolved in April 1928. The successor to the *Hyōgikai*, the Japan Labour Union National Conference (*Nihon Rōdō Kumiai Zenkoku Kyōgikai*: abbreviated as *Zenkyō*) was formed in December 1928.

Meanwhile, the 'realists' of the *Sōdōmei* continued in their efforts to mobilize working women. The creation of the *Rōdō Fujin Renmei* (Labour Women's Alliance) in 1927, was one important step. The leader of the League was Akamatsu Akiko. In 1927, Akamatsu Tsuneko[98] joined the *Sōdōmei* Women's Division, where she would continue her efforts on behalf of working women until 1940. One of Akamatsu Tsuneko's achievements was the publication of the long-awaited women's journal *Rōdō Fujin* (*Labour Woman*).[99]

Women in the *Nichirō* Unions

In the centrist *Nihon Rōdō Kumiai Dōmei*, Iwauchi Zensaku continued his efforts to mobilize women workers through the Japan Textile

Workers' Union, and its journal, *Seigi no Hikari* (*The Light of Justice*).[100] From November 1927, the Japan Textile Workers' Union co-operated with the National Women's League (*Zenkoku Fujin Dōmei*) on a committee calling for the abolition of night work for women.

After the abolition of night work for women in 1929, both companies and unions offered evening classes for women workers. In both cases, sewing, cooking, flower arranging and tea ceremony featured strongly. In other words, both companies and unions presented these evening classes as providing women workers with training in feminine accomplishments. Each set of activities, however, masked another ideological agenda. Company classes would be accompanied by lectures on moral training, which would emphasize patriotism, feminine values, loyalty to company and family, and hard work. Union classes would be accompanied by education in the ideas behind unionism. In the case of the *Sōdōmei* affiliates, patriotic values would be melded with social democratic unionism. In the case of the centrist *Nichirō* affiliates, such as the Labour Women's Night School (*Rōdō Jojuku*) run by Orimoto [Tatewaki] Sadayo in the Kameido region of Tokyo, Marxist ideas would be presented in simplified form.[101] The labour schools were thus negotiating a contradictory set of ideas about women workers. They used feminine stereotypes in order to attract women to the labour schools, and taught sewing and cooking as promised. Once in the schools, however, women were also trained as more or less militant unionists. Participants in some of the strikes of the early depression years later acknowledged the influence of the labour schools.[102]

Imagining Women Workers

Participants in left-wing organizations had largely failed to see women as workers and thus as potential comrades and unionists. Part of women's struggle for recognition within the socialist movement involved the creation of specific organizations devoted to the attainment of women's 'special demands'. It was also, however, necessary to transform the conventions of writing about women in labour movement publications.[103] Representations of women in such publications highlight the difficulty of a woman trying to speak from the position of 'worker', and once again dramatize the tension between being a woman, and trying to be a political activist.

Since the 1870s, work in cotton and silk spinning factories had been presented as a gendered patriotic activity. Factory work for women was presented as being analogous to military service for men. Companies played on notions of patriotism in propaganda directed at women workers, through company songs which described women spinning and reeling 'for the nation', and through special publications directed at women workers.[104]

Well into the 1920s, factory owners attempted to exploit workers more effectively through appeals to patriotic feeling, although workers themselves were cynical about such appeals.[105] Union organizers also, however, used the language of patriotism. This was particularly true of *Sōdōmei* affiliates: *Sōdōmei* leader Suzuki Bunji and his followers always affirmed the values of patriotism.[106]

While workers were cynical about appeals to self-sacrifice in the name of patriotism, they were able to find other justifications for their work. The fact that they were working for the good of their families made their sacrifices worthwhile – at least for some of the factory workers. In the factory workers' songs collected by labour historians and reproduced in union journals, there are frequent references to the workers' families.[107] This may take the form of a lament, in songs which describe feelings of homesickness. In other cases women workers are portrayed as martyr figures, engaging in self-sacrifice for the sake of their families. Factory owners attempted to redirect these feelings of familial obligation. In company propaganda, the factory could be presented as a surrogate family, with the factory owner as a father figure. Once again, however, workers were cynical about such appeals, and had no trouble in exposing the dubious logic behind these appeals to familial feeling.

Union organizers also identified female workers with the family in various ways. This could take the form of a paternalistic attitude towards women workers, seen most strikingly in the case of textile union leader, Iwauchi Zensaku, who referred to women workers as his 'children' and who was in turn addressed as 'father'.[108] The family could also serve as a metaphor for a community based on solidarity and co-operation, as it had for the early socialists. A poem which appeared in the fifth edition of *Seigi no Hikari* invited women workers to see the union as a surrogate family, where the union would become 'our brother and sister and our parent'.[109]

Both factory owners and union organizers tended to see women workers as future brides, filling in time before marriage. For factory owners, this meant that women workers were an expendable temporary work force, to be exploited for a few short years and easily replaced by other young women. For union organizers, this meant that women were not seen as providing a firm foundation for the creation of a strong base for the union movement.[110]

In the contributions of the male union organizers to the journal *Seigi no Hikari*, it is possible to discern a reluctance to see women as 'workers'. Women workers were seen as daughters, wives, or potential brides, rather than being addressed as fellow workers. This often led to some convoluted and original arguments for the necessity of unions. A worker from the Azuma branch reinforced the stereotype that women were only working for a few years before marriage, and expressed sympathy with women who might not be able to find a husband on their return to their villages. He argued, however, that if they would only support the union's campaign for the abolition of the night shift, they would be able to use their evenings to learn cooking, flower arranging, and all of the other skills which would help them to find a good husband![111]

Women in factories often worked twelve-hour days in dark and steamy workrooms, spending the remaining hours of the day in cramped dormitories, their freedom severely restricted. These conditions were particularly prevalent in textile factories.[112] Such conditions were described in numerous songs figuring factory workers as caged birds.[113] The major way of imagining liberation from this situation was to imagine escape. Indeed, the fantasy of escape in these songs matches the workers' preferred way of changing their situation in the earliest days of industrialization.[114]

The songs of the factory workers provided solidarity and comfort during the long working day. We could perhaps see these songs as forms of resistance, as one of the 'weapons of the weak'.[115] But what happens when such songs are taken away from the immediate context of the working day and recycled as texts?[116]

These songs were collected by labour historians and became part of the cultural resources available to represent women workers. Labour organizers recycled the imagery of workers' songs and re-presented this imagery in union journals directed at women in the textile mills. They reproduced the songs about caged birds and this trope was reinforced by visual imagery. The metaphor of the caged bird is one which is constantly referred to in the songs, illustrations and articles in union journals.[117]

Seigi no Hikari drew on journalistic representations of women workers, from such works as *Jokō Aishi* (*The Pitiful History of the Factory Girls*). One of the most heart-wrenching features of Hosoi's story of the textile workers is his collection of the songs sung by the women workers, which represent their extreme repression and exploitation.[118] It is these songs which are re-presented to the textile workers in the pages of the union journal. The following song, collected by Hosoi, was reproduced in the textile workers' journal in 1926:

I am a mill girl: rain that falls in spring
Silently sobbing on my own
When will the sky clear?
My pillow is wet with endless tears

I am a mill girl: a frail bird
Even though I have wings I can't fly away
Even though I can see the sky I'm stuck inside a cage
A tiny bird with broken wings

I am a mill girl: a fragile flower
A bud spoiled by frost
Even though spring is here I won't bloom
A tiny, tiny bud

I am a mill girl: a lonely star
Far away from my family
Twinkling in the dark, night sky
A tiny star brimming with tears.[119]

This song was thus part of a complex cycle of representations: first of all sung by the textile workers themselves, then collected by Hosoi in a work of popular journalism, and finally re-presented to the textile workers in the union journal.

It is possible to argue that these songs reflect a consciousness of these women's identity as *jokō* (factory girls).[120] It might also be possible to argue that by recycling these workers' songs, the union journals were showing respect for women's own self-representations. However, I am interested not only in the description of oppression, but in the linguistic and cultural resources available to imagine the possibility of liberation. Can these images of fragility and pathos (spring rain, fragile flowers, frail birds, lonely stars) be used to imagine the possibility of shared political action, as the basis for a political movement? As bell hooks has pointed out:

> Literature emerging from marginalised groups that is only a chronicle of pain can easily act to keep in place existing structures of domination.[121]

In the writings of at least some activists, there were attempts to appropriate the imagery of these songs for political ends. Male union leader Asō Hisashi referred to the 'caged bird' song, which was apparently popular outside the factories. Asō used this imagery to argue that all workers were in the position of caged birds. In the case of women workers, however, they were seen to suffer double imprisonment by the twin cages of class and sex. In the case of women, even if 'with their feeble strength' they were able to break out of the cage of class exploitation, they would still be subject to exploitation as women.[122]

However, the trope of imprisonment was more than a mere metaphor. Women workers were literally prevented from leaving dormitories outside of working hours, and this was one focus of union writings on women workers.[123] The abolition of the dormitory system was a standard item in union policies on women workers, and often featured as a demand in labour disputes. It was also argued that the reform or abolition of the dormitory system was a necessary condition for the development of the union movement.[124]

One dispute, which occurred in Hodogaya in November 1925, was referred to as the 'caged birds' strike. Several of the strikers' demands referred to restrictions on the freedom of women in dormitories. In addition to calling for a reduction in working hours, they demanded freedom to leave the dormitory and to meet visitors, and freedom to withdraw their own savings at will. The demand that 'workers should be allowed to return home immediately on receipt of a telegram reporting a family illness or other problem' suggests how severely workers' freedom was restricted. In this particular dispute the workers were only successful in having their working hours reduced – admittedly an important concession for workers with family responsibilities.[125] The issue of dormitories, however, would recur in labour disputes involving women workers. Eventually, in a dispute at the Tōyō Muslin factory in Kameido in May 1927, women workers did gain the right to leave the dormitory at will, a victory which has been described as having the force of a 'declaration of human rights' for women workers.[126]

The imagery of caged birds was also used to describe another group of workers: those who had been indentured into prostitution.[127] Once again, the trope of imprisonment was more than mere metaphor. As Yamakawa pointed out in her advocacy of the abolition of licensed prostitution, prostitution was a particular kind of unfree labour. Prostitution could also be used as a shorthand term for the exploitation of women under the capitalist system: women are forced into prostitution while men are forced into military service.

For factory women, there was a feeling that very little separated them from the fate of the prostitute. As E. P. Tsurumi has pointed out, in the early days of industrialization, there was little choice between being sold to a brothel and being sent to a factory to work off payments advanced to the worker's family. For later generations, women workers who left the factories were likely to end up as waitresses or in other jobs in the entertainment and hospitality industry which often slid into prostitution. Even for factory women, who were not explicitly engaged in sexual labour, sexual harassment was always a possibility, as dramatized in the workers' songs.[128]

The stereotypical image of a woman worker was a young girl, fresh from the country, filling in a couple of years before marriage. When motherhood was mentioned it was as a potentiality, as the future of these young women. The future role of these women as 'mothers of the nation' was one of the justifications for the implementation of protective legislation for women workers. Early socialists used the maternal as an image which encapsulated the caring values of a socialist society, while others linked maternal values with pacifism.[129]

In reality, however, depending on the region and industry, an increasing number of women workers in factories were married and had children. In the 1920s, the pages of *Seigi no Hikari* started to reflect this reality.[130] The maternal image often, however, involves conflict. The potential contradiction involved in being both mother and worker is dramatized in a visual representation of a mother leaving her child behind as she departs for the factory.[131] A similar sense of conflict is expressed in Gotō Miyoko's poetry from the late 1920s:

A haggard mother runs to the factory,
her child racing after her; no time to wipe his nose.[132]

Visual imagery from labour movement publications portrays an uneasy amalgam of socialist realism and allegory. It is difficult to decide whether the nursing mothers in these illustrations represent actual working-class mothers, or the abstract values of compassion which were thought to be a feature of the socialist movement (See illustration p. 70).[133]

Women factory workers were described as *jokō* (female operative, factory girl). *Jokō* was often a rather derogatory label, but there were also attempts to turn this label into a positive form of identity.[134] One such attempt was Nagai Chōzō's contribution to an early edition of *Yūai Fujin*, the journal of the *Yūaikai* Women's Division. Nagai argued that *jokō* should be respected rather than looked down on. However, in his attempt to dispel negative stereotypes of women workers, he reinforces a few more. stereotypes of feminine qualities: patience, attention to detail, tidiness, and nimble fingers.[135]

There were also attempts to validate the identity of factory girls in songs:

Don't dismiss us as factory girls
Factory girls are a treasure chest for the company (*kaisha no senryōbako*)
Don't look down on us as factory girls
When we go home we are the apple of our parents' eyes (*hakoiri musume*).[136]

An article in *Rōdō Fujin* (the *Sōdōmei* women's journal) asked women workers about their experiences in a strike at the Kanebō factory. When asked how their consciousness had changed since the strike, they spoke

of rejecting their obedient attitude to the company, of losing their fear
of strikes and unions, and of gaining understanding of how workers
were exploited by capitalists.[137]

Another woman described to an oral historian a transformation of
her consciousness of her identity as a 'factory girl' (*jokō*). Umezu
Hagiko had been the subject of an article in the company magazine
for the speed of her reeling, and she was asked to speak to the other
women working in the factory. Given this opportunity, she did not give
the expected homily on the virtues of hard work. Rather, she told the
other women that it was up to them to become awakened. She would
look back on this occasion and reflect:

> At that time factory girls (*jokō*) were looked down on, and all the feelings
> pent up in my heart must have just come out spontaneously. At that time, I
> wasn't at all abject.[138]

Thus, gaining in assertiveness was one aspect of the transformation
of the identity of 'factory girls' into an identity which gave equal weight-
ing to the fact that they were workers, members of the working class,
and potential unionists. Another step in the validation of women
workers' identity involved an assertion of the difference between
women of the working class and women of other classes, often in references to a middle-class woman wearing clothes produced by the
labour of working-class women.[139] The exploitation which is the basis
of the relationship between the working class and the ruling class was
presented graphically in the following song. Here, everything which
shines, sparkles, or glistens is connected with the representatives of class
privilege: the rich man, the general, and the rich man's mistress.

> What is it that sparkles in the glasses of the rich?
> Champagne??
> No, no, it's the sweat of the poor farmer.
> What is it that glistens on the face of the rich man's mistress?
> Diamonds??
> No, no, it's the bloody tears of the poor female factory worker.
> What is it that shines on the chest of the Minister and the General?
> A medal??
> No, no, it's the bones of the poor soldier.[140]

A contributor to the journal *Seigi no Hikari* (*The Light of Justice*) plays
on the imagery of light and darkness in order to argue for women's
strength. Tajima Hide begins with an evocation of the actual conditions
of working women, who leave home before sunrise and come home
from the factory after dark. These conditions are contrasted with the
'young ladies' of the middle classes:

Some people say that factory girls work for the nation, that they are the nation's treasure. But it is the young ladies who go to girls' schools who wear beautiful clothes, eat good food, and who grow up bathed in light. And what about the factory girls, who are said to be the nation's treasure? They are hidden away in the darkness, drained of blood and sweat, and collapse one by one.[141]

This imagery of deprivation and envy, however, is transformed into an image of strength, as Tajima assures her readers that the light of justice, like that of the sun, can never be extinguished but only hidden, and that it is in their power to regain their strength through solidarity:

It is factory girls who are doing the most important work. If all of the 730,000 factory girls were to stop working, we would find out how much power we have. Until now we have been unaware of our power. It will be easy to drive away the clouds if we use the power of unity. Until now we had forgotten about our own power. The people have chosen not to see us. Now is the time for us to show our power. Let us show our strength, to ourselves, and to the world. Let us be proud of our strength.

Only then will the light which has been hidden for so long emerge from the clouds. And then let us bring this light to all of the people.[142]

In Tajima's writing, the conventional images of pathos have still been used, but she has attempted to transform an image of deprivation into an image of power.

Some women, however, rejected the 'politics of envy'.[143] For Tajiri Okayo, a participant in a rural dispute, a focus on the differences between women of different classes diverted energy away from the struggle to transform society:

Women are the most wretched victims of the evils of capitalism. We are not only mothers of families, but mothers of humanity. We women, who have the responsibility of future life, have a mission even more precious than that of men.

Our mission is a great one.

Instead of envying wealthy women, we should wake up to the reality around us, and turn our attention to the reformation of society, for the attainment of women's demands.[144]

Union leaders, too, could occasionally transcend their paternalistic and patronizing attitudes. In Yamane Kenjirō's exhortation to the textile workers to join the union, we can see one example of a union leader addressing male and female workers in similar terms. He suggests that it is unrealistic for young women to expect to go back to the village when village life is characterized by poverty. Yamane addresses the reality of work for most families, where men and women must both work and leave their children to be minded by others. Women workers are initially addressed as *jokōsan*, but it is also clear from the content of his article that when he refers to textile workers (*bōshoku rōdōsha*) or 'we workers' (*warera rōdōsha*) he is referring to both male and female workers. This writer, at least, was able to imagine women as fellow workers and as fellow unionists. In his explanation of exploitation, Yamane refrains from using words like 'capital' or 'capitalists'.[145] He simply explains that the motivation of the wealthy is to amass further wealth, and this is why they prefer to use the cheapest labour possible, which may involve dismissing male workers and employing female workers for lesser wages. For this reason both male and female workers must join unions and show solidarity against the arrogance and selfishness of the rich. Yamane was able to explain complex ideas in simple terms, without patronizing the women workers.[146] Such images of solidarity are an obvious advance on the representations of women workers in the early union publications. The visual representations of women workers had also evolved: they were now likely to be represented in groups, standing together under the union flag.[147]

Striking Women

1930 saw an increase in the number of strikes involving women workers,[148] including strikes at Kanegafuchi factories in Ōsaka and Kōbe,[149] and the Kishiwada factory in Sakai. The Tōyō Muslin strike[150] was one of the most violent of strikes which involved thousands of workers, and has become famous as a 'women's strike'.[151] The strike lasted over 60 days, from 26 September to 21 November. Violence erupted on 24 October between the workers and hired gangs.

While left-wing pamphlets and publications portrayed the women as heroic, indeed as the vanguard of the proletariat, companies attempted to manipulate the anxieties of parents. Companies wrote to the families of striking women workers that their daughters were likely to be engaging in unseemly relationships with men, warned of the danger of pregnancy and advised that they should take their daughters back to the country before their chances of marriage were ruined.[152] The company also directed propaganda at the wives of male workers, at residents of the Kameido region, and at the striking workers themselves.[153]

The strikers were supported by the *Musan Fujin Dōmei* (Proletarian Women's League),[154] and Orimoto [Tatewaki] Sadayo's Labour Women's Night School provided a base for supporters of the strike.[155] Strike pamphlets describe the suffering of rural people in the current depression as one of the explanations for the urban factory workers' determination to see this dispute through to the end. The women workers in particular are described in heroic terms, while the 'proletarian women of Nankatsu' are urged to support their brothers and sisters in the factory:

> ... Over 3000 of our brothers and sisters at Tōyō Muslin have ... embarked on a strike in order to save themselves from starvation, and are fighting against the high-handedness of the company and the indescribable suppression by the police.
>
> The enemy which has forced the factory women into such an extreme situation, and the enemy which has caused the increasingly sorry state of our pantries are the same – the finance capitalists.
>
> So, the victory of the factory women of Tōyō Muslin, will, in the end, be a victory for all proletarian women.
>
> Please help the poor factory women win their struggle!
>
> We hope that you will come out of your kitchens, stand up together, and provide your wholehearted support.[156]

Another pamphlet elaborates:

> Consider the 60,000 retrenchments in the textile industry, and the 80% cut in wages. There have been huge retrenchments in the woollen textile trade, and Kanebō has cut wages by 40%. We have seen this in innumerable places, such as Kashiwabara and Kyōto Muslin. However, all of these disputes have failed because of the lack of a strong organization.
>
> ... In order to protect first of all their own livelihood, and, by extension, to stem the raging tide of rationalizations which threatens our one million sisters throughout the country, the 3,000 sisters at Tōyō Muslin have been united in strike action for 26 days.
>
> We of the Proletarian Women's League give our unqalified support to this struggle, in order to fulfil our duty to our class, and to defend all proletarian women against starvation.
>
> The Tōyō Muslin dispute is now intensifying, and suppression by police and the *Nihon Seigi Dan* has turned Kameido into a street of violence.
>
> Our 3000 brothers and sisters are paying a sacrifice in blood!
>
> Do not give them up to the enemy!
>
> Bring down a torrent of contributions to our fighting fund![157]

The authors of these pamphlets are intimately involved with the workers' struggle, rather than gazing on the factory women from afar. Such publications as strike pamphlets, of course, had a relatively limited circulation, restricted to the immediate area surrounding the dispute. However, the Tōyō Muslin strike, due to its length and scope, was widely reported in the media. In the *Tokyo Nichi Nichi Shinbun* (*Tokyo Daily News*), the strikers' representations of themselves as strong and brave became a feature of a report on the strike. The headline of this article quoted the posters and pamphlets seen around the factory – 'See the strength of the women workers!', 'Liberation through struggle!' – and closed on the following note:

I said goodbye to the factory girls with a feeling of respect for the impressive discipline shown by these awakened factory women. They farewelled me with the 'comrades song' complete with accompaniment.[158]

The account of the strike published in *Chūō Kōron* is perhaps more conventional, in its references to the 'caged birds' song. This commentator asks what turned these 'factory girls' (*jokō*) into 'tigers' (*tora*), and concludes that it is economic conditions which are to blame.[159]

Although the 1930 Tōyō Muslin strike was unsuccessful in terms of achieving the demands of the workers, it was important as an example of working-class militancy, and of the militancy of women workers.[160] The absolute numbers of organized women were still small, but such strikes were significant in facilitating new ways of seeing working women: as workers and as comrades.

From Worker to Activist

While women in the socialist movement were primarily seen as wives and as mothers, socialism was presented to women as mainly involving issues related to marriage, the family, and reproduction. If women could also be seen as workers, however, then they could be seen to have interests in common with their male comrades. The relationship between men and women in the socialist movement could be seen, not as a relationship between protector and protected, between activist and helpmate, but as a relationship based on comradeship. In the 1920s, male union leaders did not immediately give up their protective and patronizing attitude to women workers. Eventually, however, it became apparent that a labour movement which could not successfully mobilize the majority of its industrial work force – the women workers – would be doomed to failure. From 1929 to 1931, it was these women workers in the textile industry who bore the brunt of layoffs, and it was these women who were forced into militant action against capital. The reality of these women's militancy (albeit under the guidance of a predominantly male union leadership) was reflected in new representations of strong working women. The early 1930s also saw attempts to mobilize women outside the factories which formed the 'traditional' base for a union movement. In both Ōsaka and Tokyo, for example, there were attempts to form waitresses' unions.[161]

Thus, the process of organizing working women was necessarily accompanied by new ways of imagining working women. It is for this reason that I have been interested not only in debates about the class position of women, and discussion of the best strategies for mobilizing these women, but also in the poetic, fictional and visual representations of working women. If women could first be imagined as workers and as comrades, this was an important step in the transformation of women into activists.

One aspect of women's activism involved direct conflict with capital, as workers, and as unionists. In Chapter six I will examine socialist women's activities in engaging with state institutions: through co-operation with suffragists, in campaigns for social welfare legislation, and through collision with the repressive power of the State through the experience of surveillance and imprisonment.

CHAPTER 6

Activists

Activists. In the 1920s and 1930s, women in the socialist movement were starting to be recognized as activists, as reflected in the visual representations of assertive women in the publications directed at working women, such as this cover of the *Sōdōmei* women's journal *Rōdō Fujin*, October 1927.

When Nakasone Sadayo was arrested on May Day in 1921, the policeman mocked her,

> What sort of a woman are you! Demonstrating when you should be home looking after your children!

Nakasone Sadayo's reply was:

> What sort of a man are you! A proletarian who works for the capitalists! Take a look at yourself!

This incident, which was reported in a socialist leaflet of the times,[1] highlights one aspect of the relationship between socialist women and the State in Japan before 1945. *Sekirankai* member Nakasone Sadayo, on attempting to participate in a political demonstration, was subject to the repressive power of the State, through the agency of a policeman who questioned the feminine suitability of her behaviour. Nakasone's reply in turn reflected prevailing socialist views of the State. Her retort implied that the State represented the interests of business rather than the interests of workers or, indeed, women.

This incident illustrates that when we consider the relationship between women and the State,[2] we often envisage a 'top-down' relationship whereby it is the State which acts upon women, through repression of political activity, or through other policies related to education, work, welfare or reproduction. Also implicit in this incident is an oppositional relationship between women and the State. However, in contrast with the 'top-down' view of a State which acts upon women, it is also possible to look at the State from the point of view of women, to see how they understood the State, and how they attempted to influence the policies of State institutions.

In the case of middle-class members of such groups as the Patriotic Women's Association, no distinction was made between State interests and 'women's interests'. In contrast with groups such as the Patriotic Women's Association, which rarely challenged government policies, feminist and socialist groups often tried to influence the government. Different feminist ways of engaging with the State can perhaps best be illustrated by taking two extreme examples. In the case of suffragist Ichikawa Fusae, she came to see co-operation with the State as being in the interests of women, and was thoroughly co-opted by the militarist state. Anarchist Takamure Itsue,[3] on the other hand, envisioned small autonomous communities and a withering away of the State.

Most socialist women were positioned somewhere between these extremes. While many argued for the transformation of the existing system in some way, other social democratic women were willing to engage in campaigns for more immediate reforms. Although some socialist women concentrated their activities in the labour movement, supporting women workers in their struggles against capital, a greater number engaged more directly with State institutions, through criticism of State policies, and through attempts to influence these policies in various ways. Socialist women also engaged with the State in their comments on the Manchurian Incident of 1931, and in broader criticism of Japanese imperialism. While women in the labour movement came into direct conflict with employers through strike activities, they also addressed the State more directly, in campaigns for the implementation of effective labour legislation to supplement the inadequacies of the Factory Act of 1911 and the amended Factory Act of 1923. Whether active in the labour movement or in support of the party movement, however, socialist women first had to negotiate the factionalism of the socialist movement.

While socialists considered the class position of women, and debated the best way to mobilize women workers, liberal feminists began to move beyond individualist views of women's liberation and engage in organized group action, although this was by necessity carried out within the limitations of Article Five of the Public Peace Police Law. Hiratsuka Raichō, Sakamoto Makoto, Ichikawa Fusae and Oku Mumeo formed the New Women's Association (*Shin Fujin Kyōkai*) in 1920.[4] Like the early socialist women of the *Heiminsha*, these liberal feminists realized that the repeal of Article Five of the Public Peace Police Law was necessary for women to participate fully in social movements, and the campaign for women's freedom to participate in political organizations was the first focus of the New Women's Association.

Article Five of the Public Peace Police Law was modified in February 1922, and this made possible the formation of organizations devoted to the cause of women's suffrage. Several suffragists' organizations were formed in the years after the amendment of Article Five. In the 1920s and 1930s, there was some co-operation between suffragists and socialist activists on several issues, including conferences on women's suffrage, and campaigns for the implementation of social welfare measures. While the Taishō debates on 'motherhood protection' had involved discussion of the relationship between individual and State, this had not immediately been translated into political action. In the 1930s, however, liberal feminists and social democratic women co-operated as activists in attempting to pressure the government into the enactment of legislation to provide State assistance for supporting mothers – a demand which became more urgent with the escalation of conflict on the Chinese mainland.

By the 1930s it had become apparent to the government and

bureaucracy that women could be mobilized to support State policies in various ways. The modest patriotic organizations of the early twentieth century were now transformed into mass organizations, mobilizing women in both urban and rural areas. The patriotic women's groups were supported by Young Women's Associations, and educational activities directed at young people.[5]

A limited Bill for Women's Suffrage actually passed the Lower House in 1931, suggesting that in Japan, as in many European countries, it was thought that women might provide a further source of support for conservative governments. The Bill, however, failed to pass the Upper House. Women were not successful in achieving full political rights in Japan before the end of the Second World War. Official discourse primarily constructed women as subjects who could be mobilized to support State policies, rather than citizens who had a right to participate in shaping those policies. Socialist women did not, however, give up their aspirations to citizenship, and attempted to influence State policies in various ways during the 1930s. Many women involved in the suffrage movement attempted to gain legitimacy for their demands through co-operation with State institutions. For socialist women, however, their attitude to the State was generally more cautious. Since the beginning of the twentieth century, socialists had been subject to surveillance, censorship, arrest and imprisonment, and this would intensify in the 1930s.

Suffragism and Electoral Politics

After the formation of the New Women's Association in 1920, liberal feminists carried on a campaign for the repeal of Article Five of the Public Peace Police Law. The 'New Women' also presented a petition to the Diet, asking that men carrying venereal diseases be prevented from marrying. The petition on venereal diseases had little impact, but modifications to Article Five of the Public Peace Police Law were eventually passed by both houses. The achievement of this amendment has been attributed to the success of the campaign of the New Women's Association, but recent analyses suggest that the government and bureaucracy were also finding it increasingly useful to mobilize women in public campaigns.[6]

The modification of Article Five in 1922 made possible the creation of associations specifically devoted to the attainment of women's suffrage.[7] Suffrage was granted to all adult males over the age of twenty-five in 1925, and proletarian political parties were created to mobilize the men of the proletarian class. The removal of property qualifications for voting made it clear that women were being excluded from political participation on the grounds of sex alone. Although women could, after the revision of Article Five, attend public political meetings, they were still unable to join political parties, vote, or stand for public office. The League for the Attainment of Women's Political Rights (*Fujin San-seiken Kakutoku Kisei Dōmeikai*), led by Ichikawa Fusae, was created in 1924.[8] Other women's organizations which supported the cause of women's suffrage included the Japanese chapter of the Women's Christian Temperance Union (*Nihon Kirisuto Kyō Fujin Kyōfukai*), The Tokyo Federation of Women's Organizations (*Tokyo Rengō Fujinkai*), and the All-Kansai Federation of Women's Organizations (*Zen Kansai Fujin Rengōkai*). Teachers were also well-represented in suffragists' organizations.[9] Most suffragists demanded political power within the existing system,[10] although reformers affiliated with Christian organizations wanted to use the vote to transform immoral relations between men and women.

Socialist attitudes to women's suffrage were, however, ambivalent. The goal of suffrage could be criticized as bourgeois, distracting socialist women from the main goal of transforming society according to socialist principles. It was also, however, apparent that women would be able to participate more effectively in the socialist movement if they could attain full political rights. After the creation of the proletarian parties in the mid-1920s, all of these parties eventually created affiliated 'women's leagues' in order to mobilize the support of proletarian women. From 1928, some of these 'women's leagues' were co-operating with the suffragists on various issues.

Women's Leagues of Proletarian Parties

Several proletarian parties were formed after the enactment of Universal [Manhood] Suffrage in 1925.[11] The parties were closely aligned with the union federations and followed similar factional lines, as discussed in Chapter five. The communist-influenced *Hyōgikai* union federation supported the Labour–Farmer Party (*Rōdō Nōmin Tō*) until its dissolution after the anti-communist purge of 1928.[12] The centrist Japan Labour Union League (*Nihon Rōdō Kumiai Dōmei*) supported the Japan Labour–Farmer Party (*Nihon Rōnō Tō*), formed in December 1926. The Japan Labour–Farmer Party was joined by groups from the right and left of the proletarian movement in several mergers, and underwent several name changes in the years from 1928 to 1931.[13] The moderate *Sōdōmei* supported the Social Democratic Party (*Shakai Minshū Tō*), formed in December 1926.[14] The *Shakai Minshū Tō* merged with the centrist National Labour–Farmer Masses Party (*Zenkoku Rōnō Taishū Tō*) to form the Social Masses Party (*Shakai Taishū Tō*) in July 1932. While

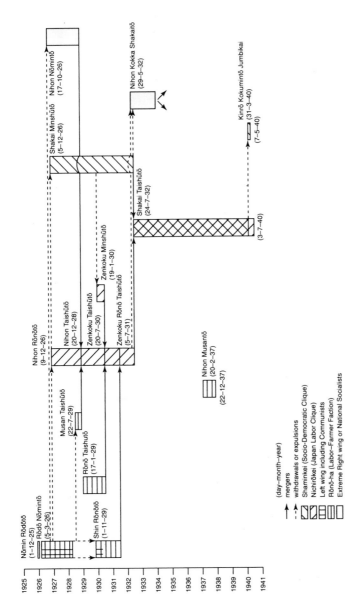

Figure 6.1 The Proletarian Party Movement
Adapted from Stephen S. Large. *Organized Workers and Socialist Politics in Interwar Japan*, Cambridge: Cambridge University Press, 1982, p. 262. For translations, see Glossary.

proletarian forces coalesced under the moderate social democratic banner of the Social Masses Party, the extreme right of the proletarian movement broke away to form the Japan National Socialist Party (*Nihon Kokka Shakai Tō*) under the leadership of Akamatsu Katsumaro in 1932. Another nationalist grouping formed the New Japan People's League (*Shin Nihon Kokumin Dōmei*) in the same year. The Social Masses Party gained 18 seats in the Diet in 1936, and in 1937 achieved 37 seats in the 466-member Diet, the highest of any pre-war proletarian party.[15]

A broad-based women's political organization, the Society for the Promotion of Women's Political Movements (*Fujin Seiji Undō Sokushin-kai*) was established under the auspices of the magazine *Shufu no Tomo* (*The Housewife's Friend*) in December 1926 but was soon superseded by the Women's Leagues attached to the various proletarian parties.[16] The Kantō Women's League (*Kantō Fujin Dōmei*) was aligned with the communist-influenced Labour–Farmer Party.[17] The Kantō Women's League was formed on 3 July 1927 but forcibly disbanded in March 1928 when official party policy argued against the existence of separate women's divisions.[18] The National Women's League (*Zenkoku Fujin Dōmei*), formed on 2 October 1927, was aligned with the centrist *Nihon Rōdō Nōmin Tō*.[19] The Social Women's League (*Shakai Fujin Dōmei*), formed in November 1927, was aligned with the moderate *Shakai Minshū Tō*. The Social Women's League changed its name to the Social Democratic Women's League (*Shakai Minshū Fujin Dōmei*) in July 1928.[20]

After the disbandment of the Kantō Women's League, those women who retained their allegiance to the 'legal' left formed the Proletarian Women's Study Group (*Musan Fujin Kenkyūkai*) in June 1928. The study group became the Proletarian Women's Alliance (*Musan Fujin Renmei*) in October 1928, and this organization formed an alliance with the centrist National Women's League (*Zenkoku Fujin Dōmei*) in January 1929, creating the Proletarian Women's League (*Musan Fujin Dōmei*). The merger of the Proletarian Women's League and Social Democratic Women's League in August 1932 resulted in the creation of the Social Masses Women's League (*Shakai Taishū Fujin Dōmei*). This organization was, in effect, the Women's League of the Social Masses Party. After the formation of the national socialist *Kokka Shakai Tō*, a women's league was formed under the leadership of Akamatsu Akiko, wife of Akamatsu Katsumaro. Akamatsu's sister Tsuneko, however, stayed with the Social Masses Women's League, which was active until 1936. The activities of these women's leagues will first be described briefly, in order of their factional alliances,[21] before moving on to a discussion of socialist women's attempts to engage with State institutions in various campaigns of the 1920s and 1930s.

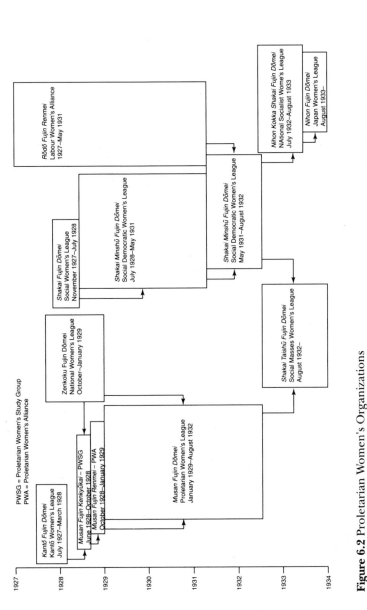

PWSG = Proletarian Women's Study Group
PWA = Proletarian Women's Alliance

Kantō Fujin Dōmei
Kantō Women's League
July 1927–March 1928

Musan Fujin Kenkyūkai – PWSG
June 1928–October 1928
Musan Fujin Renmei – PWA
October 1928–January 1929

Zenkoku Fujin Dōmei
National Women's League
October–January 1929

Musan Fujin Dōmei
Proletarian Women's League
January 1929–August 1932

Rōdō Fujin Renmei
Labour Women's Alliance
1927–May 1931

Shakai Fujin Dōmei
Social Women's League
November 1927–July 1928

Shakai Minshū Fujin Dōmei
Social Democratic Women's League
July 1928–May 1931

Shakai Minshū Fujin Dōmei
Social Democratic Women's League
May 1931–August 1932

Shakai Taishū Fujin Dōmei
Social Masses Women's League
August 1932–

Nihon Kokka Shakai Fujin Dōmei
NAtional Socialist Wome's League
July 1932–August 1933

Nihon Fujin Dōmei
Japan Women's League
August 1933–

1927
1928
1929
1930
1931
1932
1933
1934

Figure 6.2 Proletarian Women's Organizations
Adapted from Ishizuki Shizue. '1930nendai no Musan Fujin Undō', in Joseishi Sōgō Kenkyūkai (eds) *Nihon Joseishi 5: Gendai*, Tokyo: Tokyo Daigaku Shuppankai, 1990, p. 195.

Women in the *Rōnō* Faction

In Chapter five, I surveyed debates on the formation of a women's division in the *Hyōgikai* union federation, and proposals for the formation of a Women's League to mobilize women outside the union movement. Women of the *Rōnō* faction initially co-operated on the Society for the Promotion of Women's Political Movements (*Fujin Seiji Undō Sokushinkai*), and the first meeting of this society was chaired by Oku Mumeo and Tajima Hide. After factional disagreements at this meeting, however, the leftist women prepared for the creation of a women's league independent from the other factions. The Women's League Preparatory Committee issued a stirring statement in December 1926.[22] This statement reads as a direct challenge to all of the representations of women as weak and ineffectual:

> Who was it who decided that women are weak? We are not at all weak! The only reason for our weakness is that we have been shut up at home and relegated to the edges of society, and this has dispersed our strength. When all women stand up together in opposition to the discriminatory social and economic treatment [we have received] in this country, no one will be able to call us weak! That's right! When all women arise in solidarity, that is when our strength will be radiant, that is when a new age for women will be born.
>
> Now is the time when women must fight for our freedom, and make demands with a new strength and solidarity.
>
> This is why we are now planning to establish the Women's League in order to unite women from all over the country. Volunteers from all over the Kantō region have formed a preparatory committee for the formation of the Women's League. The Committee has already started preparations for an inaugural meeting.
>
> We have no doubt that this newly created Women's League is the organization that we have long been waiting for and hoping for – the organization which will fight for women's demands and women's freedom.
>
> Our comrades from all over the country!
> Join the Women's League!
> Power to women! The Women's League will shine brilliantly![23]

Despite this stirring manifesto, the activities of the group were still subject to the dictates of the Communist-influenced *Hyōgikai* union federation and the Labour–Farmer Party. The League was also supported by the Women's League of the Japan Farmers' Union. A leaflet prepared for International Women's Day in March 1927 made clear the factional position of this group. The leaflet affirmed support for the Labour–Farmer Party and criticized the moderate Social Democratic Party and the centrist Japan Labour–Farmer Party.[24]

The Kantō Women's League (*Kantō Fujin Dōmei*) was eventually formed in July 1927.[25] The inaugural meeting, held on 3 July 1927, announced a set of policies which will be familiar from the discussion of union women's divisions:

* full political rights for women, and freedom to join political parties;
* abolition of laws which discriminate on the grounds of sex;
* prohibition of night work and mining work for women;
* reform of the dormitory system;
* abolition of licensed prostitution;
* abolition of the indenture system;
* equal opportunity in education;
* abolition of sexual discrimination in wages;
* protection of children;
* maternity leave; and
* provision of free crèches.

Perhaps the only distinctive clause concerns the 'liberation from feudal restrictions in the family'.[26] The activities of the League included support for strikes, support for the Labour–Farmer Party at the elections in 1928, and the production of a newsletter.[27]

Regional committees were set up in preparation for a national structure for the Women's League, and a national meeting was planned for March 1928.[28] After further changes in party policy on women's leagues, the Kantō Women's League was forcibly disbanded in March 1928, before this national meeting could be held.[29] The League was accused of pursuing bourgeois objectives, and it was stated that women would best be occupied in mobilizing proletarian housewives and women in factories. Behind this controversy was the factionalism of the extreme left of the proletarian movement. After the dissolution of the Japan Communist Party in 1924, leftists had continued their activities in the Labour–Farmer Party and the *Hyōgikai* union federation. This group was split between those who wanted to re-form the Communist Party and those who wished to remain within the legal left of the Party movement. After the Party was re-formed, the Fukumoto faction concentrated their activities in the underground Communist movement, while Sakai Toshihiko, the Yamakawas and their followers were active in the Labour–Farmer Party and its successors. It was the reconstituted Central Committee of the Japan Communist Party which, under the influence of Comintern policy, ordered the dissolution of the *Kantō Fujin Dōmei.*[30]

Several members of the *Kantō Fujin Dōmei*, including Tajima Hide and Tanno Setsu, continued as supporters of the underground communist movement, an occupation which became more dangerous after mass arrests on 15 March 1928.[31] The Labour–Farmer Party, until now representing the legal face of the left of the proletarian movement, was banned by the Home Ministry in April 1928.[32]

The Proletarian Women's League

After the disbandment of the *Kantō Fujin Dōmei*, Tanno Setsu and Tajima Hide continued their activities in the underground communist movement. Other former members of the League kept up their connections with the left of the legal party movement. These women formed a study group known as the Proletarian Women's Study Group (*Musan Fujin Kenkyūkai*) in June 1928.[33] In addition to studying socialist writings, these women assisted in the production of a women's edition of the Labour–Farmer Party journal, *Rōnō*.[34] Extant documents include a statement condemning the licensed prostitution system. The study group became the Proletarian Women's Alliance (*Musan Fujin Renmei*) in October 1928, and was affiliated with the Proletarian Masses Party (*Musan Taishū Tō*), one of the successors of the Labour–Farmer Party.[35] The merger of the Proletarian Women's Alliance (*Musan Fujin Renmei*) with the centrist National Women's League (*Zenkoku Fujin Dōmei*) resulted in the creation of the Proletarian Women's League (*Musan Fujin Dōmei*) in January 1929.[36] By 1930 the League had 100 members, and in 1931 increased to 445 members.

Sakai [Kondō] Magara was an important member of this grouping. On many issues, the Proletarian Women's League retained a radical perspective, for example, in being one of the few groups to criticize openly the Manchurian Incident. Sakai and her colleagues also, however, displayed pragmatism in their willingness to co-operate with social democratic women and liberal feminists in campaigns for women's suffrage and for State benefits for supporting mothers.[37] Sakai was also committed to unity among the proletarian women's groups. As early as 1928, she had published an article pointing out the absurdity of operating with three proletarian parties, three union federations, and three women's leagues. It would take several more years, however, before the proposed coalition could be achieved.[38]

Women in the *Nichirō* Faction

The National Women's League (*Zenkoku Fujin Dōmei*), formed on 2 October 1927, was aligned with the centrist Japan Labour–Farmer Party and the Japan Labour Union League.[39] Office bearers included Orimoto [Tatewaki] Sadayo[40] and Iwauchi Tomie.[41] The group produced a newsletter and was active in supporting strike activities in affiliated unions, and supporting the Japan Labour–Farmer Party in the 1928 elections.[42] The League also co-operated with the Japan Textile Workers' Union on a committee lobbying for the banning of night work for women from November 1927,[43] and participated in a Joint Committee for Women's Suffrage formed in March 1928.

Iwauchi Tomie and Orimoto [Tatewaki] Sadayo were particularly active in supporting the activities of the Japan Textile Workers' union. Iwauchi Tomie's husband, Zensaku, was leader of the union and the couple managed the *Airindan*, a Christian socialist charitable organization in the Nishi Nippori neighbourhood of Tokyo. Orimoto [Tatewaki] Sadayo managed the Labour Women's Night School (*Rōdō Jojuku*) and this provided a base for support of strike activities, in particular the Tōyō Muslin strike of 1930. Orimoto would also turn to the writing of the history of working women in Japan, publishing a pamphlet on working women in Japan and contributing articles on working women to the journal *Fujin Sensen*.[44] The *Zenkoku Fujin Dōmei* formed a coalition with the Proletarian Women's Alliance (*Musan Fujin Renmei*),[45] creating the Proletarian Women's League (*Musan Fujin Dōmei*) in January 1929. This merger was marked with a joint meeting on 20 January 1929.

Social Democratic Women

The *Shakai Fujin Dōmei* (Social Women's League) was aligned with the moderate *Shakai Minshū Tō*. The Social Women's League, formed in November 1927, changed its name to the *Shakai Minshū Fujin Dōmei* (the Social Democratic Women's League) in July 1928.[46] The Social Democratic Women's League was active on working women's issues, and in the campaign for State benefits for supporting mothers. The pages of the League's journal *Minshū Fujin* express the moderate line taken by this group.[47] The first issue, for example, proclaims:

> *Minshū Fujin* will march under the banner of realism and the light of legality will shine on the road which the proletarian working women will follow.[48]

"Realism" was the slogan of the moderate *Sōdōmei* union federation and the Social Democratic Party, and signified a distancing from more radical elements of the left-wing movement. The contributors to the journal constantly reiterate that they are interested in mobilizing 'proletarian and working women' (*kinrō musan fujin*).[49]

In this moderate socialist women's journal, 'capital', or the 'bourgeoisie', are blamed for poverty, retrenchments, unemployment, and the resulting mother-child suicide incidents. However, it is the State which is called upon to provide support through unemployment relief, removal of consumption taxes, the implementation of a Mother and Child Assistance Act, and the provision of free childcare facilities. The

Mother and Child Assistance Act was discussed in the context of the necessity for birth control, and the League established the Birth Control Association (*Sanji Seigen Kyōkai*) in September 1930, under the guidance of former nurse Iwauchi Tomie. The Association was responsible for selling birth control equipment and information.[50]

The Social Democratic Women's League initially espoused policies of female suffrage; women's rights to political participation; a union law; a motherhood protection law; the prohibition of licensed prostitution; jobs for the unemployed; the abolition of consumption tax on necessary goods; and the reform of women's education.[51] By 1931, they had added calls for free crèches and maternity clinics, and improvement in maids' working conditions.[52] The Social Democratic women were quite specific in the kinds of reformist, legislative changes they demanded. In January 1931, they held meetings and engaged in 'pamphleteering' in both Tokyo and Ōsaka on the issues of women's suffrage and State assistance for supporting mothers.[53] As survival became more difficult in the years of economic depression, they also turned their attention to issues related to declining standards of living, calling for reduction in charges for gas, electricity, water, and provided support for several strikes by women workers in affiliated unions.[54]

In May 1931, the Social Democratic Women's League merged with the Women's Labour Alliance (*Rōdō Fujin Renmei*), an organization they had been co-operating with for some time.[55] The Social Democratic Women also co-operated with the Proletarian Women's League from 1930 on. The Joint Committee on Total Suffrage (*Tettei Fusen Kyōdō Iinkai*), established in October 1930, brought together women of the two groups. A public meeting held by this committee on 29 November 1930 linked two pressing concerns: suffrage and the protection of living standards.[56] The groups also co-operated on a Proletarian Women's Day in Tokyo and Ōsaka on 8 February 1931.[57]

By July 1931 the Social Democratic Women's League had 22 branches, representing a doubling in size in just a few months. The membership was 2225 by October 1931, eight times the 1929 figure. In 1932, tensions came to a head in the right wing of the proletarian movement, resulting in a split which saw the creation of the Japan National Socialist Party (*Nihon Kokka Shakai Tō*) on 29 May 1932. The Japan National Socialist Party was led by Akamatsu Katsumaro, and his wife Akamatsu Akiko left the Social Democratic Women's League to lead the Japan National Socialist Women's League (*Nihon Kokka Shakai Fujin Dōmei*), which was formed in July 1932, and changed its name to the Japan Women's League (*Nihon Fujin Dōmei*) in August 1933.[58]

Akamatsu's sister, Akamatsu Tsuneko, however, remained in the social democratic movement, and supported further coalitions in the moderate left. The Social Democratic Women's League merged with the Proletarian Women's League in August 1932, forming the Social Masses Women's League (*Shakai Taishū Fujin Dōmei*). The Social Masses Women's League provided support for the Social Masses Party, formed in August 1932 from the merger of the centrist and social democratic parties.[59]

The Social Masses Women's League

The merger of the *Musan Fujin Dōmei* and *Shakai Minshū Fujin Dōmei* in 1932 resulted in the creation of the Social Masses Women's League (*Shakai Taishū Fujin Dōmei*) in 1932. This organization, affiliated with the Social Masses Party, was active until 1936.[60] Akamatsu Tsuneko was chairperson and Sakai Magara was secretary, with Tanabe Tose as treasurer, assisted by Iwauchi Tomie, with a Central Committee of 60 members. The League called for the destruction of fascism, the granting of women's political rights, equal opportunity in education, abolition of the licensed prostitution system, paid maternity leave, nursing leave, menstruation leave, a mother-child support act, and the provision of childcare facilities.[61]

Co-operation between Socialists and Suffragists

One issue which brought together liberal feminists and women of the left was the issue of women's suffrage.[62] Although some socialist groups criticized an excessive emphasis on the suffrage as 'bourgeois', the policy statements of all of the left-wing parties, unions, women's divisions, and women's leagues included demands for women's voting rights and women's rights to political participation. This was a particular focus of the Social Democratic Women's League.[63]

Socialist women's groups also supported the campaigns of the Proletarian political parties, particularly at the first election held under Universal Manhood Suffrage in 1928. Even though women could not vote, they were exhorted to support the election of proletarian candidates who would represent the interests of the men and women of the proletarian class. Such sentiments could even be found in the left of the proletarian movement, for example in Tanno Setsu's contribution to the communist paper *Sekki* (*Red Flag*):

. . . The Diet has been dissolved, and men over twenty five have been given the right to vote. Universal [manhood] suffrage will now enable us to send representatives of the workers and peasants to the Diet.

But we women have not been given the right to vote. We do not have the right to choose our representatives. We have only a tiny bit of freedom, the freedom to get on the platform and support those who will represent the workers and the peasants in the Diet. Armed with this small freedom, women throughout the nation are battling in the electoral districts. We must win the right for women to take part in political activities and the freedom to join political parties. In order to participate in this movement, women – women workers and farm women – must stand on the platform and speak out during the election . . .[64]

A joint women's suffrage committee (*Fusen Kakutoku Kyōdō Iinkai*) was set up in December 1928 and was active until 1929. This committee brought together three women's suffrage organizations and four of the left-wing women's leagues: the Labour Women's Alliance (*Rōdō Fujin Renmei*), the Social Women's League (*Shakai Fujin Dōmei*), the Japan Association for Women's Political Rights (*Nihon Fujin Sanseiken Kyōkai*), the Kantō Women's League (*Kantō Fujin Dōmei*), the League for Women's Political Rights (*Fujin Sansei Dōmei*), the Women's Suffrage League (*Fusen Kakutoku Dōmei*), and the National Women's League (*Zenkoku Fujin Dōmei*).[65] The group was responsible for a series of public meetings on the women's suffrage issue between March and May 1928.[66]

The First National Women's Suffrage Conference was held on 27 April 1930, under the auspices of the Women's Suffrage League, with the support of the Japan Association for Women's Political Rights, the Proletarian Women's League, and the All-Kansai Women's Federation. The Proletarian Women's League was also represented at the Second National Women's Suffrage Conference on 14 February 1931.[67]

There were several further attempts to set up joint committees. The Joint Committee on Total Suffrage (*Tettei Fusen Kyōdō Tōsō Iinkai*), established in October 1930, brought together women of the Social Democratic Women's League and the Proletarian Women's League,[68] while the Allied Committee for the Attainment of Women's Suffrage (*Fusen Dantai Rengō Iinkai*), established in January 1931, brought together the Women's Suffrage League, the Japan Christian Association for Women's Suffrage (*Nihon Kirisutokyō Fujin Sanseiken Kyōkai*), the League for Women's Political Rights (*Fujin Sansei Dōmei*), and the Proletarian Women's League. These four groups were represented at the third annual National Women's Suffrage Conference in May 1932, which produced a statement condemning fascism.[69]

Socialist women were represented at national women's suffrage conferences from 1930 on, and their influence can be seen in some of the declarations issued by these conferences. Some elements of the socialist movement were, however, critical of such co-operation. The *Musan*

Fujin Dōmei's response to criticism of their co-operation with the suffragists was outlined in the League's newsletter:

> ... It is not the case that we of the *Musan Fujin Dōmei* are simply interested in suffrage and nothing else. We are working for the day when [control of] today's politics will be seized by the workers and the farmers. All of our actions – strikes, workers' schools, electoral struggles – are in preparation for that day. So, in order to prepare properly, we will take every opportunity to put forward our ideas. That is [the nature of] our movement. We have no interest in the class of women who rush after the bait of women's suffrage, and think they can solve all problems through the power of women. We think that there is nothing to be gained by throwing insults at each other. We must communicate our class consciousness to that class of women who are being moved to fight for the cause of women's suffrage. We must call out to those women who can co-operate with the class of working women. Each of these opportunities is a site for our struggle! It is from this point of view that the *Musan Fujin Dōmei* proposes this joint struggle.[70]

Several bills for women's suffrage were introduced by individual members of the Diet during the 1920s. By the end of the decade, women's suffrage had broad support within the government, culminating in a Bill presented by the Hamaguchi Cabinet in 1931. This Bill only allowed for women's voting in regional (city, town and village) assemblies, and provided for women to stand for office in local assemblies with their husband's permission. The Women's Suffrage League was opposed to this limited form of women's suffrage. Although this was passed by the Lower House, it failed to pass the more conservative House of Peers, and was subsequently overshadowed by events surrounding the Manchurian Crisis from 1931.[71]

Suffrage conferences continued until 1937, and fascism was criticized at the annual conferences, largely thanks to Proletarian members of the joint suffrage committee.[72] Suffragists and socialists campaigned together for improved labour legislation for women workers, and for State benefits for supporting mothers. Although suffrage conferences made several feminist demands, relating to women's political participation, the only demands which were listened to in 1930s Japan were those which reinforced women's maternal function. The Women's Suffrage League was forced to disband in 1940.[73]

Meanwhile, the government made its own attempts to mobilize women, in opposition to the developing alliances between socialists and suffragists. The *Fujin Dōshikai*, formed on 12 May 1930, attracted several women from the most conservative wing of the Women's Suffrage League. This was followed by the formation of the Japan Federation of Women's Associations (*Nihon Rengō Fujin Kai*) on 6 March 1931, and the formation of the Women's National Defence Organization (*Nihon*

Kokubō Fujinkai) in March 1932.[74] All of these nationalist women's organizations, along with the pre-existing Patriotic Women's Association, would merge in the Greater Japan Women's Association (*Dai Nihon Fujinkai*) in February 1942, under the system which commenced with the promulgation of the National Mobilization Law (*Kokka Sōdōin Hō*) in 1938.

The Manchurian Incident

Even before the outbreak of the Manchurian Crisis in September 1931, the Proletarian Women's League had consistently opposed imperialism.[75] At the time of the Manchurian Incident, the Proletarian Women's League attempted to mobilize women's opposition to Japanese encroachment into China. The Proletarian women planned a day of speeches on the theme of 'Women and War', but were unable to enlist the support of other socialist or suffragist groups. The Proletarian women put out their own statement opposing militarism, which explicitly rejected the emotionalism and passivity which had often been a feature of women's pacifist writings since the publication of Yosano Akiko's pacifist poem 'Kimi shini tamau koto nakare' in 1904:

> War is not a matter of individual likes and dislikes. It is something forced on us by the ruling class. For this reason it is no use saying to our husbands, brothers, and children 'do not give up your life for the Emperor' (*kimi shini tamau koto nakare*). We must say to the promoters of war : 'Do not wage war! Do not kill proletarians for the sake of your own profits!!'[76]

In the Social Democratic Women's League's statement on the Manchurian Incident in December 1931, they call on the Japanese State to take control of Manchuria from the bourgeoisie in the interests of the proletariat, and call for a special tax, the proceeds of which will be used for the families of servicemen.[77]

Several feminist leaders commented individually on these events. Suffragist Ichikawa Fusae reiterated the pacifist view that international disputes should not be solved by military means, and referred to the children who would be sacrificed to military conflict on both sides. Ichikawa believed that women, who are the 'mothers of humanity', would be most concerned to prevent such sacrifices.[78] Yamakawa Kikue, on the other hand, was more cynical about linking pacifism with women's 'peace-loving' nature:

> The refined kind of movement which calls on the peace-loving instincts of women to prevent war is, in short, nothing more than an amusement of peaceful times. Even though women may love peace and hate war, their socialization has strongly cultivated the habit of sacrificing one's personal

emotion and personal benefit for the common benefit of the society one belongs to – for what is believed to be just. In every society in every age without exception, we can observe women's attitude of self-sacrifice and martyrdom. With the same passion and excitement that they have devoted to their child's upbringing, these women show no regrets in offering their children on the altar of war, in the name of justice and the common good. A simplistic maternal love, and an attachment to a peaceful home life is preparation for the act of sacrifice to the greater needs of the group.[79]

Hiratsuka Raichō criticized the relative silence of women's groups on the Manchurian issue.[80] Takamure Itsue was also critical of the failure of most of the proletarian women's groups to mount effective criticism of the incident, and critical of those women who based their pacifism on their standpoint as mothers. Takamure herself was working towards a more philosophical understanding of war, quoting Heraclites, Plato and Marx.[81] A more radical response came from anarchist Yagi Akiko, on the occasion of the creation of the puppet state of Manchukuo in 1932. Yagi described Manchukuo as a slave state which had simply exchanged one invader for another, and called for opposition to imperialism.[82]

The failure of socialist groups to present united opposition to Japanese imperialism in Manchuria in 1931 was a sign of the gradual capitulation of the legal left. The Social Democrats, in particular, failed to promote principles of internationalism, although there was some isolated criticism of the Manchurian Incident from other proletarian groups. These tendencies were foregrounded with the formation of the Japan National Socialist Party in 1932, but even those who stayed within the Social Democratic fold were muted in their criticism of imperialism.[83] Although the Proletarian Women's League and the Social Democratic Women's League merged in 1932, their different stances on issues related to imperialism were left unresolved.[84] Socialist women, however, were united in their attempts to pressure the State to enact legislation to address the needs of working women and supporting mothers and their children.

The Mother and Child Protection Act

The issue of State assistance for supporting mothers continued to be discussed after the debate on 'motherhood protection' in the Taishō period. The progressive women's newspaper *Fujo Shinbun* referred to the issue throughout the 1920s, and set up a committee·to promote the issue in 1926.[85] The issue was also addressed in labour movement publications.[86] After 1931, and the escalation of Japanese aggression in China, calls for State assistance for supporting mothers became more urgent, as families suffered from the effects of economic depression and the problems of surviving with fathers and brothers absent in the military. Incidents of mother-child suicides focused attention on this problem.[87] Akamatsu Tsuneko reported in July 1932 that in the past two years there had been 492 incidents which had claimed the lives of 821 children.[88]

Although the need for such short-term measures as welfare provisions for supporting mothers may have been questioned by some individual socialist writers, this principle was one of the demands made by the *Shakai Taishū Fujin Dōmei* (Social Masses Women's League) in 1932. Their platform specifically mentions a *Boshi Fujo Hō* (Mother and Child Assistance Act),[89] while other proletarian groups refer to protective provisions or *bosei hogo* in general. In other words, there were philosophical differences between individuals and groups, but most were willing to support pragmatic short-term measures such as the Mother and Child Assistance Act, while maintaining their separate positions on longer-term objectives.

The Women's Suffrage League had always supported the various policies described as 'motherhood protection', and the Fifth Annual Women's Suffrage Conference in 1934 specifically demanded the introduction of a *Boshi Fujo Hō* (Mother and Child Assistance Act).[90] Representatives from both liberal and socialist groups formed the Alliance for the Promotion of a Mother and Child Protection Act (*Bosei Hogo Hō Seitei Sokushin Fujin Renmei*) in September 1934.[91] This committee was headed by former Bluestocking Yamada Waka. Yamada had been responsible for the early translations of Ellen Key's writings in the journal *Seitō*, and was said to 'embody' the principle of maternalism, although she had no children of her own.[92] Yamada was against abortion, against contraception, and raised the ire of former colleague Hiratsuka in 1931 when she advocated that women should 'return to their homes'.[93]

Sakai [Kondō] Magara was one of the socialists represented on this committee. While Yamada's promotion of State support for motherhood was linked with antagonism towards contraception and abortion, socialists often linked the issues of birth control and State assistance for supporting mothers. They argued that women should not be forced to give birth to unplanned children, and that they should have the economic means to look after the children they chose to bear.[94] Sakai had already had one confrontation with Yamada on the subject of contraception,[95] and now voiced her concern about the philosophy behind the proposed legislation:

> There is nothing wrong with being moved to feelings of sympathy, compassion or mercy by the problem of mother-child suicides. It is a different matter, however, when these feelings become the basis for a movement, and the spirit behind legislation.
> There is no need for the worship of motherhood . . .
> Rather than saying 'Protect motherhood because it is something noble',

this State, which is built by the people, should protect both motherhood and fatherhood.

Nowadays, the members of the Movement for the Creation of a Motherhood Protection Act demand, support, and call for the protection of motherhood. Could we not say that the fact that the State does not provide such protection, is proof that the State does not belong to the people?

When there is a war, and there are not enough soldiers, there are calls to bear children and to multiply. [In such times] mothers with children will be given financial assistance. Does this also come under the name of respect for motherhood, and protection of motherhood?[96]

This polemic was written for the suffragists' journal *Fusen* in October 1934. Sakai was perceptive enough to realize that such measures as the Mother and Child Assistance Act were most likely to be granted in wartime, when the family unit was being threatened. She also realized the contradiction involved in 'protecting' mothers and children, in order that they may later be sacrificed for the war effort. Given that the State is seen to be responsible for the exploitation of the proletariat as workers and as soldiers, she insists that the State should also take responsibility for women and children.

Sakai's writings on this issue show an ambivalent attitude to State institutions, which goes beyond the simplistic identification of State interests with capitalist interests, but is less sanguine about the benevolence of State institutions. By 1935 her rhetoric was framed in slightly different terms. Writing in the textile workers' paper *Seigi no Hikari*, Sakai now stated that such demands as the creation of a Mother and Child Assistance Act or an Unemployment Insurance System were worthwhile because they would cause cracks in the system, and hasten the defeat of capitalism.[97]

The Mother and Child Protection Act (*Boshi Hogo Hō*) was promulgated on 31 March 1937, and became effective on 1 January 1938.[98] The Act provided assistance for a mother (or grandmother) and child when the father had died, deserted the family, or become ill. A bill for the assistance of families of soldiers ill, wounded, or killed in war (*Gunji Fujo Hō*) was passed on the same day.[99]

We should note that this law was enacted at a time when families were being shaken by the loss of husbands, fathers and sons, and the myth of the nuclear family with father as breadwinner could no longer be sustained. The State now looked after widows in place of the absent fathers, suggesting another possible relationship between women and the State, with the State cast as patriarch. This impression is reinforced by the title of the Act. Implied in the title 'Mother and Child Protection Act' is an unequal relationship between women and the state, with women positioned as weak supplicants in need of 'protection', to be provided by a strong and benevolent State.[100]

Subtle differences in terminology appeared between different actors in this campaign. The women's newspaper *Fujo Shinbun* criticized the Home Ministry's use of the phrase *Jidō Fujo Hō* (Child Assistance Act) in draft legislation, arguing that this title ignored the issue of the welfare of mothers.[101] Such an emphasis on the links between the welfare of children and the welfare of mothers, however, suggests an inability to conceptualize issues of women's welfare independent of their roles as mothers. The women's committee formed to lobby for this legislation referred to a 'mother and child assistance act', although the committee itself was called the 'Motherhood Protection League' and articles and slogans on the issue often slipped back into the language of 'protection of motherhood' (*bosei hogo*), suggesting the difficulty of transcending this way of viewing the relationship between women and the State.

Campaigns by socialist women on labour legislation in the 1920s and 1930s employed similar language. Proletarian women's leagues and unions called for legislation for the 'protection' of women workers (*Fujin Rōdōsha Hogohō*). The proposed legislation was a response to the inadequacies of the Factory Act. These groups called for the immediate abolition of night work for women, proper paid maternity leave, and from the late 1920s also called for menstruation leave.[102]

Like liberal feminists, many socialist women were willing to attempt to engage with State institutions in order to achieve reforms in the interests of women. However, because socialist women were always conscious of the possibility of political repression, and because they were conscious of the class interests of the bureaucracy and the government, this engagement with State structures was less likely to slide into co-operation or co-optation.

There was a fine line between participation on committees formed to lobby the State for the implementation of feminist demands, and co-optation onto committees formed by the bureaucracy to mobilize women for government defined purposes. The movements for civic participation in local improvement movements mobilized many progressive women who were critical of the more overtly nationalist organizations such as the Patriotic Women's Association and the Women's National Defence Organization. Yamakawa Kikue, however, was one socialist woman who continued to criticize women's co-optation into organizations formed to promote State defined goals.[103]

Debates with Anarchist Women

While social democratic women and liberal feminists proposed statist solutions to many women's issues, anarchist women continued to question the role of the State in Marxist thought. These issues were considered in two women's intellectual journals which appeared around the turn of the decade. *Nyonin Geijutsu* (*Women's Arts*) and *Fujin Sensen* (*The Women's Front*) are usually presented as anarchist women's arts journals, but both journals published contributions from a broad spectrum of the left, including Communist Sata Ineko, Marxist Yamakawa Kikue, maternalist feminist Hiratsuka Raichō, as well as anarchists Yagi Akiko and Takamure Itsue.[104] *Nyonin Geijutsu*, edited by Hasegawa Shigure, a former contributor to the Bluestocking journal, appeared from July 1928 to June 1932.[105] *Fujin Sensen* appeared from March 1930 to June 1931.[106]

These journals provided a space for what could be called a feminist '*ana-boru ronsō*'.[107] Takamure Itsue and Yamakawa Kikue carried on a debate on the relative merits of anarchist and socialist solutions to the woman question in several intellectual journals, particularly *Fujin Kōron*.[108] They were joined by several contributors to *Nyonin Geijutsu* and *Fujin Sensen*, including some articles which descended into personal attacks on male and female socialists.[109]

Contributors to *Fujin Sensen* pointed out some of the weaknesses of socialist attempts to solve the 'woman question'. Takamure Itsue argued that because socialist thought privileged labour and the economic sphere, those activities which were the responsibility of women (childbirth and childcare) were relegated to the private sphere and thus devalued. Takamure also rejected the socialists' advocacy of public provision of childcare facilities, arguing that this, too, represented a devaluation of motherhood, as children were taken away from their mothers.[110] Takamure envisioned a society based on small autonomous communities (*museifu kyōsan shakai*)[111] close to nature, where women would share responsibility for children; she identified such an anarchist tradition in Japanese village communities.[112]

Takamure, like Hiratsuka Raichō, tended to idolise motherhood.[113] Takamure, however, identified motherhood with nature, and rejected the State support which had been advocated by Hiratsuka:

> [Takamure] called for establishment of community support and care for mothers and abolition of marriage as an institution . . .
> Believing that nature had its own order which must be honored, she argued that integral parts of nature like reproduction and childcare should be controlled by nature's own representatives – women, rather than by unnatural social institutions like marriage and the family.[114]

Contributors to *Fujin Sensen* attacked the family system in a series of articles.[115] Although Takamure explicitly addressed the question of childcare, in her rejection of public childcare facilities and her advocacy of co-operative childcare in small autonomous communities, she did not question the sexual division of labour, whereby it was women who held primary responsibility for childcare.

Takamure and Yamakawa also clashed on the subject of romantic love. While Yamakawa argued that women's economic independence was a necessary precondition for entering into a relationship on terms of freedom and independence, Takamure argued that this was impossible even in a socialist society. Takamure's ideal society was one where there was no division of labour, and any member of society could be a worker, and a politician, and an artist. Only when hierarchies were abolished would truly loving relationships be possible. Yagi Akiko commented on this debate, and questioned the view that love was a private matter, placing it rather in the context of the structure of society at large.[116]

In Hiratsuka's contribution to *Fujin Sensen*, she looked back on the two decades since the establishment of the Bluestocking journal, and traced the changes in her political position. Although she is now critical of 'capitalist' exploitation, she is not ready to embrace socialist solutions to women's problems. Like Takamure, she seems to fear that socialist solutions tend to be authoritarian solutions. Hiratsuka has now become involved with the consumers' co-operative movement, and she identifies this movement as having the potential to transform society through the feminine principles of co-operation, rather than what she sees as the masculine strategy of class struggle. Although the forms of political strategy proposed by Hiratsuka had undergone several transformations, she still sought specifically feminine strategies for political change.[117]

Like the motherhood protection debate of the Taishō period, these writings allowed further definition of the differences between socialist and other women's strategies for political change. While the Taishō debates had allowed a clear definition of the differences between liberal feminists and socialist women, the contributions to *Nyonin Geijutsu* and *Fujin Sensen* allowed discussion of the differences between anarchist and socialist views of women's issues, and much of this discussion focused on the role of the State. While anarchist and socialist women differed in the degree to which they had faith in Statist solutions to women's issues, they did share experiences of the repressive functions of State institutions.

The Repressive State

The experience of imprisonment appears in socialist women's writings from the earliest days. One of the features of Fukuda Hideko's autobiography is the extended discussion of her experiences in prison. Although her imprisonment on charges related to the Ōsaka Incident certainly reflects the repressive power of the Meiji State, her experience of imprisonment appears to have been relatively benevolent, perhaps because of her relatively privileged class background.

Kanno Suga, however, had a much more violent introduction to the powers of the police and judiciary. It seems that her poor treatment at the hands of the police in the Red Flag Incident in 1908 was one of the catalysts for her subsequent radicalization. We have a relatively detailed account of her imprisonment during the trial for the Great Treason Incident, thanks to the survival of her prison diary.[118] Kanno would become the first woman to be executed for treason in modern Japan.

The experience of imprisonment and police repression was something which united all participants in the socialist movement. Sakai Magara was conscious of this issue from her childhood, and her earliest memories included visiting her father Sakai Toshihiko in prison, and receiving a farewell letter and presents from Kanno Suga. When Sakai Magara and Nakasone Sadayo were imprisoned for distributing anti-militarist leaflets in the 1920s, Sakai was thus conscious of the links between herself and other activist women who had been imprisoned. All of these women were seen to have acted in ways which threatened the national polity: Fukuda Hideko's involvement in the Ōsaka Incident, Kōtoku and Kanno's treason plot, and Sakai and Nakasone's distribution of material containing 'dangerous thoughts'. Sakai was able to form a more tangible link, however, as she imagined Kanno's experience of imprisonment in a cell which was probably identical to her own, and remembered Kanno's poem about light shining through the barred prison window.[119]

Most of our access to the experience of women under imprisonment comes from retrospective accounts like Sakai [Kondō] Magara's. There are the semi-fictional writings of Yamanouchi Mina[120] and Sata Ineko,[121] the memoirs of such women as Tajima Hide[122] and Nakamoto Takako, and the experiences recounted in the autobiographies and the oral history interviews of the post-war period.[123] Occasionally, however, accounts of imprisonment appeared in contemporary publications. Tanno Setsu's letter to her mother from prison appeared in the women's journal *Fujin Kōron*,[124] while *Nyonin Geijutsu* published the account of a 'modern girl' who had ended up in prison after a demonstration.[125] From 1933, the newspapers also published accounts of those former communists and socialists who had committed *tenkō*: public renunciation of their left-wing views. This provided a negative example for those who were brave enough to continue in oppositional activity. What all of these accounts did was to remind activists of the increasingly strict limits placed on oppositional activity, particularly after the enactment of the Peace Preservation Law (*Chian Iji Hō*) of 1925.

Women as Activists

In addition to actively repressive policies, the government was increasingly involved in campaigns to mobilize ever more clearly-defined sectors of the population, through youth groups, women's organizations, and other patriotic organizations. By 1937, Japan was at war with China, and moving towards a state of total national mobilization. The activities of the proletarian women's divisions and suffragist organizations were soon overshadowed by these semi-official patriotic women's organizations. The *Kokubō Fujin Kai* (Women's National Defence Organization) was established in Western Japan in 1932. Although initially a private organization, the Association's fundraising activities were supported first by the media and then by the bureaucracy. While the *Aikoku Fujinkai* had largely remained an organization for (upper) middle-class women, the *Kokubō Fujin Kai* was from the start a more broad-based organization. These two patriotic women's organizations worked in parallel until their merger in 1942. While the proletarian women's organizations tried to reach women from the grass-roots level, the activities of the *Kokubō Fujin Kai* were increasingly organized from 'above'.

The first campaign by socialist women examined in this book was the campaign for the revision of Article Five of the Public Peace Law, carried out by the women of the *Heiminsha*, in a relatively optimistic time of liberal idealism. In the next three decades, socialist women would gain confidence as workers and as activists, addressing employers with demands for improved working conditions, and addressing the State with demands for legislative changes to deal with the contradictory situation of women who were workers too. The last campaign to be analysed concerned the demand for State assistance for supporting mothers, and the achievement of this particular piece of legislation suggests the limits of public discourse on women and politics in this period.

State policies in the 1930s and 1940s showed contradictory attitudes to women and their reproductive capacity. The Mother and Child Protection Act (*Boshi Hogo Hō*), which provided welfare assistance for supporting mothers, was passed in 1937. In the same year, Ishimoto Shidzue was arrested for her promotion of birth control, as part of a purge of left-wing activists. Ishimoto's promotion of birth control conflicted with increasingly pro-natalist policies. Abortion was allowed from 1940 on mainly eugenic grounds. The National Eugenics Law

(*Kokumin Yūseihō*) of 1940 was followed by the 'Outline for Establishing Population Growth Policy' in 1941. This policy allowed for the sterilization of those suffering from hereditary diseases, and the prohibition of the practice of birth control by healthy couples.[126]

In parallel with the mobilization of women for State purposes, there was an increased glorification of motherhood. In contradistinction to those feminists who had linked women's reproductive capacity with creativity and empowerment, official discourse increasingly linked maternity and nationalism. From 1940 women who produced large numbers of children were given official recognition,[127] and motherhood was glorified in school textbooks and other official publications.[128]

Socialist women had attempted to expand the representations of women, and were starting to be recognized as fellow workers and comrades within the socialist and labour movements. The strikes of the depression years brought representations of women engaged in militant labour activism out of the socialist press and into the mass media. These representations, however, had to compete with official representations which confined women within the bounds of a nationalist discourse which emphasized motherhood.

From the late 1930s, socialist women could choose public renunciation of their socialist beliefs, retreat from public activity, or engage in moderate reformist activities. Some continued in illegal underground activity, while others spent much of the war years in prison. For women who identified themselves as socialists, the relationship between individual and State, or between political organization and State, was necessarily an oppositional one. They had no illusions about the power of the State and the policing apparatus.

However, even groups and individuals who take an oppositional stance must frame their opposition in the language available to them. As E. Ann Kaplan has argued, 'women, like everybody else, can function only within the linguistic, semiotic constraints of their historical moment – within that is the discourses available to them'.[129] In previous chapters I have been exploring the discourses available to socialist women in early twentieth-century Japan. Fictional genres of writing, and the tropes and metaphors of creative writing, may also be part of the process of imagining other political possibilities, as I have briefly alluded to in previous chapters. In Chapter seven, in addition to surveying the organizational and political strategies employed by socialist women in the years from 1903 to 1937, I will examine the discursive strategies of socialist women's writings, and the language used to describe situations of repression and exploitation, and to imagine the possibility of liberation.

CHAPTER 7

Creating Socialist Women 1900–1937

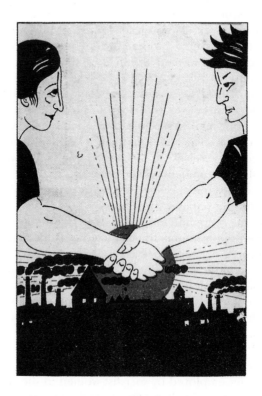

Solidarity. This cover of the textile workers' journal *Seigi no Hikari*, No. 8, 15/11/1926, portrays a working man and woman in partnership, united in a common struggle. The image of the dawn of socialism is a trope which was used in Japanese socialist iconography from the earliest days. Here, the light of the morning sun shines between the factory chimneys, aligning the allegorical meaning of the dawn with the socialist realist portrayal of the workers' own surroundings.

'... We often complain privately. And we think seriously about getting our conditions improved. However, we crumple when we have to come forward, because we have had no experience of disputes until now. We just whispered in the shadows. If we don't solve our situation, who will do it for us? It's no use waiting on the person next to you. When has anyone else ever done the slightest little thing to help us? No one has!'

The women were silent, deep in thought. Outside, the sky suddenly cleared, and a warm shaft of light came through a gap in the paper blinds.

Ushiyama broke the silence . . .'[1]

This scene is part of a fictional account of a group of factory women who come to understand their exploited position in the factory, and the necessity for women to act as a group, united in a common struggle with other workers – male and female – with the support of the union movement. This is a pivotal moment in their transformation from isolated individuals to a group of activists united by a common cause, and demonstrates the necessity of these women imagining themselves in new ways before they could countenance participation in militant action, supported by a union movement which provided organizational and conceptual backing.

In this book I have been exploring this process on a larger scale. Socialist women in early twentieth-century Japan were active in a range of political groups, from the *Heiminsha* of the 1900s to the women's divisions and women's leagues of the left-wing union federations and the proletarian political parties of the 1920s and 1930s. A major activity of the members of these groups was writing in a variety of genres: autobiography, essays, manifestos, fiction and poetry. The process of 'creating socialist women' was a threefold one, which involved the theorization of the class position of women and the political strategies for mobilizing women in the socialist and labour movements; the creation of organizational structures in order to mobilize women effectively in the labour and socialist movement; and the process of imagining women in new ways: as workers, comrades and activists rather than as wives, mothers and subjects of the Emperor. In this final chapter, I will survey the development of a movement of socialist women according to these three themes: defining a socialist and feminist position, organizing socialist women, and imagining socialist women.

Defining a Socialist and Feminist Position

There were two parallel developments from the liberal movement of the nineteenth century: socialism and feminism. The development of a socialist position on the 'woman question' came out of a conjunction of socialism and feminism, which involved bringing a gendered perspective to socialism, and a class perspective to feminism. This also involved the differentiation of a socialist position from liberal and anarchist positions.

Both socialism and feminism developed from the roots of the early liberal movement. A discursive space was opened up for feminism by the early Meiji discussions of the relationship between family and State, and women were interpellated in new ways by official pronouncements on 'good wives and wise mothers'.[2] The Meiji government privileged a patriarchal family where hierarchical gender relations were articulated into the power structures of the new State.

In this system, the nature of subjecthood was gendered, with men serving the State through conscription into the military, while women's service to the State was located in the family. Liberal theorists of the family, however, wished to see egalitarian relationships within the family and society at large. Progressive men and feminist women within the liberal movement wished to see 'freedom and people's rights' extended to include women's rights. The transformations of modernity and capitalist development provided the conditions for mobilization on the basis of gender as well as class. Both socialism and feminism developed as critiques of the limitations of liberal ideology.

As industrialization developed, this made possible mobilization on the basis of class, as workers came to realize the basic contradiction between the interests of capital and the interests of labour. While the bureaucracy looked to the German school of social policy for ways of controlling the supply of labour, and forestalling potential labour militancy, intellectuals looked to American labourism, British Utopian socialism, and European Marxism for an understanding of the relations between labour and capital.

In the early days of socialist thought in Japan, however, there was little to distinguish socialism from liberalism, and one of the first focuses of the early socialist movement was the campaign for the removal of property qualifications for the vote. Most of the early attempts at forming unions were short-lived, and a union movement on explicitly socialist principles did not really develop until after the First World War.

The first conjunction of socialism and feminism became apparent in the *Heiminsha* (the Commoners' Society) in the 1900s. A major focus of the organization was the production of several socialist newspapers: *Heimin Shinbun* (*Commoners' News*), *Chokugen* (*Plain Talk*), *Hikari* (*Light*), and *Shinkigen* (*New Age*). The range of socialist thinkers referred to in these publications attests to the eclecticism of the early socialists. Their search for a socialist understanding of the woman question is reflected in their speeches and articles on the thought of Bebel, Engels and Morgan.

While the members of the *Heiminsha* were keen to debate socialist answers to the woman question, their answers were shaped by the dominant discourses on women's place. In both mainstream society and in the socialist movement, women were primarily constructed as wives: as helpmates within the patriarchal family, as helpmates to the State through patriotic women's organizations, and helpmates to their male comrades in the socialist movement. In socialists' attempts to conceptualize a society based on co-operative principles, the family was often invoked as a metaphor for communal values, although the socialists were also willing to attempt to conceptualize new forms of the family. As far as women were concerned, however, they were rarely conceptualized outside this sphere, and articles addressed to women in the socialist movement tended to address the 'feminine' concerns of marriage and family, romance and reproduction. The sphere of interest was widened, however, when socialist men and women criticized the Patriotic Women's Association, where women were constructed as 'wives and mothers' of an increasingly militarist State.

Leftists reeled from the shock of the Great Treason Incident of the late Meiji period, and the years after 1911 are often referred to as the 'winter years' of the socialist movement. This decade also, however, saw the creation of the Bluestocking Society, a group of 'new women' who emphasized the power of feminine creativity. Socialist Yamakawa Kikue collided with these liberal feminists in the motherhood protection debate of the mid-Taishō period.

This debate provided an opportunity for the delineation of the differences between socialist and liberal solutions to the problems of the care and maintenance of children, and saw the beginnings of the articulation of a new way of linking questions of gender, State and welfare: the maternalist feminist position, initially espoused by Hiratsuka Raichō and Yamada Waka, but given further refinement in the 1930s by Hiratsuka and anarchist Takamure Itsue. The motherhood protection debate also introduced the question of class differences between women, an issue which would be addressed by socialist and communist discussions of the mobilization of women in the 1920s.

By the end of the First World War Marxism had become the most influential form of socialist thought, and more and more of the classics of Marx, Engels and Lenin were translated in the 1920s. The first complete translation of Bebel's *Woman Under Socialism* also appeared in this decade. The Russian Revolution was another major catalyst in the revival of the socialist movement after the 'winter years' following the Great Treason Incident.

The first women's division of a union was created by the *Yūaikai* friendly society in 1916, but the *Yūaikai* view of women was essentially a protective one. They saw the State and the unions as having a paternalistic role in protecting women from the excesses of capitalist exploitation. The position of women in the socialist and labour movements was not effectively theorized until the *Seiji Kenkyūkai* debates on women's issues, and the debates on women's divisions in the *Hyōgikai* union federation between 1925 and 1927. These debates considered the relationship between the class struggle and 'women's special demands'. Despite the intellectual advances made in discussions of what recent feminist theorists call 'equality versus difference',[3] and the belated recognition that women could be workers too, these theoretical gains could not immediately be translated into effective mobilization of women, due to the subordination of women's interests to the factions of the 'malestream' movement and the dictates of Comintern policy.

The malestream left-wing movement was increasingly fragmented into Marxist, Social Democratic, and eventually Nationalist Socialist factions. Women within the socialist movement chose their allegiances to one or other of these factions, and became activists in the women's divisions of unions or the women's leagues which supported the proletarian parties. Socialist women also defined their position in opposition to anarchist women and liberal feminists. The increasing refinement of these positions did not, however, preclude co-operation. A broad spectrum of anarchist, Communist and socialist women contributed to the women's arts journals *Nyonin Geijutsu* (*Women's Arts*) and *Fujin Sensen* (*The Women's Front*), and social democratic women formed alliances with liberal feminists to lobby for feminist demands.

While some women participated on committees formed to lobby the State for the implementation of feminist demands, others were co-opted on to committees formed by the bureaucracy to mobilize women for government defined purposes. Although the movements for civic participation in local improvement activities mobilized many progressive women, socialist women such as Yamakawa Kikue criticized women's co-optation into organizations formed to promote State defined goals.

The debates of the 1920s had focused on the relationship between class and gender: on the problem of integrating women's 'special demands' into the class struggle. In the late 1920s and early 1930s, debates between anarchist and socialist women focused on an issue which had been implicit in all previous debates on gender issues: the role of the State. Social Democratic women were increasingly engaged in co-operation with liberal feminists in campaigns for State solutions to women's problems (suffrage, protective labour legislation, State assistance for supporting mothers, and the public provision of medical facilities for childbearing women, family planning, and childcare facilities). Anarchist women rejected Statist solutions and envisioned autonomous, non-hierarchical communities where women could share responsibility for childcare. In the case of Takamure Itsue, this was linked with a Utopian vision, as she placed women in a more natural sphere, in communities modelled on her image of traditional Japanese villages. Like Hiratsuka Raichō, Takamure emphasized the power of women's creativity as mothers.

Socialist and anarchist women could not help but be conscious of the State. They and their comrades had been subject to the repressive power of the policing apparatus of the State from the earliest days of the leftist movement. This was usually through the sanctioned power of the bureaucracy, the police, and the legal system. Occasionally, however, they were subject to the actions of agents of the State who had gone out of control, as in the murder of Ōsugi Sakae, Itō Noe, and several labour activists by police in the disorder following the Great Kantō Earthquake of 1923.

As a result of increased repression in the 1930s, the more radical sections of the leftist movement increasingly moved underground, or even escaped overseas, while the moderate elements of the socialist movement coalesced in a united proletarian party. Some succumbed to repression and committed *tenkō*: public renunciation of their allegiance to the leftist movement.[4] From this time on, the movement entered what Japanese historians call the 'dark valley' of the 1930s and 1940s, when the light of socialism and feminism had limited power to illuminate the darkness of repression.

Organizing Socialist Women

The process of forging a theoretical conjunction of socialism and feminism was meaningless, however, without the creation of effective organizational structures and political practices which could mobilize the energies of those women who came to define themselves as 'socialist women'.

The *Heiminsha*, as we have seen, was often constructed as a surrogate family. The *Heiminsha* 'family' was seen as a space where communal values could be put into practice, in keeping with the relatively gentle brand of socialism espoused by this group. Values of co-operation and community were more apparent than the class struggle in this early socialist group. For women in the *Heiminsha*, however, the use of familial metaphors also had hierarchical connotations, and women in the socialist movement were primarily constructed as wives and lovers, daughters and sisters. This was reflected in a sexual division of labour in the day-to-day running of the *Heiminsha*, and in the different ways in which women and men contributed to the early socialist publications.

There were also attempts to create autonomous spaces for women's activities, through the Socialist Women's Seminar,[5] and through publications directed at socialist women: *Nijū Seiki no Fujin* (*Twentieth Century Woman*), *Sweet Home*, and *Sekai Fujin* (*Women of the World*). Through the *Heiminsha* women learned to practise political activity, by producing publications and selling them in public places. The novelty of these activities for women is evidenced in Matsuoka [Nishikawa] Fumiko's account of this activity in the *Commoners' News*.[6]

The liberal roots of the early socialist views of the woman question became apparent in the first public campaign by socialist women. Fukuda Hideko and her colleagues from the Commoners' Society carried out a campaign for the repeal of those articles of the Public Peace Police Law which prevented women from engaging in public political activity. These liberal demands were matched by liberal political strategies; the campaigners wrote essays in socialist publications, lobbied politicians, collected signatures, and presented petitions to the Diet.

The women of the *Sekirankai* and the *Yōkakai* carried on some of the political practices developed in the *Heiminsha*: lecture meetings, and the contribution of essays to intellectual journals. They did not, however, produce any independent publications. The women of the *Sekirankai* also participated in a new performance of socialist solidarity – the May Day demonstration – and immediately suffered the consequences of this participation: arrest, police brutality, and prosecution for the distribution of pamphlets without permission.

In a lecture meeting held to raise money for the fines incurred, Sakai Magara recounted her experiences of arrest in another incident, and used humour as a way of dealing with this experience. Nakasone Sadayo was also valorized for her feisty response to an arresting officer.[7] The practices of celebrating May Day and International Women's Day gave expression to the links between the Japanese socialists and an international movement.

These groups were important as relatively autonomous socialist women's organizations which provided further opportunities for the development of the theoretical tools and practical skills necessary for political action. The *Sekirankai* and the *Yōkakai* were not, however, successful in bridging the gap between intellectual women and working women. The unions and proletarian parties of the 1920s were engaged in attempts to bridge this gap.

The first union women's division was created by the *Yūaikai* friendly society in 1916, but the *Yūaikai* and its successor the *Sōdōmei* displayed an ambivalent attitude to women workers, taking some time to give women workers full membership. Male union organizers took a protective attitude to women workers, and were likely to see their role as providing advice on supplementary work for male unionists' wives, rather than fostering militancy among women workers – perhaps unsurprising in an organization initially devoted to promoting 'harmony' between capital and labour.

The *Hyōgikai* union federation devoted more attention to developing a socialist attitude to women workers, but the actual mobilization of women workers was hampered by the factionalism of the union movement in the 1920s. Eventually, however, women gained experience of strikes, picketing and pamphleteering, and the unions affiliated with the three main union federations – the *Sōdōmei*, *Nichirō* and *Hyōgikai* – fostered a small number of women organizers, whose activities were supported by the women's leagues of the proletarian parties.

The development of what Andrew Gordon has called a 'dispute culture' among the women and men of the labour movement[8] culminated in the militant strikes of the early depression years, when women workers in the textile industry bore the brunt of rationalization and retrenchments. Even in the strikes of the early 1930s, however, where women were portrayed as heroic figures, these activities were hampered by the splits and factions of the union movement as several unions competed for control, and the numbers of women workers organized in unions remained small.[9]

As women in the labour movement engaged in direct conflict with capital in the 1920s and 1930s, in order to gain improvements in conditions for their own workers, other women in the socialist movement supported the proletarian party movement through affiliated women's leagues, and also turned their attention to government policies.

While women in the communist movement were increasingly forced underground, social democratic women moved to closer co-operation with liberal feminists, on campaigns for women's suffrage, state assistance for supporting mothers, and improved labour legislation. Like the women of the *Heiminsha* who had lobbied for the amendment of Article Five of the Public Peace Police Law, the participants in these campaigns employed essentially liberal strategies: writing, petitioning, pamphleteering, lobbying and speeches. The achievement of legislative reform, in the shape of the Mother and Child Assistance Act in 1937, was one example of effective lobbying on liberal principles. This legislation, however, reinforced the role of a paternalistic and patriarchal State in 'protecting' women and children, and affirmed a nationalist and militarist project which circumscribed the meanings attached to the concept of motherhood.

Imagining Socialist Women

The intellectual process of creating a theoretical conjunction of socialism and feminism was thus carried out in parallel with strategies for creating suitable organizational structures for the mobilization of women in the socialist movement. Women within the socialist movement gained skills in writing and distributing publications and pamphlets, participating in demonstrations, picketing and strikes, and learning to deal with the repressive power of the State through encounters with the policing apparatus and the legal system. The proletarian arts movement was an important resource in providing the means to imagine new socialist futures peopled by new socialist women and men, through writing, theatre, and visual arts. In addition to specifically literary publications, most left-wing journals published poetry, fiction and illustrations alongside essays and theoretical discussions.[10]

Many socialist women have traced a shift in subjectivity gained in their experiences of these actions. Activist women have recorded the first speech in public, the first experience of selling magazines or distributing leaflets, or the moment when their attitude shifted from compliance to defiance.[11] Others have recorded their experiences of visiting comrades in prison, their own experiences of arrest, imprisonment or police brutality, or the experience of interrogation in court.

Often the shifts in subjectivity occasioned by these experiences are constructed retrospectively, in memoirs, reminiscences, or oral history interviews. Socialist women were also, however, engaged in an ongoing process of reconstruction of subjectivity through the contemporary writings of the socialist movement, as they tried to imagine women in new ways, or tried to facilitate the shift in subjectivity of other socialist women, through essays and fictional and poetic writings which portrayed new possibilities for the activism of socialist women. The construction of new subjectivities was carried out not only through the propositional content of these writings, but also through the use of vocabulary and metaphor, and the transformation and adaptation of existing genres of writing and visual representations.

While dominant discourses positioned women as Imperial subjects, as wives and as mothers, women attempted to reposition themselves as workers and as activists. Women were positioned in various ways according to nationalist, liberal, socialist and feminist discourses. Each of these discourses provided a limited space for the discussion of feminist issues. Socialist women, through their writings, attempted to extend the limits of this discursive space.

Speaking Positions: From Subject to Activist

Women were officially constructed as subjects of the Emperor, in a system where familial hierarchy was linked with societal hierarchy. The patriarchal family formed a crucial link in the chain of loyalty from subject to Emperor. Nationalist discourses on gender and the family constructed women as helpmates – to the family and to the nation. Although liberals, feminists and socialists aspired to active citizenship rather than passive subjecthood, their discourses were often shaped by nationalist values.

Nationalist discourse was gendered as men were trained to be good soldiers while women were trained to be 'good wives and wise mothers'. In patriotic organizations, women were seen as helpmates of the State, supporting nationalist and militarist programmes. In this context, women could attempt to speak as nationalist subjects, emphasizing their service to the nation. Within the earliest socialist organizations, too, women were constructed as helpmates to the socialist movement. While this did allow space for the socialist discussion of issues related to marriage, family, sexuality and reproduction, it was some time before it was recognized that all aspects of socialist theory and strategy could be relevant to women, who were also workers and potential activists.

The other side of the slogan 'good wives and wise mothers' involved constructions of women as mothers. Women were referred to as 'mothers of the nation'. Women as mothers, however, were primarily constructed as the objects of State protection. This attitude to the relationship between women and the State coloured both official constructions of womanhood, and the discussions of feminists who subsumed calls for State assistance for supporting mothers under the label of 'protection of motherhood'. Maternity could also be a powerful metaphor in a variety of contexts. Socialists used the maternal as a metaphor for the caring values of an ideal socialist society, while the Bluestockings used the maternal as a specifically feminine trope of creativity and empowerment. The maternal trope could also, however, be recuperated for nationalist ends, in the context of pro-natalist policies in the late 1930s and 1940s.[12]

Women were initially not seen as workers, whether in official ideology or in socialist publications. The first union federations took a protective attitude to women workers, emphasizing their identity as women rather than as workers. As women came to be recognized as workers, however, it became apparent that all aspects of socialist theory and strategy were relevant to women. It also became clear that women workers were potential comrades, unionists and activists. Women as workers gained legitimacy to engage with employers in disputes about working conditions. They also attempted to gain legitimacy to engage with the State in demands for legislative change.

But to be a woman worker was to embody a contradiction. Although women in the socialist movement gained legitimacy through being recognized as fellow workers, this did not solve the issue of women's difference from men, the existence of women's 'special demands'. Some strikes of the early Shōwa period addressed the special needs of women, through demanding that employers provide paid maternity leave and menstruation leave.[13] Women's demands for legislative change in the 1930s were attempts to deal with these needs at a State level.

Women were recognized as activists through their participation in strikes, and through their participation in campaigns for legislative change. Woman as activist could also, however, be represented as a dangerous figure. The employers who warned of the sexual promiscuity of the workers of the Toyō Muslin factory were attempting to reassert the boundaries of acceptable feminine behaviour which had been transgressed by the striking women. For the women themselves, participation in disputes occasioned subtle shifts in subjectivity, as they came to see themselves as activists. These shifts in subjectivity can be traced through an examination of the imaginative resources of the genres of socialist writing.

Identifying oneself as an activist, and engaging in political campaigns, however, did not supersede or transcend the other facets of women's lives and identities. While socialist women had brought discussion of so-called 'women's issues' into the conference rooms of the union federations and proletarian parties, many women still had to deal with the sexism of male activists in their everyday lives. Women writers in the proletarian literary movement of the 1920s and 1930s, such as Miyamoto [Chūjō] Yuriko and Sata [Kubokawa] Ineko, used fictional genres to address the relationships between men and women in the left-wing movement, and the contradictory situation of women who tried to reconcile the positions of wife, mother, worker, and activist.[14]

Oppression, Liberation and Transformation

The first stage in the transformation of socialist women's subjectivity involved the recognition of their own oppression and exploitation, and this was expressed initially through metaphors of imprisonment, a trope which had been used from the late nineteenth century in Japan.[15] The conditions of factory work were described in numerous songs figuring factory workers as caged birds, and a major way of imagining liberation from this situation was to imagine escape. Workers sang of breaking the bars of imprisonment and flying away. This fantasy of escape matched the workers' preferred way of changing their situation in the earliest days of industrialization.[16] Another textile workers' song contrasted an unnatural state of oppression and exploitation with a more innocent state. In this song, the mill girl is a bird who cannot fly away; a bud, spoiled by frost, which will never bloom.[17]

These songs provided a 'chronicle of pain', a documentation of the exploitation of these workers. Could these images of fragility and pathos be used to imagine the possibility of shared political action, as the basis for a political movement? Or did they simply 'act to keep in place existing structures of domination'?[18]

Asō Hisashi, as we have seen, used the caged bird metaphor from the workers' songs to demonstrate his arguments about the relationship between different kinds of exploitation based on sex and class. He argued that all workers were in the position of caged birds. In the case of women workers, however, they were seen to suffer double imprisonment by the twin cages of class and gender. Even if women 'with their feeble strength' were able to break out of the cage of class exploitation, they would still be subject to exploitation as women. Although Asō's article laments the seriousness of women's double oppression, rather than providing a means to imagine the transformation of that situation, it is a useful attempt to marry the imaginative resources of a local tradition with the theoretical tools of Marxist analysis. Visual representations in the union journals of the 1920s and 1930s also reworked the conventions of European socialist iconography for the local context.[19]

Another aspect of the development of a new subjectivity involved the consciousness of the differences between women of different classes, and a recognition that the privilege of the middle classes was achieved at the cost of the exploitation of the working classes. In her contributions to the textile workers' journal, *Seigi no Hikari* (*The Light of Justice*), Tajima Hide played on the imagery of light and darkness in the title of the journal. Tajima contrasted the conditions of working women, who leave home before sunrise and come home from the factory after dark, with the 'young ladies' who attend 'ladies' colleges', wear beautiful kimonos, eat good foods, and are said to 'grow up bathed in light'.[20]

Such imagery was often linked with what Carolyn Steedman has called a 'politics of envy' where the situation of working-class women was contrasted with that of middle-class women.[21] This sentiment is expressed in Sata Ineko's story, 'From the Caramel Factory', in a scene where a thirteen-year-old factory worker admires the silk kimono of the factory owner's wife.[22] In another of Sata's stories, strike participants are suddenly at a loss to know how to address their boss. It no longer seems appropriate to address him as 'Sir' after they have faced him with their demands.[23]

The imagery of deprivation and envy, however, could also be transformed into an image of strength, and the imagery of light and darkness could be used to describe the possibility of political transformation. In Tajima Hide's union movement writings, the politics of envy is transformed into the imagery of class struggle. Tajima used the conventional images of pathos, but attempted to transform an image of deprivation into an image of power and solidarity. The power of solidarity is expressed through the metaphor of the sun emerging from the clouds. In Nakamoto Takako's story 'The Number 2 Tōkyō Muslin Factory', as we have seen, a shaft of light through the factory window marks the women workers' transition from uncertainty to militancy.[24]

In this text Nakamoto is quite self-conscious about the politics of artistic production. She also portrays the factory women attending a play performed by a proletarian theatre group, which contributes to their developing political consciousness. It seems that theatre was also used as a consciousness-raising tool by unions. *Rōdō Fujin* carries the script of a performance written and performed by Hanaoka Shigeko.[25] Other works of the proletarian arts movement portrayed women engaging in such activities as pamphleteering and strikes.[26]

By the late 1920s, the world depression which also affected the Japanese textile industry meant that women workers in suburban Tokyo were in the vanguard of struggles between labour and capital. Strike pamphlets of the time make little use of poetic imagery. Rather the workers' struggle is expressed in simple language. An appeal to 'the proletarian women of Nankatsu', described the participation of women in the Tōyō Muslin strike of May 1930:

Over 3000 of our brothers and sisters at Tōyō Muslin have . . . embarked on a strike in order to save themselves from starvation, and are fighting against the high-handedness of the company and the indescribable suppression by the police.
. . . So, the victory of the factory women of Tōyō Muslin, will, in the end, be a victory for all proletarian women . . .

Another pamphlet from the same strike referred to the militancy of the striking women and men:

> ... Our 3000 brothers and sisters are paying a sacrifice in blood!
> Do not give them up to the enemy!
> Bring down a torrent of contributions to our fighting fund![27]

In these pamphlets, it is perhaps the close relationship between representation and political activism that is responsible for the strong representations of women to be found here. The reality of women's strike activity at this time made possible the representation of strong and active women, and these representations made possible the imagining of future activism by women. In these labour movement writings, there is a depth which comes from references to the lived struggles of women workers.

The Rhetoric of Feminism and Socialism

This leads us to a consideration of the relationship between the study of the language of political movements, and the study of other aspects of the mobilization of individuals under the banners of feminism, socialism, and other political ideologies. Previously, I have considered the imaginative resources of writings on women's situation and writings on the liberation of women from patriarchal and capitalist exploitation. In many of the writings that I have analysed, depth has come from intertextuality, from the use of metaphors which have shared meanings in a particular cultural context, and the creation of metaphors which attempt to transform those shared cultural meanings. Another kind of depth, however, comes from the relationship between representation and political action. As bell hooks has reminded us, 'To imagine is to begin the process that transforms reality'.[28]

Some of the writings examined employed the conventional imagery of femininity. This conventional imagery reinforced notions of passivity and decorativeness, particularly the use of floral imagery. Other metaphors contrasted the deformations of capitalist and patriarchal society with what was seen as a more natural state. This is the function of the images of the stunted flowers, the bud which will not bloom, the tiny bird who cannot fly. The imagery of imprisonment forms a similar function in depicting an exploitative situation, and becomes linked with fantasies of escape.

It would be simplistic to argue for a simple congruence between a political position and a set of rhetorical images. At times, rhetoric and political strategy certainly were mutually reinforcing. The liberal individualism of the Bluestockings was indeed expressed through the assertiveness of the first person pronoun, and images of individual genius, albeit initially divorced from a consciousness of the social. The use of maternal imagery provided a specifically feminine trope of creativity and empowerment, although such imagery could also be co-opted for nationalist purposes.

However, when socialist Sakai Toshihiko described the women of the *Heiminsha* as flowers and birds, this was at odds with the actions of a man who devoted more attention to an understanding of the woman question than most of his male comrades. On the other hand, there seems to be a congruence between the pathetic imagery of fragility and imprisonment employed by early labour organizers and the lack of a clear strategy for mobilizing the women workers whom they viewed as objects of pity and compassion, rather than as comrades in a common struggle.

Other kinds of natural imagery, however, presented a more dynamic picture. For the contributors to the feminist arts journal *Bluestocking* (*Seitō*), the imagery of nature was a means of imagining liberation. This is seen most strikingly in Yosano Akiko's often-cited poem, 'Mountain Moving Day', which uses the metaphor of subterranean volcanic activity to express the potential power of women's energy.[29]

The politics of envy, expressed in comparisons between middle-class privilege and working-class deprivation, were useful in dramatizing the inequalities of society. It was necessary for socialist women to link this envy, however, with a clear understanding of the explanations for this inequality, and strategies for transforming the society which is based on such inequalities.

The imagery of light and darkness in political and imaginative writings invoked the concept of enlightenment, *Keimō*.[30] In this context, light represented knowledge. In other writings, light was most often linked with the possibility of transformation. In the case of the Bluestockings, this referred to individual liberation, and the development of individual creativity. In labour movement writings, however, light and darkness took on class connotations, describing the contrast between middle-class privilege and working-class deprivation. Several writers used this imagery to imagine the possibility of social transformation. In the writings of Tajima Hide and Nakamoto Takako, light was linked to solidarity and the potential for shared political action.

All of these writers and activists were engaged in a complex struggle, in activities concerned with 'the micropolitics of work, home, family and sexuality', and a parallel struggle which was waged at the level of ideology and discourse. Writing was an integral part of the process of forging 'new political identities' for feminist and socialist women.[31] In analysing these writings, it has thus been necessary to link representations with the specific political struggles engaged in by these women, and the generic constraints and possibilities of particular types of political writing.[32]

Fukuda Hideko's autobiography presented the contradictory position of a female activist who aspired to the ideals of liberal individualism, while her novel *My Memories* was constrained by conventional plot structures. The poetic manifestos of Yosano Akiko, Hiratsuka Raichō and Takamure Itsue attempted to go beyond the boundaries of liberal political discourse. Labour organizers supplemented the hortatory tone of the political pamphlet and the cool tone of political debate with the imaginative resources of the artistic products of the proletarian literary arts movement.

Similar imagery and rhetorical strategies often appeared across genres, and we can trace links between the speaking positions available to feminist and socialist women in early twentieth-century Japan, the discursive strategies employed in their writings, and the political strategies they envisaged for changing their society and their own situation. We should also, however, consider the relationship between these marginal representations and mainstream discourses on women and politics. How much power did socialist and feminist writers have to challenge dominant constructions of women as wives and as mothers?[33]

In the introduction to this book, I invoked the 1970s feminist project of uncovering something which has been 'hidden from history'.[34] The existence of a movement of socialist women in early twentieth-century Japan has indeed been relatively hidden, particularly in English-language scholarship on Japan. This research has been made possible by the labour historians and feminist historians in Japan, who have attempted to preserve the documents of the labour, feminist and socialist movements, making many of them available in facsimile editions and document collections. It has thus been possible to trace the development of a movement of socialist women in early twentieth-century Japan, and to map out the individuals, organizations and publications which made up this movement.

I have also, however, realized the limitations of the metaphors of 'uncovering' in the writing of feminist history. Feminist historians do not simply reveal a pre-existing reality. We construct our own narratives of resistance and liberation. In my own case I have constructed a narrative of this movement of socialist women around a series of speaking positions, tracing a trajectory from subjection to activism, in a discussion which culminates in representations of strong women engaged in militant labour activism, structuring a narrative around my own desire for images of political transformation which can replace the imagery of feminine passivity. Following Rajeswari Sunder Rajan, I acknowledge that 'the discovery of resistance in women's writing also requires the investment of our desires and the acknowledgment of our politics as women/feminists reading'.[35]

Notes

1 Introduction

1 Dokuzen Kyōfu, *Kageyama Hidejo no Den*, Tokyo, 1887.

2 Her family name before her marriage to Fukuda Tomosaku was Kageyama, and she was known by this name at the time of the Ōsaka Incident, but because she published her autobiography under the name of Fukuda Hideko, and used this name for the rest of her life, I will use this name to refer to her from here on. For biographical details of Fukuda's life, see Murata Shizuko, *Fukuda Hideko*, Tokyo: Iwanami Shoten, 1959; Itoya Toshio, *Josei Kaihō no Senkushatachi*, Tokyo: Shimizu Shoin, 1975; Sharon L. Sievers, *Flowers in Salt: The Beginnings of Feminist Consciousness in Meiji Japan*, Stanford: Stanford University Press, 1983, Chapters 3 and 6; Sharlie Conroy Ushioda, 'Women and War in Meiji Japan: The Case Of Fukuda Hideko, *Peace and Change*, Vol. 4, No. 3, (Fall 1977), pp. 9–12; Sharlie Conroy Ushioda, 'Fukuda Hideko and the Women's World of Meiji Japan', in Hilary Conroy, et al. (eds), *Japan in Transition: Thought and Action in the Meiji Era*, Cranbury, New Jersey: Associated University Presses, 1984, pp. 276–93. I will be referring to the following edition of Fukuda's autobiography: Fukuda Hideko, *Warawa no Hanseigai*, Tokyo: Iwanami Bunkō, 1958. Translations are my own unless otherwise stated.

3 Fukuda's autobiography was obviously popular as it ran to several editions. The publisher's advertisement in *Sekai Fujin* in 1907 notes that the book is already in its fifth reprinting; *Sekai Fujin*, No. 3, p. 8, 1907 (Facsimile edition, Tokyo: Ryūkei Shosha; p. 74).

4 cf. Mikiso Hane, *Reflections on the Way to the Gallows*, Berkeley: University of California Press, 1988; p. 29.

5 She uses a literary style of writing, which employs grammatical endings derived from classical Japanese – a style removed from spoken language. However, the use of *furigana* to provide readings for Chinese characters made this writing somewhat more accessible. For an account of the transformations of literary language in the Meiji period, see: Masao Miyoshi, *Accomplices of Silence: The Modern Japanese Novel*, Berkeley: University of California Press, 1974, Chapter 1.

6 This genre of writing is discussed by Richard Bowring in 'The Female Hand in Heian Japan: A First Reading', in Domna C. Stanton (ed.), *The Female Autograph*, Chicago: University of Chicago Press, 1984, pp. 49–56.

7 Fukuzawa's autobiography was published in 1898 under the title *Fukuō Jiden*. This is discussed by Carmen Blacker, in *The Japanese Enlightenment: A Study of the Writings of Fukuzawa Yukichi*, Cambridge: Cambridge University Press, 1964, pp. 11–13.

171

8 cf. the discussion in Livia Monnet, ' "In the Beginning Woman was the Sun"': Auto-biographies of Modern Japanese Women Writers', *Japan Forum*, Vol. 1, No. 1, April 1989; and Vol. 1, No. 2, October 1989. Monnet is sensitive to the fact that women's 'self-writing', as she calls it, must be placed in the context of a long tradition of poetic diaries, and the blurring of autobiography and fiction in modern Japanese novels. However, I would argue that the generic conventions of the Heian poetic diaries were not appropriate to the writing of a political life in Meiji Japan. Bowring, in 'The Female Hand', argues that the genre of poetic diary involves a central trope of 'waiting', with the woman as passive centre. On the other hand, Fukuda's auto-biography involves a life of action. While the poetic diaries are cyclical in structure, Fukuda's autobiography is much closer to the 'quest' novel – mainly linear in struc-ture, but allowing flashbacks and other temporal manipulation for dramatic and textual effect. As I will discuss later, Fukuda's autobiography is a carefully constructed text, drawing on novelistic and melodramatic conventions. For further discussion of Fukuda's autobiography from the standpoint of genre, see Vera Mackie, 'Narratives of Struggle: Writing and the Making of Socialist Women in Japan', in Elise Tipton (ed.), *Society and State in Interwar Japan*, London: Routledge (forthcoming).

9 *Warawa no Hanseigai*, p. 11.

10 *Warawa no Hanseigai*, pp. 46–7. The biography was translated by her erstwhile fiancé, Kobayashi Kusuo.

11 Several books dealing with the heroic exploits of the Russian Nihilists appeared in Japan in the 1880s. John Crump, *The Origins of Socialist Thought in Japan*, Beckenham, Kent: Croom Helm, 1983, p. 38.

12 Several of these statements from the weekly *Heimin Shinbun* are collected in Odagiri Susumu (ed.), *Meiji Bungaku Zenshū 84: Meiji Shakai Shugi Bungaku Shū 2*, Tokyo: Chikuma Shobō, 1965, pp. 389–92. For some later statements by women in the journal *Chokugen*, see Suzuki Yūko (ed.), *Shiryō: Heiminsha no Onnatachi*, Tokyo: Fuji Shuppan, 1986, pp. 72–4; Nishikawa Fumiko, *Heiminsha no Onna: Nishikawa Fumiko Jiden*, Tokyo: Aoyamakan, 1984, Amano Shigeru (ed.), pp. 209–10. These statements will be discussed in Chapter three of this book. Such statements were also found in British socialist writing, and the genre can perhaps be traced back to the tradition of narratives of religious conversion. See Stephen Yeo, 'A New Life: The Religion of Socialism in Britain, 1883–1896', *History Workshop*, No. 4, (Autumn, 1977), pp. 11–12; Carolyn Steedman, 'Women's Biography and Autobiography: Forms of History and Histories of Form', in Helen Carr (ed.), *From My Guy to Sci-Fi: Genre and Women's Writing in the Postmodern World*, London: Pandora, 1989, p. 108.

13 Fukuda uses the word *gomu* 'rubber'. At that time, there were two ways of making artificial tortoiseshell: by painting hard rubber in suitable colours, or by using cel-luloid. I am indebted to Charles Sowerwine for clarification.

14 *Warawa no Hanseigai*, pp. 13–14.

15 Mary Mason has suggested that a doubling or splitting of the self is a characteristic of many early European women's autobiographies. See Mary G. Mason, 'The Other Voice: Autobiographies of Women Writers', in James Olney (ed.), *Autobiography: Essays Theoretical and Critical*, Princeton University Press, 1980, p. 211. Sidonie Smith also refers to 'the generic contract' which 'engages the autobiographer in a doubled subjectivity – the autobiographer as protagonist of her story and the autobiographer as narrator. Through that doubled subjectivity she pursues her fictions of selfhood by fits and starts.' Sidonie Smith, *A Poetics of Women's Autobiography: Marginality and the Fictions of Self-Representation*, Bloomington: Indiana University Press, 1987, p. 17.

16 *Warawa no Hanseigai*, pp. 70–3.

17 *Warawa no Hanseigai*, p. 14. This is not to suggest that Fukuda's mother simply pres-sured her to conform. Fukuda's mother was a respected teacher and scholar in her own right, and was largely responsible for Fukuda's education – the means by which Fukuda was able to gain a measure of independence.

18 *Warawa no Hanseigai*, p. 17; p. 22; p. 43.

19 *Warawa no Hanseigai*, p. 63.

20 *Warawa no Hanseigai*, p. 20.

21 *Warawa no Hanseigai*, p. 12.
22 *Warawa no Hanseigai*, p. 20.
23 The conjunction between modernity and the development of the autobiographical genre has been noted by Rey Chow in the Chinese context and Dipesh Chakrabarty in his discussion of Indian pasts. Rey Chow, *Woman and Chinese Modernity: The Politics of Reading Between East and West*, Minnesota: University of Minnesota Press, 1991, pp. 92–3; Dipesh Chakrabarty, 'Postcoloniality and the Artifice of History: Who Speaks for Indian Pasts?', *Representations*, 37, 1992, pp. 161–85.
24 Sidonie Smith, in *A Poetics of Women's Autobiography: Marginality and the Fictions of Self-Representation*, discusses the relationship between autobiography and liberal individualism, and the contradictions involved in women's writing of autobiography and aspiring to the ideals of liberal individualism.
25 cf. Stephen Large, 'The Romance of Revolution in Japanese Anarchism and Communism During the Taishō Period', *Modern Asian Studies*, Vol. II, No. 3, July 1977.
26 *Warawa no Hanseigai*, p. 52. The theme of embodiment in this text is discussed in more detail in Vera Mackie, "In a Woman's Body": Gender and Activism in Meiji Japan', in Vera Mackie and Freda Freiberg (eds), *Re-orienting the Body*, (forthcoming).
27 *Warawa no Hanseigai*, pp. 52–3.
28 *Warawa no Hanseigai*, pp. 74–8. On Ōi Kentarō, see Marius Jansen, 'Ōi Kentarō: Radicalism and Chauvinism', *Far Eastern Quarterly*, Vol. 2, No. 3, May 1952, pp. 305–16.
29 *Warawa no Hanseigai*, p. 15.
30 Murata, *Fukuda Hideko*, pp. 22–3.
31 *Warawa no Hanseigai*, pp. 15–16. For details of Kishida Toshiko's life, see Itoya Toshio, *Josei Kaihō no Senkushatachi*, Tokyo: Shimizu Shoin, 1975; Sievers, *Flowers in Salt*, Chapter 3. Sharon L. Sievers, 'Feminist Criticism in Japanese Politics in the 1880s: The Experience of Kishida Toshiko,' *Signs*, Vol. 6, No. 4, (Summer 1981), pp. 602–16.
32 Ushioda, 'Fukuda Hideko and the Women's World'; Sievers, *Flowers in Salt*, Chapter 6.
33 *Warawa no Hanseigai*, pp. 28–9; pp. 35–8; pp. 61–2.
34 *Warawa no Hanseigai*, pp. 94–5.
35 *Warawa no Hanseigai*, pp. 38–40; translated in Hane, *Reflections on the Way to the Gallows*, pp. 38–9.
36 Hane, *Reflections on the Way to the Gallows*, p. 39.
37 *Warawa no Hanseigai*, p. 17. See also *Warawa no Hanseigai*, p. 43
38 *Warawa no Hanseigai*, p. 44.
39 *Warawa no Hanseigai*, p. 26.
40 cf. Her account of joining her comrades at a tea house: *Warawa no Hanseigai*, p. 33.
41 *Warawa no Hanseigai*, p. 20.
42 An example of Meiji writings on popular rebellions is Komuro Shinsuke, *Tōyō Minken Hyakka Den*, [1883], edited by Hayashi Motoi, Tokyo: Iwanami Shoten, 1957. For discussion of the representation of women in peasant uprisings, see Anne Walthall, 'Devoted Wives/Unruly Women: Invisible Presence in the History of Japanese Social Protest', in Barbara Laslett, et al. (eds), *Rethinking the Political: Gender, Resistance and the State*, Chicago: University of Chicago Press, 1995, pp. 282–312; for translated accounts of women in peasant uprisings, see Anne Walthall, *Peasant Uprisings in Japan: A Critical Anthology of Peasant Histories*, Chicago: University of Chicago Press, 1991.
43 For a discussion of anarchist Kōtoku Shūsui's identification with the *shishi* ideal, see F. G. Notehelfer, *Kōtoku Shūsui: Portrait of a Japanese Radical*, Cambridge: Cambridge University Press, 1971, pp. 27–30; for a discussion of the influence of the *shishi* on theorist Kawakami Hajime, see Gail Lee Bernstein, *Japanese Marxist: A Portrait of Kawakami Hajime 1879–1946*, Cambridge, Massachusetts: Harvard Council on East Asian Studies, 1990 edn, pp. 167–73.
44 The invocation of the figure of Joan of Arc is explored in more detail in Mackie, 'In a Woman's Body'.
45 *Warawa no Hanseigai*, pp. 20–4. For more detail of the Ōsaka Incident, see Jansen, 'Ōi Kentarō', pp. 305–16.

46 *Warawa no Hanseigai*, p. 12.
47 *Warawa no Hanseigai*, pp. 94–6. Freda Freiberg has analysed a similar sense of symmetry in the 'rhyming' scenes of sisterhood which open and close Mizoguchi's fictionalised film of Fukuda's early life, *Waga Koi wa Moenu*. Freda Freiberg, 'Tales of Kageyama', *East–West Film Journal*, Vol. 6, No. 1, 1992.
48 By 'tradition', I am thinking of the concept of tradition employed by Hobsbawm and others, whereby tradition is seen not as something timeless and unchanging, but as something which is constantly reinvented and reconstituted, both by dominant groups and by those taking an oppositional stance. See Eric Hobsbawm and Terence Ranger (eds), *The Invention of Tradition*, Cambridge: Cambridge University Press, 1983; and the discussion of 'tradition' in Stuart Hall, 'Notes on Deconstructing "The Popular" ', in Raphael Samuel (ed.), *People's History and Socialist Theory*, London: Routledge & Kegan Paul, 1981, pp. 227–40. On the beginnings of a tradition of feminism in Japan, see Sievers, *Flowers in Salt*.
49 Other feminist activists refer to reading Fukuda's autobiography: cf. Nishikawa, *Heiminsha no Onna*, p. 184. Fukuda was invited to contribute to the Bluestocking journal in 1913 (see Chapter four in this book), and her death in 1927 was marked in the suffragists' journal *Fusen*, which published extracts of her autobiography.
50 Takamure Itsue, *Josei no Rekishi*, Tokyo: Kōdansha Bunko, 1972, 2 volumes; Joyce Ackroyd, 'Women in Feudal Japan', *Transactions of the Asiatic Society of Japan*, Vol. 7, No. 3, 1959, pp. 31–68; Haruko Wakita, 'Marriage and Property in Pre-modern Japan from the Perspective of Women's History', *Journal of Japanese Studies*, (Winter 1984), pp. 73–100; Hitomi Tonomura, 'Women and Inheritance in Japan's Early Warrior Society', *Comparative Studies in Society and History*, 1990, pp. 592–623.
51 Yōzō Watanabe, 'The Family and the Law: The Individualistic Premise in Modern Japanese Family Law', in Arthur Taylor von Mehren (ed.), *Law in Japan*, Cambridge, Massachusetts: Harvard University Press, 1963; Ryōsuke Ishii, *Japanese Legislation in the Meiji Era*, Tokyo: Pan-Pacific Press, The Centenary Culture Council, 1958, pp. 574–92.
52 Takamure Itsue, *Josei no Rekishi*, Vol. 2, pp. 79–83.
53 Inoue Kiyoshi, *Nihon Joseishi*, Tokyo: San'Ichi Shobō, 1967 [revised edn], pp. 202–13; E. P. Tsurumi, *Factory Girls: Women in the Thread Mills of Meiji Japan*, Princeton, New Jersey: Princeton University Press, 1990.
54 An important source of information on the earliest mills is Wada Ei's *Tomioka Nikki* (Tokyo: Kōdansha Bunko, 1976). See also Janet Hunter, 'Labour in the Japanese Silk Industry in the 1870s: The Tomioka Nikki of Wada Ei', in Gordon Daniels (ed.), *Europe Interprets Japan*, Tenterden, Kent: Paul Norbury Publications, pp. 20–5.
55 Two surveys of socialism in Japan before the Second World War (from radically different perspectives) are George Totten's *The Social Democratic Movement in Prewar Japan*, (New Haven: Yale University Press, 1966) and John Crump's *The Origins of Socialist Thought in Japan*. Studies of the labour movement include: S. S. Large, *The Rise of Labour in Japan: The Yūaikai 1912–1919*, Tokyo: Sophia University Press, 1972; S. S. Large, *Organized Workers and Socialist Politics in Interwar Japan*, Cambridge: Cambridge University Press, 1981; Andrew Gordon, *The Evolution of Labour Relations in Japan, Heavy Industry 1853–1955*, Cambridge, Massachusetts: Harvard University Press, 1985; Andrew Gordon, *Labor and Imperial Democracy in Prewar Japan*, Berkeley: University of California Press, 1991; Sheldon Garon, *The State and Labour in Modern Japan*, Berkeley: University of California Press, 1988. There have also been several studies of male individuals involved in the early development of labour and socialist politics in Japan, including: Atsuko Hirai, *Individualism and Socialism: The Life and Thought of Kawai Eijirō (1891–1944)*, Cambridge, Massachusetts: Harvard Council on East Asian Studies, 1986; Hyman Kublin, *Asian Revolutionary: The Life of Sen Katayama*, Princeton, New Jersey: Princeton University Press, 1964; F. G. Notehelfer, *Kōtoku Shūsui: Portrait of A Japanese Radical*, Cambridge: Cambridge University Press, 1971; Stephen S. Large, 'Revolutionary Worker: Watanabe Masanosuke and the Japanese Communist Party, 1922–1928', *Asian Profile*, Vol. 3, No. 4, August 1975, pp. 371–90; Gail Lee Bernstein, *Japanese Marxist: A Portrait of Kawakami Hajime 1879–1946*, Cambridge, Massachusetts: Harvard University Press, 1978; Germaine Hoston, 'Marxism

and National Socialism in Taishō Japan: The Thought of Takabatake Motoyuki', *Journal of Asian Studies*, Vol. XLIV, No. 1, November 1984, pp. 43–64; Germaine Hoston, 'Marxism and Japanese Expansionism: Takahashi Kamekichi and the Theory of "Petty Imperialism" ', *Journal of Japanese Studies*, Vol. 10, No. 1, pp. 1–30; Stephen E. Marsland, *The Birth of the Japanese Labour Movement: Takano Fusatarō and the Rōdō Kumiai Kiseikai*, Honolulu: University of Hawaii Press, 1989; Miriam Silverberg, *Changing Song: The Marxist Manifestos of Nakano Shigeharu*, Princeton, New Jersey: Princeton University Press, 1990. Particular aspects of Marxist thought are discussed in George Beckmann and Genji Ōkubo, *The Japanese Communist Party 1922–1945*, Stanford: Stanford University Press, 1969; John Dower, 'E. H. Norman, Japan and the Uses of History', in E. H. Norman, *The Origins of the Modern Japanese State*, New York: Pantheon Asia Library, 1975, John Dower (ed.), pp. 3–101; Tessa Morris-Suzuki, *A History of Japanese Economic Thought*, London: Routledge, 1989; and Germaine Hoston, *Marxism and the Crisis of Development in Prewar Japan*, Princeton, New Jersey: Princeton University Press, 1986.

56 Several writers use the label 'imperial Japan' to refer to the period from 1890 (the date when the Meiji Constitution became effective) to 1945. See Thomas Stanley's discussion of alternative periodizations of modern Japanese history. Thomas A. Stanley, 'Periodization in Modern Japanese History', *ASAA Review*, Vol. 10, No. 3, April 1987, pp. 101–5.

57 Large, *The Rise of Labour*; Large, *Organized Labour and Socialist Politics in Interwar Japan*.

58 Totten, *The Social Democratic Movement in Prewar Japan*.

59 Gordon, *The Evolution of Labour Relations in Japan*; Gordon, *Labour and Imperial Democracy in Prewar Japan*.

60 Roger Bowen, *Rebellion and Democracy in Meiji Japan*, University of California Press, 1980.

61 cf. Totten, *The Social Democratic Movement*, p. 23: '. . . those who worked in the various crafts, such as sawyers, held on to exclusive guild traditions, while the mass of women and children in textiles *hardly constituted much of a base for building trade unionism.*' [emphasis added].

62 Dorothy Robins-Mowry, *The Hidden Sun: Women of Modern Japan*, Boulder, Colorado: Westview Press, 1983, p. 38.

63 Suzuki Yūko, 'Shakai Undō Shi no Naka no Josei', *Dai Nikai Yamakawa Kikue Kinen Fujin Mondai Kenkyū Shōreikin Zōteishiki Kiroku*, Tokyo: Yamakawa Kikue Kinenkai, 1983, pp. 24–36. Suzuki herself has contributed to a re-evaluation of the participation of women in the labour and socialist movements through her own writings and analysis and by making the fruits of her research available to other researchers in the form of collections of documents and oral history interviews. See in particular, Suzuki Yūko, *Josei to Rōdō Kumiai*, Tokyo: Renga Shobō, 1991; Suzuki Yūko, *Jokō to Rōdō Sōgi*, Tokyo: Renga Shobō, 1989; Suzuki Yūko (ed.), *Shiryō: Heiminsha no Onnatachi*.

64 Yasue Aoki Kidd, *Women Workers in the Japanese Cotton Mills 1880–1920*, Cornell University East Asian Papers, 1978; Sievers, *Flowers in Salt*, Chapter 4; Tsurumi, *Factory Girls: Women in the Thread Mills of Meiji Japan*, Tsurumi, E. P.,'Female Textile Workers and the Failure of Early Trade Unionism in Japan', *History Workshop Journal*, No. 18, (Autumn, 1984).

65 Hosoi Wakizō, *Jokō Aishi*, Tokyo: 1925 (Reprinted by: Iwanami Shoten, 1954); Katayama Sen, *Nihon no Rōdō Undō*, Tokyo: Iwanami Shoten, 1952; Yokoyama Gennosuke, *Nihon no Kasō Shakai*, Tokyo: 1899 (Reprinted by: Iwanami Shoten, 1949).

66 Nancy Andrew, 'The Seitōsha: An Early Japanese Women's Organization, 1911–1916', in Albert Craig (ed.), *Papers on Japan*, Cambridge, Massachusetts: Harvard University Press, 1972; Noriko Mizuta Lippit, 'Seitō and the Literary Roots of Japanese Feminism', *International Journal of Women's Studies*, Vol. 2, No. 2, 1975, pp. 155–63; Pauline Reich and Atsuko Fukuda, 'Japan's Literary Feminists', *Signs*, Vol. 2, No. 1, (Autumn 1976).

67 Dee Ann Vavich, 'The Japanese Women's Movement: Ichikawa Fusae, Pioneer in Women's Suffrage', *Monumenta Nipponica*, Vol. XXII, Nos 3–4, 1967, pp. 402–36; Miyamoto, Ken, 'Itō Noe and the Bluestockings', *Japan Interpreter*, Vol. 10, No. 2, (Autumn 1975), pp. 190–204; S. Goldstein, and S. Shinoda, *Tangled Hair*, Lafayette, 1971;

Laurel Rasplica Rodd, 'Yosano Akiko and the Taishō Debate over the "New Woman" ', in Bernstein (ed.), *Creating Japanese Women*, pp. 175–98.

68 There was an expansion of left-identified political parties after the granting of universal male suffrage in 1925. That is, all males over the age of twenty-five could vote without property qualifications. Totten, *The Social Democratic Movement*, p. 360.

69 Inoue, *Nihon Josei Shi.*

70 Takamure Itsue, *Takamure Itsue Zenshū*, Tokyo: Rironsha, 1966–1967, Hashimoto Kenzō (ed.), 10 Vols.

71 Such publishers as Domesu Shuppan and Fuji Shuppan have released collections of documents and facsimile editions of early women's publications, while other researchers have been engaged in oral history projects among women activists in the early labour, socialist, and feminist movements. The present study would not have been possible without the ground-breaking work of these Japanese researchers.

72 The few notable pioneering exceptions include: Mary Beard, *Woman as Force in Japanese History*, Washington, DC: Public Affairs Press, 1953; Alice Mabel Bacon, *Japanese Girls and Women*, Boston: Houghton Mifflin, 1902; and Ackroyd, 'Women in Feudal Japan'.

73 cf. Rey Chow's discussion of the representation of Chinese women as 'case studies' in academic discourse: 'Violence in the Other Country: China as Crisis, Spectacle, and Woman', in Chandra Talpade Mohanty, et al. (eds), *Third World Women and the Politics of Feminism*, Bloomington: Indiana University Press, 1991, pp. 81–100.

74 For a discussion of the problems involved in describing 'women' as a trans-historical category divorced from specific circumstances, see Denise Riley, *Am I That Name? Feminism and the Category of 'Women' in History*, London: Macmillan, 1988.

75 Joyce Lebra, et al. (eds), *Women in Changing Japan*, Berkeley: University of California Press, 1976; Robins-Mowry, *The Hidden Sun: Women of Modern Japan*, Takie Sugiyama Lebra, *Japanese Women: Constraint and Fulfilment*, Honolulu: University of Hawaii Press, 1984; Ann Nakano, *Japanese Women: A Century of Living History*, Adelaide: Rigby, 1986.

76 Susan J. Pharr, *Political Women in Japan*, Berkeley: University of California Press, 1981; Alice Cook and Hiroko Hayashi, *Working Women in Japan: Discrimination, Resistance and Reform*, Cornell: Cornell University Press, 1980; Mary Saso, *Women in the Japanese Workplace*, London: Hilary Shipman, 1990; E. P. Tsurumi, *Factory Girls: Women in the Thread Mills of Meiji Japan*, Princeton, New Jersey: Princeton University Press, 1990; Janet Hunter (ed.), *Japanese Women Working*, London: Routledge, 1993.

77 Vavich, 'The Japanese Women's Movement: Ichikawa Fusae, Pioneer in Women's Suffrage'; Hélène Bowen, 'Victims as Victors, Life as Death: Representation and Empowerment in the Works of Kanno Suga and Kaneko Fumiko', Unpublished PhD Thesis, La Trobe University, 1992; Miyamoto, 'Itō Noe and the Bluestockings'; Goldstein and Shinoda, *Tangled Hair*; Rodd, 'Yosano Akiko and the Taishō Debate over the "New Woman" ' Tomoko Yamazaki, *Yamada Waka: From Prostitute to Feminist Pioneer*, Tokyo: Kōdansha International, 1985; Sievers, 'Feminist Criticism in Japanese Politics in the 1880s: The Experience of Kishida Toshiko'; Jennifer Shapcott, 'The Red Chrysanthemum: Yamakawa Kikue and the Socialist Women's Movement in Pre-War Japan', *Papers on Far Eastern History*, No. 35, March 1987, pp. 1–30.

78 Ushioda, 'Women and War in Meiji Japan: The Case Of Fukuda Hideko'; Ushioda, 'Fukuda Hideko and the Women's World of Meiji Japan'.

79 Sievers, *Flowers in Salt*, Chapter 6.

80 Hane, *Reflections on the Way to the Gallows.*

81 Large, 'The Romance of Revolution in Japanese Anarchism and Communism During the Taishō Period'.

82 E. P. Tsurumi, 'Feminism and Anarchism in Japan: Takamure Itsue, 1894–1964' *Bulletin of Concerned Asian Scholars*, Vol. 17, No. 2, April–June 1985, pp. 2–19.

83 cf. Gary Saxonhouse, 'Country Girls and Communications among Competitors in the Japanese Cotton Spinning Industry', in Hugh Patrick (ed.), *Japanese Industrialization and its Social Consequences*, Berkeley: University of California Press, 1976, pp. 97–125.

84 On related questions in the Taishō period, see: Barbara Molony, 'Activism among

Women in the Taishō Cotton Industry', in Bernstein (ed.), *Recreating Japanese Women, 1600–1945*, pp. 217–38.

85 Anna Davin, 'Women and History', in Michelene Wandor (ed.), *The Body Politic: Women's Liberation in Britain*, London: Stage 1, 1972, p. 217.

86 Sally Alexander and Anna Davin, 'Feminist History', *History Workshop*, Vol. 1, No. 1, (Spring 1976).

87 Sally Alexander, 'Women, Class and Sexual Differences in the 1830s and 1840s: Some Reflections on the Writing of a Feminist History', *History Workshop*, No. 17, (Spring 1984), p. 127.

88 Joan Wallach Scott, *Gender and the Politics of History*, New York: Columbia University Press, 1988, p. 48.

89 This problem was formulated in the following terms by E. H. Carr in 1961: 'Here I should say something about the role of the rebel or dissident in history. To set up the popular picture of the individual in revolt against society is to reintroduce the false antithesis between society and the individual. No society is fully homogeneous. Every society is an arena of social conflicts, and those individuals who range themselves against existing authority are no less products and reflexions of the society than those who uphold it . . .' E. H. Carr, *What is History?*, Harmondsworth: Pelican, 1961, p. 52.

90 Subjectivity has been defined by Lieven, as follows: ' "Subjectivity" is the general term for all of those attributes (intentionality, desire, awareness, etc.) which make us human "subjects" – i.e., "individuals", whose existence is bound up with that of our human bodies, and who reflect on ourselves as living among others. Materialist theories of subjectivity are opposed to the notion of a "transcendental" subject, an individuality which somehow pre-exists social relations, or exists independently of them; rather, subjectivity is socially constructed, it changes historically as societies change, and is always being reconstructed.' E. Lieven, 'Subjectivity, Materialism, and Patriarchy', in Cambridge Women's Studies Group, *Women in Society*, London: Virago, 1981, p. 257.

91 Alexander, 'Women, Class and Sexual Differences', p. 132.

92 Chandra Talpade Mohanty, 'Cartographies of Struggle: Third World Women and the Politics of Feminism', in Mohanty, et al. (eds), *Third World Women and the Politics of Feminism*; Zathia Pathak and Rajeswari Sunder Rajan, 'Shahbano', in Judith Butler and Joan W. Scott (eds), *Feminists Theorize the Political*, New York: Routledge, 1992, pp. 257–79; Rajeswari Sunder Rajan, *Real and Imagined Women: Gender, Culture and Postcolonialism*, London: Routledge, 1993.

93 Mohanty draws on Benedict Anderson's notion of an 'imagined community'. While Anderson was, of course, referring to the modern construct of the nation, Mohanty uses this concept to refer to feminism as an 'imagined community' of women united in a common struggle. She also refers to the concept of 'communities of resistance', in an attempt to go beyond individualist notions of agency. Mohanty, 'Cartographies of Struggle', pp. 4–5.

94 'The relations of power I am referring to are not reducible to binary oppositions or oppressor/oppressed relations. I want to suggest that it is possible to retain the idea of multiple, fluid structures of domination which intersect to locate women differently at particular historical conjunctures, while at the same time insisting on the dynamic oppositional agency of individuals and collectives and their engagement in "daily life". It is this focus on dynamic oppositional agency that clarifies the intricate connection between systemic relationships and the directionality of power . . . However, systems of domination operate through the setting up of (in Dorothy Smith's terms) particular, historically specific "relations of ruling" (Smith, 1987, p. 2). It is at the intersections of these relations of ruling that . . . feminist struggles are positioned. It is also by understanding these intersections that we can attempt to explore questions of consciousness and agency without naturalizing either individuals or structures.' Mohanty, 'Cartographies of Struggle'; p. 13; citing Dorothy Smith, *The Everyday World as Problematic: A Feminist Sociology*, Boston: Northeastern University Press, 1987; p. 2.

95 Mohanty, 'Cartographies of Struggle'; p. 34.

96 Mohanty, 'Cartographies of Struggle'; pp. 35–6.

97 Mohanty, 'Cartographies of Struggle'; p. 21.

98 My definition of activism differs from that employed by Barbara Molony in her article on 'activism' in the Taishō cotton industry. Molony defines activism as 'the opposite of passivity', a definition which seems unnecessarily broad, particularly as the term 'agency' can be used to denote an individual's control over his or her own circumstances. I prefer to reserve the term activism to describe women's attempts to transform their situation through collective action. I argue that for women to see themselves as workers was a necessary first step in women's transformation into activists. It was also necessary for others to recognise women as workers before they could be recognised as potential comrades in collective action. cf. Barbara Molony, 'Activism among Women in the Taishō Cotton Industry', p. 218. For other attempts to define the possibilities for women's collective action, see several chapters in Laslett, et al. (eds), *Rethinking the Political: Gender, Resistance and the State*, in particular the chapter by Louise Tilly.

99 cf. Griselda Pollock, 'Feminism/Foucault – Surveillance/Sexuality', in Norman Bryson, Michael Ann Holly and Keith Moxey (eds), *Visual Culture: Images and Interpretations*, Hanover and London: Wesleyan University Press, 1994, p. 13; and p. 3: 'While investigating the possible ways to theorize about the inevitable relations that exist between the social formation and specific representations that are our domain of study in art history, for instance, we could do well to consider the "cultural" as a space of representation, shaped by social forces that are specifically articulated in modes peculiar to the cultural sphere. Instead, therefore, of deriving meaning for culture from some other source – from the social or the economic – we attend to the ways in which such forces are enacted, performed, staged, and articulated in these specific practices of representation, to how these forces effectively constitute the relations they articulate. There is thus no prior place in which the meanings of cultural forms are made, which art then expresses, replicates, defers to. The cultural is actively producing meaning by its own social, semiotic, and symbolic procedures and imperatives. These meanings are materially constituted in discourses and practices – the technologies of class, to borrow a phrase from Foucault.'

100 Lynda Nead, *Myths of Sexuality: Representations of Women in Victorian Britain*, Oxford: Basil Blackwell, 1988, p. 4.

101 cf. Helen Carr (ed.), *From My Guy to Sci-Fi: Genre and Women's Writing in the Postmodern World*; Anne Cranny-Francis, *Feminist Fiction: Feminist Uses of Generic Fiction*, Cambridge: Polity Press, 1990.

102 These archives include the Ōhara Social Research Institute at Hōsei University, the Women's Suffrage Centre, Tokyo University's Meiji Newspaper and Magazine Collection, and the Ōya Sōichi Library.

103 Sheila Rowbotham, *Women, Resistance and Revolution*, London: Allen Lane, 1972; Sheila Rowbotham, et al., *Beyond the Fragments: Feminism and the Making of Socialism*, London: Merlin Press, 1979; Barbara Taylor, *Eve and the New Jerusalem*, London: Virago, 1984; Mandy Leveratt, 'Feminism and Socialism in England 1883–1900', *Lilith*, No. 2, Winter 1985, pp. 6–29.

104 Charles Sowerwine, *Sisters or Citizens? Women and Socialism in France Since 1876*, Cambridge: Cambridge University Press, 1982.

105 Marilyn Boxer and Jean Quataert (eds), *Socialist Women: European Socialist Feminism in the Nineteenth Century*, New York: Elsevier North-Holland, 1978; Jane Slaughter and Robert Kern (eds), *European Women on the Left: Socialism, Feminism, and the Problems Faced by Political Women, 1880 to the Present*, Westport, Connecticut: Greenwood Press, 1981; Jean Quataert, *Reluctant Feminists in German Social Democracy, 1885–1917*, Princeton, New Jersey: Princeton University Press, 1979; Renate Pore, *A Conflict of Interest: Women in German Social Democracy, 1919–1933*, Westport, Connecticut: Greenwood Press, 1981; Richard Evans, *Comrades and Sisters: Feminism, Socialism, and Pacifism in Europe, 1870–1945*, Brighton, Sussex: Wheatsheaf Books, 1987; Sonia Kruks, et al. (eds), *Promissory Notes: Women in the Transition to Socialism*, New York: Monthly Review Press, 1989.

106 Joy Damousi, *Women Come Rally: Socialism, Communism and Gender in Australia, 1890–1955*, Melbourne: Oxford University Press, 1994; Patricia Grimshaw, 'The

"Equals and Comrades of Men"?: *Tocsin* and "the Woman Question"', in Susan Magarey, et al. (eds), *Debutante Nation: Feminism Contests the 1890s'*, Sydney: Allen & Unwin, 1993, pp. 100–13.

107 cf. Sheila Rowbotham, *Hidden From History*, London: Pluto Press, 1973.

2 Imperial Subjects

1 The relevant regulations are translated in: W. W. McLaren, (ed.), 'Japanese Government Documents', *Transactions of the Asiatic Society of Japan*, Vol. LXII, Part II, 1914, pp. 529–57: *Tosho Kaihan no Kitei* (Regulations Governing the Publication of Books), 1869; *Shuppan Jōrei* (Book and Press Regulations) 1869; Newspaper Regulations 1873; Newspaper Press Law, 1875; Newspaper Regulations, 1887; Publication Regulations, 1887.

2 For details of Mori's life and thought, see Ivan Hall, *Mori Arinori*, Cambridge: Cambridge University Press, 1971, *passim*. For an account of the founding of the Meirokusha, see David Huish, 'Meiroku Zasshi: Some Grounds for Reassessment', *Harvard Journal of Asiatic Studies*, Vol. 32, 1972; pp. 208–29; The full text of the journal is translated by William Braisted, *Meiroku Zasshi: Journal of the Japanese Enlightenment*, Cambridge, Massachusetts: Harvard University Press, 1976. The *Meiroku Zasshi* writings on women have also been surveyed by Sievers, *Flowers in Salt*, pp. 16–25.

3 Bowen, *Rebellion and Democracy*, p. 5.

4 For a discussion of the early Meiji discussions of concubinage and other legal policies concerning sexuality, see Hayakawa Noriyo, 'Sexuality and the State: The Early Meiji Debate on Concubinage and Prostitution', in Vera Mackie (ed.), *Feminism and the State in Modern Japan*, Melbourne: Japanese Studies Centre, 1995, pp. 31–40.

5 Mitsuda Kyōko, 'Kindaiteki Boseikan no Juyō to Henkei: Kyōiku suru Haha kara Ryōsai Kenbo e', in Wakita Haruko (ed.), *Bosei o Tou: Rekishiteki Henkō*, Tokyo: Jinbun Shoin, 1985, Vol. 2, pp. 107–8.

6 It has been pointed out that almost all of the *Meirokusha* members had studied Confucianism as well as 'Western learning'. For details of individual members of the *Meirokusha*, see Braisted, *Meiroku Zasshi*, pp. xxiii–xxxiii, and Kōsaka Masaaki, *Japanese Thought in the Meiji Era*, Tokyo: Pan-Pacific Press, 1958, pp. 85–133.

7 Mori Arinori, 'Saishōron', *Meiroku Zasshi*, No. 15, November 1874, in Maruoka Hideko (ed.), *Nihon Fujin Mondai Shiryō Shūsei*, Tokyo: Domesu Shuppan, 1977, Vol. 8, pp. 73–7; and translated in Braisted', *Meiroku Zasshi*, pp. 189–91.

8 Sakatani Shiroshi 'Shōsetsu no utagai', *Meiroku Zasshi*, No. 32, March 1875; translated in Braisted, *Meiroku Zasshi*, pp. 392–9.

9 Sievers, *Flowers in Salt*, p. 22.

10 Nakamura Masanao, 'Zenryō naru haha o tsukuru setsu', *Meiroku Zasshi*, March 1875, No. 33, in *Nihon Fujin Mondai Shiryō Shūsei*, Vol. 15, pp. 348–50; and translated in Braisted, *Meiroku Zasshi*, pp. 401–4.

11 Mori Arinori, 'Saishōron', *Meiroku Zasshi*, No. 32, 1875; translated in Braisted, *Meiroku Zasshi*, p. 399.

12 Katō Hiroyuki, 'Fūfu Dōken no Ryūhei ron', *Meiroku Zasshi*, No. 31, March 1875; in *Nihon Fujin Mondai Shiryō Shūsei*, Vol. 8, pp. 77–9; and translated in Braisted, *Meiroku Zasshi*, pp. 376–7.

13 Fukuzawa Yukichi, 'Danjo Dōsū Ron', *Meiroku Zasshi*, March 1875, No. 31; in *Nihon Fujin Mondai Shiryō Shūsei*, Vol. 8, p. 79; quoted in Sievers, *Flowers in Salt*, p. 21. For discussion of Fukuzawa's life and thought, see Blacker, *The Japanese Enlightenment*.

14 Fukuzawa Yukichi, *Gakumon no Susume*, cited in Blacker, *The Japanese Enlightenment*, p. 69.

15 As a challenge to the dominance of such writings as Confucian Scholar Kaibara Ekken's *Onna Daigaku (Greater Learning for Women)*, Fukuzawa penned: *Nihon Fujin Ron (On Japanese Women)* and *Hinkōron* in 1885; *Danjo Kōsai Ron (On Relations Between Men and Women)* in 1886; *Onna Daigaku Hyōron (A Critique of Greater Learning for Women)* and *Shin Onna Daigaku (The New Greater Learning for Women)* in 1899. For

discussion of these writings, see Blacker, *The Japanese Enlightenment,* pp. 67–89; Sievers, *Flowers in Salt,* pp. 18–25; Kiyooka Eiichi, *Fukuzawa Yukichi on Japanese Women: Selected Writings,* Tokyo: University of Tokyo Press, 1988.

16 As most of the contributors to the *Meiroku Zasshi,* with the notable exception of Fukuzawa Yukichi, were public servants and bureaucrats, they were in a position to influence and even implement government policy. Mori Arinori, for example, was to serve as Minister for Education; Nishimura Shigeki was appointed Chief of the Compilation Section of the Ministry of Education in 1873 and lectured on Western Books to the Meiji Emperor. Katō Hiroyuki, Tsuda Mamichi and Nishi Amane also held government positions. Hall, *Mori Arinori;* Blacker, *The Japanese Enlightenment,* p. 32.

17 McLaren, 'Japanese Government Documents', p. 427: 'It is impossible to print all the memorials which were sent in to the government between 1874 and 1881, petitioning for the establishment of a National Assembly. In the first nine months of 1880 no less than thirty petitions were received by the *Genrō-in,* of which twenty-three were forwarded to the Council of State for consideration . . . The expression of the public mind on the subject was not by any means confined to petitions and memorials, but after 1877 found its way into the press to an extent which is surprising.'

18 The Charter Oath was proclaimed in the name of the Emperor Meiji in April 1868. The following general principles were stated in the oath: 'By this oath we set up as our aim the establishment of the national weal on a broad basis and the framing of a constitution and laws. 1 Deliberative assemblies shall be widely established and all matters decided by public discussion. 2 All classes shall unite in vigorously carrying out the administration of affairs of state. 3 The common people, no less than the civil and military officials, shall each be allowed to pursue his own calling so that there may be no discontent. 4 Evil customs of the past shall be broken off and everything based upon the just laws of nature. 5 Knowledge shall be sought throughout the world so as to strengthen the foundations of imperial rule.' Translated in Ryūsaku Tsunoda, et al., *Sources of Japanese Tradition,* New York: Columbia University Press, 1964; Vol. II, p. 137.

19 Roger Bowen has discussed the participation of commoners in the Freedom and Popular Rights Movement, and the efforts made to disseminate liberal ideas through political societies, discussion groups, study groups, and the composition of songs on the theme of popular rights. Bowen, *Rebellion and Democracy in Meiji Japan,* p. 179.

20 Totten, *The Social Democratic Movement in Prewar Japan,* p. 18.

21 Karen Offen, 'Liberty, Equality and Justice for Women: The Theory and Practice of Feminism in 19th Century Europe', in Renate Bridenthal, et al. (eds), *Becoming Visible: Women in European History,* Boston: Houghton Mifflin, 1987, 2nd edn, p. 336.

22 Bowen, *Rebellion and Democracy in Meiji Japan;* pp. 180–5; Richard Evans, *The Feminists,* Croom Helm: London, 1977; pp. 13–39; Taylor, *Eve and the New Jerusalem,* pp. 1–18. In recent feminist writing it has been argued that the exclusion of women from early liberal discourse was more than an oversight. Rather, patriarchal values form the very basis of liberal discourse. See Carole Pateman, *The Sexual Contract,* London: Polity Press, 1988, *passim.*

23 Bowen, *Rebellion and Democracy in Meiji Japan;* pp. 120–1: 'The free rural market of late Tokugawa, Smith shows, likewise demonstrated such aspects of capitalistic society as occupational migration and mobility; employment contracts; competitive hiring practices; competition to secure adequate supplies of raw materials; a small-producer hatred of government-supported monopolies; the concentration of wealth and political power in the hands of large landholders; and wide-scale commercial farming . . . "Such men were far from being peasants with an abacus," Smith writes. Instead, "we find them in conflict with government over its intervention in local affairs, in matters concerning village common land, irrigation rights and the selection of headmen . . ." Local political autonomy, "a more open system above," and unrestricted rights of commerce were the "liberties" *demanded* by the rural beneficiaries

of the expansion of the market economy.' cf. T. C. Smith, *The Agrarian Origins of Modern Japan*, Stanford: Stanford University Press, 1959.

24 For discussion of peasant rebellions during the Tokugawa period, see Stephen Vlastos, *Peasant Protests and Uprisings in Tokugawa Japan*, Berkeley: University of California Press, 1986; Herbert Bix, *Peasant Protest in Japan: 1590–1884*, New Haven: Yale University Press, 1986; Walthall, *Peasant Uprisings in Japan: A Critical Anthology of Peasant Histories*. Roger Bowen, in *Rebellion and Democracy in Meiji Japan*, discusses the participation of commoners in some early Meiji rebellions which drew on the notions of 'freedom and popular rights'.

25 Bowen, *Rebellion and Democracy in Meiji Japan*, pp. 116–25.

26 On the reception of Herbert Spencer's ideas in Japan, see Yamashita Shigekazu, 'Herbert Spencer and Meiji Japan', in Hilary Conroy, et al. (eds), *Japan in Transition: Thought and Action in the Meiji Era, 1868–1912*, Cranbery, New Jersey: Associated University Presses, 1984; pp. 77–95; on the reception of other liberal thinkers, see J. Pittau, *Political Thought in Early Meiji Japan 1868–1889*, Cambridge, Massachusetts: Harvard University Press, 1967, p. 112; Sievers, *Flowers in Salt*, p. 16.

27 Bowen, *Rebellion and Democracy in Meiji Japan*, p. 109: 'Common to most of these [petitions to the government] was a notion of natural right that would have as its positive expression the institutions of self-government, local autonomy, and the equality of the classes.'

28 Bowen, *Rebellion and Democracy in Meiji Japan*, p. 108. See also the work of Irokawa Daikichi, who has researched the regional liberal societies and study groups which were involved in producing alternative draft constitutions on liberal principles: Irokawa Daikichi, 'Freedom and the Concept of People's Rights', *Japan Quarterly*, Vol. XIV, No. 2, April–June 1967, pp. 175–83; Irokawa Daikichi (ed.), *Minshū Kenpō no Sōzō: Uzumoreta Kusa no Ne no Ninmyaku*, Tokyo: Hyōronsha, 1970.

29 Translation of announcement in: Ishii, *Japanese Legislation in the Meiji Era*, pp. 720–1.

30 For discussion of the development of Tokutomi's thought, see K. P. Pyle, *The New Generation in Meiji Japan: Problems of Cultural Identity 1885–1895*, Stanford: Stanford University Press, 1969, pp. 140–1; Takamure Itsue, *Josei no Rekishi*, p. 99; Yamashita Shigekazu, 'Herbert Spencer and Meiji Japan', pp. 81–2; John D. Pierson, 'The Early Liberal Thought of Tokutomi Sohō: Some Problems of Western Social Theory in Meiji Japan', *Monumenta Nipponica*, Vol. XXIX, 1974; pp. 199–224; John D. Pierson, *Tokutomi Sohō 1863–1957: A Journalist for Modern Japan*, Princeton, New Jersey: Princeton University Press, 1980; Chapter IV, pp. 125–51; Kōsaka Masaaki, *Japanese Thought in the Meiji Era*, pp. 201–10.

31 Bowen defines *heiminshugi* in the following terms: 'Heiminshugi, or "commonerism"', was one shorthand characterization of the period used to refer to the ideological and social underpinnings of wide-scale commoner participation in the popular rights movement; democratic populism, perhaps, no less captures the essential meaning.' Bowen, *Rebellion and Democracy in Meiji Japan*, p. 125. For further discussion of the meaning of *heiminshugi*, see Kōsaka, *Japanese Thought in the Meiji Era*, p. 207. Heimin refers to the new 'commoner' class which replaced the old status groups of merchants, peasants and artisans after the Meiji Restoration. The élite of the samurai class retained some privileges under the name of *kizoku* (nobility), while members of the former outcaste class were labelled as *Shin-heimin* or 'New Commoners'.

32 One of the early socialist groups, as I will discuss later, called itself the *Heiminsha* (Commoners' Society), and published a newspaper called the *Heimin Shinbun* (*Commoners' News*). Pyle reports that such socialist pioneers as Kōtoku Shūsui and Sakai Toshihiko described the influence of Tokutomi and the *Kokumin no Tomo* on the development of their political ideas. Pyle, *The New Generation*, p. 47.

33 Nobutaka Ike, *The Beginnings of Political Democracy in Japan*, Baltimore: Johns Hopkins Press, 1950; Donald Keene, 'The Meiji Political Novel', in *Dawn to the West: Japanese Literature of the Modern Era*, New York: Henry Holt and Company, 1984, pp. 76–95; G. T. Shea, *Leftwing Literature in Japan: A Brief History of the Proletarian Literary Movement*, Tokyo: Hōsei University Press, 1964, p. 5.

34 Bowen, *Rebellion and Democracy in Meiji Japan*, pp. 204–5. For a discussion of the ideas of Ueki Emori, see Ienaga Saburō, *Ueki Emori Kenkyū*, Tokyo: Iwanami Shoten, 1960.
35 Bowen, *Rebellion and Democracy in Meiji Japan*, pp. 208–10. For a discussion of alternative draft constitutions, see Pittau, *Political Thought in Early Meiji Japan*, pp. 99–130.
36 Ueki Emori, 'Minken Inaka Uta', in Ienaga Saburō (ed.), *Meiji Bungaku Zenshū 12*, Tokyo: Chikuma Shobō, pp. 128–9; translated in Bowen, *Rebellion and Democracy*, pp. 206–8; see also G. T. Shea, *Leftwing Literature in Japan: A Brief History of the Proletarian Literary Movement*, Tokyo: Hōsei University Press, 1964, p. 6. I have modified Bowen's translation slightly as he uses 'man' and 'men' for the gender-neutral '*hito*' and '*ningen*'. In Shea's translation he has used feminine pronouns for the caged bird.
37 Kusunose Kita, 'Nōzei no Gi ni Tsuki Goshireigan no koto', *Tokyo Nichinichi Shinbun*, 31/1/1879, in *Nihon Fujin Mondai Shiryō Shūsei*, Vol. 8, pp. 102–3; discussed in Maruoka Hideko, *Fujin Shisō Keisei Shi Nōto*, Tokyo: Domesu Shuppan, 1985 edn, Vol. 1, pp. 34–5; Sievers, *Flowers in Salt*, pp. 29–30.
38 Maruoka Hideko, *Fujin Shisō Keisei Shi Nōto*, Vol. 1, pp. 35–41; Itoya Toshio, *Josei Kaihō no Senkushatachi*; Sievers, 'Feminist Criticism in Japanese Politics in the 1880s, pp. 602–16.
39 Sievers, *Flowers in Salt*, p. 41.
40 Sievers, *Flowers in Salt*, p. 34.
41 Itoya Toshio, *Josei Kaihō no Senkushatachi*, pp. 42–4.
42 Takamure Itsue, *Josei no Rekishi*, Vol. 2, pp. 54–5.
43 E. J. Kinmonth, *The Self-Made Man in Meiji Japanese Thought*, Berkeley: University of California Press, 1981; pp. 27–9.
44 'The *gōnō* [wealthy farmer] advocates of Freedom and People's Rights took the ideal of primitive Confucianism to consist in the ideology of the love of Emperors Yao and Shun for the people – the ideology of "dynastic change" which stated that incompetent emperors should abdicate or be replaced, and that the absolutism of the sovereign was not the natural "will of heaven", and also the utopian vision of the simple society in which people live in happy contentment, as the "will of Heaven." The *gōnō* then, by joining this ideology with the revolutionary ideology of Europe and America (the modern doctrine of natural rights) and the doctrine of joint rule by sovereign and people, formed the ideology of Freedom and People's Rights.' Irokawa, 'Freedom and the Concept of People's Rights', p. 181.
45 Andrew Gordon discusses the use of such concepts as *giri* (obligation) by participants in twentieth-century labour disputes, and concludes that 'Japanese cultural values' could 'work to sanction resistance to authority'. Andrew Gordon, *Labour and Imperial Democracy in Prewar Japan*, p. 73.
46 Pittau, *Political Thought in Early Meiji Japan*, p. 233.
47 Nishimura Shigeki, 'An Explanation of Right', *Meiroku Zasshi*, 1875, translated in Braisted, *Meiroku Zasshi*; pp. 510–13. See also Donald Shively, 'Nishimura Shigeki: A Confucian View of Modernization' in Marius Jansen (ed.), *Changing Japanese Attitudes To Modernization*, Princeton, New Jersey: Princeton University Press, 1965, pp. 193–241.
48 Ishii Ryosuke, *Japanese Legislation in the Meiji Era*, p. 579: 'The translation of the French word *droit civil* into Japanese was another special problem, apparently, since it is said that the equivalent Japanese word *minken*, which was created by Mitsukuri, was opposed by members of the first Civil Code Committee on the ground that common people were not entitled to any such thing as rights.'
49 'There were partisans of *minken* (the rights of the people) and partisans of *kokken* (the rights of the state); some emphasised the independence of the individual, and others emphasised the subordination of individual rights in order to maintain national independence.' Katō Shūichi, 'Japanese Writers and Modernization', in Jansen (ed.), *Changing Japanese Attitudes To Modernization*, p. 425.
50 For different nuances of the word *kokumin*, see Carol Gluck, *Japan's Modern Myths*; pp. 48–9, 242–3; Gordon, *Labour and Imperial Democracy*; pp. 17–18, 89–90, 285–290, 311–25.
51 Pittau, *Political Thought in Early Meiji Japan*, p. 129.
52 Ike, *The Beginnings of Political Democracy in Japan*, p. 113.

53 In 1890, the electorate numbered 450 000, or 1.1 per cent of the population. Those who paid 15 yen per annum in direct taxes were enfranchised. Gluck, *Japan's Modern Myths*, p. 67.

54 Andrew Barshay, *State and Intellectual in Japan: The Public Man in Crisis*, Berkeley: University of California Press, 1988, p. 3. Barshay argues that the imbalance in power relations between 'the people' and the bureaucracy is encapsulated in the phrase *kanson minpi* 'revere the officials and despise the people', a phrase originally used to refer to representatives of the feudal bureaucracy, but which also came to be applied to the modern bureaucrats of the Meiji system. For further discussion of *kanson minpi*, see Gluck, *Japan's Modern Myths*, pp. 60–72; pp. 227–46.

55 Hideo Tanaka and Malcolm Smith, *The Japanese Legal System*, Tokyo: University of Tokyo Press, 1976; p. 637.

56 The Constitution of 1890, translation in Tanaka and Smith, *The Japanese Legal System*, pp. 16–24.

57 Tanaka and Smith, *The Japanese Legal System*, p. 631; Nagai Michio, 'Westernisation and Japanisation: the Early Meiji Transformation of Education', in D. Shively (ed.), *Tradition and Modernisation in Japanese Culture*, Princeton, New Jersey: Princeton University Press, 1971; p. 73.

58 Gordon, *Labor and Imperial Democracy in Prewar Japan*, p. 15.

59 Nagai, 'Westernisation and Japanisation: the Early Meiji Transformation of Education', p. 41.

60 Takamure, *Josei no Rekishi*, pp. 67–8. It was not until the early twentieth century that female students' attendance rates passed 90 per cent. Tachi Kaoru quotes the following attendance rates for girls: 1873: approx. 15 per cent; 1888: approx. 28 per cent; 1903: 90 per cent. Tachi Kaoru, 'Ryōsai Kenbo', in Joseigaku Kenkyūkai (eds), *Kōza Joseigaku 1: Onna no Imēji*, Tokyo: Keisō Shobō, 1984, p. 188.

61 Robins-Mowry, *The Hidden Sun*, p. 41.

62 Official translation of the Imperial Rescript on Education reproduced in Gluck, *Japan's Modern Myths*, p. 121. For discussion of the process leading up to the promulgation of the Imperial rescript on Education, see Gluck, *Japan's Modern Myths*, pp. 102–56; Shively, 'Nishimura Shigeki: A Confucian View of Modernization', pp. 193–241.

63 Gluck, *Japan's Modern Myths*, p. 127.

64 Mitsuda Kyōko, 'Kindaiteki Boseikan no Juyō to Henkei', p. 122; Gluck, *Japan's Modern Myths*, pp. 129–32.

65 Tachi Kaoru, 'Ryōsai Kenbo', p. 187.

66 Nagai, 'Westernisation and Japanisation: the Early Meiji Transformation of Education', p. 76.

67 Gluck, *Japan's Modern Myths*, p. 265.

68 Ike, *The Beginnings of Political Democracy in Japan*, pp. 197–8.

69 Watanabe Yōzō, 'The Family and the Law'; Ishii, *Japanese Legislation in the Meiji Era*, pp. 574–92; Tanaka and Smith, *The Japanese Legal System*; Kōsaka, *Japanese Thought in the Meiji Era*, pp. 360–74.

70 Pyle, *The New Generation*, p. 137.

71 Ishii, *Japanese Legislation in the Meiji Era*, p. 591.

72 Ueki Emori, 'Ikanaru minpō o seitei subeki ka', *Kokumin no tomo*, 22/8/1889–2/9/1889, *Nihon Fujin Mondai Shiryō Shūsei*, Vol. 5, pp. 383–7.

73 Hozumi Yatsuka, 'Minpō idete, chūkō horobu', *Hogaku Shinpō*, No. 5, 1891, reprinted in *Nihon Fujin Mondai Shiryō Shūsei*, Vol. 5, pp. 237–39.

74 Benedict Anderson, *Imagined Communities: Reflections on the Origins and Spread of Nationalism*, London: Verso, 1983, p. 19: 'If nation-states are widely conceded to be "new" and "historical", the nations to which they give political expression always loom out of an immemorial past.'

75 Pyle, *The New Generation*, pp. 131–6.

76 Wakita Haruko, 'Marriage and Property in Pre-modern Japan from the Perspective of Women's History', pp. 73–100.

77 Smith, *The Agrarian Origins of Modern Japan*, *passim*.

78 Wakita, 'Marriage and Property in Pre-modern Japan from the Perspective of Women's History'.
79 Gluck, *Japan's Modern Myths*, pp. 258–9.
80 Anderson, *Imagined Communities, passim*.
81 Barshay, *State and Intellectual in Meiji Japan*, p. 4.
82 Regulations for Political Meetings and Associations, 1880; Revised Regulations for Political Meetings and Associations, 1882; Hōan Jōrei (Peace Preservation Ordinance), 1887; Revision of Public Meeting Regulations, 1889; McLaren, 'Japanese Government Documents', pp. 495–505.
83 The Combination Law of 1851 prohibited women from taking part in political meetings or joining political associations in most parts of Germany. Similar legislation was enacted in Austria in 1867. Evans, *The Feminists*, p. 94; p. 105.
84 Sievers, *Flowers in Salt*, p. 51; Sharon H. Nolte and Sally Ann Hastings, 'The Meiji State's Policy Toward Women, 1890–1910', in Bernstein (ed.), *Recreating Japanese Women*, pp. 154–5.
85 Regulations concerning Household Registration were promulgated as early as 1871. Gluck, *Japan's Modern Myths*, p. 187.
86 Ishii, *Japanese Legislation in the Meiji Era*, p. 669.
87 Kazuo Hatoyama and Saburō Sakamoto, 'Japanese Personal Legislation', in Shigenobu Ōkuma (ed.), *Fifty Years of New Japan*, New York: E. P. Dutton, 1909, Vol. 1, p. 278.
88 Ishii, *Japanese Legislation in the Meiji Era*, pp. 685–91.
89 Ishii, *Japanese Legislation in the Meiji Era*, pp. 666–74.
90 For a survey of premodern marriage and divorce practices, see Hatoyama and Sakamoto, 'Japanese Personal Legislation', pp. 251–80.
91 Ishii, *Japanese Legislation in the Meiji Era*, pp. 671–4.
92 Takamure, *Josei no Rekishi*, p. 70; Sievers, *Flowers in Salt*, p. 13.
93 Takamure, *Josei no Rekishi*, p. 71; Braisted, *Meiroku Zasshi*, p. 114.
94 Such a gendering of nationalist discourse is also true of other countries. In India, where nationalist discourse was developed in opposition to Western imperialism, the conflict between 'Eastern' tradition and 'Western' modernity was often framed in gendered terms, and focused on women's role within the family. See the discussion of these issues in Kumari Jayawardena, *Feminism and Nationalism in the Third World*, London: Zed Press, 1986, *passim*; Partha Chatterjee, 'The Nationalist Resolution of the Women's Question', in Kumkum Sangari and Sudesh Vaid (eds), *Recasting Women: Essays in Indian History*, New Brunswick: Rutgers, 1990, pp. 233–53; Dipesh Chakrabarty, 'The Difference-Deferral of (a) Colonial Modernity: Public Debates on Domesticity in British Bengal', *History Workshop Journal*, No. 36, (Autumn 1993), pp. 1–34. For a brief discussion of the role of women as the embodiment of tensions between 'tradition' and 'modernity' in the Japanese context, see Sievers, *Flowers in Salt*, pp. 10–15.
95 The Women's Temperance League was established in 1886 and its journal *Tōkyō Fujin Kyōfū Zasshi* commenced publication in 1888. The Red Cross was established in 1887.
96 Sievers, *Flowers in Salt*, pp. 87–113. Murakami, *Nihon no Fujin Mondai*, pp. 88–90.
97 Several feminist leaders were connected with this school or educated there, including Shimizu Toyoko, Ōtsuka Kanaoko, Nogami Yaeko. Maruoka Hideko, *Fujin Shisō Keisei Shi Nōto*, Vol. 1, p. 45.
98 *Jogaku Zasshi* commenced publication on 20 July 1885. Its first editor was Kondō Kenzō. Iwamoto took over as editor on Kondō's death in 1886. Oka Mitsuo, *Kono Hyakunen no Onnatachi: Jaanarizumu Joseishi*, Tokyo: Shinchō Sensho, 1983, p. 29. For a detailed study of Iwamoto and his editorship of *Jogaku Zasshi*, see Nobeji Kiyoe, *Josei Kaihō Shisō no Genryū: Iwamoto Zenji to Jogaku Zasshi*', Tokyo: Azekura Shobō, 1984, *passim*.
99 For discussion of *Jogaku Zasshi* and *Bungakukai*, see Kōsaka, *Japanese Thought in the Meiji Era*, pp. 261–9. *Bungakukai* appeared from 1893–98.
100 Noguchi, 'Love and Death in the Early Modern Novel', p. 161; Takamure, *Josei no Rekishi*, pp. 76–8.

101 Ueki Emori, 'Minpō jō oyobi sono ta ni okeru fūfu no kenri', *Jogaku Zasshi*, No. 171, in *Nihon Fujin Mondai Shiryō Shūsei*, Vol. 5, pp. 378–1.
102 Hatoyama Kazuo, 'Danjo dōken yori otto no shin'yū ni naru', *Jogaku Zasshi*, No. 115 (facsimile edition: Kyōto: Rinsen Shoten, 1967, 16 volumes); Takamure, *Josei no Rekishi*, p. 84.
103 Kitamura Tōkoku, 'Ensei shika to Josei', *Jogaku Zasshi*, 1892; Noguchi, 'Love and Death in the Early Modern Novel: Japan and America', p. 169.
104 Miki Sukako, 'Meiji no Fujin Zasshi o Tadoru', in Kindai Josei Bunka Shi Kenkyū Kai (eds), *Fujin Zasshi no Yoake*, Tokyo: Taikūsha, 1989, p. 87.
105 Shimizu Toyoko, 'Naze ni joshi wa seidan shūkai ni sancho suru to o yurusarezaru nari', *Jogaku Zasshi*, No. 228, 30 August, 1890; 'Naite Aisuru Shimai ni tsugu', *Jogaku Zasshi*, No. 234, October 11, 1890 (supplement); Iwamoto Zenji, 'Joshi no Seidan Bōchō', *Jogaku Zasshi*, No. 225, 1890.
106 Iwamoto Zenji, 'Shasetsu: Tsutsushimite Chokugo o Haidoku shi Tatematsuru', *Jogaku Zasshi*, No. 238, 8/11/1890; cited in Nobeji, *Josei Kaihō Shisō no Genryū: Iwamoto Zenji to Jogaku Zasshi*, p. 25.
107 Murakami Nobuhiko, 'Fujin Mondai to Fujin Kaihō Undō', *Iwanami Kōza Nihon Rekishi, 18: Kindai*, Tokyo: Iwanami Shinsho, 1972.
108 Noguchi, 'Love and Death in the Early Modern Novel', p. 169.
109 On Higuchi Ichiyō see: Nakamura, *Japanese Fiction in the Meiji Era*, p. 75; Robert Lyons Danly, *In the Shade of Spring Leaves*; Victoria Vernon, *Daughters of the Moon: Wish, Will and Social Constraint in Fiction by Modern Japanese Women*, Berkeley, California: Institute of East Asian Studies, 1988, pp. 35–68.
110 Kinmonth, *The Self-Made Man in Meiji Japanese Thought*, pp. 147–8.
111 Nakamura Mitsuo, *Japanese Fiction in the Meiji Era*, Tokyo: Kokusai Bunka Shinkō kai, 1966; pp. 64–70.
112 Tachi Kaoru, 'Ryōsai Kenbo', pp. 195–6.
113 Takamure, *Josei no Rekishi*, pp. 79–83.
114 It should be added, however, that oppositional groups may also have tried to appropriate the language of Confucianism. cf. Irokawa's discussion of the use of Confucianist concepts in the Freedom and Popular Rights Movement. Irokawa, 'Freedom and the Concept of People's Rights', p. 181.
115 Tachi Kaoru, 'Ryōsai Kenbo', pp. 192–3. The number of women enrolled in higher schools was 286 in 1882, 2363 in 1888, 12 000 in 1900, and 75 000 in 1912.
116 Tachi Kaoru, 'Ryōsai Kenbo', p. 195. I would agree with Tachi's assertion that specific appeals were made to women of different classes, although the familial ideology promoted among young single working women seems somewhat different in content from *ryōsai kenbo* ideology, which was much more relevant to middle- and upper-class women who did not engage in paid work.
117 Nolte and Hastings, 'The Meiji State's Policy Toward Women', pp. 151–6.
118 Nolte and Hastings put forward this point of view in the following (unfortunately unsourced) paragraph: 'Yet the ban on joining political organisations actually suggests a third image of woman, one neither innocent nor rebellious but responsible and authoritative. The ban placed women in the same category as public figures, including military men, public and private school teachers and students, and shrine and temple officers. The grouping implied that women were like civil servants whose political activity would be inappropriate or whose responsibilities so weighty as to preclude their participation. Gradually conservatives inside and outside the government would elaborate on the idea that wives were public figures, veritable officers of the state in its microcosm, the home. Their mission was a noble one that transcended petty partisan politics. Thus, the justification of women's political exclusion was primarily in terms of their home and family duties, and not of their physical, mental, or moral incapacity.' Nolte and Hastings, 'The Meiji State's Policy Toward Women, 1890–1910', p. 156.
119 On the development of concepts of public and private in European bourgeois culture, see Leonore Davidoff and Catherine Hall, *Family Fortunes: Men and Women of the English Middle Class*, London: Hutchinson, 1987; Jean Bethke Elshtain, *Public*

Man: Private Woman, Oxford: Robertson, 1981; Eva Gamarnikow, et al. (eds), *The Public and the Private*, London: Heinemann, 1983; Philippe Ariès, et al., *A History of Private Life*, Cambridge, Massachusetts: The Belknap Press, 5 volumes, 1987–1991.

120 See Barshay's discussion of the development of notions of public and private in Japan. Barshay argues that the concept of 'private' in Japan was opposed to 'public' in the meaning of governmental or official. Unfortunately, Barshay does not elaborate on possible connections between gender relations and the development of concepts of public and private in the Japanese context: Barshay, *State and Intellectual in Japan*.

3 Wives

1 Matsuoka [Nishikawa] Fumiko,'Fujin no honsei to shakai shugi', *Shūkan Heimin Shinbun*, 20/11/1904.

2 Odagiri Susumu, 'Kaidai', in Odagiri (ed.), *Meiji Bungaku Zenshū 84: Meiji Shakai Shugi Bungaku Shū 2*, pp. 416–17; Totten, *The Social Democratic Movement in Prewar Japan*, pp. 16–31.

3 For discussion of the early disputes by female textile workers, see Tsurumi, *Factory Girls*, pp. 50–8, pp. 112–20.

4 Large, *Organized Workers and Socialist Politics in Interwar Japan*, p. 12.

5 On the development and activities of the *Shakai Seisaku Gakkai*, see Hirai, *Individualism and Socialism: The Life and Thought of Kawai Eijirō (1891–1944)*; Kublin, *Asian Revolutionary: The Life of Sen Katayama*, pp. 136–8; Garon, *The State and Labour in Modern Japan*, pp. 25–6.

6 Translated in Kublin, *Asian Revolutionary*, p. 137.

7 Kōsaka, *Japanese Thought in the Meiji Era*, pp. 208–9.

8 Abe Isoo lists at least ten Japanese publications on socialism which appeared between 1893 and 1901. Abe Isoh [Isoo], 'Socialism in Japan', in Ōkuma Shigenobu (ed.), *Fifty Years of New Japan*, New York: E. P. Dutton, 1909, Volume II, pp. 494–512.

9 In 1882, a group on the left of the liberal movement called itself the *Tōyō Shakai Tō* (Oriental Socialist Party), but its activities were short-lived. After only a few months the government ordered its disbandment. John Crump, *The Origins of Socialist Thought in Japan*, Beckenham, Kent: Croom Helm, 1983, p. 39.

10 *Rōdō Sekai* was established in 1897 and appeared in various formats until 1902. *Shakai Shugi* appeared from March 1903 to December 1904, and *Shūkan Shakai Shinbun* appeared between June 1907 and August 1911. Miyake Yoshiko, 'Rekishi no naka no jendaa: Meiji Shakaishugisha no Gensetsu ni arawareta Josei, Josei Rōdōsha', in Hara Hiroko, et al. (eds), *Jendaa (Library Sokan Shakaigaku 2)*, Tokyo: Shinseisha, 1994, p. 146.

11 Yokoyama, *Nihon no Kasō Shakai*.

12 'Shokkō Shokun ni Kisu', in Katayama Sen, *Nihon no Rōdō Undō*, Tokyo: Iwanami Shoten, 1952, pp. 18–27; partial translation in Tsunoda, Ryūsaku, et al., *Sources of Japanese Tradition*, New York, Columbia University Press, 1952, Volume II, pp. 300–4.

13 For an analysis of the portrayal of women workers in *Rōdō Sekai* and *Shokkō Jijō*, see Suzuki, *Josei to Rōdō Kumiai*, pp. 10–24. See also Miyake Yoshiko's analysis of the publications *Rōdō Sekai*, *Shakai Shinpō*, and *Shūkan Shakai Shinbun* from the perspective of feminist discourse analysis. Miyake, 'Rekishi no naka no jendaa', pp. 141–65.

14 Article 17 stated that: 'No one shall commit violence or threaten others or publicly slander others for the purposes in the following paragraphs or seduce or incite others for the purpose of paragraph 2, following: 1 In order to let others join, or to prevent others from joining, an organization which aims at cooperative action concerning conditions of work or remuneration. 2 In order to make an employer discharge workers, or to make him reject applications for work or to make him refuse an offer of employment with a view to organizing a lockout or a strike. 3 In order to compel the other party to agree to the conditions of work or remuneration.' Translation in: Large, *The Rise of Labour in Japan: The Yūaikai 1912–19*, p. 3.

15 For details of Meiji period legislation related to control of publications and political activities, see Elise Tipton, *Japanese Police State: Tokkō in Interwar Japan*, Sydney: Allen & Unwin, 1990, pp. 55–62; Richard Mitchell, *Thought Control in Prewar Japan*, Ithaca: Cornell University Press, 1976; Richard Mitchell, *Censorship in Imperial Japan*, Princeton, New Jersey: Princeton University Press, 1983.

16 Tipton, *Japanese Police State*, p. 58.

17 These included Kōtoku Shūsui's *Nijū Seiki no Kaibutsu: Teikoku Shugi* (Imperialism: The Spectre of the Twentieth Century: 1901) and *Shakai Shugi Shinzui* (The Essence of Socialism: 1903), Katayama Sen's *Waga Shakai Shugi* (My Socialism: 1903), Katayama Sen and Nishikawa Kōjirō's *Nihon no Rōdō Undō* (The Japanese Labour Movement: 1901), Abe Isoo's *Shakai Mondai Kaishaku Hō* (The Solution to Social Problems: 1901), *Shakai Tō* (The Socialist Party) by Nishikawa Kōjirō, and Yano Ryūkei's *Shin Shakai* (New Society). Odagiri Susumu, 'Kaidai', p. 416.

18 Ōkōchi Kazuo, 'Kaisetsu', in *Gendai Nihon Shisō Taikei: Shakai Shugi*, Tokyo: Chikuma Shobō, 1962; cited in Odagiri Susumu, 'Kaidai', pp. 416–17.

19 Ishikawa Sanshirō and Kōtoku Shūsui, *Nihon Shakai Shugi Shi*, cited in Kōsaka, *Japanese Thought in the Meiji Era*, p. 208.

20 The newspaper had a print run of between 3700 and 8000 depending on the issue. The first issue appeared in November 1903. Itoya Toshio, *Kanno Suga*, Tokyo: Iwanami Shoten, 1970, p. 35. (Facsimile edition: Meiji Bunken Shiryō Kankōkai (eds), *Meiji Shakai Shugi Shiryō Shū: Bessatsu 3, Shūkan Heimin Shinbun*, Tokyo.)

21 For the importance of the Russo–Japanese War in the development of Japanese socialism and pacifism, see Nobuya Bamba, and John F. Howes, *Pacifism in Japan: The Christian and Socialist Tradition*, Vancouver: University of British Columbia, 1978, *passim*; Hyman Kublin, 'Japanese Socialists and the Russo–Japanese War', *Journal of Modern History*, Vol. XXII, No. 4, December 1950.

22 See the discussion of the importance of the Hibiya riots in Gordon, *Labor and Imperial Democracy*, pp. 26–62.

23 Facsimile edition: Meiji Bunken Shiryō Kankōkai (eds), *Meiji Shakai Shugi Shiryō Shū*: Vol. 1.

24 'Yo wa ika ni shite shakaishugisha to narishi ka', in Odagiri (ed.), *Meiji Shakai Shugi Bungaku Shū 2*, pp. 389–92.

25 Yamaguchi Koken, 'Yo wa ika ni shite shakaishugisha to narishi ka', *Shūkan Heimin Shinbun*, No. 44; reproduced in Odagiri (ed.), *Meiji Shakai Shugi Bungaku Shū 2*, pp. 391–2.

26 On the connections between religion and socialism in the British context, see Yeo, 'A New Life: The Religion of Socialism in Britain, 1883–1896', pp. 5–56.

27 Sakai Toshihiko, 'Yo wa ika ni shite shakaishugisha to narishi ka', *Shūkan Heimin Shinbun*, No. 8; reproduced in Odagiri (ed.), *Meiji Shakai Shugi Bungaku Shū 2*, pp. 389–90.

28 Facsimile edition: Meiji Bunken Shiryō Kankōkai (eds), *Meiji Shakai Shugi Shiryō Shū*, Vol. 3.

29 Facsimile edition: Meiji Bunken Shiryō Kankōkai (eds), *Meiji Shakai Shugi Shiryō Shū*, Vol. 2. The imagery of light was played on in various ways in the journal *Hikari*. The masthead bore an almost pictorial representation of the ideograph for 'light', and several poems used the imagery of light: Yamaguchi Koken, 'Hikari no Kuni', *Hikari*, No. 1, p. 1; Josephine Conger Kaneko, 'The Light', *Hikari*, No. 5, 20/1/1906, p. 1. Kaneko's poem appeared in both English and Japanese versions on the front cover of issue 5. The imagery of light in early socialist writings is discussed in Vera Mackie, *Imagining Liberation: Feminism and Socialism in Early Twentieth Century Japan*, Papers in Feminist Cultural Studies No. 1, Women's Research Centre, University of Western Sydney: Nepean, 1995.

30 Facsimile edition: Meiji Bunken Shiryō Kankōkai (eds), *Meiji Shakai Shugi Shiryō Shū*, Vol. 4.

31 It should also be said that Kōtoku's often liberal views on women's issues in print were not matched by his private conduct.

32 Kinoshita's activities were not restricted to the *Heiminsha* circle. Itoya recounts that

Kinoshita gave a speech entitled 'Danjo Kōfuku Hikaku Ron' (A Comparison of the Happiness of Men and Women) at a national meeting of the *Nihon Kirisutokyō Kyōfūkai* (Japan Women's Christian Temperance Union), held in the Kanda district of Tokyo. On finishing his speech, he brandished a copy of the weekly *Heimin Shinbun*, proclaiming that this publication held the basic answers to the resolution of the 'woman question'. Itoya, *Kanno Suga*, pp. 41–2.

33 Suzuki Yūko (ed.), *Sakai Toshihiko Josei Ron Shū*, Tokyo: San'Ichi Shobō, 1983, p. 387.

34 Suzuki Yūko (ed.), *Shiryō: Heiminsha no Onnatachi*, Tokyo: Fuji Shuppan, 1986, p. 12.

35 *Katei Zasshi* was established in April 1903 by Sakai Toshihiko. It appeared until July 1909, under a series of editors, including Sakai, Ōsugi Sakae, and Nishimura Shozan. Hori Yasuko was also involved in the production of the *Katei Zasshi* from its first issue. Miki Sukako, 'Meiji no Fujin Zasshi o Tadoru', pp. 75–9; *Katei Zasshi*, facsimile edition: Tokyo: Fuji Shuppan, 1983.

36 'Jokō no Dōmei Higyō', *Shūkan Heimin Shinbun*, No. 3, 29/1/1903, p. 2; 'Kōjo no Gyakutai', *Shūkan Heimin Shinbun*, No. 4, 6/12/1903, p. 2; 'Jokō no Dōmei', *Shūkan Heimin Shinbun*, No. 51, 30/10/1904, p. 2; 'Kōjo Gyakutai', *Chokugen*, Vol. 1, No. 22, 25/9/1906; etc.

37 'Jokō no Uta', *Shūkan Heimin Shinbun*, No. 9, 10/1/1904, p. 5; Koken, 'Kōjo no Uta', *Shūkan Heimin Shinbun*, No. 59, 15/12/1904, p. 5; Kokensei, 'Bōseki Kōjo', *Chokugen*, Vol. 2, No. 31, 3/9/1905, p. 4.

38 Early titles include: *Kakumei Fujin* (Revolutionary Women), Tokyo: Heiminsha Bunkō, 1905; and Yamaguchi Koken, *Shakai Shugi to Fujin* (Women and Socialism), Tokyo: Heiminsha Bunkō, 1905.

39 On the participation of women in the *Heiminsha*, see Suzuki (ed.), *Shiryō: Heiminsha no Onnatachi*; Nishikawa, *Heiminsha no Onna: Nishikawa Fumiko Jiden*, pp. 56–75; Murata, *Fukuda Hideko*, pp. 100–7; Ōki Motoko. 'Meiji Shakai Shugi Undō to Josei', in Joseishi Sōgō Kenkyūkai (eds), *Nihon Josei Shi 4: Kindai*, Tokyo: Tokyo Daigaku Shuppankai, 1990, pp. 115–48; Sievers, *Flowers in Salt*, pp. 114–38.

40 *Nijūseiki no Fujin* was established on 1 February 1904, with Kawamura Haruko and Imai Utako as publisher and editor. Endō [Iwano] Kiyoko later took over the editorship. After a brief hiatus, the magazine reappeared in May 1906, and the final edition was published in November 1906. Miki Sukako, 'Meiji no Fujin Zasshi o Tadoru', p. 79. Extant issues of *Nijūseiki no Fujin* are held in Tokyo University's Meiji Newspaper and Magazine Collection.

41 *Sekai Fujin* seems to have been able to gain support from all factions of the socialist movement. Among *Sekai Fujin*'s supporters, Suzuki Yūko lists Christian socialists Ishikawa Sanshirō and Abe Isoo, social democrat Sakai Toshihiko, anarcho-syndicalist Kōtoku Shūsui, and Nishikawa Fumiko, Sugaya Iwako, and Kamikawa Matsuko, who displayed a commitment to both feminism and socialism. Suzuki Yūko (ed.), *Shiryō Heiminsha no Onnatachi*, p. 17.

42 Fukuda had made contact with the socialists after she moved into the same neighbourhood as Sakai Toshihiko in 1901. Itoya Toshio reports that Fukuda introduced Sakai to Katō Tokijirō who, with Kojima Ryūtarō, provided funding for the establishment of the *Heimin Shinbun* in 1903. See Itoya Toshio, 'Kaisetsu', in Fukuda, *Warawa no Hanseigai*, pp. 113–15.

43 Fukuda Hideko, *Warawa no Omoide*, Tokyo, 1905, reprinted in Odagiri (ed.), *Meiji Bungaku Zenshū 84: Meiji Shakai Shugi Bungaku Shū 2*, pp. 3–56.

44 Sharon Sievers refers to the *Heiminsha* women as the 'kitchen crew'. Sievers, *Flowers in Salt*, p. 125.

45 Suzuki, *Shiryō: Heiminsha no Onnatachi*, p. 16.

46 Matsuoka Fumiko, 'Heiminsha no Katei', *Shūkan Heimin Shinbun*, No. 60, 1/1/1905, reproduced in Suzuki (ed.), *Shiryō: Heiminsha no Onnatachi*, pp. 53–5.

47 Sakai Toshihiko, however, seems to have taken an interest in improving the practical conditions of the work of the 'kitchen crew', in purchasing, for example, a device to simplify the process of washing rice. cf. Nishikawa Fumiko, 'Kometogi Kikai no

Ohanashi', *Heimin Shinbun*, No. 63, 22/5/1905, reproduced in Suzuki, *Shiryō: Heiminsha no Onnatachi*, p. 56. Sakai, indeed, was distinguished as one of the male socialists in the early twentieth century who showed a prolonged commitment to pursuing answers to 'the woman question'. cf. Suzuki Yūko, 'Sakai Toshihiko no Josei Ron Nōto', *Undō Shi Kenkyū*, No. 12, August 1983; Suzuki (ed.), *Sakai Toshihiko Josei Ron Shū*.

48 Matsuoka Fumiko, 'Heiminsha no Katei', in Suzuki, *Shiryō: Heiminsha no Onnatachi*, p. 55.

49 Matsuoka [Nishikawa] Fumiko, 'Yūshi no Gofujin ni Gosōdan Itashimasu', *Shūkan Heimin Shinbun*, No. 60, 1/1/1905, reproduced in Suzuki, *Shiryō: Heiminsha no Onnatachi*, p. 53.

50 Suzuki, *Shiryō: Heiminsha no Onnatachi*, pp. 72–3. Nobuoka's account of the reasons for her interest in socialism will be discussed below. Nobuoka later married Sakai Toshihiko, and is also known under the name Sakai Tameko.

51 For details of Kanno Suga's connection with the *Heiminsha*, see Itoya, *Kanno Suga*, Chapter II; Sharon Sievers, *Flowers in Salt*, pp. 139–62. See also Kondō Magara's reminiscences of Kanno in Kondō, *Watashi no Kaisō*, Vol. 1, pp. 114–17, pp. 189–91. For a comprehensive study of Kanno Suga's life and works, see Hélène Bowen, 'Victims as Victors, Life as Death: Representation and Empowerment in the Works of Kanno Suga and Kaneko Fumiko'.

52 Suzuki, *Shiryō: Heiminsha no Onnatachi*, pp. 72–4.

53 Nishikawa Fumiko 'Ika ni shite shakaishugi sha to narishi ka', *Chokugen*, Vol. 2, No. 12, 23/4/1905, reprinted in *Nishikawa Fumiko Jiden*, pp. 209–10, see also *Nishikawa Fumiko Jiden*, p. 57.

54 Nobuoka Tameko, 'Ika ni shite shakaishugi sha to narishi ka', *Chokugen*, Vol. 2, No. 12, 23/4/1905, Reproduced in Suzuki Yūko (ed.), *Shiryō: Heiminsha no Onnatachi*, pp. 72–3.

55 Sugaya Iwako, 'Ika ni shite shakaishugi sha to narishi ka', *Chokugen*, Vol. 2, No. 12, 23/4/1905, Reproduced in Suzuki Yūko (ed.), *Shiryō: Heiminsha no Onnatachi*, p. 73. For biographical details, see Suzuki Yūko (ed.), *Shiryō: Heiminsha no Onnatachi*, pp. 32–3.

56 Kamikawa Matsuko, 'Ika ni shite shakaishugi sha to narishi ka', *Chokugen*, Vol. 2, No. 12, 23/4/1905, Reproduced in Suzuki (ed.), *Shiryō: Heiminsha no Onnatachi*, pp. 73–4. Kamikawa employs quite similar imagery in another article published at the same time: Kamikawa Matsuko, 'Aa mujō, kotō no shita ni', *Nyoran*, Hiroshima: Hiroshima Jogakkō Dōshikai, No. 2, 5/2/1905, reprinted in Suzuki, pp. 75–7. For biographical details, see Suzuki, pp. 43–6.

57 This brief account is somewhat reminiscent of Fukuda Hideko's extended treatment of her meetings with a female beggar in her autobiography, as previously discussed in Chapter one.

58 Matsuoka [Nishikawa] Fumiko, 'Fujin no honsei to shakai shugi', *Shūkan Heimin Shinbun*, 20/11/1904, reprinted in *Nishikawa Fumiko Jiden*, p. 206. This was the content of Nishikawa's speech to the Socialist Women's Seminar (*Shakai Shugi Fujin Kōen*), 6/11/1904, as reported in 'Shakai Shugi Fujin Kōen (Honsha)', *Shūkan Heimin Shinbun*, No. 54, 10/11/1904.

59 Barbara Taylor explains the consequences of this tendency in the writings of the Utopian socialist women: '[There was] an unresolved tension between the desire to minimize sexual difference and the need to re-assert it in women's favour. This tension was particularly acute within socialist rhetoric, since the very qualities which were considered quintessentially female were also those which the Owenites wished to see generalized across the population: love, compassion, generosity, charity. A good woman, it was implied, was a born communist.' Taylor, *Eve and the New Jerusalem*, pp. 30–1.

60 Compare this view of socialism with Ōsugi Sakae's autobiographical account, where he relates his understanding that it was necessary to renounce pacifism in order to embrace socialism: 'Simultaneously [with my disillusion with Christianity] I came to doubt the principle of nonresistance, the "turn the other cheek" that is an essential

quality of religion and that I had begun unconsciously to embrace. Thus I could now embrace pure socialism and the class struggle.' *The Autobiography of Ōsugi Sakae*, edited and translated by Byron K. Marshall, Berkeley: University of California Press, 1992, p. 125. Arahata Kanson, in his autobiography, also reflects on the contradiction between belief in the class struggle and the statement of pacifist principles. Arahata Kanson, *Kanson Jiden*, Tokyo: Iwanami Shoten, 1975, Vol. 1, pp. 99–107.

61 Suzuki, *Shiryō: Heiminsha no Onnatachi*, pp. 277–90: *Nishikawa Fumiko Jiden*, pp. 57–8, pp. 206–8; Sievers, *Flowers in Salt*, p. 120. It is tempting to make a connection between this activity and the women's group established by Fukuda and other liberal women in Okayama. Murata, *Fukuda Hideko*, pp. 22–3.

62 'Shakai Shugi Fujin Kōen no Ki', *Shūkan Heimin Shinbun*, 21/2/1904, cited in Ōki Motoko, 'Meiji Shakai Shugi Undō to Josei', p. 120.

63 'Shakai Shugi Fujin Kōen', *Shūkan Heimin Shinbun*, No. 12, 31/1/1904. Speakers at the first session were Kinoshita Naoe, Sakai Toshihiko and Nishikawa Kōjirō.

64 'Katei ni Okeru Kaikyū Seido', speech presented in two parts on 13/1/1904 and 3/3/1904; reported in 'Shakai Shugi Fujin Kōen no Ki', *Shūkan Heimin Shinbun*, No. 15, 21/2/1904, No. 19, 20/3/1904. See also Sakai Toshihiko, 'Katei ni Okeru Kaikyū Seido', *Katei Zasshi*, Vol. 2, No. 2, 2/2/1904; Vol. 2, No. 4, 2/4/1904; 'Oyako no Kankei', speech presented on 12/3/1904; reported in 'Shakai Shugi Fujin Kōen Daisankai', *Shūkan Heimin Shinbun*, No. 19, 20/3/1904; 'Onnarashiki to wa nan zo ya', speech presented on 9/4/1904; reported in 'Shakai Shugi Fujin Kōen (Heiminsha)', *Chokugen*, Vol. 2, No. 11, 20/3/1904.

65 'Fujin Mondai No Chūshinten', speech presented on 13/2/1904; reported in 'Shakai Shugi Fujin Kōen no Ki', *Shūkan Heimin Shinbun*, No. 15, 21/2/1904.

66 Christian Socialist Ishikawa Sanshirō stated that the purpose of socialism was to bring the 'freedom of love' (*ai no jiyū*) to all of humanity, and thought this was particularly suited to women's vocation of 'creating love' (*Ai no jitsugen o tenshoku to suru fujin*). Ishikawa Sanshirō, 'Fujin no Tenshoku', speech presented on 12/3/1904; reported in 'Shakai Shugi Fujin Kōen Daisankai', *Shūkan Heimin Shinbun*, No. 19, 20/3/1904.

67 'Kakumei Undō to Fujin', speech presented on 12/6/1904, reported in 'Shakai Shugi Fujin Kōen', *Shūkan Heimin Shinbun*, No. 32, 19/6/1904.

68 Sakai Toshihiko, 'Bebel no Fujin Ron' Part 1, speech presented on 7/5/1905; reported in 'Fujin Kōenkai (Heiminsha)', *Chokugen*, Vol. 2, No. 15, 14/5/1905.

69 Matsuoka [Nishikawa] Fumiko, 'Fujin no honsei to shakai shugi'; see p. 94, p. 105.

70 Yamaguchi Koken later referred to the activities of those women who had 'nurtured the knowledge of socialism, and who were all enthusiastic preachers'. He mentioned: Fukuda Hideko, Sakai [Nobuoka] Tameko, Nishikawa Fumiko, Hori Yasuko, Teramoto [Oguchi] Michiko, and Kamikawa Matsuko. Yamaguchi Koken, 'Nihon Shakai Shugi Undō Shi', *Kaizō*, October 1919, cited in Suzuki Yūko (ed.), *Shiryō: Heiminsha no Onnatachi*, p. 8.

71 Matsuoka [Nishikawa] Fumiko, 'Shizuka Gozen no Ohanashi', Summary of speech presented to the Heiminsha; *Shūkan Heimin Shinbun*, No. 58, 18/11/1904, reproduced in Suzuki (ed.), *Shiryō: Heiminsha no Onnatachi*, pp. 57–9. Shizuka Gozen was the mistress of Yoshitsune, who was captured while fleeing Yoritomo's forces with Yoshitsune. She displayed her defiance of Yoritomo's authority by proclaiming her love for Yoshitsune, when ordered to dance by Yoritomo. Shizuka's life was spared, but her son (by Yoshitsune) was killed at birth on Yoritomo's orders. See Margaret Fukazawa Benton, 'Hōjō Masako: The Dowager Shōgun', in Chieko Irie Mulhern, *Heroic with Grace: Legendary Women of Japan*, New York: M. E. Sharpe, 1991, pp. 181–7.

72 Sugaya Iwako, 'Genji Monogatari ni okeru Josei', speech reported in 'Shakai Shugi Fujin Kōen (Heiminsha)', *Chokugen*, Vol. 2, No. 6, 12/3/1905, p. 6.

73 Murai Tomoyoshi, 'Nihon Fujin ni Taisuru Nidaimeisō' (part one), speech presented to the Socialist Women's Seminar, 13/2/1904, reported in 'Shakai Shugi Fujin Kōen no Ki', *Shūkan Heimin Shinbun*, No. 15, 21/2/1904; reproduced in Suzuki, *Shiryō: Heiminsha no Onnatachi*, pp. 277–80.

74 Sakai Toshihiko, 'Ryōsai Kenbo Shugi'; Imai Utako, 'Fujin no Chii', *Nijūseiki no Fujin*, Vol. 1, No. 7; 1/8/1904; H. A. Sei, 'Tate yo Shimai', *Sekai Fujin*, Vol. 1, No. 1, p. 7;

Kamikawa Matsuko, 'Ori ni Furete', *Sekai Fujin*, Vol. 1, No. 3, 1/2/1907, p. 5; etc.
75 cf. Nishikawa [Matsuoka] Fumiko, 'Yoshiwara Kenbutsu no Ki', *Chokugen*, 11/6/1905, also reprinted in *Nishikawa Fumiko Jiden*, pp. 210–11.
76 Writers on these issues included Nishimura Shozan, Sugaya Iwako, Kamikawa Matsuko and Endō Yūshirō. Miki Sukako, 'Meiji no Fujin Zasshi o Tadoru', pp. 76–8.
77 *Shinshin Fujin* appeared from February 1913 to September 1923, and was often presented as a rival to *Seitō* (Bluestocking). Nishikawa's writings in this journal will be referred to in Chapter four.
78 Imai Utako, 'Tsuma to shite no Joshi', *Nijū Seiki no Fujin*, Vol. 1, No. 9, 1/10/1904; reprinted in Suzuki (ed.), *Shiryō: Heiminsha no Onnatachi*, pp. 85–7. For biographical details of Hatoyama, see Tachi, 'Ryōsai Kenbo'.
79 Imai Utako, 'Ikeru Fujin', *Nijūseiki no Fujin*, No. 1, 1904.
80 Imai Utako, 'Fujin no Chii', *Nijūseiki no Fujin*, Vol. 1, No. 7, 1/8/1904, reprinted in Suzuki, *Shiryō: Heiminsha no Onnatachi*, pp. 83–5.
81 Sugako [Kanno Suga], 'Fujin to Dokusho', *Muroo Shinpō*, No. 540, 9/12/1905; reprinted in Sekiyama Naotarō (ed.), *Shoki Shakai Shugi Shiryō*, Tokyo, 1959, pp. 119–20; partial translation in Sievers, *Flowers in Salt*.
82 Asahiyama Sei [Ishikawa Sanshirō], 'Jiyū Ren'ai Shiken', *Shūkan Heimin Shinbun*, No. 45, 18/9/1904, p. 1, also reprinted in Hayashi Shigeru and Nishida Taketoshi (eds), *Nihon Heimin Shinbun Ronsetsu Shū*, Tokyo: Iwanami Shoten, 1961. See also Kōtoku Shūsui's criticism of marriage: Kōtoku Shūsui, 'Fujin Shōkan', *Sekai Fujin* No. 2, 15/1/1907, p. 2.
83 Matsuoka Fumiko, 'Yoshiwara Kenbutsu no Ki'. On the 'Bluestockings' visit to the Yoshiwara, see Horiba Kiyoko, *Seitō no Jidai*, Tokyo: Iwanami Shoten, 1988, pp. 112–13.
84 Ibara Hanako, 'Shōgi o Awaremu', *Sekai Fujin*, No. 23, 5/3/1909, p. 3.
85 See also Yamaguchi Gizō, 'Shakaishugi to Inbaifu', *Shūkan Heimin Shinbun*, No. 21, 3/4/1904, p. 7. For the views of later socialist writers on prostitution, see Chapter five.
86 'Shasetsu: Kyōsan Shakai no Katei', *Sekai Fujin*, No. 31, 5/12/1908, p. 1.
87 *Fujin Mondai* (The Woman Question), published in 1907, explicitly mentions Carpenter, Engels, Bebel and Rappaport. *Danjo Kankei no Shinka* (The Progress of Relations Between Men and Women) has been described as a history of women in Japan, drawing on Engels' *The Origins of the Family, Private Property and the State*. Suzuki, *Sakai Toshihiko Josei Kaihō Ronshū*, p. 391.
88 Abe Isoo, 'Joshi to Iden', *Sekai Fujin*, No. 32, 5/1/1909, p. 2.
89 The phrase was used by a writer in *Fujo Shinbun*; 'Ryōsai Kenbo', *Fujo Shinbun*, No. 159, 1904. See also Kanno Suga, 'Hiji Teppō', *Muroo Shinpō*, 15/4/1906, reprinted in Sekiyama (ed.), *Shoki Shakai Shugi Shiryō*, pp. 162–3, partial translation in Sievers, *Flowers in Salt*, p. 149; Nishikawa Fumiko, 'Nihon Shōrai no katei', *Shinshin Fujin*, 1914, reprinted in *Nishikawa Fumiko Jiden*, pp. 244–7.
90 Sakai Toshihiko, 'Heiminsha yori', *Chokugen*, Vol. 2, No. 12, 23/4/1905, quoted in Suzuki Yūko (ed.), *Shiryō: Heiminsha no Onnatachi*, p. 28. In the same article, Sakai, who was usually sensitive on matters related to gender relations, reveals a reliance on conventional literary imagery when he describes the women of the *Heiminsha* as 'flowers', employing a different floral image for each woman. *Heiminsha* stalwarts Nishikawa Fumiko and Nobuoka Tameko are the plum and cherry blossoms, while the other women are wisteria and peony, the chrysanthemum and Chinese bell-flower. Women are said to enliven the place like birds or like butterflies. Comrades come and go, 'some to enjoy the fragrance, some to gain courage for new political campaigns, some to gain relief from the fatigue of long campaigns'.
91 See the discussion of Yamaguchi Koken's, 'Yo wa ika ni shite.shakaishugisha to narishi ka', p. 100. For the use of the analogy between family and society in other socialist movements, see Barbara Taylor's discussion of British Utopian Socialism and Charles Sowerwine's discussion of women and socialism in France. Taylor, *Eve and the New Jerusalem*, p. 244; Sowerwine, *Sisters or Citizens? Women and Socialism in France Since 1876*, p. 31.

92 Kinoshita Naoe, 'Hi no Hashira', *Tokyo Mainichi Shinbun*, January–March 1904, repro-
    duced in: Yamagiwa Keiji (ed.), *Kinoshita Naoe Zenshū*, Tokyo: Kyōbunkan, 1990–1995,
    10 Vols, vol 1.
93 This discussion follows Shea, *Leftwing Literature in Japan*, pp. 17–20.
94 Shea, *Leftwing Literature in Japan*, p. 20.
95 Ushioda has focused on the pacifist sentiments expressed in the novel. Ushioda,
    'Women and War in Meiji Japan: the Case of Fukuda Hideko'.
96 Fukuda, *Warawa no Omoide*, p. 54.
97 Women writers in the proletarian literary movement of the 1920s and 1930s, such
    as Miyamoto [Chūjō] Yuriko and Sata [Kubokawa] Ineko, would address the rela-
    tionships between men and women in the left-wing movement, and the contradictory
    position of women who tried to reconcile the positions of wife, mother, worker, and
    activist.
98 Wakita Haruko, et al. (eds), *Nihon Josei Shi*, Tokyo: Yoshikawa Kōbunkan, 1986, p. 223.
    For accounts of the history of this organization, see Jane Mitchell, 'Women's National
    Mobilization in Japan: 1901–1942', unpublished Honours Thesis, University of Ade-
    laide, 1986; Sharon H. Nolte and Sally Ann Hastings, 'The Meiji State's Policy Towards
    Women, 1890–1910', in Bernstein (ed.), *Recreating Japanese Women*, pp. 151–74.
99 For discussion of the activities of Japanese women's organizations at the time of the
    Russo–Japanese War, see Miki Sukako, 'Meiji no Fujin Zasshi o Tadoru', pp. 68–74;
    Wakita Haruko, et al. (eds), *Nihon Josei Shi*, pp. 222–5.
100 Sakai Toshihiko, 'Ryōsai Kenbo Shugi': '. . . The view that "women should simply
    stay in the home, obey their husbands, and bear and bring up children", is an
    ideology which pushes women into the home and makes them the slaves of men.
    Ryōsai Kenbo ideology is, in other words, a method of training slaves for the nation
    of men (*danshi koku*).'
101 Kinoshita Naoe, 'Sameyo Fujin', *Chokugen*, Vol. 2, No. 12, 23/4/1905, p. 1, also repro-
    duced in Hayashi and Nishida (eds), *Nihon Heimin Shinbun Ronsetsu Shū*, pp. 73–7;
    Kōtoku Shūsui, 'Fujin to Seiji', speech given to the Socialist Women's Seminar, sum-
    marized in *Shūkan Heimin Shinbun*, 22/5/1904; full text in *Katei Zasshi*, No. 6, 1904,
    pp. 17–22.
102 Kōtoku, 'Fujin to Seiji'.
103 Kōtoku, 'Fujin to Sensō', *Katei Zasshi*, No. 3, pp. 6–10.
104 Kōtoku, 'Fujin to Seiji'.
105 For biographical details and reminiscences of Imai Utako and Kawamura Haruko,
    see Nishikawa Fumiko, *Jiden*; Suzuki Yūko, *Shiryō: Heiminsha no Onnatachi*, pp. 31–2.
106 Despite its name, the *Hokkaidō Fujin Dōshikai* was based in Tokyo. See the promo-
    tional statement on the founding of the organization, which bears an address in the
    Kōjimachi ward of Tokyo; reproduced in Suzuki, *Shiryō: Heiminsha no Onnatachi*,
    p. 31.
107 cf. Imai Utako, 'Ikeru Fujin', *Nijūseiki no Fujin*, No. 1, 1904, p. 4.
108 The year 1904 saw a spate of books on the theme of Women and War, discussed in
    more detail in Vera Mackie, 'Gender and Nationalism in Imperial Japan', paper
    presented at the Summer School on Nationalism and National Identities, Humanities
    Research Centre, Australian National University, February 1996.
109 Imai Utako, 'Fujin to sensō', *Nijūseiki no Fujin*, No. 2, 1904, pp. 2–3.
110 Suzuki Yūko, *Shiryō: Heiminsha no Onnatachi*, p. 31.
111 See also the discussion of Imai's articles p. 59: Imai Utako, 'Tsuma to shite no Joshi';
    Imai Utako, 'Ikeru Fujin'.
112 Suzuki Sumuko traces the development of modern nursing in Japan, from the
    domestic conflicts of the early Meiji period, through the Japanese Red Cross's
    involvement in Japan's conflicts in Russia and China. Suzuki mentions that Florence
    Nightingale was idolized in Japan until the xenophobia of the 1930s, and my reading
    of women's magazines of the early twentieth century confirms this. Suzuki Sumuko,
    'Jūgun Kangofu', *Jūgoshi Nōto*, No. 3, 1979, pp. 1–8. Florence Nightingale is one of
    the famous women profiled in *Sekai Fujin*, and is also mentioned as a role model in
    Fukuda Hideko's novel, *My Memories*. Fukuda, *Warawa no Omoide*, p. 14.

113 It was not until the late 1930s that State support for widows and supporting mothers was achieved. The campaign for this legislation will be discussed in Chapter six.

114 Published in the literary journal *Myōjō* (Venus) September 1904, and reprinted in the *Chokugen* women's edition, 23/4/1905, p. 9; English translation in Bamba and Howes, *Pacifism in Japan.* The ensuing controversy is traced in Jay Rubin, *Injurious to Public Morals: Writers and the Meiji State,* University of Washington, 1984, pp. 55–9.

115 Rubin, *Injurious to Public Morals,* p. 57.

116 Ōtsuka Kanaoko, 'Ohyakudo Mōde', *Taiyō,* November 1905. This was also reprinted in *Chokugen,* Vol. 2, No. 15, 14/5/1905, p. 5; and more recently reprinted in Yamada Seizaburō, *Puroteraria Bungaku Shi,* Vol. 1, Tokyo: Rironsha, 1977, p. 128: Chifuku Hanako, 'Chōchin Gyōretsu to Rōbo no Koe', *Muroo Shinpō,* 12/9/1904, reprinted in Maruoka Hideko, *Fujin Shisō Keisei Shi Nōto,* Vol. 1, Tokyo: Domesu Shuppan, pp. 51–2.

117 Christian pacifist Uchimura Kanzō had also chosen a female protagonist as a focus for anti-war sentiment in his poem written at the time of the Sino–Japanese War: 'Yamome no Joya' (The Widow's New Year's Eve), *Fukuin Shinpō,* 25 December 1896, translation in John F. Howes, 'Uchimura Kanzō: The Bible and War', in Bamba and Howes, *Pacifism in Japan,* pp. 102–3. See the visual representation of gendered responses to the Russo–Japanese War in Figure 3.

118 cf. Genevieve Lloyd's discussion of the tension between citizenship and motherhood: Genevieve Lloyd, 'Selfhood, War and Masculinity', in Carole Pateman and Liz Gross (eds), *Feminist Challenges: Social and Political Theory,* Sydney: Allen & Unwin, 1986, pp. 63–76.

119 'Shasetsu: Seijijō ni okeru Fujin no Jiyū', in *Sekai Fujin,* No. 2, 15 January 1907; a slightly different translation appears in Sievers, *Flowers in Salt,* p. 114.

120 cf. Lisa Tickner's discussion of Caroline Watts' poster 'The Bugler Girl': 'The Artists' Suffrage League primed the Manchester Guardian to explain to its readers how "the Amazon who stands on the battlements of the fort may be said to be heralding the new day of which the sun is just seen rising".' Lisa Tickner, *The Spectacle of Women: Imagery of the Suffrage Campaign 1907–1914,* London: Chatto & Windus, 1987, p. 211; Eric Hobsbawm discusses the image of the dawn of socialism in 'Man and Woman: Images on the Left', in *Worlds of Labour: Further Studies in the History of Labour,* London: Weidenfeld & Nicolson, 1984, p. 74, p. 89.

121 Miki Sukako, 'Meiji no Fujin Zasshi o Tadoru', p. 86; Suzuki, *Shiryō: Heiminsha no Onnatachi,* pp. 14–16. Several writers point out that, although Iwamoto Zenji and Shimizu Toyoko had expressed criticism of the provisions of the *Shūkai oyobi Seisha Hō* (Law on Political Assembly and Association) of 1890 (the precursor of the Public Peace Police Law) in the pages of the *Jogaku Zasshi,* this did not develop into an organized movement.

122 'Fujin no Seiji Undō ni Kansuru Seigan', *Shūkan Heimin Shinbun,* 29/1/1905, reprinted in Suzuki, *Shiryō: Heiminsha no Onnatachi,* p. 292.

123 For accounts of this campaign, see Kodama Katsuko, 'Heiminsha no Fujintachi ni yoru Chian Keisatsu Hō Kaisei Seigan Undō ni Tsuite', *Rekishi Hyōron,* No. 323, 1977; Kodama Katsuko, *Fujin Sanseiken Undō Shōshi,* Tokyo, Domesu Shuppan, 1981, pp. 29–34; Suzuki, *Shiryō: Heiminsha no Onnatachi,* pp. 14–16; Miki Sukako, 'Meiji no Fujin Zasshi o Tadoru', pp. 86–90; Sievers, *Flowers in Salt,* pp. 122–34. Relevant documents are reproduced in: Ichikawa Fusae (ed.), *Nihon Fujin Mondai Shiryō Shūsei,* Vol. 2, Tokyo: Domesu Shuppan, 1977, pp. 131–220; relevant documents from the socialist press are reproduced in Suzuki, *Shiryō* pp. 291–303. An autobiographical account from someone involved in the campaign appears in Nishikawa Fumiko, *Heiminsha no Onna: Nishikawa Fumiko Jiden.*

124 cf. the motto of the early French women's organization *Le Droit des Femmes:* 'no duties without rights: no rights without duties'. Sowerwine, *Sisters or Citizens?,* p. 24.

125 'Shasetsu: Seijijō ni okeru Fujin no Yōkyū', *Sekai Fujin,* No. 1, 1/1/1907; 'Gikai Shokun ni Atau', Sekai Fujin, No. 3, 1/2/1907, p. 1.

126 'Fujin no Yōkyū', *Shūkan Heimin Shinbun,* No. 62, 13/1/1905; in Suzuki, *Shiryō: Heiminsha no Onnatachi,* pp. 291-2.

127 'Seijijō ni okeru Fujin no Jiyū'.
128 Evidence from Lewis Henry Morgan's research into primitive societies was used by Engels in framing his argument in the *Origins of the Family, Private Property and the State.* Morgan's *Ancient Society* was first published in 1877. Engels' *Origin of the Family, Private Property and the State* first appeared in 1884. Lewis Henry Morgan, *Ancient Society,* New York: Henry Holt & Co, 1877; Friedrich Engels, *The Origins of the Family, Private Property and the State,* 1884 (reprinted in London: Lawrence & Wishart, 1972).
129 'Seijijō ni okeru Fujin no Jiyū'.
130 What is at stake here is not so much the accuracy of the evidence provided by Morgan and Engels – this has been challenged by various scholars – but the opportunity their writings provided for the imagining of radically different forms of social organization. For critical discussion of the works of Morgan and Engels, see Annette Kuhn, 'Structures of Patriarchy and Capital in the Family', in Annette Kuhn and AnnMarie Wolpe (eds), *Feminism and Materialism: Women and Modes of Production,* London: Routledge & Kegan Paul, 1975; Karen Sacks, 'Engels Revisited: Women, the Organization of Production, and Private Property', in Rayna R. Reiter (ed.), *Toward an Anthropology of Women,* New York: Monthly Review Press, 1975; Janet Sayers, et al. (eds), *Engels Revisited: New Feminist Essays,* London: Tavistock, 1987; Rosalind Coward, *Patriarchal Precedents: Sexuality and Social Relations,* London: Routledge & Kegan Paul, 1983.
131 'Shasetsu: Nijū no Tatakai', *Sekai Fujin,* No. 4, 15/2/1907, p. 1. Maruoka Hideko has identified the influence of Bebel's ideas in this editorial. Excerpts from August Bebel's *Woman Under Socialism* were translated by Sakai Toshihiko and Kōtoku Shūsui in 1904 under the title *Fujin Ron.* A more complete translation by Yamakawa Kikue appeared in 1923. Maruoka Hideko, *Fujin Shisō Keisei Shi Nōto,* Vol. 1, pp. 53–5.
132 Maruoka Hideko recognizes that this editorial represented an advance on previous understandings of the woman question, but points out that there is no specific solution offered. Rather, the writer expresses faith that the destruction of class society will result in the emancipation of women. Maruoka Hideko, *Fujin Shisō Keisei Shi Nōto,* Vol. 1, p. 54.
133 'Fujin to Kizoku', *Nikkan Heimin Shinbun,* No. 62, 30/3/1907, reprinted in Suzuki, *Shiryō: Heiminsha no Onnatachi,* pp. 301–2.
134 'Fujin to Kizoku'.
135 One article in the *Heimin Shinbun* on the progress of the campaign reports that Fukuda and Imai visited sympathetic parliamentarians, and also Count Itagaki. 'Fujin Seiji Undō no Yōkyū', *Nikkan Heimin Shinbun,* No. 5, 15/1/1907. See also, Fukuda Hideko, 'Undō Nisshi', *Sekai Fujin,* No. 3, 1/2/1907, p. 2.
136 The Japanese socialist women were certainly aware of the activities of the suffragettes, which were reported regularly in *Sekai Fujin.* See the *Kaigai Jiji* (Overseas Topics) column of *Sekai Fujin:* No. 1, 1/1/1907, p. 3; No. 3, 1/2/1907, p. 3; No. 7, 1/4/1907, p. 3; No. 21, 1/1/1908, p. 3; No. 22, 5/2/1908, p. 2; No. 24, 5/4/1908, p. 2; No. 25, 5/6/1908, p. 10, No. 26, 5/7/1908, p. 2; No. 28, 5/9/1908, p. 3.
137 The next campaign for the modification of Article Five was carried out by the *Shin Fujin Kyōkai* (New Women's Association) in the 1920s. The New Women's Association developed from the activities of the liberal feminist *Seitōsha* (Bluestocking Society) which will be referred to in Chapter four. The provisions of Article Five relating to women were eventually modified in 1922, making possible the creation of the first organizations devoted to the attainment of women's suffrage.
138 Kublin, *Asian Revolutionary,* p. 143. Katayama Sen, *Nihon no Rōdō Undō,* pp. 324–6.
139 Murata Shizuko, *Fukuda Hideko,* p. 104.
140 See the discussion of Kōtoku's early articles on women and politics, pp. 58–9.
141 Kōtoku Shūsui, 'Fujin Kaihō to Shakai Shugi', *Sekai Fujin,* No. 16, 1/9/1907, p. 1; summarized by Sievers, *Flowers in Salt,* p. 131.
142 For accounts of this incident, see Sakai Toshihiko, *Nihon Shakai Shugi Undō Shi,* Tokyo: 1954, pp. 148–50; Arahata Kanson, *Kanson Jiden,* pp. 274–80; Itoya, *Kanno Suga;* pp. 105–33. In English, see Kublin, *Asian Revolutionary,* pp. 203–6; Thomas A. Stanley, *Ōsugi Sakae: Anarchist in Taishō Japan,* Cambridge, Massachusetts: Harvard

Council on East Asian Studies, 1982, pp. 43–7. For discussion of women's involvement in the incident, see Suzuki, *Shiryō: Heiminsha no Onnatachi*, pp. 20–4; Nishikawa Fumiko, *Heiminsha no Onna*; Sievers, *Flowers in Salt*, pp. 153–5.

143 For biographical details of Ōsuka Satoko and Ogure Reiko, see Suzuki, *Shiryō: Heiminsha no Onnatachi*, pp. 46–9.

144 Sanshirō, 'Sekishokki, Kokushokki', *Sekai Fujin*, No. 26, 5/7/1908, p. 4; 'Nishikawa Fumiko shi no Kikoku', *Sekai Fujin*, No. 27, 5/8/1908, p. 2, etc.

145 Suzuki, *Shiryō: Heiminsha no Onnatachi*, p. 42. When questioned about her radicalization in the Great Treason Trial, she explained: 'I was put in jail in the Red Flag Incident. Though it was not a major incident, socialists were given severe sentences: Sakai Toshihiko was sentenced two years for no reason. From these experiences, my anger grew, and I came to realize that ordinary methods could never be successful; against such a government . . .' Sievers, *Flowers in Salt*, p. 160.

146 For accounts of this incident, see F. G. Notehelfer, *Kōtoku Shūsui: Portrait of a Japanese Radical*, Cambridge: Cambridge University Press, 1971; Bowen, 'Victims as Victors', pp. 240–73.

147 In her early writings in the *Murō Shinpō*, Kanno describes herself as a 'socialist', in the all-inclusive sense of the word in the early 1900s in Japan. Although her anarchist philosophy at the time of her death was probably outside the bounds of what was understood as socialism in 1910 in Japan, she deserves mention in this study for her connections with the *Heiminsha*, and for the effects of the Great Treason Incident on the socialist movement as a whole. For a detailed study of Kanno's life and works see Bowen, 'Victims as Victors'.

148 Sievers, *Flowers in Salt*, p. 140, p. 221; Bowen, 'Victims as Victors'.

149 See Nishikawa Fumiko's account of distributing leaflets and selling newspapers with Nobuoka [Sakai] Tameko: Nishikawa Fumiko, 'Shinbun Uri no Ki', *Chokugen*, Vol. 2, No. 5, 5/3/1905, reproduced in Suzuki (ed.), *Shiryō: Heiminsha no Onnatachi*, pp. 61–3.

150 For discussion of the use of public space by women in other political campaigns, see Martha Vicinus, 'Male Space and Women's Bodies: The English Suffragette Movement', in Judith Friedlander, et al. (eds), *Women in Culture and Politics: A Century of Change*, Bloomington: Indiana University Press, 1986, pp. 209–22; Martha Vicinus, *Independent Women: Work and Community for Single Women – 1850–1920*, London: Virago, 1985, pp. 262–8; Joy Damousi, 'Socialist Women and Gendered Space: The Anti-Conscription and Anti-War Campaigns of 1914–1918', *Labour History*, No. 60, May 1991, pp. 1–15; Joy Damousi, 'The Gendering of Labour History', 1992 Roger Joyce Memorial Lecture, History Institute of Victoria, 1992.

151 I have found Andrew Gordon's concept of the development of a 'dispute culture' among the working class useful in this context. Gordon traces how disputes were organized, and 'how the dispute culture of the 1920s, consisting of knowledge of this form of action and the ability to carry it out, spread among workers concurrently with the building of a union movement.' Gordon, *Labor and Imperial Democracy*, p. 159.

152 See Nobuoka [Sakai] Tameko's account of being followed by a detective: Nobuoka Tameko, 'Tantei-san to Ohanami', *Chokugen*, Vol. 2, No. 12, 23/4/1905, reproduced in Suzuki (ed.), *Shiryō: Heiminsha no Onnatachi*, pp. 66–7; Matsuoka [Nishikawa] Fumiko, 'Utsunomiya no Shōsoku: Gokuchū no Nishikawa Kōjirō', *Nikkan Heimin Shinbun*, No. 31, 22/2/1907, reproduced in Suzuki (ed.), *Shiryō: Heiminsha no Onnatachi*, pp. 63–4; Fukuda Hideko, 'Ishikawa-ani o Okuru', *Sekai Fujin* No. 9, 1/5/1907, p. 1; Nobuoka [Sakai] Tameko, 'Saiban Iiwatashi no Kōei', *Nihon Heimin Shinbun*, No. 18, 20/2/1908; reproduced in Suzuki (ed.), *Shiryō Heiminsha no Onnatachi*, pp. 67–9; Nobuoka [Sakai] Tameko, 'Yuibunsha Yori', *Kumamoto Hyōron*, No. 28, 5/7/1908, in Suzuki (ed.), *Shiryō: Heiminsha no Onnatachi*, pp. 70–1.

153 Sievers, *Flowers in Salt*, p. 121: 'And the tiny band of socialists developed a new routine: sending off and welcoming back their comrades on the way to prison.'

4 Mothers

1 Hiratsuka Raichō, 'Bosei hogo no shuchō wa irai shugi ni arazu – Yosano, Kaetsu Joshi e', *Fujin Kōron*, Vol. 3, No. 5, 1918, in *Nihon Fujin Mondai Shiryō Shū sei*, Vol. 8, p. 232.

2 Sharon H. Nolte and Sally Ann Hastings, 'The Meiji State's Policy Towards Women, 1890–1910', in Bernstein (ed.), *Recreating Japanese Women*, p. 152.

3 Nolte and Hastings, 'The Meiji State's Policy Towards Women', p. 174; cf. discussion of the health of women workers in: Andō Tarō, 'Shokkō no Torishimari oyobi hogo', *Taiyō*, No 2, 5/12/1896, pp. 55–9; cited in Garon, *The State and Labour*, p. 26.

4 For discussion of the use of this term, see Gluck, *Japan's Modern Myths*, pp. 27–9; Garon, *The State and Labour*, pp. 23–9.

5 H. D. Harootunian, 'Introduction: A Sense of an Ending and the Problem of Taishō', in B. S. Silberman and H. D. Harootunian (eds), *Japan in Crisis: Essays on Taishō Democracy*, Princeton, New Jersey: Princeton University Press, 1974, p. 24: 'In July of 1910, while the [Great Treason] trial was still being argued, Kawada Shirō's The Woman's Problem (*Fujin Mondai*) became the object of "intellectual management", because it threatened to undermine the family system. It "spontaneously went out of print" and speedily slipped into obscurity.' In September 1910, the journal *Hototogisu* was banned on the publication of Ichinomiya Takiko (Kiuchi Tei)'s story 'Onna', which included a rejection of the family system. Horiba Kiyoko (ed.), *Seitō Josei Kaihō Ron Shū*, Tokyo: Iwanami Shoten, p. 11. Sharon Nolte also discusses examples of censorship of criticism of the family system in 'Individualism in Taishō Japan', *Journal of Asian Studies*, Vol. XLIII, No. 4, August 1984, pp. 674–5.

6 Garon, *The State and Labour*, p. 12.

7 For interpretations of the significance of the death of the Meiji Emperor and the end of the Meiji era, see Gluck, *Japan's Modern Myths*, pp. 213–46; Harootunian, 'A Sense of an Ending and the Problem of Taishō', pp. 3–28.

8 The reign of the Taishō emperor lasted from 1912 to 1926. For discussions of the applicability of the term, 'Taishō democracy', see Silberman and Harootunian, *Japan in Crisis: Essays on Taishō Democracy*; Gordon, *Labor and Imperial Democracy*, pp. 5–10.

9 Takeshi Ishida, 'The Development of Interest Groups and the Pattern of Political Modernization in Japan', in Robert E. Ward (ed.), *Political Development in Modern Japan*, Princeton, New Jersey: Princeton University Press, 1968; cited in Large, *The Rise of Labour*, p. 191.

10 Andrew Gordon, who describes the term Taishō democracy as 'chronologically inaccurate and analytically empty', prefers to use the term 'imperial democracy' to describe the contradictory nature of mass political activity in the years from 1905. Gordon, *Labor and Imperial Democracy*, p. 5.

11 On the development of the *Yūaikai*, see Large, *The Rise of Labour in Japan*, passim; Iwao F. Ayusawa, *A History of Labor in Modern Japan*, Honolulu: East–West Center Press, 1966, pp. 98–101.

12 Garon, *The State and Labour*, p. 33.

13 On the influence of the Russian Revolution on Japanese unionists and socialists, see Large, *The Rise of Labour*, pp. 96–109; pp. 145–62; Gail Lee Bernstein, 'The Russian Revolution, the early Japanese Socialists, and the Problem of Dogmatism', *Studies in Comparative Communism*, Vol. 9, No. 4, pp. 327–48.

14 For discussion of the rice riots of 1918, see Michael Lewis, *Rioters and Citizens: Mass Protest in Imperial Japan*, Berkeley: University of California Press, 1987, passim.

15 In 1919, The name of the organization was changed to the Dai Nihon Rōdō Sōdōmei *Yūaikai* (Friendly Society Greater Japan General Federation of Labour). In 1921, *Yūaikai* (Friendly Society) was dropped from the title. On the transformation of the *Yūaikai* see Large, *The Rise of Labor*; Gordon, *Labor and Imperial Democracy*, pp. 146–8.

16 Women worked in mines in Japan until well into the twentieth century. See: Mikiso Hane, *Peasants, Rebels and Outcastes: The Underside of Modern Japan*, New York, Pantheon, 1988, pp. 227–45; Regine Mathias, 'Female Labour in the Japanese Coal-mining Industry', in Janet Hunter (ed.), *Japanese Women Working*, London: Routledge, 1993, pp. 98–121; Morisaki Kazue, *Makkura*, Tokyo: San Ichi Shobō, 1977; Idegawa Yasuko, *Hi o Unda Onnatachi: Onna Kōfu Kara no Kikigaki*, Fukuoka: Yoshi Shobō, 1984. On the development of legislation in the mining industry, see Ayusawa, *A History of Labor in Modern Japan*, pp. 105–6. The text of the *Kōgyō Jōrei*, and other documents relevant to factory legislation, appear in Akamatsu Ryōko (ed.), *Nihon Fujin Mondai Shiryō Shūsei*, Tokyo: Domesu Shuppan, 1977, Vol. 3, pp. 285–376.
17 Ayusawa, *A History of Labor in Modern Japan*, pp. 106–7.
18 These Councils included representatives of bureaucracy, business and academia. Garon, *State and Labour*, p. 21.
19 Kojima Tsunehisa, *Dokyumento Hataraku Josei: Hyakunen no Ayumi*, Tokyo: Kawade Shobō Shinsho, 1983, pp. 52–3.
20 Garon, *State and Labour*, p. 23.
21 This draft is reproduced in: Katayama Sen, *Nihon no Rōdō Undō*, Tokyo: Iwanami Shoten, 1952, pp. 40–8; translated in Stephen E. Marsland, *The Birth of the Japanese Labour Movement: Takano Fusatarō and the Rōdō Kumiai Kiseikai*, Honolulu: University of Hawaii Press, 1989, pp. 204–10. See also Kublin, *Asian Revolutionary*, pp. 125–8. For an account of this draft, and criticisms by an official of the Department of Agriculture and Commerce, see Ernest Foxwell, 'The Protection of Labour in Japan', *The Economic Journal*, 11, March 1901, pp. 106–24. Foxwell's account is based on: Saitō Kashiro, *La Protection Ouvrière au Japon, Projet de Loi et Enquête Personelle*, Paris: Ancienne Maison L. Larose et Forcelle, 1900.
22 For details of the *Rōdō Kumiai Kiseikai* campaign on Factory legislation, see Katayama Sen, *Nihon no Rōdō Undō*, pp. 39–52; Marsland, *The Birth of the Japanese Labour Movement*, pp. 104–11.
23 Saitō, p. 18, cited in Foxwell, p. 108: '. . . quand j'ai visité des diverses provinces, je n'ai jamais constaté en pratique ces relations familières et affectieuses dont on nous parle'; on the protection of women workers, see Foxwell, p. 116.
24 Kublin, *Asian Revolutionary*, p. 125; Foxwell, p. 106.
25 Nōshōmushō Kankōkai, *Shokkō Jijō*, Tokyo: Meicho Kankōkai, 1967; Yokoyama Gennosuke, *Nihon no Kasō Shakai*, Tokyo: Kyōbunkan, 1899 (Reprinted by: Iwanami Shoten, 1949); Hane, *Peasants, Rebels & Outcastes*, pp. 181–4.
26 *Shūkan Fujo Shinbun* was established in 1901 by Fukushima Shirō. For details of the founding see Fukushima Miyoko, 'Shūkan Fujo Shinbun ni miru 1930nendai Fujin Zasshi no Teikō to Zasetsu', *Agora*, No. 24, 20/5/1981; pp. 129–31; Murakami Nobuhiko, 'Fujin Mondai to Fujin Kaihō Undō', *Iwanami Kōza Nihon Rekishi, No. 18: Kindai 5*, p. 230.
27 'Shasetsu: Kōjo no Gyakutai', *Fujo Shinbun*, No. 121, 1/9/1902, p. 1.
28 cf. Anna Davin, 'Imperialism and Motherhood', *History Workshop Journal*, Spring 1978, p. 17: 'Comparisons could also be made with imperial rivals, who without accusations of socialism had successfully turned the attention of the State to national and particularly children's health. Japan (a very recent newcomer to the club of imperialist powers) was often quoted in this context, as at the annual congress of the Sanitary Institute in 1904, (where members were told apropos of the medical inspection of schoolchildren) that in Japan every schoolchild was under medical supervision, and that first aid and hygiene were taught in school. Japan also was "in no danger of race suicide", mothers there were not "shrinking from maternity as in other lands".'
29 Garon, *State and Labour in Modern Japan*, p. 28.
30 Ayusawa, *A History of Labor in Modern Japan*, p. 107.
31 Garon, *State and Labour in Modern Japan*, p. 28. Oka, *Kōjōhōron*, Tokyo: Yūhikaku, 1917 (revised edn), p. 209; Janet Hunter, 'Textile Factories, Tuberculosis and the Quality of Life in Industrializing Japan', in Janet Hunter (ed.), *Japanese Women Working*, pp. 69–97.

32 For a comprehensive discussion of opinions on the abolition of night work in the cotton spinning industry, see: Janet Hunter, 'Factory Legislation and Employer Resistance: The Abolition of Night Work in the Cotton Spinning Industry', in Tsunehiko Yui and Keiichirō Nakagawa (eds), *Japanese Management in Historical Perspective*, Tokyo: University of Tokyo, 1989, pp. 243–72.

33 Nolte and Hastings have argued that Japan did not have the same anxieties about the fitness of working-class mothers as was apparent in Britain at the turn of the century. However, it seems to me that the anxiety about the danger of the spread of tuberculosis from female factory workers reflects a similar anxiety about the health of the recruits who would support Japan's imperialist ambitions. Nolte and Hastings, 'The Meiji State's Policy Towards Women', p. 173; Anna Davin, 'Imperialism and Motherhood', *passim.*

34 Kojima, *Hataraku Josei*, pp. 54–5.

35 Ayusawa, *A History of Labor in Modern Japan*, p. 111.

36 Kanatani, 'Rōdōsha hogohō henkō shi ni miru bosei hogo', pp. 47–8; Large, *Organized Workers and Socialist Politics*, p. 54; Hane, *Peasants, Rebels and Outcastes*, p. 183. The 1923 amendment reduced the maximum working time to eleven hours, raised the minimum age of workers from twelve to fifteen, and extended the jurisdiction of the law to cover all factories employing more than ten workers.

37 Sakurai Kinue, *Bosei Hogo Undōshi*, Tokyo: Domesu Shuppan, 1987, pp. 41–2.

38 Oka, *Kōjōhōron*, p. 210.

39 Kanatani Chieko, 'Rōdōsha hogohō henkō shi ni miru bosei hogo', *Agora*, No. 89, 10/8/84, pp. 39–66; Tanino Setsu, *Fujin kōjō kantoku kan no kiroku*, Tokyo: Domesu Shuppan, Tokyo, 1985, pp. 269–77. The 1926 amendment increased maternity leave to four weeks before parturition, and six weeks after; although a woman could return to work after four weeks with a doctor's approval, Sakurai, *Boseihogo Undōshi*, p. 41.

40 The attainment of these provisions in various industries is surveyed in Yamaguchi Miyoko and Maruoka Hideko (eds), *Nihon Fujin Mondai Shiryō Shūsei*, Vol. 10, Tokyo: Domesu Shuppan, Tokyo, 1981.

41 Oka, *Kōjōhōron*, p. 208.

42 Oka, *Kōjōhōron*, pp. 218–19.

43 Several writers have recently discussed the relationship between citizenship and waged work. Given the different relationship of men and women to waged work in early twentieth-century Japan, it is unsurprising that they should also have differing relationships to the concept of citizenship. cf. Nancy Fraser, 'What's Critical about Critical Theory? The Case of Habermas and Gender', in Seyla Benhabib and Drucilla Cornell (eds), *Feminism as Critique*, Cambridge: Polity Press, 1987; Nancy Fraser, 'Women, Welfare and the Politics of Need Interpretation', in *Unruly Practices: Power, Discourse and Gender in Contemporary Social Theory*, Cambridge: Polity Press, 1989.

44 Garon, *State and Labour in Modern Japan*, p. 30, citing Oka, *Kōjōhōron*: 'Oka likened the legislation to "our imperially bestowed Constitution [of 1889] which was granted to, rather than demanded by, the people".'

45 This criticism was made by Suzuki Bunji in 1916. See Large, *The Rise of Labour*, p. 73, citing Suzuki Bunji, 'Sangyō jō no rikken seiji', *Rōdō oyobi Sangyō*, 1/3/1916, pp. 2–9: '[Suzuki stated that] in Japan, feudal notions about society made a mockery of constitutional government. He added that in the industrial world, too, the capitalists dominated the workers with disdain for their rights. He accused the government of failing to consult the persons most affected by factory legislation – the workers themselves. He concluded, "such autocratic, feudal, bureaucratic ideas point up the fallacious notions which contradict the execution of constitutional government in contemporary society".' In other words, Suzuki's criticism questioned the very legitimacy of the State which valued capital accumulation above the democratic rights of the people.

46 On the development of the *Yūaikai*, see Large, *The Rise of Labour in Japan*, *passim*; Ayusawa, *A History of Labor in Modern Japan*, pp. 98–101.

47 The journal's name was changed to *Rōdō oyobi Sangyō* in 1915.

48 Translation in Ayusawa, *A History of Labour in Modern Japan*, p. 99.

49 The growth of the *Yūaikai* has been traced by Stephen Large: 'By 1913 it had expanded from a fifteen-man organization in Tokyo into one claiming 1,295 members in a growing network of branches throughout Japan. By the end of 1915, the membership was 7,000 and by April 1917, it had climbed to over 20,000. In 1919, the Yūaikai rolls numbered around 30,000 workers.' Large, *Organized Workers and Socialist Politics*, p. 17.

50 Suzuki Yūko, *Josei to Rōdō Kumiai*, pp. 25–100; Large, *The Rise of Labour in Japan*, pp. 71–2.

51 Initially, there was no restriction made, but in 1913, a category of 'associate member' was created for women. This was revised in 1917, after protest by women workers. Large, *The Rise of Labour*, p. 72; Gordon, *Labor and Imperial Democracy*, p. 92; Tsurumi, 'Female Textile Workers', p. 26.

52 '*Yūaikai* Fujinbu Kisoku', reproduced in Suzuki, *Josei to Rōdō Kumiai*, pp. 45–6.

53 Major contributors to the women's journal were Suzuki Bunji, Hirasawa Keishichi, Yutani Jirōshichi, Miura Gakudō, Sakamoto Masao, and Inaba Aiko. Yoshioka Yayoi, Kawaguchi Aiko and Misumi Suzuko also contributed articles at times. Suzuki, *Josei to Rōdō Kumiai*, pp. 50–9. Contents of the supplement to *Rōdō oyobi Sangyō* are listed on pp. 60–2 of Suzuki's book. At the time of writing, no extant issues of the women's supplement had been found.

54 Soeda Juichi, 'Ikka no Shufu no Suru Koto', *Yūai Fujin*, No. 2, pp. 38–9.

55 Suzuki, *Josei to Rōdō Kumiai*, p. 45.

56 '*Yūaikai* Fujinbu Shui', reproduced in Suzuki, *Josei to Rōdō Kumiai*, p. 45.

57 cf. Suzuki Bunji, 'Makoto no Onna no Fumiyuku Beki Michi', *Yūai Fujin*, No. 1, 6/7/1916, p. 5: 'A true woman's true value is in having an internal attitude of determination and power, but in appearing outwardly gentle, and consoling and encouraging her husband.'

58 'Henshū dayori', *Yūai Fujin*, No. 1, 6/7/1916, p. 96.

59 Suzuki Bunji, 'Rōdōsha no tachiba yori Kōjōhō o Hyōsu', *Rōdō oyobi Sangyō*, 1/6/1916, pp. 2–10; cited in Large, *The Rise of Labour*, p. 73.

60 'Iyo iyo Kōjōhō Jisshi: Onna Kodomo Tasukaru', *Yūai Fujin*, No. 2, June 1916, pp. 90–1.

61 'Iyo iyo Kōjōhō Jisshi', pp. 90–1.

62 Founders of the journal included Hiratsuka, Yasumochi Yoshiko, Nakano Hatsu, and Kiuchi Tei. Horiba Kiyoko, *Seitō no Jidai*, Tokyo: Iwanami Shoten, 1988, pp. 60–3. On the Bluestockings, see Ide Fumiko, *Seitō no Onnatachi*, Tokyo: Setouchi Harumi, *Seitō*; Horiba Kiyoko, *Seitō no Jidai*; Andrew, 'The Seitōsha – an early Japanese women's organisation 1911–1916'; Lippit, 'Seitō and the Literary Roots of Japanese Feminism', pp. 155–63; Reich and Fukuda, 'Japan's Literary Feminists – the Seitō Group'; Sharon H. Nolte, *Liberalism in Modern Japan: Ishibashi Tanzan and His Teachers, 1905–1960*, Berkeley: University of California Press, 1987, pp. 97–105; Sievers, *Flowers in Salt*, Chapter 8; Vera Mackie, 'Feminist Politics in Japan', *New Left Review*, January–February 1988, pp. 56–7.

63 Andrew, 'The Seitōsha', pp. 50–3.

64 Lippit, 'Seitō and the Literary Roots of Japanese Feminism', p. 155.

65 Nolte, *Liberalism in Modern Japan*, pp. 95–7; Nolte, 'Individualism in Taishō Japan', pp. 672–7.

66 Other writers have also compared the early *Seitō* writings with 'consciousness raising'. See Tachi Kaoru, 'Kenkyū Nōto: Hiratsuka Raichō to Ofudesaki', *Ochanomizu Joshi Daigaku Josei Bunka Shiryōkan Hō*, No. 7, 1986, p. 105; Kanda Michiko, 'Jiritsu no Keisei to Katei – Hratsuka Raichō o Chūshin to Shite', in *Onnatachi no Yukue*, Tokyo: Keisō Shobō, 1982.

67 Yosano Akiko, 'Sozorogoto', *Seitō*, Vol. 1, No. 1, 1911, p. 1. Translation in Laurel Rasplica Rodd, 'Yosano Akiko and the Taishō debate over the "New Women" ', in Bernstein, *Recreating Japanese Women*, p. 180.

68 Yosano Akiko, 'Sozorogoto', p. 2: 'Ichininshō nite nomi monokakabaya/ware wa onago zo/ichininshō nite nomi monokakabaya/ware wa ware wa'. See the discussion of the later verses in Ide, *Seitō no Onnatachi*, pp. 12–16.

69 Hiratsuka Raichō, 'Genshi Josei wa Taiyō de atta', *Seitō*, Vol. 1, No. 1, p. 37. For discussion of the use of metaphors of the sun and the moon for the feminine, see Tachi Kaoru, 'Kenkyū Nōto: Hiratsuka Raichō to Ofudesaki', *Ochanomizu Joshi Daigaku Josei Bunka Shiryōkan Hō*, No. 7, 1986, pp. 103–12. Similar polarities appear in European thought, where the sun may also be used as a metaphor for individual creativity and transcendence, while the moon's reflected light has been linked with women's imitative nature. Bram Dijkstra has outlined the use of these images in *fin-de-siècle* European culture: '[T]he moon had come to stand for everything that was truly feminine in the world. The moon, too, after all, existed only as a "reflected entity". It had no light of its own, just as woman, in her proper function had existence only as the passive reflection of male creativity. The sun was Apollo, the god of light, the moon, Diana, his pale echo in the night.' Bram Dijkstra, *Idols of Perversity: Images of Feminine Evil in Fin-de-Siècle Culture*, Oxford: Oxford University Press, 1986, p. 122.

70 Hiratsuka Raichō, 'Genshi Josei wa Taiyō de atta', p. 41; p. 49; p. 50; p. 52.

71 The metaphor of the sun, however, had multivalent connotations in Japan, which also drew on the Taoist cosmology, whereby the Sun represented the masculine principle of Yang, and the moon represented the feminine principle of Yin. Hiratsuka could thus draw on a complex series of associations from Japanese, Daoist and European traditions. For further discussion of the metaphorical language of Japanese feminism, see Mackie, *Imagining Liberation: Feminism and Socialism in Early Twentieth Century Japan*.

72 Hiratsuka Raichō, 'Genshi Josei wa Taiyō de atta', p. 38.

73 Hiratsuka Raichō, 'Genshi Josei wa Taiyō de atta', p. 42.

74 Hiratsuka Raichō, 'Genshi Josei wa Taiyō de atta', pp. 42–7.

75 Rodd, 'Yosano Akiko and the Taishō debate over the "New Woman"', p. 175.

76 On these incidents, see: Horiba Kiyoko, *Seitō no Jidai*, pp. 112–13, p. 199.

77 Tsubouchi's lecture was reported in the *Waseda Kōen* journal, and he later reworked the material in a book on 'The So-Called New Woman'. Tsubouchi Shōyō, 'Kinsei Geki ni Mietaru Atarashiki Onna', *Waseda Kōen*, Vol. 1, Nos 5–7, 1911; Tsubouchi Shōyō, *Iwayuru Atarashii Onna*, Tokyo: Seimidō, 1912; cited in Horiba, *Seitō no Jidai*, p. 51. For further discussion of the concept of the 'New Woman' in Japan, see Yamada Takako, 'Atarashii Onna', in Joseigaku Kenkyūkai (eds), *Kōza Joseigaku 1: Onna no Iméji*, Tokyo: Keisō Shobō, 1984, pp. 210–34.

78 *Seitō*, Vol. 3, No. 4, p. 156, English version in Reich and Fukuda, 'Japan's Literary Feminists – the Seitō Group', p. 288.

79 *Seitō*, Vol. 1, No. 1, p. 110; Vol. 2, p. 91; Vol. 2, No. 1, supplement.

80 *Seitō*, Vol. 4, No. 1, supplement.

81 Andrew, 'The Seitōsha', p. 56.

82 Fukuda Hideko, 'Fujin Mondai no Kaiketsu', *Seitō*, Vol. 3, No. 2, 1913, Supplement, p. 1; translated excerpts in Sievers, *Flowers in Salt*, p. 178; Hane, *Reflections on the Way to the Gallows*, p. 33.

83 Itō's life is discussed in Large, 'The Romance of Revolution', Miyamoto Ken, 'Itō Noe and the Bluestockings', pp. 190–204. For the reasons for the change in editorship, see Ide Fumiko, *Seitō no Onnatachi*.

84 *Seitō*, Vol. 3, No. 9, supplement, p. 1; Vol. 3, No. 11, p. 53.

85 *Seitō*, Vol. 3, Nos 11–12; Vol. 4, Nos 7–10; Vol. 5, No. 2.

86 *Seitō*, Vol. 4, No. 5, supplement.

87 Lippit, 'Seitō and the Literary Roots of Japanese Feminism', p. 161; *Seitō*, Vol. 15, No. 8, p. 30; Vol. 6, Nos 1–2. On prostitution, see interview with Yamakawa in Rekishi Hyōron Henshūbu, *Kindai Nihon Joseishi e no Shōgen*, pp. 16–17.

88 Two issues of 1913 were banned – one carrying Fukuda's article on the solution to the woman question and one carrying Raichō's article attacking the family system. Andrew, 'The Seitōsha', p. 56.

89 Although the period of publication of *Seitō* (1911 to 1916) includes the beginnings of the First World War, the *Seitō* group was distinguished by an almost complete lack

of interest in issues of war and peace. Hiratsuka herself notes this lack in her autobiography. Hiratsuka Raichō, *Genshi Josei wa Taiyō de atta*, Tokyo: Ōtsuki Shoten,
Tokyo, 1971, Vol. 2, pp. 568–70.

90 Saika Kotoko, 'Senka', *Seitō*, Vol. 5, No. 10; quoted in Hiratsuka Raichō, *Genshi Josei
wa Taiyō de atta*, Vol. 2, pp. 568–70.

91 *Shin shin fujin* was established in 1913, and published for just over ten years. Few
issues of this journal survived the Tokyo Earthquake of 1923, but some issues are
held in the Ōhara Social Research Institute. Nishikawa's writings have been collected
as an appendix to her autobiography: Nishikawa, *Heiminsha no onna: Nishikawa Fumiko
Jiden*.

92 Aims of the *Shinshin fujin kai*, Nishikawa Fumiko Jiden, p. 137.

93 'Fujin to Heiwa', *Shinshin fujin: Heiwa gō*, 1/10/1914.

94 'Fujin to shakai mondai', *Shinshinfujin*, 1/3/1920, Jiden, p. 271.

95 *Atarishiki onna no yuku beki michi*, 1913, quoted in *Jiden*, pp. 377–8.

96 Nishikawa Fumiko, *Atarishiki onna no yuku beki michi*; quoted in *Jiden*, pp. 377–8.

97 Nishikawa Fumiko, 'Nihon shōrai no katei', *Shinshin fujin*, 1914, reprinted in *Nishi-
kawa Fumiko Jiden*, pp. 244–7. The phrase *ryōfu kenfu* was also used by a writer in *Fujo
Shinbun*, No. 159; and by Kanno Suga in *Muroo Shinpō*, 15/4/1906. I am indebted to
Hélène Bowen for pointing out Kanno's use of this phrase.

98 This debate is surveyed in: Maruoka, *Fujin Shisō Keisei Shi Nōto*, Vol. 1, pp. 105–27;
Kōuchi Nobuko, ' "Bosei Hogo Ronsō" no Rekishiteki Igi: "Ronsō" Kara "Undō"
e no tsunagari'. *Rekishi Hyōron*, No. 195, November 1966, pp. 28–41; Kōuchi Nobuko.
'Kaidai', in Kōuchi Nobuko (ed.), *Shiryō: Bosei Hogo Ronsō*, Tokyo: Domesu Shuppan,
1984, pp. 289–320; Sakurai Kinue, *Bosei Hogo Undōshi*, pp. 48–52; Kanatani Chieko,
'Ima Bosei Hogo Ronsō o Toinaoshi: Yosano Akiko Kara Manabu Mono', *Onna to
Otoko no Joseiron*, No. 7, 1991, pp. 28–45; Diana Bethel, 'Visions of a Humane Society:
Feminist Thought in Taishō Japan', *Feminist International*, No. 2, 1980; Vera Mackie,
'Motherhood and Pacifism in Japan, 1900–1937', *Hecate*, Vol. 14, No. 2, 1988, pp. 37–
8; Barbara Molony, 'Equality versus Difference: The Japanese Debate Over Mother-
hood Protection, 1915–1950', in Janet Hunter (ed), *Japanese Women Working*, London:
Routledge, 1993, pp. 122–9.

99 *Fujo Shinbun*, editorial, 14/3/1904, p. 1. See also: 'Shasetsu: Senshisha no Izoku', *Fujo
Shinbun*, No. 281, 25/9/1905, p. 1.

100 For documents related to this debate, see *Nihon Fujin Mondai Shiryō Shūsei*, Vol. 8,
pp. 231–62, Kōuchi, *Shiryō: Bosei Hogo Ronsō*, *passim*.

101 Fukushima Shirō, 'Bosei o hogo seyo', *Fujo Shinbun* 20/4/1917; 'Bosei o hogo seyo
(futatabi)', *Fujo Shinbun* 27/4/1917; reprinted in Fukushima Shirō, *Fujinkai Sanjūgonen*, Tokyo, 1935 [facsimile edition, Tokyo: Fuji Shuppan, 1984], pp. 161–5.

102 Fukushima, 'Bosei o hogo seyo', p. 161.

103 Fukushima, 'Bosei o hogo seyo (futatabi)'; pp. 162–3. The theme would be continued
in several subsequent editorials. See 'Bosei hogo no hoken', *Fujo Shinbun*, 28/6/
1918; reprinted in *Fujinkai Sanjūgonen*, pp. 165–7; 'Boseiai no kakuchō', *Fujo Shinbun*,
10/1/1926; reprinted in *Fujinkai Sanjūgonen*, pp. 167–9; 'Bosei Hogo no Kyūyō', *Fujo
Shinbun*, 7/2/1926, reprinted in *Fujinkai Sanjūgonen*, pp. 171–2; 'Joken setsu to Boseihogo setsu', *Fujo Shinbun* 26/4/1931, reprinted in *Fujinkai Sanjūgonen*, pp. 175–6;
'Boseiai no kakuchō (futatabi)', *Fujo Shinbun*, 16/4/1933; reprinted in *Fujinkai Sanjūgonen*, pp. 169–70. Later editorials refer to the creation of a committee to lobby
for the creation of a Mother and Child Assistance Act. See the discussion of this
campaign in Chapter six.

104 Yosano Akiko, 'Shieiroku', *Fujin Kōron*, Vol. 3, No. 3, March 1918, excerpted in
Kōuchi, *Shiryō: Bosei Hogo Ronsō*, pp. 85–6; cited in Rodd, 'Yosano Akiko and the
Taishō Debate over the 'New Woman', p. 192.

105 Yosano Akiko, 'Nebatsuchi Jizō', *Taiyō*, Vol. 24, March–August 1918; excerpts in
Nihon Fujin Mondai Shiryō Shūsei, Vol. 8, pp. 233–9.

106 Hiratsuka Raichō, 'Bosei hogo no shuchō wa irai shugi ni arazu', p. 231.

107 Hiratsuka, 'Bosei hogo no shuchō wa Irai shugi ni arazu', p. 232.

108 See the discussion of these issues in Marilyn Lake, 'Mission Impossible: How Men

Gave Birth to the Australian Nation – Nationalism, Gender and Other Seminal Acts, *Gender and History*, Vol. 4, No. 3, (Autumn 1992), pp. 305–22.

109 'Bosei Hogo no Hoken', pp. 166–7.

110 cf. Caroline Rowan, 'Mothers. Vote Labour! The State, the Labour Movement and Working-Class Mothers, 1900–1918', in Rosalind Brunt and Caroline Rowan (eds), *Feminism, Culture and Politics*, London, Lawrence and Wishart, 1982, p. 82: 'If childrearing and housewifery were civic duties, they could demand civic rights in return.'

111 Yosano Akiko, 'Nebatsuchi Jizō', *Taiyō*, Vol. 24, No. 7, 1918, in *Nihon Fujin Mondai Shiryō Shūsei*, Vol. 8, pp. 233–9.

112 Yosano, 'Nebatsuchi Jizō', p. 234.

113 For discussion of Yamada's contribution to the debate, see Yamazaki Tomoko, *Ameyuki-san no Uta: Yamada Waka no Sūki naru Shōgai*, Tokyo: Bungei Shunjū, 1981, pp. 213–15; Yamazaki Tomoko, *The Story of Yamada Waka: From Prostitute to Feminist Pioneer*, Tokyo: Kodansha, 1985, pp. 129–30.

114 Yamada Waka, 'Kongo no Fujin Mondai o Teishōsu', original publication details unclear, reproduced in Kōuchi, *Shiryō: Bosei Hogo Ronsō*, pp. 91–5. See also Yamada Waka, 'Fujin o Madowasu Fujinron', *Bunka Undō*, No. 100, October/November 1918, in Kōuchi, *Shiryō: Bosei Hogo Ronsō*, pp. 168–76.

115 Similar issues were discussed in other national contexts. See Rowan, 'Mothers. Vote Labour!'; Janet Evans, 'The Communist Party of the Soviet Union and the Women's Question: The case of the 1936 Decree "In Defence of Mother and Child"', *Journal of Contemporary History*, Vol. 16, 1981, pp. 757–75; Gisela Bock and Pat Thane (eds), *Maternity and Gender Policies: Women and the Rise of the European Welfare States, 1880s–1950s*, London: Routledge, 1991; Lake, 'Mission Impossible'.

116 For details of Yamakawa Kikue's life and work, see Ezashi Akiko, *Sameyo Onnatachi*, Tokyo: Ōtsuki Shoten, 1980, pp. 122–39; Rekishi Hyōron Henshūbu, *Kindai Nihon Joseishi e no Shōgen*, Tokyo: Domesu Shuppan, 1979, pp. 9–48; Kondō [Sakai] Magara, *Watashi no Kaisō*, Tokyo: Domesu Shuppan, 1981, Vol. 2, pp. 182–5; Jennifer Shapcott, 'The Red Chrysanthemum: Yamakawa Kikue and the Socialist Women's Movement in Pre-war Japan', *Papers on Far Eastern History*, No 35, March 1987, pp. 1–30.

117 Yamakawa Kikue, 'Yosano, Hiratsuka Ryōshi no ronsō', *Fujin Kōron*, Vol. 3, No. 7, 1918, in *Nihon Fujin Mondai Shiryō Shūsei*, Vol. 8, p. 239–48. For discussion of Ellen Key's influence on Japanese feminism, see Kaneko Sachiko, 'Taishōki ni okeru seiyō josei kaihō ron juyō no hōhō – Ellen Key *Ren'ai to kekkon* o tegakari ni', *Shakai Kagaku Jaanaru*, No. 24, October 1985.

118 Yamakawa, 'Yosano, Hiratsuka Ryōshi no ronsō', p. 241.

119 Yamakawa, 'Yosano, Hiratsuka Ryōshi no ronsō', p. 245.

120 Yamakawa, 'Yosano, Hiratsuka Ryōshi no ronsō', p. 242.

121 Yamada Waka, 'Fujin no Kaihō to wa', *Fujin to Shinshakai*, No. 3, May 1920, p. 10. Some copies of *Fujin to Shinshakai* are held in the Ōhara Social Research Institute. (Nos 3–9 (May–November 1920), 11–13 (January–March 1921)).

122 Barbara Molony, in 'Equality versus Difference: The Japanese Debate Over Motherhood Protection, 1915-1950', concentrates on the notion of equality versus difference, and discusses what she calls the 'body-centred' emphasis of much of the discussion of 'motherhood protection' from 1915 to 1950. In the following, I shall argue that the use of the one label, *bosei hogo*, for several different areas of social policy obscures the fact that what is often being discussed has more to do with social structures than biological difference. For recent feminist discussions of 'equality versus difference', see Shane Phelan, 'Specificity: Beyond Equality and Difference', *Differences: A Journal of Feminist Cultural Studies*, Vol. 3, No. 1, 1991; Carol Lee Bacchi, *Same Difference*, Sydney: Allen & Unwin, 1991; Joan Scott, 'Deconstructing Equality versus Difference; or, The Uses of Post-Structuralist Theory for Feminism', *Feminist Studies*, Vol. 14, No. 1, (Spring 1988); [revised as 'The Sears Case', in Joan Scott, *Gender and the Politics of History*, New York: Columbia University Press, 1988]; Gisela Bock and Susan James (eds), *Beyond Equality and Difference: Citizenship, Feminist Politics and Female Subjectivity*, London: Routledge, 1992.

123 cf. Rowan, 'Mothers Vote Labour!', p. 60: 'If one regards the family as a key site of patriarchal power relations, albeit as a result of historical development, rather than biological inevitability, then state intervention in the family can be seen as the point of intersection of class and gender struggle and the point at which tensions and contradictions between the two are likely to be most evident.'

124 For discussions of the concept of 'motherhood' in early twentieth-century Japan see Kanō Mikiyo, *Jiga no Kanata e: Kindai o Koeru Feminizumu*, Tokyo: Shakai Hyōronsha, 1990; Kōuchi Nobuko, (ed.), *Bosei Hogo Ronsō*; Suzuki Yūko, *Joseishi o Hiraku 1: Haha to Onna*, Tokyo: Miraisha, 1989; Tachi Kaoru, 'Kindai Nihon no Bosei to Feminism – Bosei no Kenri kara Ikujiken e', in Hara Hiroko and Tachi Kaoru (eds), *Bosei kara Jisedai Ikuseiryoku e: Umisodateru Shakai no Tame ni*, Tokyo: Shinyōsha, 1991; Wakita Haruko, (ed.), *Bosei o Tou: Rekishiteki Henkō*, Vol. 2, Kyōto: Jinbun Shoin, 1985. For more recent considerations of this issue, see Aoki Yayoi, (ed.), *Bosei to wa Nani ka?*, Tokyo: Kaneko Shobō, 1986; Ōhinata Masami, *Bosei no Kenkyū*, Tokyo: Kawashima Shoten, 1988.

125 cf. Zathia Pathak and Rajeswari Sunder Rajan, 'Shahbano', in Judith Butler and Joan W. Scott (eds), *Feminists Theorize the Political*, New York: Routledge, 1992, pp. 262–6.

126 On the implications of discourses of protection, Fraser quotes Judith Stiehm: 'As Judith Stiehm has argued, this division between male protectors and female protected introduces further dissonance into women's relation to citizenship. It confirms the gender subtext of the citizen role. And the view of women as in need of men's protection "underlies access not just to . . . the means of destruction, but also [to] the means of production – witness all the 'protective' legislation that has surrounded women's access to the workplace – and [to] the means of reproduction, [witness] women's status as wives and sexual partners".' ; Judith Stiehm, 'The Protected, the Protector, the Defender,' in Judith Hicks Stiehm (ed.), *Women and Men's Wars*, New York: Pergamon Press, 1983, cited in Nancy Fraser, 'What's Critical about Critical Theory? The Case of Habermas and Gender', p. 44.

127 Hiratsuka Raichō, Sakamoto Makoto, Ichikawa Fusae and Oku Mumeo formed the *Shin Fujin Kyōkai* (New Women's Association) in 1920. The activities of the *Shin Fujin Kyōkai* will be discussed in Chapter six. Robins-Mowry, *The Hidden Sun: Women of Modern Japan*, pp. 66–7.

128 Ichikawa Fusae and others formed the League for the Attainment of Women's Political Rights (*Fujin Sanseiken Kakutoku Kisei Dōmeikai*) in 1924. The League's name was changed to *Fusen Kakutoku Dōmei* (Women's Suffrage League) in April 1925. The issue of women's suffrage will be discussed in Chapter six.

5 Workers

1 Yamakawa Kikue, 'Rōdō Fujin no Genzai to Sono Shōrai', *Nihon Hyōron*, February 1919, reprinted in Yamakawa's book, *Onna no Tachiba Kara*, under the title 'Rōdō Kaikyū no Shimai e'. This version is reproduced in Suzuki Yūko (ed.), *Josei: Hangyaku to Kakumei to Teikō to*, Tokyo: Shakai Hyōronsha, 1990, pp. 54–9. Subsequent citations refer to this version.

2 Yamakawa, 'Rōdō Kaikyū no Shimai e', p. 55. This is reminiscent of the anxiety expressed by early British socialists on the effects on workers of working with machines: William Morris, 'Attractive Labour', *Commonweal*, June Supplement, 1885, p. 49, cited in Anne Cranny-Francis, *The Body in the Text*, Melbourne: Melbourne University Press, 1995, p. 91.

3 Yamakawa, 'Rōdō Kaikyū no Shimai e', p. 56.

4 Compare with Sandra Dijkstra's account of pioneering French feminist Flora Tristan's realization of her connection with the working class. Sandra Dijkstra, *Flora Tristan: Feminism in the Age of George Sand*, London: Pluto Press, 1992, pp. 129–33.

5 Yamakawa, 'Rōdō Kaikyū no Shimai e', p. 58. This incident is also described at length in Yamakawa's autobiography, *Onna Nidai no Ki*, Tokyo: Heibonsha, 1972. On class

differences dramatized in spatial terms, see my discussion of Fukuda Hideko's autobiography, Chapter one, Introduction.

6 Yamakawa, 'Rōdō Kaikyū no Shimai e', pp. 58–9.

7 Yamakawa was most active, however, as a writer, translator, and interpreter of socialist
ideas. In 1919 she published *The Triumph of Women*, a work heavily indebted to the
ideas of August Bebel. (Yamakawa Kikue, *Fujin no Shōri*, Tokyo: Nihon Hyōronsha,
1919.) Although Bebel's ideas had been influential since the days of the *Heiminsha*,
it was not until 1923 that Yamakawa's full translation of *Woman and Socialism*
appeared, under the title, *Fujinron* (On Women). By 1928, Yamakawa had also translated works of Gorky, Radek, Lenin and Kollontai. For a full listing of Yamakawa's
writings, see Sotozaki Mitsuhiro and Okabe Masako (eds), *Yamakawa Kikue no Kōseki*,
Tokyo: Domesu Shuppan, 1979.

8 On the *ana-boru ronsō*, see Thomas A. Stanley, *Ōsugi Sakae: Anarchist in Taishō Japan*,
Cambridge, Massachusetts: Harvard University Council on East Asian Studies, 1982,
pp. 128–41.

9 Tajima Hide, *Hitosuji no Michi: Fujin Kaihō no Tatakai Gojūnen*, Tokyo: Aoki Shoten,
1968, p. 138; Inumaru Giichi, 'Nihon ni okeru Marukusu shugi Fujinron no Ayumi:
Senzenhen', in Joseishi Sōgō Kenkyūkai (eds) *Nihon Joseishi 5: Gendai*, Tokyo: Tokyo
Daigaku Shuppankai, pp. 149–92.

10 On the *Rōnō-Kōza debates*, see Hoston, Germaine, *Marxism and the Crisis of Development
in Prewar Japan*, Princeton, New Jersey: Princeton University Press, 1986, *passim*. For
some comments on the relevance of women's work to the 'Japanese capitalism
debate', see Janet Hunter, 'Introduction', in Hunter (ed) *Japanese Women Working*,
pp. 2–3.

11 Robins-Mowry, *The Hidden Sun*, p. 75.

12 On the participation of women in the *Suiheisha*, see Suzuki Yūko, *Suiheisen o Mezasu
Onnatachi*, Tokyo: Domesu Shuppan, 1987.

13 Large, *Organized Workers and Socialist Politics*, pp. 45–53.

14 On Nakasone Sadayo, see Ezashi, *Sameyo Onnatachi*, pp. 96–120; Watanabe and
Suzuki, *Tatakai ni Ikite*, pp. 34–5; Kondō, *Watashi no Kaisō*, Vol. 2, pp. 48–51; on Sakai
Magara, See Kondō, *Watashi no Kaisō*, *passim*; Watanabe Etsuji and Suzuki Yūko (eds),
Tatakai ni Ikite: Senzen Fujin Rōdō Undō e no Shōgen, Tokyo: Domesu Shuppan, 1980,
pp. 8–38. Ezashi, *Sameyo Onnatachi*, pp. 30–50.

15 For a detailed discussion of the splits, see Large, *Organized Workers and Socialist Politics*,
pp. 62–71, pp. 108–9. See Figure 5.1, page 261 for the factions of the pre-war union
movement.

16 The Social Democratic (*Shaminkei*) clique was based in the *Sōdōmei* Union Federation
and the Social Democratic Party (*Shakai Minshū Tō*). The centrist (*Nichirō*) clique
was based in the Japan Labour Union League (*Nihon Rōdō Kumiai Dōmei*) and the
Japan Labour–Farmer Party (*Nihon Rōdō Nōmin Tō*). The left-wing (*Rōnō-ha*) clique
was based in the left-wing *Hyōgikai* Union Federation and the Labour–Farmer Party
(*Rōdō Nōmin Tō*). These factions are discussed in detail in Large, *Organized Workers
and Socialist Politics*, pp. 111–18. In this chapter I will mainly be concerned with
women's participation in the labour organizations, and the debates surrounding
strategies for mobilizing women workers. The proletarian political parties and their
affiliated women's leagues will be discussed in Chapter six.

17 Garon, *State and Labour*, p. 43. For further discussion of the importance of the ILO
to the Japanese labour movement before the Second World War, see Nakayama
Kazuhisa, *I.L.O. Jōyaku to Nihon*, Tokyo: Iwanami Shoten, 1983, pp. 12–18.

18 The minimum size of factory covered by the law was changed from fifteen workers
to ten workers, meaning that 11 per cent more factories came under the jurisdiction
of the law. The minimum age of workers was raised from twelve to fifteen years old.
The maximum permissible hours to be worked by women and minors was lowered
from twelve hours to eleven hours. The principle of the abolition of night work for
women was reiterated, but postponed again. Large, *Organized Workers and Socialist
Politics*, p. 54; Sakurai, *Bosei Hogo Undōshi*, pp. 42–8.

19 Hunter, 'Factory Legislation and Employer Resistance', pp. 243–72.

20 Gordon, *Labor and Imperial Democracy*, pp. 140–1; Garon, *State and Labour*, pp. 123–30.
21 Rather than attempting to give a comprehensive picture of the demographics of women's work, I have tried to identify some features of women's employment which are relevant to socialist attempts to mobilize women workers. The information in this section comes from the following sources: Barbara Molony, 'Activism among Women in the Taishō Cotton Industry', in Gail Lee Bernstein (ed.), *Recreating Japanese Women, 1600–1945*, pp. 217–38; Margit Nagy, 'Middle-Class Working Women During the Interwar Years', in Bernstein, *Recreating Japanese Women*, pp. 199–216; Mariko Asano Tamanoi, 'Songs as Weapons: The Culture and History of *Komori* (Nursemaids) in Modern Japan', *Journal of Asian Studies*, Vol. 50, No. 4, November 1991, pp. 793–817; Kathleen Uno, 'One Day at a Time: Work and Domestic Activities of Urban Lower-Class Women in Early Twentieth Century Japan', in Hunter (ed.), *Japanese Women Working*, pp. 37–68; Regine Mathias, 'Female Labour in the Japanese Coal-Mining Industry', in Hunter (ed.), *Japanese Women Working*, pp. 98–121; Kōnosuke Odaka, 'Redundancy Utilized: The Economics of Female Domestic Servants in pre-War Japan, in Hunter (ed.), *Japanese Women Working*, pp. 16–36.
22 One attempt to address this problem is: Maruoka Hideko, *Nihon Nōson Fujin Mondai*, Tokyo: Kōyō Shoin, 1937.
23 Odaka, 'Redundancy Utilized', p. 17.
24 Odaka, 'Redundancy Utilized', p. 17.
25 Barbara Molony notes that relatively few women in factories in the 1920s returned to villages after leaving one place of employment. Most went on to other factory employment, or other kinds of waged work, or stayed in the city as housewives after marrying a fellow worker. Molony, 'Activism among Women in the Taishō Textile Industry', p. 224.
26 Uno, 'One Day at a Time', pp. 41–2.
27 The number of licensed prostitutes remained around 50 000 in the Taishō and Shōwa periods. It is estimated that similar numbers worked as *geisha*, or as waitresses. Sheldon Garon, 'The World's Oldest Debate? Prostitution and the State in Imperial Japan, 1900–1945, *American Historical Review*, June 1993, p. 714.
28 Nagy, 'Middle-Class Working Women', pp. 201–4.
29 Silverberg, Miriam, 'The Modern Girl as Militant', in Bernstein (ed.) *Recreating Japanese Women*, pp. 239–66; Barbara Hamill Sato, 'The *Moga* Sensation: Perceptions of the *Modan Gāru* in Japanese Intellectual Circles During the 1920s', *Gender and History*, Vol. 5, No. 3, (Autumn 1993), pp. 363–81.
30 Although 1920 was the first time May Day had been celebrated with a public demonstration, the members of the *Heiminsha* had marked May Day in a modest fashion from 1905. See Tanaka Sōgorō (ed.), *Shiryō: Nihon Shakai Undō Shi*, Tokyo: Tōzai Shuppansha, 1948, Vol. 1, pp. 508–9. On the history of May Day as an international workers' celebration, see Eric Hobsbawm, 'Mass-Producing Traditions: Europe 1820–1914', in Hobsbawm and Ranger (eds), *The Invention of Tradition*, pp. 283–6. On the incorporation of May Day into the tradition of the Japanese labour movement, see Gordon, *Labor and Imperial Democracy*. The participation of women in Japan's May Day celebrations will be discussed below. The last May Day celebration of this period was in 1935.
31 The founding members of the *Sekirankai* included Sakai Magara and her step-mother Sakai Tameko, Takatsu Tayoko, Kutsumi Fusako, Akitsuki Shizue, Kitagawa Chiyo, Hashiura Haruko and Hashiura Riku, with Yamakawa Kikue and Itō Noe acting as advisors. For the development of the *Sekirankai*, see Ezashi, Akiko *Sameyo Onnatachi*, *passim*; interview with Kondō [Sakai] Magara in Watanabe and Suzuki, *Tatakai ni Ikite*, pp. 8–33; interview with Yamakawa Kikue in Rekishi Hyōron Henshūbu, *Kindai Nihon Joseishi e no Shōgen*, pp. 42–3; Tajima, *Hitosuji no Michi*, pp. 61–6; Kondō, *Watashi no Kaisō*, Vol. 2, pp. 185–9; Vol. 2, pp. 7–62, pp. 98–134; Shapcott, 'The Red Chrysanthemum'; Yamakawa, *Fujin Undō Shōshi*, pp. 137–141. On Sakai Tameko, see Ezashi, *Sameyo Onnatachi*, pp. 30–50; Kondō, *Watashi no Kaisō*, Vol. 1, pp. 101–3; on Takatsu Tayoko, see Ezashi, *Sameyo Onnatachi*, pp. 52–71; Suzuki Yūko, *Hiroshima-ken Josei Undō Shi*, Tokyo: Domesu Shuppan, 1985, pp. 69–76; Watanabe and Suzuki,

Tatakai ni Ikite, pp. 35–6; Kondō, *Watashi no Kaisō*, Vol. 2, pp. 37–47; on Kutsumi Fusako, see Makise Kikue, *Kutsumi Fusako no Koyomi: Meiji Shakai Shugi kara Zoruge Jiken e*, Tokyo: Shisō no Kagakusha, 1975; Ōtake Hitoko, *Haha to Watashi: Kutsumi Fusako to no Hibi*, Tokyo: Tsukiji Shokan, 1984; Ezashi, *Sameyo Onnatachi*, pp. 162–92; Watanabe and Suzuki, *Tatakai ni Ikite*, p. 34; Kondō, *Watashi no Kaisō*, Vol. 1, pp. 122–38; on Akitsuki Shizue, see Ezashi, *Sameyo Onnatachi*, pp. 234–41; Watanabe and Suzuki, *Tatakai ni Ikite*, p. 33; on Kitagawa Chiyo, see Ezashi, *Sameyo Onnatachi*, pp. 194–211; Watanabe and Suzuki, *Tatakai ni Ikite*, p. 36; on Hashiura Haruko, see Ezashi, *Sameyo Onnatachi*, pp. 74–93; Watanabe and Suzuki, *Tatakai ni Ikite*, p. 34; Makise Kikue, *Kikigaki: Hitamuki no Onnatachi–Musan Undō no Kage ni*, Tokyo: Asahi Shinbunsha, 1976, pp. 7–28; translated excerpts of Makise's interview with Hashiura appear in Hane (ed.), *Reflections on the Way to the Gallows*; on Hashiura Riku, see Ezashi, *Sameyo Onnatachi*, pp. 74–93.

32 Yamakawa Kikue, *Fujin Undō Shōshi*, p. 123.

33 'Fujin ni Gekisu', held in Ōhara Social Research Institute, reproduced in Ezashi, *Sameyo Onnatachi*, pp. 23–4; Kondō, *Watashi no Kaisō*, Vol. 2, pp. 58–9; slightly modified from translation in Shapcott, 'The Red Chrysanthemum', p. 13.

34 The prostitute could also serve as a metaphor for the exploitation of the proletarian class as a whole. See Shea's discussion of Hayama Yoshiki's story, 'Inbaifu' (Prostitute), which appeared in the proletarian literary journal *Bungei Sensen* in November 1925: Shea, *Leftwing Literature in Japan*, pp. 154–6.

35 Ezashi, *Sameyo Onnatachi*, pp. 87–8.

36 Watanabe and Suzuki, *Tatakai ni Ikite*, pp. 9–10.

37 For accounts of this evening, see Ezashi, *Sameyo Onnatachi*, pp. 39–41; interview with Kondō [Sakai] Magara in Watanabe and Suzuki *Tatakai ni Ikite*, pp. 19–20; Yamakawa, *Nihon Fujin Undō Shōshi*. Yamakawa reports that the speeches were stopped by police, but this does not match Ezashi's account, which includes details of Sakai Magara's speech, based on contemporary newspaper accounts. Yamakawa may have been thinking of the first International Women's Day meeting which was disbanded by police (see p. 105).

38 For accounts of this lecture series, see Ezashi, *Sameyo Onnatachi* Watanabe and Suzuki, *Tatakai ni Ikite*, pp. 20–1.

39 Other speakers included Kutsumi Fusako, Nakasone Sadayo, Fujimori Seikichi, Eguchi Kan, and Akita Ujaku.

40 Yamakawa, *Fujin Undō Shōshi*, p. 123; Ezashi, *Sameyo Onnatachi*, p. 42.

41 The conflict between the New Women's Association and the *Sekirankai* is discussed in Shapcott, 'The Red Chrysanthemum', pp. 16–23. See also Kondō, *Watashi no Kaisō*, Vol. 2, pp. 98–101; Yamakawa Kikue, *Fujin Undō Shōshi*, p. 116.

42 Yamakawa Kikue, 'Shin Fujin Kyōkai to Sekirankai', *Taiyō*, Vol. 27, No. 9, July 1921; reprinted in Maruoka Hideko (ed.), *Nihon Fujin Mondai Shiryō Shūsei*, Vol. 8, pp. 265–9.

43 Oku Mumeo, 'Watashitachi no Shuchō to Tachiba: Yamakawa Kikue no "Shin Fujin Kyōkai to Sekirankai" o Yomite', *Taiyō*, Vol. 27, No. 21, August 1921; reprinted in *Nihon Fujin Mondai Shiryō Shūsei*, Vol. 8, pp. 269–72.

44 Ezashi, *Sameyo Fujin*, pp. 65–8.

45 Ezashi, *Sameyo Fujin*, p. 47; Kondō Magara, *Watashi no Kaisō*, Vol. 2, pp. 123–8; Watanabe and Suzuki, *Tatakai ni Ikite*, pp. 22–4.

46 Tajima, *Hitosuji no Michi*, pp. 77–81; Yamada Seizaburō, *Puroretaria Bungaku Shi*, Tokyo: Rironsha, Vol. 1, pp. 344–5; *Tokyo Nichi Nichi Shinbun*, 3/9/1925, morning edition, p. 9; cited in Makise, *Hitamuki no Onnatachi*, pp. 30–1. Several of the speakers used pseudonyms. Kaneko Hiroko was the pseudonym of doctor Sasaki Haru. Tajima Hide used the name Miyake Hideko; Tanno Setsu used the name Minato Chie; and Kawakami Ai used the name Takeda Toshi. The names of Nakasone Sadayo and Yamakawa Kikue appeared on the brochure, and it may have been Yamakawa's name which attracted the attention of the anti-communist agitators. Tajima Hide was a woman who for a time worked in both the liberal women's movement and the socialist movement, but eventually concentrated her activities in the left of the socialist

movement, moving to the illegal Communist party in the late 1920s. Tajima, *Hitosuji no Michi*, pp. 78–9.

47 *Tane Maku Hito: Musan Fujin Gō – Kokusai Fuin Dē Kinen*, March 1923.
48 Such criticisms have been made by several of the activists of the 1920s. See Tajima Hide, *Hitosuji no Michi*, pp. 63–4; Yamakawa Kikue, *Fujin Undō Shōshi*; and comments by Shapcott, 'The Red Chrysanthemum'.
49 Yamakawa Hitoshi, 'Musan Kaikyū no Hōkō Tenkan', *Zen'ei*, July–August 1922.
50 Ezashi, *Sameyo Onnatachi*, p. 135. On Tanno Setsu, see Large, 'The Romance of Revolution'; Tajima, *Hitosuji no Michi*, pp. 96–8; *Tanno Setsu: Kakumei Undō ni Ikiru*; excerpts translated in Hane, *Reflections on the Way to the Gallows*.
51 The decision to participate in this federation was influenced by the new policy of going 'to the masses'. Yamakawa Kikue, after her scathing attack on such bourgeois feminist organizations as the New Women's Association, was now advising socialist women's participation in mainstream organizations. Tajima Hide, *Hitosuji no Michi*, pp. 104–9.
52 Large, *Organized Workers and Socialist Politics*, p. 53.
53 The following policies were approved at the Second Convention of the *Seiji Kenkyūkai*, in April 1925: ' the society should (1) prepare a draft program for the proletarian party to be, (2) speed the organization of such a party, (3) campaign for the abolition of the newly passed Peace Preservation Law, and (4) demand that women be given the right to participate in politics'. Totten, *The Social Democratic Movement*, p. 55.
54 As Miyake Yoshiko points out, describing women's needs as 'specific' or 'special' implies the universalism of male demands. Miyake, 'Rekishi no naka no jendaa', p. 147.
55 Yamakawa Kikue, 'Fujin no Tokushu Yōkyū ni tsuite', June 1925; later published in Yamakawa Hitoshi and Kikue, *Musansha Undō to Fujin no Mondai*, Tokyo: Hakuyōsha, 1928; reproduced in *Nihon Fujin Mondai Shiryō Shūsei*, Vol. 8, pp. 275–86. Subsequent citations refer to this version.
56 Yamakawa Kikue, 'Fujin no Tokushu Yōkyū ni tsuite'.
57 By this time Japan has control of both Korea and Taiwan, with trading interests in Manchuria.
58 Yamakawa Kikue, 'Fujin no Tokushu Yōkyū ni tsuite', pp. 279–80.
59 Yamakawa Kikue, 'Fujin no Tokushu Yōkyū ni tsuite', pp. 280–1.
60 Maruoka Hideko, *Fujin Shisō Keisei Shi Nōto*, pp. 145–6.
61 Yamakawa Kikue, 'Fujin no Tokushu Yōkyū ni tsuite', p. 283.
62 This discussion has similarities with the arguments of the women of the Ladies National Association of Great Britain, who campaigned for the repeal of the Contagious Diseases Acts under the leadership of Josephine Butler. Judith R. Walkowitz, *Prostitution and Victorian Society: Women, Class and the State*, Cambridge: Cambridge University Press, 1982, pp. 67–147.
63 On the activities of women in the *Sōdōmei/Yūaikai*, see Suzuki, *Josei to Rōdō Kumiai*, *passim*; On the activities of women in the *Hyōgikai*, see Sakurai Kinue, 'Hyōgikai Fujinbu no Katsudō ni tsuite', Parts 1–3; *Rekishi Hyōron*, March 1976; March 1977; October 1977.
64 Suzuki, *Josei to Rōdō Kumiai*, p. 69.
65 On Nomura Tsuchino, see Suzuki Yūko, *Josei to Rōdō Kumiai*, p. 80; on Yamanouchi Mina see Yamanouchi Mina, *Yamanouchi Mina Jiden: Jūnisai no Bōseki Jokō kara no Shōgai*, Tokyo: Shinjuku Shobō, 1975.
66 The new Federation was administered by a Central Executive Committee, and an Executive Committee which comprised twenty-five members elected to represent the regional councils. In 1920, the prefix 'Greater' was removed on the grounds of connections with imperialist tendencies. In 1921, 'Yūaikai' was removed from the name. Large, *Organized Workers and Socialist Politics*, pp. 25–6.
67 Suzuki, *Josei to Rōdō Kumiai*, pp. 76–7.
68 Tanaka Takako was due to be the Government's adviser on women workers at the forthcoming International Labour Conference. On Tanaka [Takanashi] Takako's career, see Nolte, *Liberalism in Modern Japan*, pp. 118–28.

69 Suzuki, *Josei to Rōdō Kumiai*, pp. 78–81. 'Yūaikai Fujinbu Taikai ni Mezametaru Jokō: Komochi ya Kataage no Kien Banjō', *Tokyo Asahi Shinbun*, 6/10/1919, cited in Maruoka Hideko, *Fujin Shisō Keisei Shi Nōto*, Tokyo: Domesu Shuppan, 1975, Vol. 1, p. 133; Itō Noe, 'Fujin Rōdōsha Taikai', *Rōdō Undō*, No. 2, 13/11/1919, cited in: Suzuki, *Josei to Rōdō Kumiai*, p. 79. The speeches appeared in the November 1919 issue of the union journal, *Rōdō oyobi Sangyō*. The journal *Fujin Sekai*. (World of Women) also carried Kikuchi's article under the dramatic title, 'The Cries of Working Mothers'. Yamanouchi wrote about 'The Cries of Women in Dormitories' in the same issue. Kikuchi Hatsu, 'Komochi Jokō no Sakebi'; Yamanouchi Mina, 'Kishuku Jokō no Sakebi', *Fujin Sekai*, December 1919; cited in Suzuki, *Josei to Rōdō Kumiai*, p. 81.

70 On Ichikawa's resignation, see Suzuki, *Josei to Rōdō Kumiai*, pp. 81–6; interview with Ichikawa Fusae in Rekishi Hyōron Henshūbu, *Nihon Kindai Joseishi e no Shōgen*, pp. 52–3.

71 Suzuki, *Josei to Rōdō Kumiai*, p. 87.

72 'Zadankai: Rōdō Undō no naka no Senkuteki Joseitachi', *Undōshi Kenkyū*, No. 11, February 1983; excerpted in Suzuki, *Josei to Rōdō Kumiai*, pp. 88–91. See also Tajima Hide's comments on the 'feudal' attitudes of men in the labour movement. Tajima, *Hitosuji no Michi*, p. 97.

73 Tajima, *Hitosuji no Michi*, pp. 116–20. The *Sōdōmei* was administered by two large regional councils in Eastern and Western Japan. For further details of the *Sōdōmei* administrative structure, see Large, *Organized Workers and Socialist Politics*.

74 On Komiyama Tomie's life and work, see interview with Komiyama in: Etsuji and Suzuki (eds), *Undō ni Kaketa Onnatachi: Senzen Fujin Undō e no Shōgen*, 1980, pp. 8–52.

75 Tajima, *Hitosuji no Michi*, p. 118.

76 Saitō Ken'ichi, 'Yagyō Kinshi no Hanashi', *Seigi no Hikari*, No. 5, 18/8/1926, pp. 14–16; 'Fujin Yōnen Rōdōsha no Yagyō Kinshi', *Seigi no Hikari*, No. 13, 15/11/1926; Sakurai, *Bosei Hogo Undōshi*, pp. 48–9.

77 Sakurai Kinue notes the influence of the third annual meeting of the Profintern in 1924, which produced a list of ten demands related to the struggle of working women. Yamakawa Kikue was responsible for translating Profintern and Comintern policy on women and work into Japanese. Sakurai Kinue, *Bosei Hogo Undōshi*, p. 54.

78 'Fujin Kyōgikai Tēze', October 1925; reproduced in *Nihon Fujin Mondai Shiryō Shūsei*, Vol. 3, pp. 422–6.

79 For a discussion of similar issues with respect to the Australian Communist Party, see Joy Damousi, ' "The Woman Comrade": Equal or Different?', *Women's History Review*, Vol. 2, No. 3, 1993, pp. 387–94.

80 'Fujin Kyōgikai Tēze', p. 425.

81 Inumaru Giichi, 'Nihon ni okeru Marukusu shugi Fujinron', p. 161.

82 Fujin Kyōgikai Tēze, p. 425.

83 Inumaru, 'Nihon ni okeru Marukusu shugi Fujinron', pp. 157–8.

84 Yoshimura-sei, 'Fujinbu to iu Dokuritsu Bumon no Hitsuyō Ikaga', *Rōdō Shinbun*, No. 19, 1926.

85 Itō Manabu [Watanabe Masanosuke], 'Rōdō Kumiai no Fujinbu wa Naze ni Hitsuyō ka' Fujinbu Fuhitsuyō Ronsha ni Hantaisu', Tokyo Gōdō Rōdō Kumiai Shuppanbu, March 1926; in *Nihon Fujin Mondai Shiryō Shūsei*, Vol. 8, pp. 286–9. Yamakawa Hitoshi, 'Musan Seitō to Fujin no Yōkyū', in Yamakawa Hitoshi and Kikue, *Musansha Undō to Fujin no Mondai*, Tokyo: Hakuyōsha, October 1928.

86 Nihon Rōdō Kumiai Hyōgikai Shuppan Rōdō Kumiai, 'Fujinbu Haishi Ron ni Hantaisu', Shuppan Rōdō Kumiai Kyōiku Shuppanbu, March 1926, in *Nihon Fujin Mondai Shiryō Shūsei*, Vol. 8, pp. 291–5.

87 Tōkyō Gōdō Rōdō Kumiai [Tanno Setsu], 'Nihon Rōdō Kumiai Hyōgikai Sōhonbu Fujinbu Setchi narabi ni Fujinbu Katsudō Tōitsu ni Kansuru Ketsugian', April 1924; reproduced in *Nihon Fujin Mondai Shiryō Shūsei*, Vol. 8, pp. 296–7.

88 'Fujinbu Katsudō Tōitsu ni Kansuru Ketsugian', *ibid*.

89 Large, 'The Romance of Revolution', pp. 458–9. Inumaru, 'Nihon ni okeru Marukusu shugi Fujinron', pp. 163–4.

90 Yamakawa Kikue, 'Fujin Dōmei to Kumiai Fujinbu', August 1926; reproduced in *Nihon Fujin MondaiShiryō Shūsei*, Vol. 8, pp. 297–303. Yamakawa's statement was included in the *Hyōgikai* discussion papers on the Women's Division issue, and published in Yamakawa Hitoshi and Kikue, *Musansha Undō to Fujin no Mondai*. See also Nihon Rōdō Kumiai Hyōgikai Ōsaka Chihō Hyōgikai Shikkō Iinkai, 'Fujinbu ni Kansuru ken', October 1926.

91 Yamakawa, 'Fujin Dōmei to Kumiai Fujinbu', p. 301, p. 302.

92 Yamakawa, 'Fujin Dōmei to Kumiai Fujinbu,' p. 298. The phrase is presented in both English (work among women) and Japanese (*fujin no aida ni okeru shigoto*).

93 It is also possible to question how far these debates influenced the activities of the 'malestream' organizations and publications. Inumaru Giichi reports that the Marxist journal *Marukusushugi* only ran five articles on women's issues between 1926 and 1929, while its successor, *Puroretaria Kagaku* carried only one article on women's issues. Inumaru Giichi, 'Nihon ni okeru Marukusu shugi Fujinron', p. 159.

94 It will be remembered that the 1922 revision of Article Five had made it possible for women to attend and speak at public meetings, but women were still prevented from becoming members of political parties.

95 While socialists in urban areas attempted to mobilize factory workers, there were also attempts to mobilize tenant farmers and farm labourers. As the majority of the population was still engaged in agricultural labour, this was obviously an important constituency for the socialist movement, and the best strategy for organizing rural workers was a vital question for socialist theory. Those in rural areas were often seen to carry the remnants of feudal ideology most strongly, particularly with respect to women. Rural areas were also, however, the site for various militant protests: rice riots and tenant farmer disputes in the contemporary period, and a history of peasant uprisings dating back to the Tokugawa period.

   The *Nihon Nōmin Kumiai* (Japan Farmers' Union) was formed in 1922, and a women's division was established in 1927. A statement on the activities of the women's division was produced in June 1927. The specific situation of rural women is set out first of all. Rural women, who work alongside their husbands in farm labour, are said to be an integral part of the rural movement. While women have often shown their bravery in disputes, they have not always been mobilized effectively. They should be seen as part of a special action unit (*tokubetsu katsudō butai*), rather than simply as a reserve army of labour (*rōdōryoku no hojū butai*). In this document the question of the sexual division of labour is addressed more directly than in most of the union documents. While union documents often mentioned women's double burden, they rarely mentioned strategies for addressing this problem. The Farmers' Union, however, states that there is no reason to take the sexual division of labour for granted. When men and women are engaged in a common struggle, it may be equally appropriate for men to cook and for women to take up the hoe. Policies of the women's division also address the question of childcare, specifically mentioning the need for communal crèches for the busy season.

   Other policies mentioned are similar to the other proletarian women's organizations: female suffrage, paid maternity leave for working women, and the provision of free clinics for pregnant women. However, it is seen to be most appropriate for a Women's League (*Fujin Dōmei*) to address these issues. The Women's Division of the Farmers' Union should support the activities of the consumers' co-operative and the women's league, and facilitate the participation of women in rural disputes. This statement makes several advances in its portrayal of women as equal partners in rural struggles.

   A full discussion of socialist attempts to mobilize women and men in rural areas is unfortunately outside the scope of the present study, but the importance of rural areas for any political movement in Japan should be remembered. Maruoka, *Nihon Nōson Fujin Mondai*; Maruoka, *Fujin Shisō Keisei Shi Nōto*, pp. 155–6; Watanabe and Suzuki, *Tatakai ni Ikite*, pp. 139–41; Makise, *Hitamuki no Onnatachi*, pp. 116–30; Nihon Nōmin Kumiai Chūō Jōnin Iinkai, 'Fujinbu Kakuritsu ni kansuru Shirei', in *Nihon Fujin Mondai Shiryō Shūsei*, Vol. 8, pp. 317–19.

96 The first dispute calling for menstruation leave was carried out by women conductors

on Tokyo public transport in July 1928. Sakurai, *Bosei Hogo Undō Shi*, pp. 56–9.

97 Sakurai, *Bosei Hogo Undō Shi*, p. 57.

98 Akamatsu Akiko was the wife of Akamatsu Katsumaro. On Akamatsu Akiko's life and work, see interview with Akamatsu Akiko in: Watanabe and Suzuki, *Undō ni Kaketa Onnatachi*, pp. 81–106. Akamatsu Tsuneko was the sister of Akamatsu Katsumaro. While Akamatsu Katsumaro and his wife Akiko moved towards national socialism, Tsuneko continued in the social democratic movement. On Akamatsu Tsuneko's life and work, see Akamatsu Tsuneko Kenshōkai, *Zassō no Yō ni Takumashiku: Akamatsu Tsuneko no Ashiato*, Tokyo, 1977.

99 *Rōdō Fujin* (Facsimile edition: Tokyo: Hōsei Daigaku Ōhara Shakai Mondai Kenkyūjo Sōdōmei Gojūnen Shi Kankō Iinkai, 1978–1985, 6 Vols).

100 The textile workers' union affiliated with the Sōdōmei was the Kantō Textile Workers Union. After the second split Iwauchi left to join the Nihon Rōdō Kumiai Dōmei, and organized textile workers under the Japan Textile Workers' Union. *Seigi no Hikari* continued under the umbrella of the Japan Textile Workers' Union. Relevant documents and newsletters of both these unions are held in the Ōhara Social Research Institute.

101 See interviews with Tatewaki Sadayo in Rekishi Hyōron Henshūbu, *Nihon Kindai Joseishi e no Shōgen*, p. 169, pp. 177–9; Watanabe and Suzuki, *Tatakai ni Ikite*, pp. 194–210; and Tatewaki Sadayo, *Aru Henreki no Jijōden*, Tokyo: Sōdō Bunka, 1980.

102 Watanabe and Suzuki, *Tatakai ni Ikite*, pp. 194–210.

103 I will be drawing on publications directed at women workers in the 1920s, including *Seigi no Hikari* (The Light of Justice), produced by the *Nichirō* affiliated Japan Textile Workers' Union; *Rōdō Fujin* (Labour Woman), the journal of the *Sōdōmei* Women's Division; and *Mirai* (Future), produced by Tajima Hide, from the left of the proletarian movement. Copies of the journal of the Nihon Bōshoku Rōdō Kumiai, *Seigi no Hikari*, 1926–1935 are held in the Ōhara Social Research Institute. Tajima Hide established the Women's Work Research Institute (*Fujin Rōdō Chōsajo*) and started publishing the monthly journal *Mirai*, in March 1926. Extant issues of *Mirai* are held in the Ōhara Social Research Institute. Tajima, *Hitosuji no Michi*, pp. 124–38; Maruoka, *Fujin Shisō Keiseishi Nōto*, pp. 141–3.

104 Company songs and publications in the Meiji period are analysed in Tsurumi, *Factory Girls*, pp. 93–6.

105 See, for example, women workers' accounts of company moral training sessions, published in the July 1929 issue of *Rōdō Fujin*. Hikichi Harue, 'Shinyagyō ni kawaru Shūyōdan'; Takagi Toshiko, 'Shūyōdan no Naimaku', *Rōdō Fujin*, No. 20, July 1929; reproduced in Suzuki, *Josei to Rōdō Kumiai*, pp. 156–9.

106 Large, *The Rise of Labour*; Suzuki, *Josei to Rōdō Kumiai*.

107 cf. 'Jokō no Uta: Jokō Aishi no Naka Yori', *Seigi no Hikari*, No. 3, pp. 24–8.

108 Iwauchi revealed his attitudes to women workers in a later interview with Watanabe Etsuji. While sincere in his efforts to reach women workers through the Japan Textile Workers' Union, through the journal *Seigi no Hikari*, and through a pamphlet directed at women workers (Iwauchi Zensaku, *Jokōsan ni Okuru*, Tokyo: Nihon Rōdō Sōdōmei Kantō Bōshoku Rōdō Kumiai, 25/7/1926; held in Ōhara Social Research Institute), Iwauchi believed that these women were different from male workers, and that any discussion of socialism had to be introduced carefully. In speeches, he would commence with funny stories, before steering the discussion to a simplified explanation of socialism and unionism. Watanabe and Suzuki, *Tatakai ni Ikite*, pp. 180–5.

109 Kawamatsu Kaneko, 'Watashi no Kokoro no Yorokobi', *Seigi no Hikari*, No. 5, p. 11.

110 This picture of women workers was no longer accurate by the 1920s and 1930s. Barbara Molony points out that many workers stayed in factory employment after marriage, and 'even during the depression-ridden 1930s, only 22.5 per cent of the mill workers of rural origin returned to the farm'. Barbara Molony, 'Activism among Women in the Taishō Cotton Industry', *op. cit.*

111 *Seigi no Hikari*, No. 2, 18/5/1926.

112 Conditions were often more bearable in other industries. See interviews with women workers in Watanabe and Suzuki, *Tatakai ni Ikite*, Makise, *Hitamuki no Onnatachi*.

113 cf. the song in Yamamoto Shigemi, *Aa Nomugi Tōge*, pp. 388–9; translation in Tsurumi, *Factory Girls*, pp. 98–9. A version of this song is reproduced in *Seigi no Hikari*, No. 3, pp. 24–8.

114 In 1897, it was estimated that 45 per cent of female workers and 42 per cent of male workers in cotton factories left their jobs before a year was up. Tsurumi, *Factory Girls*, p. 154.

115 cf. Tamanoi, 'Songs as Weapons: The Culture and History of *Komori* (Nursemaids) in Modern Japan', pp. 793–817; James C. Scott, *Weapons of the Weak: Everyday Forms of Peasant Resistance*, Newhaven: Yale University Press, 1985.

116 Factory workers' songs have been used by E. P. Tsurumi in *Factory Girls*, as an archive from which to gain evidence of working conditions and attitudes of women workers during the Meiji period. In this chapter I am interested in the transformation of this aspect of oral culture into text. Once the women workers' songs have been reproduced in works of labour history or in union journals, they become part of the cultural repertoire of images of women workers, and are divorced from their immediate context. It is the use of such imagery within labour movement writings in the 1920s that I analyse in this chapter.

117 See, for example, the diary of a female factory worker illustrated by a caged bird. Ogura Michiko, 'Jokō no Nikki', *Seigi no Hikari*, No. 3, pp. 12–13.

118 Hosoi Wakizō, *Jokō Aishi*, Tokyo: Iwanami Bunkō, 1954. Workers' songs were also collected in: Taishūtō Jigyōbu (eds), *Puroretaria Kashū*, 23/5/1931.

119 *Seigi no Hikari*, No. 2, 18/5/1926, p. 25.

120 cf. Tsurumi, *Factory Girls*, pp. 194–7.

121 Bell hooks, 'Narratives of Struggle', in Philomena Mariani (ed.) *Critical Fictions: The Politics of Imaginative Writing*, Bay Press: Seattle, 1991, p. 59.

122 Asō Hisashi, 'Nijū no Kusari', *Seigi no Hikari*, No. 3 pp. 4–6. See also Kamijō Aiichi's article on Japan's working women, where, in discussing the problem posed for the union movement by the relative inaccessibility of women in dormitories, he quite naturally uses the caged bird metaphor to describe these women. Kamijō Aiichi, 'Nihon no Fujin Rōdōsha', *Seigi no Hikari*, No. 4, 15/7/1926, p. 4.

123 *Hyōgikai* organizer Watanabe Masanosuke (writing under the pen-name Itō Manabu), for example, described the situation of women workers in factory dormitories as ' a system of imprisonment which accompanies the traffic in human beings' (*jinshin baibai o tomonau kankin seido*). Tōkyō Gōdō Rōdō Kumiai Nankatsu Shibu (Itō Manabu), 'Kishukusha Seido Teppai Undō ni Kansuru Ketsugian', April 1926; in *Nihon Fujin Mondai Shiryō Shūsei*, Vol. 8, pp. 295–6.

124 Kamijō Aiichi, 'Nihon no Fujin Rōdōsha', p. 6.

125 Makise, *Hitamuki no Onnatachi*, pp. 54–5.

126 Suzuki, *Jokō to Rōdō Sōgi*, pp. 27–8; Gordon, *Labor and Imperial Democracy*, p. 225.

127 See Nishikawa Fumiko, 'Yoshiwara Kenbutsu no Ki', in Chapter 3, p. 53. See also Iwauchi Tomie's account of women from the licensed quarters who came to the Airindan for help after the earthquake of 1923. They were described in the press as 'caged birds who had been set free' (*hanatareta kagi no tori*). The Airindan was a Christian socialist organization in the Nippori region of Tokyo, managed by Iwauchi Zensaku and Iwauchi Tomie. Watanabe and Suzuki, *Tatakai ni Ikite*, p. 127–8.

128 Tsurumi, *Factory Girls*, p. 89, p. 98, pp. 144–5.

129 For a detailed discussion of the use of maternal imagery, see Vera Mackie, 'Motherhood and Pacifism in Japan, 1900–1937', *Hecate*, Vol. 14, No. 2, 1988, *passim*.

130 Kamijō Aiichi, 'Nihon no Fujin Rōdōsha', *Seigi no Hikari*, No. 4, 15/7/1926, pp. 5–6.

131 Cover of *Seigi no Hikari*, No. 2, 1926.

132 Gotō Miyoko, *I Am Alive*, Oakland University: Katydid Books, 1988, p. 34.

133 See the discussion of maternal imagery in European socialist publications in Eric Hobsbawm, 'Man and Woman: Images on the Left', in *Worlds of Labour: Further Studies in the History of Labour*, London: Weidenfeld & Nicolson, p. 97.

134 Both Suzuki Yūko and E. P. Tsurumi have traced the transformation of the identity of *jokō*. In particular, see: Tsurumi, *Factory Girls*; Suzuki, *Josei to Rōdō Kumiai*.

135 Nagai Chōzō, 'Otagai ni Sonkei Seyo', *Yūai Fujin*, No. 2, p. 9.
136 *Seigi no Hikari*, No. 3, p. 24. Similar songs appear in Yamamoto Shigemi, *Aa Nomugi Tōge*. One verse is translated in Tsurumi, *Factory Girls*, p. 97.
137 'Shimai wa kaku no gotoku seichō shita', *Rōdō Fujin*, No. 31, June 1930.
138 Interview with Umezu Hagiko, in Makise, *Hitamuki no Onnatachi*, p. 53.
139 In the following poem from *Seigi no Hikari*, there is an implicit notion of class consciousness, employing images of the differences between women: 'My eyes have been opened/The clothes worn by that young lady/Have been produced by the sweat of my labour', *Seigi no Hikari*, No. 1, 20/4/1926. A similar sentiment is given fictional expression in Sata Ineko's story, 'From the Caramel Factory', in a scene where a thirteen-year-old factory worker admires the silk kimono of the factory owner's wife. Sata Ineko, 'Kyarameru Kōjō Kara', *Puroretaria Bungaku*, March 1928, in Itō Tadashi, et al. (eds), *Nihon Gendai Bungaku Zenshū*, Vol. 83, pp. 206–12. For discussion of this story, see Vernon, *Daughters of the Moon: Wish, Will and Social Constraint in the Fiction of Japanese Women*, pp. 74–86; Gordon, *Labor and Imperial Democracy in Prewar Japan*, p. 226.
140 This song has been attributed to Takatsu Tayoko and her husband Takatsu Seidō. Kondō, *Watashi no Kaisō*, Vol. 2, pp. 39–40. There is, however, an earlier citation of the song in Kinoshita Naoe's novel *Ryōjin no Jihaku*, which was serialized in the *Mainichi Shinbun* between 1904 and 1906. The song also appeared in a collection of socialist poetry in 1906. See Matsumoto Katsuhira, *Nihon Shakai Shugi Engeki Shi: Meiji Taishō Hen* Tokyo: Chikuma Shobō: 1975, pp. 156–7.
141 Tajima Hide, 'Hikari ni Mukaite', *Seigi no Hikari*, 2; 18/5/1926, p. 4.
142 Tajima Hide, 'Hikari ni Mukaite', p. 6.
143 See the discussion of the 'politics of envy', one element of working-class attitudes to the middle class, in: Carolyn Steedman, *Landscape for a Good Woman: A Story of Two Lives*, London: Virago, 1986, p. 7.
144 Tajiri Okayo, *Mirai*, No. 4, June 1926, in Maruoka, *Fujin Shisō Keisei Shi Nōto*, pp. 155–6.
145 Other contributions to *Seigi no Hikari* did offer explanations of terms like 'labour union', 'labour movement', 'strike', 'capital', 'proletariat', 'exploitation', 'class', etc. The first issue, for example, carried the start of a series on labour unions, an explanation of May Day (the 'workers' festival'), a profile of Robert Owen, and a report on union activities. Later issues would have a similar range of educational articles alongside fiction and poetry.
146 Yamane Kenzaburō, 'Bōshoku Rōdōsha yo Jikaku Seyo!', *Seigi no Hikari*, No. 1, 20/4/1926. Yamane's discussion is quite similar to the arguments used in Iwauchi Zensaku's pamphlet addressed to factory women; Iwauchi Zensaku, *Jokōsan ni Okuru*, Tokyo: Nihon Rōdō Sōdōmei Kantō Bōshoku Rōdō Kumiai, 25/7/1926, pp. 31–2.
147 *Seigi no Hikari*, No. 4, 15/7/1926. See also the illustration on p. 128.
148 In 1930, it was reported that the number of women participating in strikes in some industries exceeded the number of males. In the dyeing and weaving industry, 14 444 women participated in disputes, about double the male figure of 7616. Several strikes were said to involve women only, and strikes spread to such occupations as waitresses, actresses, dancers, models, nurses, shop assistants, and geisha. Hasegawa Kōichi, 'Honpō ni okeru Fujin Rōdō Undō no Sūsei to sono Kentō', *Shakai Seisaku Jihō*, No. 135, October 1931, cited in Ishizuki Shizue, '1930nendai no Musan Fujin Undō', in Joseishi Sōgō Kenkyūkai (eds), *Nihon Joseishi 5: Gendai*, Tokyo: Tokyo Daigaku Shuppankai, p. 199.
149 See the special 'Kanebo' issue of *Rōdō Fujin*, June 1930.
150 On the Tōyō Muslin strike, see Suzuki, *Jokō to Rōdō Sōgi*, passim; Gordon; *Labor and Imperial Democracy*, pp. 243–5; interview with Tatewaki Sadako in Rekishi Hyōron Henshūbu, *Nihon Kindai Joseishi e no Shōgen*, p. 169, pp. 171–3; interview with Nakada Koharu in Watanabe and Suzuki, *Tatakai ni Ikite*, pp. 141–5; pp. 156–8; Kawano Mitsu, 'Jokō Ketsuruiki', *Chūō Kōron*, Vol. 46, No. 9, September 1931, in *Nihon Fujin Mondai Shiryō Shūsei*, Vol. 3, pp. 405–12; *Shakai Undō no Jōkyo*, Vol. 6, pp. 608–11; Imazu Kane

and Wada Machiko, 'Onna Higyō Jissenki', *Fujin Kōron*, July 1930, cited in Watashi-tachi no Rekishi o Tsuzuru Kai, *Fujin Zasshi Kara Mita 1930nendai*, Tokyo: Dōjidaisha, 1987, p. 40.

151 Of the 2649 workers on strike, 2181 were women. Watanabe and Suzuki, *Tatakai ni Ikite*, p. 142.

152 Such a connection between women's militancy and the danger of sexual promiscuity has been identified in other national contexts. See for example, Jacquelyn Dowd Hall, in 'Disorderly Women: Gender and Labour Militancy in the Appalachian South', *Journal of American History*, September 1986, p. 375: 'There is nothing extraordinary about this association between sexual misbehaviour and women's labour militancy. Since strikers are often young single women who violate gender conventions by invading public space customarily reserved for men (and sometimes frequented by prostitutes) – and since female aggressiveness stirs up fears of women's sexual power – opponents have often undercut union organizing drives by insinuations of prostitution or promiscuity.'

153 Watanabe and Suzuki, *Tatakai ni Ikite*, p. 144. Suzuki, *Jokō to Rōdō Sōgi*, pp. 20–3.

154 The Proletarian Women's League was one of the Women's Leagues formed to mobilize proletarian women, who could not become full members of political parties. These women's leagues will be discussed in more detail in Chapter six.

155 Watanabe and Suzuki, *Tatakai ni Ikite*, p. 143.

156 Pamphlet produced by the Proletarian Women's League (*Musan Fujin Dōmei*), October 1930, held in Ōhara Social Research Institute.

157 Musan Fujin Dōmei, *Tōyō Muslin Sōgi ōen Nyūsu*, No. 1, 8/10/1930; held in Ōhara Social Research Institute; reproduced in Suzuki, *Jokō to Rōdō Sōgi*, pp. 85–7. The *Nihon Seigi Dan* (Japan League of Justice) was an ultranationalist organization which was hired to intimidate the strikers.

158 *Tokyo Nichi Nichi Shinbun*, 26/9/1930; cited in Suzuki, *Jokō to Rōdō Sōgi*, p. 18. The singing of revolutionary songs in this dispute has been commented on in reminiscences of the strike, suggesting that the labour movement had some success in countering the pathos of the women's own songs. Watanabe and Suzuki, *Tatakai ni Ikite*, p. 144.

159 Kawano Mitsu, 'Jokō Ketsuruiki', pp. 405–12.

160 Suzuki Yūko also argues that the strikes of the early 1930s were part of the creation of a new view of the *jokō*: as a class-conscious, combative woman worker, rather than the pathetic figure portrayed by Yokoyama Gennosuke and Hosoi Wakizō. Suzuki also reminds us that, despite this militancy, the absolute numbers of unionized women workers was still small. Suzuki, *Jokō to Rōdō Sōgi*, pp. 116–17.

161 Ishizuki Shizue, '1930nendai no Musan Fujin Undō', pp. 201–2.

6 Activists

1 Nakasone Sadayo, *Fujin Mondai*, Tokyo: Musansha, 8/6/1921; Ezashi, Akiko, *Sameyo Onnatachi*, p. 96.

2 This discussion has been informed by recent Anglophone discussions of feminist theories of the State, although the main focus of the chapter will be the ways in which Japanese socialist women engaged with the State as activists and what this implied about their views of the State. The relevant literature includes: Nira-Yuval Davis and Flora Anthias (eds), *Woman: Nation: State*, London: Macmillan, 1989; Anna Yeatman, *Bureaucrats, Technocrats, Femocrats*, Sydney: Allen & Unwin, 1992; Sophie Watson (ed.), *Playing the State*, Sydney: Allen & Unwin, 1989. Parts of this chapter draw on a briefer discussion of socialist women's engagement with State institutions: Vera Mackie, 'Engaging with the State: Socialist Women in Imperial Japan', in Mackie (ed.) *Feminism and the State in Modern Japan*, pp. 61–77.

3 For details of Ichikawa Fusae's life, see Ichikawa Fusae, *Jiden: Senzen Hen*, Tokyo: Shinjuku Shobō, 1974; Vavich, 'The Japanese Women's Movement'; Patricia Murray, 'Ichikawa Fusae and the Lonely Red Carpet', *Japan Interpreter*, Vol. 10, No. 2, Autumn 1975; for details of Takamure Itsue's life and work, see Kano Masanao and Horiba

Kiyoko, *Takamure Itsue*, Tokyo: Asahi Shinbunsha, 1977; Nishikawa Yūko, *Mori no Ie no Miko: Takamure Itsue*, Tokyo: Shinchōsha, 1982; Tsurumi, 'Feminism and Anarchism in Japan'.

4 Hiratsuka announced the formation of the Association at a public meeting in 1919. The organization was formally inaugurated on 28 March 1920 and was active until the end of 1922. Robins-Mowry, *The Hidden Sun*, pp. 66–7.

5 Sharon H. Nolte, 'Women's Rights and Society's Needs: Japan's 1931 Suffrage Bill', *Comparative Studies in Society and History*, 1986, pp. 710–12; Sheldon Garon, 'Women's Groups and the Japanese State: Contending Approaches to Political Integration, 1890–1945', *Journal of Japanese Studies*, Vol. 19, No. 1, 1993, pp. 20–8.

6 Garon, 'Women's Groups and the Japanese State', pp. 16–25.

7 Campaigns leading up to the modification of Article Five are discussed in Tajima, *Hitosuji no Michi*, pp. 56–61; Nolte, 'Women's Rights and Society's Needs', pp. 695–705; Garon, 'Women's Groups and the Japanese State', pp. 16–19.

8 The name of the organization was changed to the *Fusen Kakutoku Dōmei* (Women's Suffrage League) in April 1925. The Association's monthly journal *Fusen* (Women's Suffrage) appeared from 1927, and had a print run of around 2000 copies. On the history of the pre-war campaign for women's suffrage, see Kodama, *Fujin Sanseiken Undō Shōshi, passim.*

9 Nolte, 'Women's Rights and Society's Needs', p. 692, pp. 697–9.

10 cf. Nolte's comments on the suffragists: 'Guarding the public welfare verged perilously close to statism, and the suffragists asked for the vote in order to fulfil their duties as Japanese subjects.' Nolte, 'Women's Rights and Society's Needs', p. 701.

11 See Figure 6.1, p. 133 for the factions of the pre-war proletarian party movement.

12 This left-wing grouping is known as the *Rōnō-ha* clique. There were attempts to reform a legal left-wing party after the dissolution of the Labour–Farmer Party. The Proletarian Masses Party (*Musan Taishū Tō*) was formed in August 1928, but merged with the centrist group in December 1928. Remaining elements of the former *Rōnō Tō* made several short-lived attempts to form a new left-wing party.

13 This centrist grouping is known as the *Nichirō* clique. Subsequent mergers resulted in the formation of the Japan Masses Party (*Nihon Taishū Tō*) in 1928, National Masses Party (*Zenkoku Taishū Tō*) in 1930, and the National Labour–Farmer Masses Party (*Zenkoku Rōnō Taishū Tō*) in 1931.

14 This Social Democratic grouping is known as the Shaminkei clique. A more accurate translation of Shakai Minshū Tō would perhaps be 'Social People's Party', but I will follow other writers in translating this as 'Social Democratic Party', first to distinguish this grouping from the 'Social Masses Party' (Shakai Taishū Tō), and second to reflect the moderate social democratic emphasis of the group.

15 Large, *Organized Workers and Socialist Politics*, pp. 101–19, Gordon, *Labor and Imperial Democracy*, pp. 199–203.

16 The fifty members of this organization included Oku Mumeo, Nagashima Yōko, Sakamoto Makoto, Iwauchi Tomie, Tajima Hide, Akamatsu Akiko and Sakai Magara. Kondō [Sakai] Magara, *Watashi no Kaisō*, Vol. 2, pp. 34–6. A public meeting was chaired by Oku Mumeo and Tajima Hide. Tajima, *Hitosuji no Michi.*

17 Members included Tajima Hide, Nozaka Taki, and Tanno Setsu: Maruoka, *Fujin Shisō Keiseishi Nōto*, p. 151.

18 Kondō, *Watashi no Kaisō*, Vol. 2, p. 35.

19 Members included Iwauchi Tomie, Kikugawa Shizuko, Orimoto [Tatewaki] Sadayo.

20 Members included Akamatsu Akiko, Murakami Hide, Yamada Yasu, and Fujita Takako.

21 For a diagrammatic representation of these organizations, see Ishizuki, '1930nendai no Musan Fujin Undō', p. 195. A simplified diagram appears in p. 135, Figure 6.2.

22 Members of the preparatory committee included Tajima Hide, Nozaka Ryō, and Tanno Setsu, and members of the Women's Division of the Japan Farmers' League and the Women's Division of the *Hyōgikai*. See Nihon Rōdō Kumiai Hyōgikai Chūō Jōnin Iinkai, 'Fujin Undō ni Kansuru Ikensho', December 1926; in *Nihon Fujin*

NOTES (PAGES 137–139)   215

Mondai Shiryō Shūsei, Vol. 8, pp. 304–16. Documents relevant to this committee are also held in the Ōhara Social Research Institute.

23 Fujin Dōmei (Kantō) Sōritsu Junbi Iinkai, 'Zenkoku Sanzenman no Josei ni Uttau: Fujin Dōmei no Seiritsu ni Tsuite', December 1926, in *Nihon Fujin Mondai Shiryō Shūsei*, Vol. 8, p. 317.

24 Fujin Tōronkai, 'Dai Rokkai Kokusai Fujin Dē o Kinen Seyo!', March 1927, reproduced in Tajima, *Hitosuji no Michi*, pp. 256–7.

25 Documents relevant to the Kantō Women's League are held in the Ōhara Social Research Institute.

26 *Rōnoto Fujin Iinkai Nyūsu*, No. 6, 1927, cited in Tajima, *Hitosuji no Michi*, pp. 156–7. Tajima was Secretary of the Kantō Women's League, and the Steering Committee, chaired by Niizuma Itoko, included Tanno Setsu, Nozaka Ryō, Yamanouchi Mina, Nakada Koharu, Yanagi Tsuru and Hashimoto Kikuyo.

27 Tajima, *Hitosuji no Michi*, pp. 159–63.

28 Fujin Dōmei Zenkoku Soshiki Sokushin Iinkai 'Fujin Dōmei no Hata no Shita ni', reproduced in Tajima, *Hitosuji no Michi*, pp. 258–9.

29 'Nihon Kyōsantō no Fujin Taisaku', Tajima, *Hitosuji no Michi*, pp. 259–62; 'Fujin Dōmei no Soshiki ni Tsuite', *Akahata*, No. 4, 15/3/1928; reproduced in Tajima, *Hitosuji no Michi*, pp. 262–4.

30 Tajima, *Hitosuji no Michi*, pp. 163–70; Inumaru, 'Nihon ni okeru Marukusu shugi Fujinron', pp. 164–7.

31 Kondō, *Watashi no Kaisō*, Vol. 2, p. 35; Makise and Yamanouchi (eds), *Tanno Setsu: Kakumei Undō ni Ikiru*, p. 147; Tajima, *Hitosuji no Michi*.

32 Large, *Organized Workers and Socialist Politics*, p. 142.

33 Kondō, *Watashi no Kaisō*, Vol. 2, pp. 140–4; p. 193. See also miscellaneous documents of the Proletarian Women's Study Group in the Ōhara Social Research Institute.

34 Kondō, *Watashi no Kaisō*, Vol. 2, pp. 68–70; p. 141; p. 193; Rekishi Hyōron Henshūbu, *Kindai Nihon Josei e no Shōgen*, pp. 43–4.

35 Kondō, *Watashi no Kaisō*, Vol. 2, p. 144; Ishizuki, '1930nendai no Musan Fujin Undō', p. 195. See also documents relevant to the Proletarian Women's Alliance in the Ōhara Social Research Institute.

36 Kondō, *Watashi no Kaisō*, Vol. 2, pp. 144–50. Copies of the League's newsletter, *Musan Fujin Dōmei Tōsō News*, which appeared from February 1929, are held in the Ōhara Social Research Institute. The 1929 Committee was chaired by Iwauchi Tomie, with Ōshima Tokiko as Treasurer, and a central committee of 27 members. On the new committee in 1930, Iwauchi continued as chair, assisted by Sakai Magara as Secretary and Teramoto Tsuru as Treasurer. Ishizuki, '1930nendai no Musan Fujin Undō', p. 195.

37 Kondō, *Watashi no Kaisō*, Vol. 2, pp. 70–1, pp. 173–6.

38 Kondō [Sakai] Magara, 'Gōdō wa Fujin Kara', *Fujin Undō*, March 1928; in Kondō, *Watashi no Kaisō*, Vol. 2, pp. 195–8.

39 Members of the Committee included Orimoto [Tatewaki] Sadayo as Secretary, Iwauchi Tomie with responsibility for Recruitment and Publicity, and Kikugawa Shizuko as Treasurer. On the activities of the National Women's League, see Watanabe and Suzuki, *Tatakai ni Ikite*, pp. 134–6: Rekishi Hyōron Henshūbu, *Kindai Nihon Joseishi e no Shōgen*, pp. 167–9. The *Zenkoku Fujin Dōmei News* (Nos 2–4, November 1927–April 1928) and other relevant documents are held in the Ōhara Social Research Institute.

40 For details of Orimoto's activities, see Tatewaki, *Aru Henreki no Jijōden*; interviews with Orimoto [Tatewaki] Sadayo in: Watanabe and Suzuki (eds), *Tatakai ni Ikite*, pp. 194–210; Rekishi Hyōron Henshūbu (eds), *Kindai Nihon Joseishi e no Shōgen*, pp. 167–9; Inumaru, 'Nihon ni okeru Marukusu shugi Fujinron', pp. 167–72.

41 For details of Iwauchi Tomie's activities, see Watanabe and Suzuki (eds), *Tatakai ni Ikite*, pp. 95–161.

42 *Zenkoku Fujin Dōmei News*, No. 4, April 1928.

43 The Factory Act of 1911 had banned night work for women under the age of twenty between the hours of 10 p.m. and 4 a.m. The ban, however, was not to be implemented until fifteen years after the Act was promulgated in 1916. Exemptions could

be granted which allowed women to work until 11 p.m. and night work was allowed where a two-shift system was in operation. The Revised Factory Act of 1923 provided for the abolition of night work for all women after 1926, but this too was postponed until an Imperial decree of June 1926 prohibited night work for women, to be effective on 1 July 1929. Hunter, 'Factory Legislation and Employer Resistance: The Abolition of Night Work in the Cotton Spinning Industry', pp. 247–8.

44 Orimoto Sadayo, *Rōdō Fujin Mondai*, Tokyo: Musansha, 19/9/1929.

45 This group was affiliated with the Proletarian Masses Party (*Musan Taishū Tō*), formed after the dissolution of the *Rōnō Tō*. Relevant documents are held in the Ōhara Social Research Institute.

46 Members included Akamatsu Akiko, Murakami Hide, Yamada Yasu, and Fujita Takako.

47 Copies of *Minshū Fujin*, the journal of the *Shakai Minshū Fujin Dōmei* (Nos 1–33: 25/11/1928–25/3/1932) and other relevant documents are held in the Ōhara Social Research Institute.

48 *Minshū Fujin*, No 1, 25/11/1928.

49 The use of this hybrid phrase is interesting. The Social Democratic clique tended to refer to the *kinrō kaikyū* (labouring class), which included not only the proletariat, but also salaried workers who may own a small amount of property. Their political strategies were closer to the liberal end of the spectrum. The centrist and leftist cliques, on the other hand, championed the *musan kaikyū* (propertyless class), and espoused a more revolutionary strategy. The use of the phrase *kinrō musan fujin* to describe the constituency of the Social Democratic Women's League seems to suggest a desire to be as inclusive as possible. On the distinction between *kinrō kaikyū* and *musan kaikyū*, see Large, *Organized Workers and Socialist Politics*, pp. 112–13.

50 The issue of birth control is mentioned in *Minshū Fujin* from late 1929, and is often linked with the promotion of the Mother and Child Assistance Act. See also Ishizuki, '1930nendai no Musan Fujin Undō', p. 202. Documents relevant to this birth control association are held in the Ōhara Social Research Institute.

51 *Zassō no Yō ni Takumashiku*, p. 106.

52 *Minshū Fujin*, No. 30, p. 1. See also articles in *Rōdō Fujin*: e.g. 'Raigikai ni Teishutsu no Uwasa aru Fujin Kōminken ni tsuite', *Rōdō Fujin*, No. 33, September 1930, pp. 2–3.

53 *Zassō no Yō ni Takumashiku*, p. 107; *Minshū Fujin*, No. 18.

54 Suzuki Yūko, 'Tachiagaru Onnatachi', in *Jūgoshi Nōto*, No. 2, 1978, pp. 61–3.

55 'Gōdō Taikai o Mukauru ni Saishite', *Minshū Fujin*, No. 23, May 1931. The Working Women's League had been formed on 10 July 1927, under the auspices of the moderate *Sōdōmei* Union Federation, and led by Akamatsu Tsuneko. The Committee of the amalgamated organization had Akamatsu Akiko as Secretary/Treasurer, Matsuoka Katsuyo responsible for Finance, and a management committee including Akamatsu Tsuneko, Abe Shizue and Nishio Fusano. A new committee in 1932 was chaired by Akamatsu Tsuneko, with Abe Shizue as Secretary and Matsuoka Katsuyo as Treasurer. Ishizuki, '1930nendai no Musan Fujin Undō', p. 195.

56 Ishizuki, '1930nendai no Musan Fujin Undō', pp. 196–9.

57 Akamatsu Tsuneko, Abe Shizue, Sakai Magara, and Iwauchi Tomie were arrested on this day. Kondō, *Watashi no Kaisō*, Vol. 2, p. 147; *Zassō no Yō ni Takumashiku*, p. 107.

58 Ishizuki, '1930nendai no Musan Fujin Undō', p. 213; Watashitachi no Rekishi o Tsuzuru Kai, *Fujin Zasshi kara Mita 1930nendai*, pp. 38–9.

59 Kondō, *Watashi no Kaisō*, Vol. 2, pp. 70–1.

60 Kondō, *Watashi no Kaisō*, Vol. 2, p. 149.

61 A new committee, formed in 1935, was chaired by Iwauchi Tomie, with Sakai Magara as Treasurer, asssisted by a steering committee of Akamatsu Tsuneko, Abe Shizue and three others. Ishizuki, '1930nendai no Musan Fujin Undō', p. 195; Kondō, *Watashi no Kaisō*, Vol. 2, pp. 70–1; *Shakai Undō no Jōkyō*, Vol. 6, pp. 685–6.

62 Liberal feminist activities and socialist women's activities are often presented as being antithetical, but examples of co-operation can be found in several national contexts. See, for example, Ellen Carol DuBois, 'Working Women. Class Relations, and Suffrage Militance: Harriot Stanton Blanch and the New York Women Suffrage Movement, 1894–1909', *Journal of American History*, Vol. 74, No. 1, June 1987.

63 'Tettei Fusen no Kakutoku', *Minshū Fujin*, No. 2, p. 1; Akamatsu Akiko, 'Moshi Fujin ni Kōminken ga Ataerareta Naraba', *Minshū Fujin*, No. 2; Suzuki Haruko, 'Tettei fusen tō wa nanika', *Minshū Fujin*, No. 2; 'Kōminken no kakutoku e', *Minshū Fujin*, No. 3, p. 1; 5, 'Fujin Kōminken Enzetsukai', *Minshū Fujin*, No. 5; etc.

64 Tanno Setsu, *Sekki*, 15/3/1928; translation in Hane, *Reflections on the Way to the Gallows*, pp. 193–4.

65 *Zenkoku Fujin Dōmei News*, No. 4, April 1928.

66 Ichikawa Fusae 'Kaisetsu', *Nihon Fujin Mondai Shiryō Shūsei*, Vol. 2, pp. 46–7.

67 Kano, 'Fusen Kakutoku Dōmei no Seiritsu', pp. 78–9; Sakai [Kondō] Magara, 'Watashi no Mita Taikai', *Fusen*, May 1930, in Kondō, *Watashi no Kaisō*, Vol. 2, pp. 160–4.

68 *Zassō no Yō ni Takumashiku*, p. 107.

69 Katō Akemi, 'Onnatachi no Yōkyū o Kakagete', *Jūgoshi Nōto*, No. 2, 1978, pp. 64–5.

70 'Rengō Iinkai ni Tsuite', *Musan Fujin Tōsō News*, No. 1, 1/4/1932, reprinted in Suzuki Yūko, 'Manshū Jihen to Musan Fujin Undō', *Jūgoshi Nōto*, No. 3, 1979, p. 60.

71 Nolte, 'Women's Rights and Society's Needs', pp. 703–10; Garon, 'Women's Groups and the Japanese State', pp. 28–35.

72 Suzuki, 'Manshū Jihen to Musan Fujin Undō', p. 60.

73 Kano, 'Fusen Kakutoku Dōmei no Seiritsu', p. 69.

74 Kano, 'Fusen Kakutoku Dōmei no Seiritsu', pp. 81–2.

75 Their stance was outlined in 'Rōdōsha Nōmin no Gyakusatsu Sensō Zettai Hantai', *Zenkoku Taishū Shinbun Gōgai Musan Fujinban*, 8/3/1931, and 'Teikokushugi Sensō Zettai Hantai', *Musan Fujin Dōmei Tōsō Hōkoku*, 2/4/1931; held in Ōhara Social Research Institute, and cited in Ishizuki, '1930nendai no Musan Fujin Undō', p. 204–5.

76 Musan Fujin Dōmei, 'Sensō Hantai ni taisuru Seimeisho', 18/12/1931, held in Ōhara Social Research Institute and cited in Suzuki, 'Manshū jihen to musan fujin undō', pp. 58–66). See also Sandra Wilson, 'Women's Responses to the Manchurian Crisis', chapter of unpublished doctoral thesis, 'Popular Responses to the Manchurian Crisis', Oxford University, 1990; Kondō, *Watashi no Kaisō*, Vol. 2, pp. 148–9; Ishizuki, '1930nendai no Musan Fujin Undō', pp. 205–13. Ishizuki takes a broad view of women's responses to the Manchurian Crisis, considering not only statements on the Incident itself, but also the responses of women's groups to the worsening economic situation of the early 1930s.

77 Shakai Minshū Fujin Dōmei Chūō Shikkō Iinkai, *Man-mō mondai ni kansuru seimeisho*, 11/12/1931; held in Ōhara Social Research Institute and reprinted in Suzuki, 'Manshū Jihen to Musan Fujin Undō', p. 62–3. See also 'Man-mō Mondai Taisaku o Kyōgi Shita Kinkyū Chūō Shikkō Iinkai', *Minshū Fujin*, No. 31, 25/12/1931; 'Shōwa Shichinen wa Ika ni Tatakawareru beki ka', *Minshū Fujin*, No. 31, 25/12/1931.

78 Ichikawa Fusae, 'Fujin no Honsei no Tachiba o Oite', *Asahi Shinbun*, 18/11/1931, cited in 'Shiryō: Jihen o kō Miru', *Jūgoshi Nōto*, No. 3, p. 54.

79 Yamakawa Kikue, 'Manshū no Jūsei', *Fujin Kōron*, November 1931; in Suzuki (ed.), *Yamakawa Kikue Josei Kaihō Ronshū*, p. 45. Suzuki notes that this paragraph was deleted when the article was reprinted in a collection of Yamakawa's writings in 1933. Suzuki, *Josei: Hangyaku to Kakumei to Teikō to*, p. 210, note 3. On related themes, see Yamakawa Kikue, 'Nachisu to Fujin', *Yomiuri Shinbun*, 5/12/1935; 'Sensō to Fujin', *Jiyū*, November 1937, in Suzuki (ed.), *Yamakawa Kikue Josei Kaihō Ronshū*, pp. 94–103.

80 Hiratsuka Raichō, 'Manshū Jihen to Fujintachi no Taido', *Miyako Shinbun*, 27/12/1931, cited in 'Shiryō: Jihen o kō Miru', *Jūgoshi Nōto*, No. 3, pp. 54–5.

81 Takamure Itsue, 'Heiwa to Fujin', *Shūkan Fujo Shinbun*, 31/1/1932 and 7/2/1932; cited in 'Shiryō: Jihen o kō Miru', *Jūgoshi Nōto*, No. 3, pp. 52–7.

82 Yagi Akiko, 'Manshūkoku Kensetsu to wa', *Nōson Seinen*, No. 5, March 1932, cited in 'Shiryō: Jihen o kō Miru', *Jūgoshi Nōto*, No. 3, p. 57.

83 On the attitudes of proletarian parties and union federations to the Manchurian Incident, see Large, *Organized Workers and Socialist Politics*, pp. 153–6.

84 Ishizuki, '1930nendai no Musan Fujin Undō', pp. 224–5.

85 'Boshi Fujo Hō Seitei Sokushinkai Shushi', *Fujo Shinbun*, 25/4/1926, in *Fujinkai Sanjūgonen*, pp. 176–9. See also 'Boseiai no Kakuchō', *Fujo Shinbun*, 15/10/1926, reprinted in *Fujinkai Sanjūgonen*, pp. 167–8; and 'Boseiai no Kakuchō (futatabi)', *Fujo Shinbun*, 16/4/1933, reprinted in *Fujinkai Sanjūgonen*, pp. 169–70.

86 cf. Akamatsu Tsuneko, 'Fujin no Seiji Kesshaken to Boshi Fujo Hō no Mondai', *Rōdō Fujin*, January 1930, pp. 6–7.

87 'Bosei Hogo no Kyūyō', *Fujo Shinbun*, 7/2/1926, reprinted in *Fujinkai Sanjūgonen*, pp. 170–2. The issue of mother-child suicides was also discussed other women's journals: *Fusen*, Vol. 4, No. 6, 1930, cited in Kano, 'Fusen Kakutoku Dōmei no Seiritsu', p. 79; Hiratsuka Raichō, 'Fujin Sensen ni Sanka Shite', *Fujin Sensen*, February 1930, p. 36; *Minshū Fujin*, No. 13, 25/6/1930. See also Hara Yasuichi, *Itamashiki Oyako Shinjū no Jissō*, Tokyo: Zaisan Hōjin Shakai Kyōkai, August 1932; held in Ōhara Social Research Institute.

88 *Zassō no Yō no Takumashiku*, p. 111.

89 Kondō, *Watashi no Kaisō*, Vol. 2, pp. 70–1.

90 *Nihon Fujin Mondai Shiryō Shūsei*, Vol. 2, p. 60.

91 The name was shortened to the Motherhood Protection Alliance (*Bosei Hogo Renmei*) in 1935. Relevant documents are reproduced in *Nihon Fujin Mondai Shiryō Shūsei*, Vol. 2, pp. 474–96.

92 Yamazaki, *The Story of Yamada Waka*, pp. 129–36.

93 Hiratsuka Raichō, 'Ichini no handō josei', *Fujin Sensen*, June 1930, pp. 42–3.

94 Ishizuki, '1930nendai no Musan Fujin Undō', p. 202.

95 Sakai [Kondō] Magara, 'Ningen bōtoku!', *Sanji Chōsetsu Hyōron*, May 1925, in Kondō, *Watashi no Kaisō*, Vol. 2, pp. 188–94.

96 Sakai [Kondō] Magara, 'Bosei hogo seitei undō ni kisu', *Fusen*, October 1934, in Kondō, *Watashi no Kaisō*, Vol. 2, p. 173.

97 Sakai [Kondō] Magara, 'Boshi Fujo Hō no hanashi,' *Seigi no Hikari*, No. 53, 1/1/1935, in Kondō, *Watashi no Kaisō*, Vol. 2, p. 174.

98 *Nihon Fujin Mondai Shiryō Shūsei*, Vol. 2, pp. 488–90.

99 Vavich, 'The Japanese Women's Movement'.

100 cf. Hilary Land's comments on social legislation directed at women as mothers: 'It is clear that women have often gained social entitlements as mothers, but it is often *motherhood* as a social category that has been recognised rather than the needs of individual mothers . . . Furthermore, governments have been much more inclined to recognise women as mothers when they were also wives.' Hilary Land, 'Introduction', *Gender and History*, Vol. 4, No. 3, (Autumn 1992), p. 284; Denise Riley, *War in the Nursery: Theories of the Child and Mother*, London: Virago, 1983.

101 'Bosei Hogo no Hon'i', *Fujo Shinbun*, 4/11/1926, reprinted in *Fujinkai Sanjūgonen*, pp. 172–4.

102 Sakurai, *Bosei Hogo Undōshi*, pp. 58–65; Molony, 'Equality versus Difference: The Japanese Debate Over Motherhood Protection, 1915–1950', p. 135.

103 Yamakawa Kikue, 'Fujin no Kokusaku Kyōryoku', *Fujin Kōron*, October 1938; 'Seifu no Josei Chōyō: Tashika na Ayumi de Tadashii Hōkaku e', *Tokyo Asahi Shinbun*, 24/6/1939; 'Fujin no Kokutai Kōdō', *Tokyo Asahi Shinbun*, 25/6/1939, 'Shintaiseika Fujin no Chii to Yakuwari', *Nihon Hyōron*, September 1940, in Suzuki (ed.), *Yamakawa Kikue Josei Kaihō Ronshū*, pp. 128–48.

104 On the anarchist women's arts journal, *Nyonin Geijutsu*, see Ogata Akiko, *Nyonin Geijutsu no Hitobito*; Ogata Akiko, *Nyonin Geijutsu no Sekai*, Tokyo: Domesu Shuppan, 1980; 'Nyonin Geijutsu ni kiku Hataraku Onnatachi no Koe', *Jūgoshi Nōto*, No. 2, 1978, pp. 52–6; Miriam Silverberg, 'The Modern Girl as Militant', in Bernstein (ed.), *Recreating Japanese Women*, pp. 250–5.

105 Facsimile edition: Tokyo: Ryūkei Shosha, 1981.

106 Facsimile edition: Tokyo: Ryokuinbō, 1983.

107 The debates between anarchists and bolshevists of the 1920s are referred to as the '*ana-boru ronsō*'. On the women's '*ana-boru ronsō*', see Tsurumi, 'Feminism and Anarchism', pp. 9–12.

108 Tsurumi, 'Feminism and Anarchism', pp. 9–11.

109 See for example, Matsumoto Masae, 'Buru Otoko no Kamen o Hagu', Sumai Sueko, 'Maruha no Orekireki', Shōchi Saiko, 'Wagakuni no Marukusu Fujin no Zunō Haiken', parts 1–4, *Fujin Sensen.*

110 Takamure Itsue, 'Fujin Sensen ni Tatsu', *Fujin Sensen*, No. 1, March 1930; pp. 8–16; cited in Yoneda Sayoko, 'Boseishugi no Rekishiteki Igi: *Fujin Sensen* Jidai no Hiratsuka Raichō o Chūshin ni', in Joseishi Sōgō Kenkyūkai (eds), *Nihon Joseishi 5: Gendai*, Tokyo: Tokyo Daigaku Shuppankai, p. 135. See also Takamure Itsue, 'Kaikyū Dōtoku to Museifu Dōtoku: Toku ni Fujin no Tame ni', *Fujin Sensen*, No. 9, pp. 6–11.

111 Takamure Itsue, 'Museifushugi no Mokuhyō to Senjutsu: Genka Museifushugi Sensen no Seiri ni Kansuru Shiken', *Fujin Sensen*, April 1930, pp. 30–6.

112 A similar idealization of village communities can be found in the writing of Itō Noe, who brought an anarchist perspective to the Bluestocking journal. See for example, Itō Noe, 'Museifu no jijitsu', *Itō Noe Zenshū*, Vol. 2, Gakugei Shorin, Tokyo, p. 464.

113 Hiratsuka also contributed to *Fujin Sensen*, and many similarities can be identified between Hiratsuka and Takamure. The connections between Hiratsuka and Takamure have been traced by Tsurumi. In addition to their philosophical affinities, they are also linked by their use of both polemical and poetic genres of writing in order to express their feminist ideas. See for example, Takamure Itsue's 'Leaving Home Poem' (Iede no Shi). Hiratsuka Raichō, *Genshi Josei wa Taiyō de atta*, Tokyo: Ōtsuki Shoten, Vol. 4, pp. 281–3; Tsurumi, 'Feminism and Anarchism, pp. 7–8.

114 Tsurumi, 'Feminism and Anarchism', p. 8.

115 Takamure Itsue, 'Katei Hiteiron', *Fujin Sensen*; No. 2, Matsumoto Masae, 'Sei Seikatsu no Keizaigakuteki Kansatsu: Fujin Undō to shite no Katei Hitei', *Fujin Sensen*, No. 9, pp. 14–19.

116 Yamakawa Kikue, 'Keihin tsuki Tokkahin to shite no Onna', *Fujin Kōron*, January 1928; Takamure Itsue, 'Yamakawa Kikue shi no Ren'aikan o Nanzu', *Fujin Kōron*, May 1928; Yagi Akiko, 'Ren'ai to Jiyū Shakai', *Jiyū Rengō Shinbun*, No. 29, 1/11/1928. Yagi's contribution refers to the controversy created by Hayashi Fusao's translation of Aleksandra Kollontai's fiction in 1927. These three articles are reproduced in Ezashi Akiko (ed.), *Ai to Sei no Jiyū: Ie kara no Kaihō*, Tokyo: Shakai Hyōronsha, 1989, pp. 190–213.

117 See Hiratsuka Raichō, 'Fujin Sensen ni Sanka shite', *Fujin Sensen*, 1930, pp. 34–9; and Yoneda Sayoko's discussion of Hiratsuka's political position in 'Boseishugi no Rekishiteki Igi', *passim.*

118 Discussed in detail in Hélène Bowen, 'Victims as Victors'. Kanno's prison poetry is discussed in Hélène Bowen, 'Women and Treason in Prewar Japan: The Prison Poetry of Kanno Suga and Kaneko Fumiko', *Lilith*, No. 5, (Spring 1988), pp. 9–25.

119 Kondō, *Watashi no Kaisō*, Vol. 2, pp. 39–40.

120 Yamanouchi Mina, 'The Night of the Stars', translated in Hane Mikiso, *Reflections on the Way to the Gallows.*

121 Sata Ineko, 'Kurenai,' *Fujin Kōron*, January–June 1936, reproduced in Itō Tadashi, et al. (eds), *Nihon Gendai Bungaku Zenshū 83: Sata Ineko, Tsuboi Sakae*, Tokyo: Kōdansha, 1964, pp. 147–245; excerpts translated in Yukiko Tanaka (ed.), *To Live and To Write: Selections by Japanese Women Writers 1913–1918*, Seattle: Seal Press, 1987, pp. 167–80.

122 Tajima, *Hitosuji no Michi.*

123 Makise Kikue, *Hitamuki no Onnatachi*; Watanabe and Suzuki (eds), *Tatakai ni Ikite – Senzen Fujin Undō e no Shōgen*; Watanabe and Suzuki (eds), *Undō ni kaketa Onnatachi*; Yamashiro Tomoe, *Toraware no Onnatachi*, Tokyo: Komichi Shobō, 1980, 11 Vols; Hane, *Reflections on the Way to the Gallows.*

124 Tanno Setsu, 'Gokuchū Yori Haha ni Kisu', *Fujin Kōron*, cited in Watashitachi no Rekishi o Tsuzuru Kai, *Fujin Zasshi Kara Mita 1930nendai*', p. 40.

125 'Ryūchijō no modan gāru', *Nyonin Geijutsu*, Vol. 2, No. 12, pp. 77–81, cited in Silverberg, 'The Modern Girl as Militant', p. 255.

126 Yoshiko Miyake, 'Doubling Expectations: Motherhood and Women's Factory Work in the 1930s and 1940s', in Bernstein (ed.), *Recreating Japanese Women*, p. 278.

Miyake's article includes a survey of State policies concerned with women's maternal capacity in the late 1930s and 1940s.

127 Miyake, 'Doubling Expectations', p. 279.

128 Muraki Kazuko, 'Shōka wa yo ni tsure', *Jūgoshi Nōto*, No. 3, 1979, pp. 9–24.

129 E. Ann Kaplan, *Motherhood and Representation: The Mother in Popular Culture and Melodrama*, London: Routledge, 1992, p. 16.

7 Creating Socialist Women 1900–1937

1 Nakamoto Takako, 'Tōmosu Daini Kōjō', Part 5, *Nyonin Geijutsu*, May 1932, p. 137. I have discussed this story in more detail in Mackie, *Imagining Liberation*, and Mackie, 'Narratives of Struggle'.

2 cf. Victor Koschmann's comments on Nolte and Hastings' essay on the Meiji State's policies on women: 'Without actually citing Louis Althusser's theory of ideology, the authors show how the Meiji state called upon women – "interpellated" them in Althusser's language – as historical subjects to advance national purposes.' J. Victor Koschmann, 'Review of Recreating Japanese Women, 1600–1945', *Journal of Japanese Studies*, Vol. 18, No. 2, (Summer 1992), p. 532; citing Louis Althusser, *For Marx*, London: Verso Books, 1977, p. 173.

3 For recent feminist discussions of 'equality versus difference', see Chapter four, note 122.

4 On this period, see Kazuko Tsurumi, *Social Change and the Individual: Japan Before and After World War II*, Princeton, New Jersey: Princeton University Press, 1979.

5 Even the Socialist Women's Seminar, however, was relatively dominated by men, both as speakers and as audience members. The lecture series did, though, give some women their first opportunity for public speaking, and provided a forum for the discussion of feminist issues.

6 Nishikawa Fumiko, 'Shinbun Uri no Ki', *Chokugen*, Vol. 2, No. 5, 5/3/1905, reproduced in Suzuki (ed.), *Shiryō: Heiminsha no Onnatachi*, pp. 61–3.

7 This incident is discussed in the opening to Chapter six.

8 Andrew Gordon, *Labor and Imperial Democracy*, p. 159.

9 Ishizuki, '1930nendai no Musan Fujin Undō', p. 200.

10 On the proletarian literary movement, see Shea, *Leftwing Literature in Japan*; Yanaga, *Japan Since Perry*, pp. 484–8; Iwamoto Yoshio. 'Aspects of the Proletarian Literature Movement', in Silberman and Harootunian (eds), *Japan in Crisis*, pp. 156–82; Silverberg, *Changing Song*, pp. 29–44; Vernon, *Daughters of the Moon: Wish, Will and Social Constraint in the Fiction of Japanese Women*, Berkeley, pp. 87–8. Several of the women involved with this movement became well-known literary figures in the post-War period, including Sata Ineko, Hirabayashi Taiko, Miyamoto Yuriko and Hayashi Fumiko.

11 See interview with Umezu Hagiko, quoted in Chapter five.

12 Yoshiko Miyake, 'Doubling Expectations: Motherhood and Women's Factory Work in the 1930s and 1940s', in Bernstein (ed.), *Recreating Japanese Women*, pp. 267–95.

13 Sakurai, *Bosei Hogo Undō Shi*, pp. 56–9.

14 Shocking evidence of the masculinism of men in the Communist party has been revealed in post-War discussions of the so-called 'housekeeper' issue. It seems that the Party made a practice of using women sympathetic to the cause as 'housekeepers'. They were assigned to live with male activists, giving them legitimacy as part of a married couple. In addition to household labour, the women would often engage in paid work to support the man, and often be expected to sleep with him. In the worst cases, the women would be entreated to work as cafe waitresses. Although this was not the subject of discussion in the left-wing press of the time, the practice is dramatized in novels. More recently, women of the Party have revealed their experiences in oral history interviews and memoirs. See interviews in Makise, *Hitamuki no Onnatachi*; and Nakamoto Takako, *Waga Ai*. Murakami Nobuhiko has written a particularly passionate indictment of such practices. Murakami Nobuhiko, *Nihon no Fujin Mondai*, Tokyo: Iwanami Shoten, pp. 152–62.

15 See the discussion of Kishida Toshiko's '*Hakoiri Musume*' in Chapter two, p. 28.

16 Tsurumi, *Factory Girls*, p. 154.

17 *Seigi no Hikari*, No. 2, 18/5/1926, p. 25; discussed in Chapter 5, page 116.

18 bell hooks, 'Narratives of Struggle', in Philomena Mariani (ed.), *Critical Fictions: The Politics of Imaginative Writing*, Bay Press: Seattle, 1991; p. 59.

19 See for example, representations of 'dawn' over the factories, such as the illustration on p. 154.

20 Tajima Hide, 'Hikari ni Mukaite', *Seigi no Hikari*, 2; 18/5/1926.

21 Steedman, *Landscape for a Good Woman: A Story of Two Lives*, p. 7.

22 Sata Ineko, 'Kyarameru Kōjō Kara', *Puroretaria Bungaku*, March 1928, in Itō Tadashi, et al. (eds), *Nihon Gendai Bungaku Zenshū*, Vol. 83, pp. 206–12.

23 Kubokawa [Sata] Ineko, 'Kanojora no Kaiwa', *Senki*, June 1928; pp. 100–7.

24 Nakamoto Takako, 'Tōmosu Daini Kōjō', pp. 161–2.

25 Hanaoka Shigeko, 'Haha wa Kuruu', *Rōdō Fujin*, No. 31, June 1930.

26 Kubokawa [Sata] Ineko, 'Biramaki'. See also Kubokawa [Sata] Ineko, 'Kanbu Jokō no Namida', *Kaizō*, January 1931; 'Shōkanbu', *Bungei Shunjū*, August 1931, 'Kitō', *Chūō Kōron*, October 1931, 'Kyōsei Kikoku', *Chūō Kōron*, October 1931; cited in Miriam Silverberg, 'The Modern Girl as Militant'. Kubokawa [Sata] Ineko, 'Kanojora no Kaiwa'.

27 Strike pamphlets, held in Ōhara Social Research Institute, reproduced in Suzuki Yūko, *Jokō to Rōdō Sōgi*.

28 bell hooks, 'Narratives of Struggle'.

29 Yosano Akiko, 'Sozorogoto', *Seitō*, 1911, Vol. 1, No. 1, p. l.

30 The period in the late nineteenth century when Japan's political and social institutions is referred to as *Keimōki. Keimō* literally means 'enlightening the darkness'. Blacker, *The Japanese Enlightenment: A Study of the Writings of Fukuzawa Yukichi*, p. 32.

31 Mohanty, 'Cartographies of Struggle', pp. 34–6.

32 Carr (ed.), *From My Guy to Sci-Fi: Genre and Women's Writing in the Postmodern World*.

33 As we have noted in Chapter six, representations of women engaged in labour activism did enter the mass media and intellectual journals at the time of the textile strikes of the depression years. Miriam Silverberg has also discussed the representations of the 'modern girl', the successor to the 'new woman' of the Taishō period. Silverberg argues that autonomy and militancy was one aspect of the representation of the 'modern girl'. Her discussion of the sexualized image of the modern girl also suggests that the modern girl was a dangerous figure who had to be recuperated into the acceptable bounds of femininity. Miriam Silverberg, 'The Modern Girl as Militant', in Bernstein (ed.), *Recreating Japanese Women*, pp. 263–6.

34 cf. Rowbotham, *Hidden From History*.

35 Rajan, *Real and Imagined Women: Gender, Culture and Postcolonialism*, p. 3.

Glossary

Individuals

Abe Isoo (1866–1949), Christian socialist, member of *Shakai Shugi Kenkyūkai, Heiminsha*, professor at Waseda University, member of Lower House.

Abe Shizue (1899–1974), active in Social Democratic women's organizations.

Akamatsu Akiko, wife of Akamatsu Katsumaro, member of *Shakai Minshū Fujin Dōmei*, who later moves to the right in the *Kokka Shakai Fujin Dōmei*.

Akamatsu Katsumaro (1894–1953), founder of *Shinjinkai*, active in *Sōdōmei* and *Shakai Minshū Tō*, later moves to the right in the *Kokka Shakai Tō*, brother to Akamatsu Tsuneko; married to Akamatsu Akiko.

Akamatsu Tsuneko (1897–1965), member of *Shakai Minshū Fujin Dōmei*, postwar Diet member, sister of Akamatsu Katsumaro.

Akita Ujaku (1883–1962), leader of proletarian literature movement.

Akitsuki Shizue, member of *Sekirankai*, arrested for distributing leaflets on May Day 1921.

Aoyama Kikue, see Yamakawa Kikue.

Arahata Kanson (Katsuzō) (1887–1981), member of *Heiminsha* who turns to anarchism, lover of Kanno Suga (1881–1911), contributor to *Muroo Shinpō* and other socialist publications.

Arahata Katsuzō, see Arahata Kanson.

Asō Hisashi (pseudonym: Asan Kaisuke) (1891–1940), active in Nichirō faction of union movement.

Chūjō Yuriko, see Miyamoto Yuriko.

Emile Boissonade (1825–1910), French legal scholar commissioned to prepare Meiji Civil Code.

Endō (Iwano) Kiyoko (1882–1920), contributor to socialist press including *Nijū Seiki no Fujin*. Participant in early campaign for revision of Article Five of the Public Peace Police Law which restricted women's political activities, marries writer Iwano Hōmei, contributes to *Seitō*.

Fujimori Seikichi (1892–1977) proletarian writer.

Fujita Takako, active in *Shakai Minshū Fujin Dōmei*.

Fukuda (Kageyama) Hideko (1865–1927), imprisoned for involvement in Ōsaka Incident, released on amnesty celebrating the promulgation of the Meiji Constitution, active in *Heiminsha*. Editor of *Sekai Fujin*, participant in early campaign for revision of Article Five of the Public Peace Police Law which restricted women's political activities.

Fukuda Tomosaku (1865–1899), socialist, husband of Fukuda Hideko.

Fukuzawa Yukichi (1835–1901), liberal thinker and founder of Keiō University, contributor to debates on the family in the Meiroku Zasshi.

Gotō Miyoko (1898–1975), poet involved in proletarian *tanka* movement.

Hasegawa Shigure, a former contributor to the Bluestocking journal, editor of *Nyonin Geijutsu*.

Hashiura Haruko (1899–1979), member of *Sekirankai*, arrested for distributing leaflets on May Day 1921, later withdraws from socialist movement.

Hashiura Riku (?–1923), member of Sekirankai.

Hatoyama Haruko, (1861–1938), active in Patriotic Women's Association.

Hayashi Fumiko (1903–1951) writer with anarchist connections, contributor to *Nyonin Geijutsu*.

Higuchi Ichiyō (1872–1896), poet and novelist in late nineteenth century, member of *Bungakukai* literary circle and contributor to *Bungakukai* journal.

Hirabayashi Taiko (1905–1971) writer with anarchist connections, member of *Kantō Fujin Dōmei*, *Musan Fujin Kenkyū Kai* and *Musan Fujin Renmei*.

Hiratsuka Haru(ko), see Hiratsuka Raichō.

Hiratsuka Raichō (Haruko) (1886–1971) founding editor of *Seitō*, founding member of *Seitōsha* and *Shin Fujin Kyōkai*, participant in 'motherhood protection debate'.

Hori Yasuko, contributor to *Seitō*, married to Ōsugi Sakae, sister of Sakai Toshihiko's first wife Hori Miwako (who died in 1904).

Hosoi Wakizō (1897–1925), textile worker and member of proletarian literature movement, author of *Jokō Aishi*, (The Pitiful History of the Female Factory Workers), published in 1925.

Hozumi Yatsuka, conservative commentator on legal issues.

Ibara Hanako, contributor to *Sekai Fujin*.

Ichikawa Fusae (1893–1981), secretary of Yūaikai women's division who later devotes her life to suffragism, member of House of Councillors for much of the post-war period.

Imai Utako (?–1968), publisher of *Nijūseiki no Fujin*, participant in early campaign for revision of Article Five of the Public Peace Police Law which restricted women's political activities.

Ishikawa Sanshirō (pen-name: Asahiyama), Christian socialist, member of *Heiminsha*, contributor to *Sekai Fujin*.

Ishimoto (Katō) Shidzue (1897–), birth control campaigner, author of autobiography *Facing Two Ways*, marries Communist Katō Kanjū in 1944 after divorce from Baron Ishimoto, member of House of Councillors for much of the postwar period.

Itō Noe (1895–1923), anarchist, contributor to and later editor of *Seitō*. Partner of Ōsugi Sakae and killed with Ōsugi in aftermath of 1923 earthquake.

Iwamoto Zenji (Yoshiharu), principal of the women's school *Meiji Jogakuin*, and founder of the women's education journal *Jogaku Zasshi*.

Iwano Kiyoko, see Endō Kiyoko.

Iwauchi Tomie (1898–1986), member of *Zenkoku Fujin Dōmei*, married to Iwauchi Zensaku.

Iwauchi Zensaku, leader of the Sōdōmei-affiliated *Kantō Bōshoku Rōdō Kumiai* (Kantō Textile Workers' Union), moves to *Nichirō* faction after second split and continues activities in *Nihon Bōshoku Rōdō Kumiai* (Japan Textile Workers' Union).

Kageyama Hideko, see Fukuda Hideko.

Kamichika Ichiko (1888–1981), writer, member of Seitōsha, lover of Ōsugi Sakae, contributor to *Nyonin Geijutsu*.

Kamijō Aiichi (1894–1969) active in Nichirō faction of union movement.

Kamikawa Matsuko (1885–1936), contributor to socialist press, participant in early campaign for revision of Article Five of the Public Peace Police Law which restricted women's political activities, involved in Red Flag Incident.

Kaneko Shigeri, suffragist.

Kanno Suga (pseudonym Yūgetsu) (1881–1911), contributor to *Muroō Shinpō* and other socialist publications, lover of Kōtoku Shūsui, executed as conspirator in Great Treason Incident.

Katayama Sen (1859–1933), author of *The Labour Movement in Japan*, founder of Rōdō Kumiai Kiseikai and editor of *Rōdō Sekai*, active in international communist movement.

Katō Hiroyuki (1836–1916), contributor to debates on the family in the *Meiroku Zasshi*, President of Tokyo University, member of Genrōin and Privy Council.

Katō Shidzue, see Ishimoto Shidzue.

Kawamura Haruko (?–1913), editor of *Nijūseiki no Fujin*, participant in early campaign for revision of Article Five of the Public Peace Police Law which restricted women's political activities.

Kinoshita Naoe (1869–1937), active in universal suffrage movement, member of *Heiminsha*, founder of Christian socialist journal *Shinkigen*, author of several socialist novels, leaves socialist movement.

Kishida (Nakajima) Toshiko (1861–1901), early liberal feminist, contributor to liberal newspapers and known for public speaking on behalf of liberal movement.

Kitagawa Chiyoko, member of *Sekirankai*.

Kobayashi Kusuo (1858–1920), liberal activist involved in Ōsaka Incident, engaged to Fukuda Hideko.

Komiyama Tomie, active in *Sōdōmei* until first split, then moves to *Hyōgikai*.

Kondō (Sakai) Magara (1903–83), member of *Sekirankai*; *Musan Fujin Kenkyū Kai*, editor of *Akai Hoshi*, daughter of Sakai Toshihiko; married to Kondō Kenji.

Kōtoku Chiyoko (1875–1960), participant in early campaign for revision of Article Five of the Public Peace Police Law which restricted women's political activities, wife of Kōtoku Shūsui.

Kōtoku Shūsui (Denjirō) (1871–1911), founding member of *Heiminsha* who turns to anarchism, husband of Kōtoku Chiyoko, lover of Kanno Suga, executed as conspirator in Great Treason Incident.

Kubokawa Ineko, see Sata Ineko.

Kubushiro Ochimi (1882–1972), suffragist.

Kusunose Kita (1833–1920), woman associated with liberal movement who demands voting rights in local assembly in 1878.

Kutsumi Fusako (1890–1980) member of *Sekirankai*; *Musan Fujin Dōmei*; *Fusen Kyōdō Undō*; active in *Sōdōmei* until split, moves to *Hyōgikai* and illegal Communist party, involved in Sorge spy incident.

Matsumoto Masae, contributor to *Fujin Sensen*.

Matsuoka Fumiko, see Nishikawa Fumiko.

Matsuoka Komakichi (1881–1958), active in Social Democratic Union organizations.

Matsuoka Kōson, first husband of Matsuoka (Nishikawa) Fumiko.

Mitamura Shirō, active in *Hyōgikai*, opposed to creation of women's division.

Mitsukuri Rinshō, legal scholar commissioned in 1870 to translate the French Civil Code into Japanese.

Miyamoto (Chūjō) Yuriko (1899–1951), communist writer, active in proletarian literature movement, contributor to *Hataraku Fujin*.

Mori Arinori (1847–89), founding member of Meirokusha, and contributor to debates on the family in the *Meiroku Zasshi*, became Minister of Education in 1885.

Murai Tomoyoshi (1861–1944), *Heiminsha* member, Christian socialist.

Nabeyama Sadachika (1901–), active in *Hyōgikai* and communist movement, opposed to creation of women's division, commits *tenkō* (renunciation of communism) in 1933.

Nakajima Toshiko, see Kishida Toshiko.

Nakamoto Takako (1903–1991), Communist underground sympathiser and writer.

Nakamura Masanao (Keiu) (1832–91), contributor to debates on the family in the *Meiroku Zasshi*, translator of Samuel Smiles' *Self-Help* and J. S. Mill's *On Liberty*.

Nakanomyō Ine (1894–1981), member of *Sekirankai*, arrested on May Day 1921 for distributing leaflets.

Nakasone (Ogata) Sadayo, member of *Sekirankai*, arrested with Sakai Magara for distributing subversive leaflets to army, later withdraws from socialist movement.

Nishikawa (Matsuoka) Fumiko (1882–1960), member of *Heiminsha*, participant in early campaign for revision of Article Five of the Public Peace Police Law which restricted women's political activities, founder of *Shin Shin Fujin Kai*, editor of *Shin Shin Fujin* 1913–23, married to Matsuoka Kōson and Nishikawa Kōjirō.

Nishikawa Kōjirō (Mitsujirō) (1876–1940), member of *Heiminsha* and contributor to socialist newspaper *Hikari*, second husband of Nishikawa Fumiko, later withdraws from socialist movement.

Nishimura Shigeki (1828–1902), Confucian scholar, contributor to debates on the family in the *Meiroku Zasshi*.

Nobuoka (Sakai) Tameko (1872–1959), member of *Heiminsha*, becomes second wife of Sakai Toshihiko and step-mother of Sakai Magara. Participant in early campaign for revision of Article Five of the Public Peace Police Law which restricted women's political activities, involved in Red Flag Incident.

Nogami Yaeko (1885–1985), writer, contributor to *Seitō*.

Nomura Tsuchino, active in *Sōdōmei*.

Nozaka (Kuzuno) Ryō (1896–1971), active in *Sōdōmei* until split, then moves to *Hyōgikai* and underground communist movement. Imprisoned 1928–29, wife of Communist leader Nozaka Sanzō.

Ogata Sadayo, see Nakasone Sadayo.

Oguchi Michiko (?–1962), active in *Heiminsha*.

Ogure Reiko (1890–1977), involved in Red Flag Incident.

Ōi Kentarō (1843–1922), liberal involved in Ōsaka Incident, lover of Fukuda Hideko, founder of *Dai Nihon Rōdō Kyōkai* (Greater Japan Labour Association).

Oku (Wada) Mumeo (1895–), founding member of *Shin Fujin Kyōkai*, suffragist, founder of journal *Shokugyō Fujin*, active in co-operative movement in post-war Japan.

Okumura Ioko (1845–1907), founder of Patriotic Women's Association.

Orimoto Sadayo, see Tatewaki Sadayo.

Ōsugi Sakae (1885–1923), anarchist, editor of *Kindai Shisō* and *Bunmei Hihyō*, lover of Itō Noe and Kamichika Ichiko; married to Hori Yasuko; murdered with his nephew and his partner Itō Noe after Great Kantō earthquake.

Ōsuka Satoko (1881–1913), involved in Red Flag Incident.

Sakai Magara, see Kondō Magara.

Sakai Tameko, see Nobuoka Tameko.

Sakai Toshihiko (1871–1933), socialist writer who also wrote extensively on women and socialism, founder of Communist party, subsequently active to the left of the 'legal' socialist movement.

Sakamoto (Takada) Makoto (1899–1954), founding member of *Shin Fujin Kyōkai*.

Sakatani Shiroshi, contributor to debates on the family in the *Meiroku Zasshi*.

Sata (Kubokawa) Ineko (1904–), member of Communist Arts Federation, contributor to *Puroretaria Geijutsu*, *Senki*, married to Kubokawa Tsurujirō.

Shimizu Toyoko (pen-name Shikin), contributor to *Jogaku Zasshi*.

Sugaya Iwako (1875–1929), member of *Heiminsha*, contributor to socialist press.

Sugiura Keiichi (1893–), active in *Hyōgikai*, opposed to creation of women's division.

Suzuki Bunji (1885–1946), founder of *Yūaikai*.

Tajima Hide (1901–1976), involved in *Shin Fujin Kyōkai* and later active in left wing of labour movement, active in Working Women's Research Bureau, contributes to *Seigi no Hikari* and produces the journal *Mirai*.

Takamure Itsue (1894–1964), anarchist and feminist historian, editor of *Fujin Sensen* and contributor to *Nyonin Geijutsu* and other publications.

Takatsu Masamichi (Seidō) (1893–), communist, married to Takatsu Tayoko.

Takatsu Tayoko (1896–1924), member of *Sekirankai*, married to Takatsu Masamichi (Seidō).

Tamura Toshiko (1884–1945) writer, contributor to *Seitō*.

Tanino Setsu, labour inspector in pre-war period.

Tanno Setsu (1902–1987), labour organiser, active in *Sōdōmei* until split, then moves to *Hyōgikai*, member of illegal Communist party, married to Watanabe Masanosuke.

Tatewaki (Orimoto) Sadayo (1904–90), member of *Zenkoku Fujin Dōmei*, managed the Labour Women's Night School (*Rōdō Jojuku*). Published a pamphlet on working women in Japan and contributed articles on working women to the journal *Fujin Sensen*.

Teramoto Michiko, see Oguchi Michiko.

Tokutomi Sohō (Iichirō) (1863–1957), founder of *Minyūsha* and editor of *Kokumin no Tomo*.

Tomii Tora (Otora) (1865–1885), liberal feminist, friend of Kishida Toshiko and Fukuda Hideko.

Ueki Emori (1857–1892), liberal thinker and commentator on women's issues.

Umezu (Nakahira) Hagiko (1904–) textile worker and union organiser.

Wada Ei (1857–1929), author of *Tomioka Nikki*, one of the earliest accounts of work in a textile mill.

Wada Mumeo, see Oku Mumeo.

Watanabe Masanosuke (1899–1928), communist labour activist, active in *Hyōgikai*, supports creation of women's division, married to Tanno Setsu, dies in Taiwan in 1928.

Yagi Akiko (1895–1983), anarchist writer.

Yajima Kajiko (1833–1925), founder of Japan Women's Christian Temperance Union.

Yamada Waka (1879–1957), contributor to *Seitō* and other publications, active in Motherhood Protection League.

Yamaguchi Koken (Gizō) (1883–1920), member of *Heiminsha*, contributor to socialist newspaper *Hikari*.

Yamakawa (Aoyama) Kikue (1890–1980), socialist writer, author and translator of numerous books on socialism and the woman question. Early member of underground communist movement but continues in the *Rōnō* faction of socialist movement, active in motherhood protection debate and in debates on union policies on women workers. Married to Yamakawa Hitoshi.

Yamakawa Hitoshi (1880–1958), early member of underground communist movement but continues in the *Rōnō* faction of the socialist movement. Editor of *Rōnō* journal, active in *Hyōgikai*, supports creation of women's division, married to Yamakawa Kikue.

Yamamoto Kenzō (1895–1942), active in *Hyōgikai*, opposed to creation of women's division.

Yamanouchi Mina (1900–   ), labour organizer and labour historian, active in *Sōdōmei* until split, then moves to *Hyōgikai*.

Yokoyama Gennosuke (1871–1915), journalist, author of *Nihon no Kasō Shakai*.

Yosano Akiko (1878–1924) feminist poet and critic, member of *Seitōsha*, contributor to 'motherhood protection debate'.

Organizations

Aikoku Fujin Kai (Patriotic Women's Association), formed 24 February 1901. In 1902, the organization started publishing its own journal *Aikoku Fujin* (*Patriotic Woman*). By the end of the Russo–Japanese War, the membership of the Patriotic Women's Association had leapt from an initial 45 000 to 463 000. By 1912 the organization had 816 609 members, making it the largest women's organization in the Meiji period. It continued until February 1942 when it was incorporated into the *Dai Nihon Fujin Kai* (Greater Japan Women's Association).

Bosei Hogo Hō Seitei Sokushin Fujin Renmei (Alliance for the Promotion of a Mother and Child Protection Act), formed in September 1934, committee headed by former Bluestocking Yamada Waka. The name was shortened to *Bosei Hogo Renmei* (Motherhood Protection Alliance) in 1935.

Bosei Hogo Renmei, see *Bosei Hogo Hō Seitei Sokushin Fujin Renmei*.

Dai Nihon Fujin Kai (Greater Japan Women's Association), mass nationalist women's organization created through merger of pre-existing organizations in February 1942.

Fujin Dōshikai, State-sponsored women's organization, formed 12 May 1930.

Fujin Sanseiken Kakutoku Kisei Dōmeikai (The League for the Attainment of Women's Political Rights) formed in 1924. The name of the organization was changed to the *Fusen Kakutoku Dōmei* (Women's Suffrage League) in April 1925.

Fujin Seiji Undō Sokushinkai (Society for the Promotion of Women's Political

Movements), broad-based but short-lived women's political organization formed in December 1926. The fifty members of this organization included Oku Mumeo, Nagashima Yōko, Sakamoto Makoto, Iwauchi Tomie, Tajima Hide, Akamatsu Akiko and Sakai Magara.

Fusen Dantai Rengō Iinkai (Allied Committee for the Attainment of Women's Suffrage), established in January 1931, brought together the Women's Suffrage League, the Japan Christian Association for Women's Suffrage (*Nihon Kirisutokyō Fujin Sanseiken Kyōkai*), the League for Women's Political Rights (*Fujin Sansei Dōmei*), and the Proletarian Women's League (*Musan Fujin Dōmei*). These four groups were represented at the third annual National Women's Suffrage Conference in May 1932, which produced a statement condemning fascism.

Fusen Kakutoku Dōmei (Women's Suffrage League), see *Fujin Sanseiken Kakutoku Kisei Dōmeikai.*

Fusen Kakutoku Kyōdō Iinkai (Joint Women's Suffrage Committee), set up in December 1928 and was active until 1929. This committee brought together three women's suffrage organizations and four of the left-wing women's leagues: the Labour Women's Alliance (*Rōdō Fujin Renmei*), the Social Women's League (*Shakai Fujin Dōmei*), the Japan Association for Women's Political Rights (*Nihon Fujin Sanseiken Kyōkai*), the Kantō Women's League (*Kantō Fujin Dōmei*), the League for Women's Political Rights (*Fujin Sansei Dōmei*), the Women's Suffrage League (*Fusen Kakutoku Dōmei*), and the National Women's League (*Zenkoku Fujin Dōmei*).

Heiminsha (Commoners' Society), early socialist organization, formed in 1903.

Hyōgikai, see *Nihon Rōdō Kumiai Hyōgikai.*

Kantō Bōshoku Rōdō Kumiai (Kantō Textile Workers' Union), affiliated with Sōdōmei.

Kantō Fujin Dōmei (Kantō Women's League), aligned with the communist-influenced Rōnō Tō, formed 3 July 1927 but forcibly disbanded in March 1928 when official party policy argued against the existence of separate women's leagues. Members of the preparatory committee included Tajima Hide, Nozaka Ryō, and Tanno Setsu, and members of the Women's Division of the Japan Farmers' League and the Women's Division of the Hyōgikai.

Meirokusha, intellectual organization formed in 1873, where members held lecture meetings and published lectures in *Meiroku Zasshi.*

Min'yūsha (Friends of the Nation), an organization led by Tokutomi Sohō which published *Kokumin no Tomo* and *Kokumin Shinbun.*

Musan Fujin Dōmei (Proletarian Women's League), created from the merger of the *Musan Fujin Renmei* and the *Zenkoku Fujin Dōmei* in January 1929. By 1930 the League had 100 members, increasing to 445 members in 1931. It merged with the *Shakai Minshū Fujin Dōmei* in August 1932 to create the *Shakai Taishū Fujin Dōmei* (Social Masses Women's League).

Musan Fujin Kenkyūkai (Proletarian Women's Study Group), formed in June 1928 after the disbandment of the Kantō Women's League by those women who retained their allegiance to the 'legal' left. The study group became the Proletarian Women's Alliance (*Musan Fujin Renmei*), in October 1928, and this organization formed an alliance with the centrist National Women's League (*Zenkoku Fujin Dōmei*), in January 1929, creating the Proletarian Women's League (*Musan Fujin Dōmei*).

Musan Fujin Renmei, see *Musan Fujin Kenkyūkai.*

Musan Taishū Tō (Proletarian Masses Party), formed in August 1928 after dissolution of Rōnō Tō, merges with *Nihon Rōnō Tō* in December 1928.

Nichirō, see *Nihon Rōdō Kumiai Dōmei.*

Nihon Bōshoku Rōdō Kumiai, Japan Textile Workers' Union, affiliated with Nichirō.

Nihon Fujin Dōmei, see *Nihon Kokka Shakai Fujin Dōmei.*

Nihon Kirisutokyō Fujin Kyōfūkai (Japan Women's Christian Temperance Union), established in 1886.

Nihon Kokka Shakai Fujin Dōmei (Japan National Socialist Women's League), formed in July 1932, and changed its name to the Japan Women's League (*Nihon Fujin Dōmei*) in August 1933.

Nihon Kokka Shakai Tō (Japan National Socialist Party), rightist party formed by Akamatsu Katsumaro in 1932.

Nihon Kokubō Fujinkai (Japan Women's National Defence Organization), nationalist women's organization formed in March 1932. It continued until its incorporation into the *Dai Nihon Fujin Kai* (Greater Japan Women's Association) in February 1942.

Nihon Kyōsantō (Japan Communist Party), formed in July 1922, disbanded in 1924 after government crackdowns in the summer of 1923, and was not re-formed until December 1926.

Nihon Rengō Fujin Kai (Japan Federation of Women's Associations), formed 6 March 1931.

Nihon Rōdō Kumiai Dōmei (Japan Labour Union League, abbreviated as *Nichirō*), centrist labour union federation, formed after the second *Sōdōmei* split in December 1926.

Nihon Rōdō Kumiai Hyōgikai (Japan Labour Unions Council, abbreviated as *Hyōgikai*) formed when Communist elements split from *Sōdōmei* on 25 May 1925, the site of a debate on the necessity of a women's division in 1925, *Hyōgikai* dissolved in April 1928.

Nihon Rōdō Kumiai Zenkoku Kyōgikai (Japan Labour Union National Conference, abbreviated as *Zenkyō*), successor to *Hyōgikai*, formed in December 1928.

Nihon Rōdō Sōdōmei, (Japan General Federation of Labour), abbreviated as *Sōdōmei*), moderate social democratic union federation; see *Yūaikai.*

Nihon Rōnō Tō (Japan Labour–Farmer Party), political party affiliated with the *Nichirō* clique, formed in December 1926, merges with *Musan Taishū Tō* in December 1928.

Nihon Shakai Shugi Dōmei (Japan Socialist League) formed in December 1920 but disbanded within six months.

Nihon Shakai Tō (Japan Socialist Party) formed in February 1906 by members of both the Christian and materialist factions, declared its intention to pursue legal, parliamentary means to social change, and survived until 1907.

Rōdō Fujin Renmei (Women's Labour Alliance), formed in 1927, affiliated with *Sōdōmei*, merges with *Shakai Minshū Fujin Dōmei* in May 1931.

Rōdō Kumiai Kiseikai (Society for the Promotion of Labour), established in 1897.

Rōdō Nōmin Tō (Labour–Farmer Party, abbreviated to *Rōnō Tō*), party affiliated with the Hyōgikai union federation, to the left of the 'legal left', formed in 1926 banned in April 1928.

Sanji Seigen Kyōkai (Birth Control League) formed in September 1930, under the auspices of the *Shakai Minshū Fujin Dōmei.*

Seiji Kenkyūkai, see *Seiji Mondai Kenkyūkai.*

Seiji Mondai Kenkyūkai (Political Issues Research Association, later shortened to *Seiji Kenkyūkai*, Political Research Association) formed in December 1923 in preparation for the formation of a proletarian political party which would represent both workers and tenant farmers.

Seitōsha (Bluestocking Society), women's organization which supported the Bluestocking journal from 1911 to 1916.

Sekirankai, socialist women's organization, formed in April 1921, members of this organization participate in May Day 1921, several women arrested.

Shakai Fujin Dōmei (Social Women's League), formed in November 1927, was aligned with the moderate *Shakai Minshū Tō*, changed its name to the *Shakai Minshū Fujin Dōmei* (Social Democratic Women's League) in July 1928.

Shakai Minshū Fujin Dōmei: Shakai Fujin Dōmei changes its name to *Shakai Minshū Fujin Dōmei* in July 1928. Members included Akamatsu Akiko, Murakami Hide, Yamada Yasu, and Fujita Takako. Merges with the Women's Labour Alliance (*Rōdō Fujin Renmei*) in May 1931. The Committee of the amalgamated organization had Akamatsu Akiko as Secretary/Treasurer, Matsuoka Katsuyo responsible for Finance, and a management committee including Akamatsu Tsuneko, Abe Shizue and Nishio Fusano. By July 1931 the Social Democratic Women's League had 22 branches, representing a doubling in size in just a few months. The membership was 2225 by October 1931, eight times the 1929 figure. A new committee in 1932 was chaired by Akamatsu Tsuneko, with Abe Shizue as Secretary and Matsuoka Katsuyo as Treasurer.

Shakai Minshū Tō (Social Democratic Party), formed in December 1926, affiliated with the moderate Sōdōmei union federation. [A more accurate translation of Shakai Minshū Tō would perhaps be 'Social People's Party', but I will follow other writers in translating this as 'Social Democratic Party', first to distinguish this grouping from the 'Social Masses Party' (*Shakai Taishū Tō*), and second to reflect the moderate social democratic emphasis of the group.] The *Shakai Minshū Tō* merged with the centrist National Labour–Farmer Masses Party (*Zenkoku Rōnō Taishū Tō*) to form the Social Masses Party (*Shakai Taishū Tō*) in July 1932.

Shakai Minshutō (Social Democratic Party), formed in 1901 and immediately banned. Not to be confused with the *Shakai Minshū Tō* formed in 1926.

Shakai Shugi Kenkyūkai (Society for the Study of Socialism), established in 1898, reformed as the Socialist Association (*Shakai Shugi Kyōkai*) in 1900.

Shakai Shugi Kyōkai (Socialist Association), formed in 1900 from *Shakai Shugi Kenkyūkai*.

Shakai Taishū Fujin Dōmei, formed from the merger of the *Musan Fujin Dōmei* and the *Shakai Minshū Fujin Dōmei* in August 1932, aligned with *Shakai Taishū Tō*. Akamatsu Tsuneko was chairperson and Sakai Magara was secretary, with Tanabe Tose as treasurer, assisted by Iwauchi Tomie, with a Central Committee of 60 members. A new committee, formed in 1935, was chaired by Iwauchi Tomie, with Sakai Magara as Treasurer, assisted by a steering committee of Akamatsu Tsuneko, Abe Shizue and three others.

Shakai Taishū Tō (Social Masses Party), formed in July 1932 from merger of *Shakai Minshū Tō* and *Zenkoku Rōnō Taishū Tō*.

Shaminkei clique, social democratic clique, see *Sōdōmei* and *Shakai Minshū Tō*.

Shin Fujin Kyōkai (New Women's Association), formed by Hiratsuka Raichō, Ichikawa Fusae, Oku Mumeo and Sakamoto Makoto. Hiratsuka announced the formation of the Association at a public meeting in 1919.

The organization was formally inaugurated 28 March 1920 and was active until the end of 1922.

Shin Nihon Kokumin Dōmei (New Japan People's League), nationalist party formed in 1932.

Shokkō Giyūkai (Knights of Labour), early labour organization.

Sōdōmei, see *Nihon Rōdō Sōdōmei.*

Suiheisha (Levellers' Society), an organization devoted to the liberation of the former outcaste class, formed in 1922.

Tettei Fusen Kyōdō Tōsō Iinkai (Joint Struggle Committee for Total Women's Suffrage), established in October 1930, brings together women from the Social Democratic Women's League and the Proletarian Women's League.

Tōkyō Fujin Rengōkai (Tokyo Federation of Women's Organizations), a broad-based federation, initially formed to co-ordinate relief activities in the aftermath of the Great Kantō Earthquake of 1923.

Yōkakai (Eighth Day Society), socialist women's organization involved in activities related to celebration of International Women's Day in Japan on 8 March 1923. Related activities included a women's edition of the proletarian literary journal *Tane Maku Hito.*

Yūaikai (Workers' Friendly Society), established under the leadership of Suzuki Bunji in 1912, renamed the *Dai Nihon Rōdō Sōdōmei-Yūaikai* (Greater Japan General Federation of Labour-Friendly Society) in September 1919, and finally *Nihon Rōdō Sōdōmei* (Japan General Federation of Labour), usually abbreviated as *Sōdōmei.* Women's division formed in 1916, revived in 1925.

Zen Kansai Fujin Rengōkai (All-Kansai Federation of Women's Organizations).

Zenkoku Fujin Dōmei (National Women's League), formed 2 October 1927, aligned with the centrist *Nichirō* faction; merges with the *Musan Fujin Renmei* in January 1929 to form the *Musan Fujin Dōmei.* Members of the Committee included Orimoto [Tatewaki] Sadayo as Secretary, Iwauchi Tomie with responsibility for Recruitment and Publicity, and Kikugawa Shizuko as Treasurer.

Zenkoku Rōnō Taishū Tō (National Labour–Farmer Masses Party), formed in 1920, merges with Shakai *Minshū Tō* in July 1932 to form the *Shakai Taishū Tō.*

Zenkyō, see *Nihon Rōdō Kumiai Zenkoku Kyōgikai.*

Publications

Akahata, see *Sekki.*

Akai Hoshi (*Red Star*), published by Musansha, (ed.), Sakai Magara, November 1926–September 1931.

Bungakukai, literary journal which appeared from 1893–1898.

Chokugen (*Plain Talk*), socialist newpaper, women's edition produced 23 April 1905.

Fujin Sensen (*The Women's Front*), published by Musan Fujin Geijutsu Renmei, (ed.), Takamure Itsue, March 1930–June 1931.

Fujo Shinbun (*Women's Newspaper*), progressive women's newspaper, edited by Fukushima Shirō, 1901–1940.

Fujin to Shinshakai (*Women and New Society*), (ed.) Yamada Waka, 1920–1921.

Heimin Shinbun (*Commoners' News*), newspaper produced by the *Heiminsha*, appears in various versions between 1903 and 1910. The weekly *Heimin Shinbun* appeared from November 1903–January 1905.

Hikari (*Light*), publication produced by the materialist faction including Nishikawa Kōjirō and Yamaguchi Koken, after the split in the *Heiminsha*.

Jiyū no Tomoshibi (*The Torch of Freedom*), liberal newspaper.

Jogaku Zasshi (*Women's Education Journal*), (ed.) Iwamoto Zenji.

Katei Zasshi (*Family Magazine*), founded by Tokutomi Sohō in 1892. [Not to be confused with the socialist journal of the same name].

Katei Zasshi (*Family Magazine*), established in April 1903 by Sakai Toshihiko. It appeared until July 1909, under a series of editors, including Sakai, Ōsugi Sakae, and Nishimura Shozan. Hori Yasuko was also involved in the production of the *Katei Zasshi* from its first issue.

Kokumin no Tomo (*The Nation's Friend*), newspaper associated with the Minyūsha.

Meiroku Zasshi, early Meiji intellectual journal.

Mirai (*Future*), journal of Fujin Rōdō Chōsajō, (ed.) Tajima Hide, Nos 1–9, March 1926–January 1927.

Nihon (*Japan*), nationalist newspaper.

Nijūseiki no Fujin (*Twentieth Century Women*), early socialist women's paper, established 1 February 1904, with Kawamura Haruko and Imai Utako as publisher and editor. Endō [Iwano] Kiyoko later took over the editorship. After a brief hiatus, the magazine reappeared in May 1906, and the final edition was published in November 1906.

Nyonin Geijutsu (*Women's Arts*), journal of Musan Fujin Geijutsu Renmei, edited by Hasegawa Shigure, 1928–1932.

Rōdō (*Labour*), Sōdōmei journal, produces women's supplement from April 1924.

Rōdō oyobi Sangyō (*Labour and Industry*), Yūaikai-Sōdōmei journal.

Rōdō Sekai (*Labour World*) was established by Katayama Sen and others in 1897 and appeared in various formats until 1902.

Rōnō, journal of the Labour–Farmer Party, produces women's edition.

Seigi no Hikari (*The Light of Justice*), journal of Nihon Bōshoku Rōdō Kumiai, Nos 1–72, 1926–1935.

Seitō (*Bluestocking*), feminist literary journal founded and edited by Hiratsuka Raichō, later edited by Itō Noe.

Sekai Fujin (*Women of the World*), socialist women's newspaper, (ed.) Fukuda Hideko, from 1907–1909.

Sekki (*Red Flag*), Communist party newspaper.

Shakai Shugi (*Socialism*) appeared from March 1903–December 1904.

Shin Kigen (*New Era*), publication produced by Christian socialists after the split in the *Heiminsha*.

Shinshin Fujin (*The True New Woman*) appeared from February 1913–September 1923, edited by former *Heiminsha* member Nishikawa Fumiko.

Shūkan Shakai Shinbun (*Weekly Social Newspaper*) appeared June 1907–August 1911.

Suiito Hōmu (*Sweet Home*), socialist women's paper of 1904, no issues extant.

Tane Maku Hito (*The Sower*), proletarian literary journal.

Yorozu Chōhō (*Complete Morning Report*), newspaper which employed Sakai Toshihiko and Kōtoku Shūsui until they left to form the *Heiminsha* after disagreements over the reporting of relations with Russia.

Yūai Fujin (*Yūai Woman*), journal of the Yūaikai Women's Division, August 1916–February 1917; July 1917–June 1918. Later renamed *Rōdō Fujin* (*Labour Woman*).

Select Bibliography

Primary Sources

Primary sources consulted for this book are held in the Meiji Newspaper and Magazine Collection at Tokyo University, the Ōhara Social Research Institute at Hōsei University, and the Ichikawa Fusae Memorial Centre in Tokyo. Details appear in relevant footnotes. In particular, the newsletters and documents of the following organizations have been consulted: Kantō Fujin Dōmei; Shakai Minshū Fujin Dōmei; Musan Fujin Dōmei; Musan Fujin Kenkyūkai; Musan Fujin Renmei; Nihon Kokka Shakai Fujin Dōmei; Rōdō Jojuku; Sanji Seigen Kyōkai; Sekirankai; Shakai (Minshū) Fujin Dōmei; Shakai Taishū Fujin Dōmei; Zenkoku Fujin Dōmei.

Journals and pamphlets:

Akai Hoshi, Tokyo: Musansha, Sakai Magara (ed.), November 1926– September 1931.

Doi Naosaku, *Tsūzoku Fujin Mondai*, Tokyo: Mita Shibu Kenkyūkai Shuppanbu, 1924.

Dokuzen Kyōfu, *Kageyama Hidejo no Den*, Tokyo, 1887.

Hara Yasuichi, *Itamashiki Oyako Shinjū no Jissō*, Tokyo: Zaisan Hōjin Shakai Kyōkai, August 1932; held in Ōhara Social Research Institute.

Iwauchi Zensaku, *Jokōsan ni Okuru*, Tokyo: Nihon Rōdō Sōdōmei Kantō Bōshoku Rōdō Kumiai, 25/7/1926; held in Ōhara Social Research Institute.

Mirai, Tokyo: Fujin Rōdō Chōsajō, Tajima Hide (ed.), Nos 1–9, March 1926– January 1927; held in Ōhara Social Research Institute.

Nakasone Sadayo, *Fujin Mondai*, Tokyo: Musansha, 8/6/1921; held in Ōhara Social Research Institute.

Nijūseiki no Fujin, Tokyo: Hokkaidō Fujin Dōshikai, Nos 1–4, 7, 9; February 1904–October 1904; extant issues held in Meiji Newspaper and Magazine Collection, University of Tokyo.

Seigi no Hikari, Tokyo: Nihon Bōshoku Rōdō Kumiai, Nos 1–72, 1926–1935, held in Ōhara Social Research Institute.

Shinshin Fujin, Tokyo: Shinshin Fujinkai, Nishikawa Fumiko (ed.); February

1913–September 1923. Some issues are held in the Ōhara Social Research Institute, Hōsei University.

Yamakawa Hitoshi and Kikue, *Musansha Undō to Fujin no Mondai*, Tokyo: Hakuyōsha, October 1928.

Yamakawa Kikue, Sakai Magara, Nakasone Sadayo, Ide Toshi, *Musan Fujin e*, Tokyo: Chōryūsha Shuppanbu, 1925.

Journals available in facsimile editions:

Chokugen (facsimile edition: Rōdō Undōshi Kenkyūkai (eds), *Meiji Shakai Shugi Shiryō Shū 1*, Tokyo: Meiji Bunken Shiryō Kankōkai, 1960).

Fujin Sensen, Tokyo: Musan Fujin Geijutsu Renmei, Takamure Itsue (ed.), March 1930–June 1931 (facsimile edition: Tokyo: Ryokuin Shobō, 1983).

Fujo Shinbun, Fukushima Shirō (ed.), 1901–1941.

Heimin Shinbun, 1903–5 (facsimile edition: Rōdō Undōshi Kenkyūkai (eds). *Meiji Shakai Shugi Shiryō Shū: Bessatsu 3*, Tokyo: Meiji Bunken Shiryō Kankōkai, 1960).

Hikari (facsimile edition: Rōdō Undōshi Kenkyūkai (eds), *Meiji Shakai Shugi Shiryō Shū 2*, Tokyo: Meiji Bunken Shiryō Kankōkai, 1960).

Jogaku Zasshi (facsimile edition: Kyōto: Rinsen Shoten, 1967, 16 Vols.)

Katei Zasshi, April 1903–July 1909, (facsimile edition: Tokyo: Fuji Shuppan, 1983).

Nyonin Geijutsu, Tokyo: Musan Fujin Geijutsu Renmei, Hasegawa Shigure (ed.), 1928–1931 (facsmile edition: Tokyo: Ryūkei Shosha, 1981).

Rōdō Fujin (facsimile edition: Tokyo: Hōsei Daigaku Ōhara Shakai Mondai Kenkyūji Sōdōmei Gojūnen Shi Kankō Iinkai, 6 Vols, 1978–85).

Seitō, 1911–16 (facsimile edition: Tokyo: Meiji Bunken, 10 Vols, 1970).

Sekai Fujin, 1907–1909 (facsimile edition: Tokyo: Ryūkei Shosha).

Shinkigen (facsimile edition: Rōdō Undōshi Kenkyūkai (eds). *Meiji Shakai Shugi Shiryō Shū 3*, Tokyo: Meiji Bunken Shiryō Kankōkai, 1960).

Yūai Fujin, Tokyo: Yūaikai, August 1916–February 1917; July 1917–June 1918 (facsimile edition: Tokyo: Hōsei Daigaku Ōhara Shakai Mondai Kenkyūji Sōdōmei Gojūnen Shi Kankō Iinkai, 3 Vols, 1978–80).

Autobiographies, Memoirs, Collected Works, Monographs

Arahata Kanson, *Kanson Jiden*, Tokyo: Iwanami Shoten, 1975.

Fukuda Hideko, *Warawa no Hanseigai*, Tokyo: 1904 (reprinted by: Iwanami Shoten, 1958).

Fukuda Hideko, *Warawa no Omoide*, Tokyo, 1905; reprinted in Odagiri Susumu (ed.), *Meiji Bungaku Shū 84: Meiji Shakai Shugi Bungaku Shū 2*, Tokyo: Chikuma Shobō, 1965.

Hiratsuka Raichō, *Genshi Josei wa Taiyō de Atta – Hiratsuka Raichō Jiden*, Tokyo: Ōtsuki Shoten, 4 Vols, 1971.

Hosoi Wakizō, *Jokō Aishi*, Tokyo: 1925 (reprinted by: Iwanami Shoten, 1954).

Ichikawa Fusae, *Ichikawa Fusae Jiden: Senzen Hen*, Tokyo: Shinjuku Shobō, 1974.

Itō Noe, *Itō Noe Zenshū*, Tokyo: Gakugei Shorin, 2 Vols, 1973.

Katayama Sen, *Nihon no Rōdō Undō*, Tokyo: Iwanami Shoten, 1952.

Nishikawa Fumiko. *Heiminsha no Onna: Nishikawa Fumiko Jiden*, Amano Shigeru (ed.), Tokyo: Aoyamakan, 1984.

Sakai Toshihiko, *Sakai Toshihiko Josei Ron Shū*, Suzuki Yūko (ed.), Tokyo: San-Ichi Shobō, 1983.

Taishūtō Jigyōbu (eds), *Puroretaria Kashū*, 23/5/1931.

Tajima Hide, *Hitosuji no Michi: Fujin Kaihō no Tatakai Gojūnen*, Tokyo: Aoki Shoten, 1968.

Tanino Setsu, *Fujin kōjō kantoku kan no kiroku*, Tokyo: Domesu Shuppan, Tokyo, 1985.

Tatewaki Sadayo, *Aru Henreki no Jijōden*, Tokyo: Sōdō Bunka, 1980.

Wada Ei, *Tomioka Nikki*, Tokyo: Kōdansha Bunkō, 1976.

Yamakawa Kikue, *Onna Nidai no Ki*, Tokyo: Heibonsha, 1972.

Yamakawa Kikue, *Yamakawa Kikue Josei Kaihō Ronshū*, Tokyo: Iwanami Shoten, Suzuki Yūko (ed.), 1984.

Yamakawa Kikue, *Yamakawa Kikue Shū*, Tokyo: Iwanami Shoten, Tanaka Sumiko and Yamakawa Shinsaku (eds), 11 Vols, 1981–2.

Yamanouchi Mina, *Yamanouchi Mina Jiden: Jūnisai no Bōseki Jokō kara no Shōgai*, Tokyo: Shinjuku Shobō, 1975.

Yokoyama Gennosuke, *Nihon no Kasō Shakai*, Tokyo: Kyōbunkan 1899 (reprinted by: Iwanami Shoten, Tokyo: 1949).

Document Collections

Ezashi Akiko (ed.), *Ai to Sei no Jiyū: Ie kara no Kaihō*, Tokyo: Shakai Hyōronsha, 1989.

Hayashi Shigeru and Nishida Taketoshi (eds), *Nihon Heimin Shinbun Ronsetsu Shū*, Tokyo: Iwanami Shoten, 1961.

Ienaga Saburō (ed.), *Meiji Bungaku Zenshū 12*, Tokyo: Chikuma Shobō, 1965.

Kanō Mikiyo (ed.), *Jiga no Kanata e: Kindai o Koeru Feminizumu*, Tokyo: Shakai Hyōronsha, 1990.

Kōuchi Nobuko (ed.), *Shiryō: Bosei Hogo Ronsō*, Tokyo: Domesu Shuppan, 1984.

Odagiri Susumu (ed.), *Meiji Bungaku Zenshū 84: Meiji Shakai Shugi Bungaku Shū 2*, Tokyo: Chikuma Shobō, 1965.

Ogata Akiko and Nagahara Kazuko (eds), *Feminizumu Ryōran: Fuyu no Jidai e no Hōka*, Tokyo: Shakai Hyōronsha, 1990.

Sekiyama Naotarō (ed.), *Shoki Shakai Shugi Shiryō*, Tokyo, 1959.

Suzuki Yūko (ed.), *Shiryō: Heiminsha no Onnatachi*, Tokyo: Fuji Shuppan, 1986.

Suzuki Yūko (ed.), *Josei: Hangyaku to Kakumei to Teikō to*, Tokyo: Shakai Hyōronsha, 1990.

Tanaka Sōgorō (ed.), *Shiryō: Nihon Shakai Undō Shi*, Tokyo: Tōzai Shuppansha, 2 Vols, 1948.

Yuzawa, K., et al. (eds), *Nihon Fujin Mondai Shiryō Shūsei*, Tokyo: Domesu Shuppan, 10 Vols, 1976–1980.

Oral Histories

Makise Kikue, *Hitamuki no Onnatachi*, Tokyo: Asahi Shinbunsha, 1976.

Rekishi Hyōron Henshūbu, *Kindai Nihon Joseishi e no Shōgen*, Tokyo: Domesu Shuppan, 1979.

Watanabe Etsuji and Suzuki Yūko (eds), *Tatakai ni Ikite – Senzen Fujin Undō e no Shōgen*, Tokyo: Domesu Shuppan, 1980.

Watanabe Etsuji and Suzuki Yūko (eds), *Undō ni kaketa Onnatachi*, Tokyo: Domesu Shuppan, 1980.

Secondary Sources: Japanese

Akamatsu Tsuneko Kenshōkai, *Zassō no Yō ni Takumashiku: Akamatsu Tsuneko no Ashiato*, Tokyo, 1977.

Ezashi Akiko, *Sameyo Onnatachi*, Tokyo: Ōtsuki Shoten, 1980.

Fukushima Miyoko, 'Shūkan Fujo Shinbun ni miru 1930nendai Fujin Zasshi no Teikō to Zasetsu, *Agora*, No. 24, 20/5/1981, pp. 114–42.

Horiba Kiyoko, *Seitō no Jidai*, Tokyo: Iwanami Shoten, 1988.

Ide Fumiko, *Seitō no Onnatachi*, Tokyo: Kaien Shobō, 1975.

Inoue Kiyoshi, *Nihon Josei Shi*, Tokyo: San'Ichi Shobō, 1967 [revised edition; original edition: 1948].

Inumaru Giichi, 'Nihon ni okeru Marukusu shugi Fujinron no Ayumi: Senzen-hen', in Joseishi Sōgō Kenkyūkai (eds), *Nihon Joseishi 5: Gendai*, Tokyo: Tokyo Daigaku Shuppankai, 1990, pp. 149–92.

Ishizuki Shizue, '1930nendai no Musan Fujin Undō', in Joseishi Sōgō Kenkyūkai (eds), *Nihon Joseishi 5: Gendai*, Tokyo: Tokyo Daigaku Shuppankai, 1990, pp. 193–226.

Itoya Toshio, *Kanno Suga*, Tokyo: Iwanami Shoten, 1970.

Itoya Toshio, *Josei Kaihō no Senkushatachi*, Tokyo: Shimizu Shoin, 1975.

Joseishi Sōgō Kenkyūkai (eds), *Nihon Joseishi*, Tokyo: Tokyo Daigaku Shuppan-kai, 1990, 5 Vols.

Kanatani Chieko, 'Rōdōsha hogohō henkō shi ni miru bosei hogo', *Agora*, No. 89, 10/8/84, pp. 39–66.

Kaneko Sachiko, 'Taishōki ni okeru seiyō josei kaihō ron juyō no hōhō – Ellen Key *Ren'ai to kekkon* o tegakari ni', *Shakai Kagaku Jaanaru*, No. 24, October 1985.

Kano Masanao, 'Fusen Kakutoku Dōmei no Seiritsu to Tenkai: Manshū Jihen no Boppatsu Made', *Nihon Rekishi*, No. 319, 1974, pp. 68–85.

Kano Masanao and Horiba Kiyoko, *Takamure Itsue*, Tokyo: Asahi Shinbunsha, 1977.

Kindai Josei Bunka Shi Kenkyū Kai (eds), *Fujin Zasshi no Yoake*, Tokyo: Taikūsha, 1989.

Kodama Katsuko, *Fujin Sanseiken Undō Shōshi*, Tokyo: Domesu Shuppan, 1981.

Kōuchi Nobuko, '"Bosei Hogo Ronsō" no Rekishiteki Igi: "Ronsō" Kara "Undō" e no Tsunagari', *Rekishi Hyōron*, No. 195, November 1966, pp. 28–41.

Makise Kikue, *Kutsumi Fusako no Koyomi: Meiji Shakai Shugi kara Zoruge Jiken e*, Tokyo: Shisō no Kagakusha, 1975.

Matsumoto Katsuhira, *Nihon Shakai Shugi Engeki Shi: Meiji Taishō Hen*, Tokyo: Chikuma Shobō, 1975.

Miki Sukako, 'Meiji no Fujin Zasshi o Tadoru', in Kindai Josei Bunka Shi Kenkyū Kai (eds), in *Fujin Zasshi no Yoake*, Tokyo: Taikūsha, 1989.

Miyake Yoshiko, 'Rekishi no naka no jendaa: Meiji Shakaishugisha no Gensetsu ni arawareta Josei, Josei Rōdōsha', in Hara Hiroko et al. (eds), *Jendaa (Library Sokan Shakaigaku 2)*, Tokyo: Shinseisha, 1994, pp. 141–165.

Murakami Nobuhiko, 'Fujin Mondai to Fujin Kaihō Undō', *Iwanami Kōza Nihon Rekishi, 18: Kindai*, Tokyo: Iwanami Shinsho, 1972.

Murakami Nobuhiko, *Nihon No Fujin Mondai*, Tokyo: Iwanami Shinsho, 1978.

Murata Shizuko, *Fukuda Hideko*, Tokyo: Iwanami Shoten, 1959.
Nishikawa Yūko, *Mori no Ie no Miko: Takamure Itsue*, Tokyo: Shinchōsha, 1982.
Nobeji Kiyoe, *Josei Kaihō Shisō no Genryū: Iwamoto Zenji to Jogaku Zasshi*, Tokyo: Azekura Shobō, 1984.
Ogata Akiko, *Nyonin Geijutsu no Sekai*, Tokyo: Domesu Shuppan, 1980.
Ogata Akiko, *Nyonin Geijutsu no Hitobito*, Tokyo: Domesu Shuppan, 1981.
Ōki Motoko. 'Meiji Shakai Shugi Undō to Josei', in Joseishi Sōgō Kenkyūkai (eds), *Nihon Josei Shi 4: Kindai*, Tokyo: Tokyo Daigaku Shuppankai, 1990, pp. 115–48.
Sakurai Kinue, 'Hyōgikai Fujinbu no Katsudō ni tsuite', Parts 1–3; *Rekishi Hyōron*, March 1976; March 1977; October 1977.
Sakurai Kinue, *Bosei Hogo Undōshi*, Tokyo: Domesu Shuppan, 1987.
Sotozaki Mitsuhiro and Okabe Masako (eds), *Yamakawa Kikue no Kōseki*, Tokyo: Domesu Shuppan, 1979.
Suzuki Yūko, 'Tachiagaru Onnatachi', *Jūgoshi Nōto*, No. 2, 1978, pp. 61–3.
— 'Manshū Jihen to Musan Fujin Undō', *Jūgoshi Nōto*, No. 3, 1979.
— 'Sakai Toshihiko no Josei Ron Nōto', *Undō Shi Kenkyū*, No. 12, August 1983.
— 'Shakai Undō Shi no Naka no Josei', *Dai Nikai Yamakawa Kikue Kinen Fujin Mondai Kenkyū Shōreikin Zōteishiki Kiroku*, Tokyo: Yamakawa Kikue Kinenkai, 1983, pp. 24–36.
— *Joseishi o Hiraku 1: Haha to Onna*, Tokyo: Miraisha, 1989.
— *Jokō to Rōdō Sōgi*, Tokyo: Renga Shobō, 1989.
— *Josei to Rōdō Kumiai*, Tokyo: Renga Shobō, 1991.
Tachi Kaoru, 'Ryōsai Kenbo', in Joseigaku Kenkyūkai (eds), *Kōza Joseigaku 1: Onna no Imêji*, Tokyo: Keisō Shobō, 1984.
Tachi Kaoru, 'Kenkyū Nōto: Hiratsuka Raichō to Ofudesaki', *Ochanomizu Joshi Daigaku Josei Bunka Shiryōkan Hō*, No. 7, 1986.
Takamure Itsue, *Takamure Itsue Zenshū*, Hashimoto Kenzō (ed.), Tokyo: Rironsha, 1966–67, 10 Vols.
Takamure Itsue, *Josei no Rekishi*, Tokyo: Kōdansha Bunkō, 1972, 2 Vols.
Wakita Haruko (ed.), *Bosei o Tou: Rekishiteki Henkō*, Kyōto: Jinbun Shoin, 1985, 2 Vols.
Wakita Haruko et al. (eds), *Nihon Josei Shi*, Tokyo: Yoshikawa Kōbunkan, 1986.
Watashitachi no Rekishi o Tsuzuru Kai, *Fujin Zasshi Kara Mita 1930nendai*, Tokyo: Dōjidaisha, 1987.
Yamada Seizaburō, *Puroretaria Bungaku Shi*, Tokyo: Rironsha, 2 Vols.
Yamada Takako, 'Atarashii Onna', in Joseigaku Kenkyūkai (eds), *Kōza Joseigaku 1: Onna no Imêji*, Tokyo: Keisō Shobō, 1984, pp. 210–34.
Yamamoto Shigemi, *Aa Nomugi Tōge*, Tokyo, 1977.
Yoneda Sayoko, 'Boseishugi no Rekishiteki Igi: *Fujin Sensen* Jidai no Hiratsuka Raichō o Chūshin ni', in Joseishi Sōgō Kenkyūkai (eds), *Nihon Joseishi 5: Gendai*, Tokyo: Tokyo Daigaku Shuppankai, pp. 115–48.

Secondary Sources: English

Ackroyd, Joyce, 'Women in Feudal Japan', *Transactions of the Asiatic Society of Japan*, Third Series, Vol. 7, No. 3, November 1959, pp. 31–68.
Anderson, Benedict, *Imagined Communities: Reflections on the Origins and Spread of Nationalism*, London: Verso, 1983.

Ayusawa, Iwao, F., *A History of Labor in Modern Japan*, Honolulu: East–West Center Press, 1966.

Bamba, Nobuya and Howes, John F., *Pacifism in Japan: The Christian and Socialist Tradition*, Vancouver: University of British Columbia Press, 1978.

Barshay, Andrew, *State and Intellectual in Japan: The Public Man in Crisis*, Berkeley: University of California Press, 1988.

Beckmann, George and Ōkubo, Genji, *The Japanese Communist Party 1922–1945*, Stanford: Stanford University Press, 1969.

Bernstein, Gail Lee, *Japanese Marxist: A Portrait of Kawakami Hajime 1879–1946*, Cambridge, Massachusetts: Harvard Council on East Asian Studies, 1990 edn.

Bernstein, Gail Lee (ed.), *Recreating Japanese Women, 1600–1945*, Berkeley: University of California Press, 1991.

Bethel, Diana, 'Visions of a Humane Society: Feminist Thought in Taishō Japan', *Feminist International*, No. 2, 1980.

Blacker, Carmen, *The Japanese Enlightenment: A Study of the Writings of Fukuzawa Yukichi*, Cambridge: Cambridge University Press, 1964.

Bock, Gisela and James, Susan (eds), *Beyond Equality and Difference: Citizenship, Feminist Politics and Female Subjectivity*, London: Routledge, 1992.

Bowen [Raddeker], Hélène, 'Women and Treason in Prewar Japan: The Prison Poetry of Kanno Suga and Kaneko Fumiko', *Lilith*, No. 5, (Spring 1988), pp. 9–25.

Bowen [Raddeker], Hélène, 'Victims as Victors, Life as Death: Representation and Empowerment in the Works of Kanno Suga and Kaneko Fumiko', Unpublished PhD Thesis, La Trobe University, 1992.

Bowen, Roger, *Rebellion and Democracy in Meiji Japan*, Berkeley: University of California Press, 1980.

Bowring, Richard, 'The Female Hand in Heian Japan: A First Reading', in Domna C. Stanton (ed.), *The Female Autograph*, Chicago: University of Chicago Press, 1984, pp. 49–56.

Braisted, William (ed./trans.), *Meiroku Zasshi: Journal of the Japanese Enlightenment*, Cambridge, Massachusetts: Harvard University Press, 1976.

Chakrabarty, Dipesh, 'Postcoloniality and the Artifice of History: Who Speaks for Indian Pasts?', *Representations*, 37, 1992, pp. 161–85.

Chakrabarty, Dipesh, 'The Difference-Deferral of (a) Colonial Modernity: Public Debates on Domesticity in British Bengal', *History Workshop Journal*, No. 36, (Autumn 1993), pp. 1–34.

Chatterjee, Partha, 'The Nationalist Resolution of the Women's Question', in Kumkum Sangari and Sudesh Vaid (eds), *Recasting Women: Essays in Indian History*, New Brunswick: Rutgers, 1990, pp. 233–53.

Chow, Rey, 'Violence in the Other Country: China as Crisis, Spectacle, and Woman', in Chandra Talpade Mohanty, et al. (eds), *Third World Women and the Politics of Feminism*, Bloomington: Indiana University Press, 1991, pp. 81–100.

Chow, Rey, *Woman and Chinese Modernity: The Politics of Reading Between East and West*, Minnesota: University of Minnesota Press, 1991.

Conroy, Hilary, et al. (eds), *Japan in Transition: Thought and Action in the Meiji Era, 1868–1912*, Cranbery, New Jersey: Associated University Presses, 1984.

Coward, Rosalind, *Patriarchal Precedents: Sexuality and Social Relations*, London: Routledge & Kegan Paul, 1983.

Cranny-Francis, Anne, *Feminist Fiction: Feminist Uses of Generic Fiction*, Cambridge: Polity Press, 1990.

Crump, John, *The Origins of Socialist Thought in Japan*, Beckenham, Kent: Croom Helm, 1983.

Damousi, Joy, 'Socialist Women and Gendered Space: The Anti-Conscription and Anti-War Campaigns of 1914–1918', *Labour History*, No. 60, May 1991, pp. 1–15.

Damousi, Joy, '"The Woman Comrade": Equal or Different?', *Women's History Review*, Vol. 2, No. 3, 1993, pp. 387–94.

Damousi, Joy, *Women Come Rally: Socialism, Communism and Gender in Australia, 1890–1955*, Melbourne: Oxford University Press, 1994.

Davin, Anna, 'Imperialism and Motherhood', *History Workshop*, (Spring 1978), pp. 9–65.

Dijkstra, Bram, *Idols of Perversity: Images of Feminine Evil in Fin-de-Siècle Culture*, Oxford: Oxford University Press, 1986.

Dijkstra, Sandra, *Flora Tristan: Feminism in the Age of George Sand*, London: Pluto Press, 1992.

Dower, John, 'E. H. Norman, Japan, and the Uses of History', in E. H. Norman, *The Origins of the Modern Japanese State*, (ed. John Dower), New York: Pantheon Asia Library, 1975.

Freiberg, Freda, 'Tales of Kageyama', *East–West Film Journal*, Vol. 6, No. 1, 1992.

Garon, Sheldon, *The State and Labour in Modern Japan*, Berkeley: University of California Press, 1988.

Garon, Sheldon, 'The World's Oldest Debate? Prostitution and the State in Imperial Japan, 1900–1945' *American Historical Review*, June 1993, pp. 710–32.

Garon, Sheldon, '"Women's Groups and the Japanese State" Contending Approaches to Political Integration, 1890–1945', *Journal of Japanese Studies*, Vol. 19, No. 1, 1993, pp. 5–41.

Gluck, Carol, *Japan's Modern Myths: The Ideology of the Late Meiji Period*, Princeton, New Jersey: Princeton University Press, 1985.

Goldstein, S. and Shinoda, S., *Tangled Hair*, Lafayette, 1971.

Gordon, Andrew, *Labor and Imperial Democracy in Prewar Japan*, Berkeley: University of California Press, 1991.

Gordon, Andrew, *The Evolution of Labour Relations in Japan, Heavy Industry 1853–1955*, Cambridge, Massachusetts: Harvard University Press, 1985.

Hane, Mikiso, *Peasants, Rebels and Outcastes: The Underside of Modern Japan*, New York: Pantheon, 1983.

Hane, Mikiso (ed.), *Reflections on the Way to the Gallows: Rebel Women in Prewar Japan*, Berkeley: University of California Press, 1988.

Harada, S., *Labour Conditions in Japan*, New York: Columbia University Press, New York, 1928.

Harootunian, H. D., 'Introduction: A Sense of an Ending and the problem of Taishō', in B. S. Silberman and H. D. Harootunian (eds), *Japan in Crisis: Essays on Taishō Democracy*, Princeton, New Jersey: Princeton University Press, 1974, pp. 3–28.

Hatoyama, Kazuo and Sakamoto Saburō, 'Japanese Personal Legislation', in Ōkuma Shigenobu (eds), *Fifty Years of New Japan*, New York: E. P. Dutton, 1909, Vol. 1, pp. 251–80.

Hayakawa Noriyo, 'Sexuality and the State: The Early Meiji Debate on Concubinage and Prostitution', in Vera Mackie (ed.), *Feminism and the State in*

Modern Japan, Melbourne: Japanese Studies Centre, 1995, pp. 31–40.

Hirai, Atsuko, *Individualism and Socialism: The Life and Thought of Kawai Eijirō (1891–1944)*, Cambridge, Massachusetts: Harvard Council on East Asian Studies, 1986.

Hobsbawm, Eric and Ranger, Terence (eds), *The Invention of Tradition*, Cambridge: Cambridge University Press, 1983.

Hobsbawm, Eric, 'Man and Woman: Images on the Left', in *Worlds of Labour: Further Studies in the History of Labour*, London: Weidenfeld & Nicolson, 1984.

Hoston, Germaine, *Marxism and the Crisis of Development in Prewar Japan*, Princeton, New Jersey: Princeton University Press, 1986.

Hunter, Janet, 'Factory Legislation and Employer Resistance: The Abolition of Night Work in the Cotton Spinning Industry', in Tsunehiko Yui and Keiichirō Nakagawa (eds), *Japanese Management in Historical Perspective*, Tokyo: University of Tokyo, 1989, pp. 243–72.

Hunter, Janet, 'Labour in the Japanese Silk Industry in the 1870s: The Tomioka Nikki of Wada Ei', in Gordon Daniels (ed.), *Europe Interprets Japan*, Tenterden, Kent: Paul Norbury Publications, pp. 20–5.

Ike Nobutaka, *The Beginnings of Political Democracy in Japan*, Baltimore: Johns Hopkins Press, 1950.

Irokawa Daikichi, 'Freedom and the Concept of People's Rights', *Japan Quarterly*, Volume XIV, No. 2, April–June 1967, pp. 175–83.

Ishii Ryosuke, *Japanese Legislation in the Meiji Era*, Tokyo: Pan-Pacific Press, The Centenary Culture Council, 1958.

Ishimoto Shidzue, *Facing Two Ways: The Story of My Life*, New York: Farrar and Rinehart, 1935 (reprinted by: Stanford: Stanford University Press, 1986).

Iwamoto, Yoshio, 'Aspects of the Proletarian Literature Movement', in B. S. Silberman, and H. D. Harootunian (eds), *Japan in Crisis: Essays on Taishō Democracy*, Princeton, New Jersey: Princeton University Press, 1974, pp. 156–82.

Jansen, Marius, 'Ōi Kentarō: Radicalism and Chauvinism', *Far Eastern Quarterly*, Vol. 2, No. 3, May 1952, pp. 305–16.

Kaneko Fumiko, *The Prison Memoirs of a Japanese Woman*, trans. Jean Inglis, New York: M. E. Sharpe, 1991.

Keene, Donald, *Dawn to the West: Japanese Literature of the Modern Era*, New York: Henry Holt and Company, 1984.

Kidd, Yasue Aoki, *Women Workers in the Japanese Cotton Mills 1880–1920*, Cornell University East Asian Papers, 1978.

Kinmonth, Earl J., *The Self-Made Man in Meiji Japanese Thought*, Berkeley: University of California Press, 1981.

Kiyooka Eiichi, *Fukuzawa Yukichi on Japanese Women: Selected Works*, Tokyo: University of Tokyo Press, 1988.

Kōsaka, Masaaki, *Japanese Thought in the Meiji Era*, Tokyo: Pan-Pacific Press, The Centenary Culture Council, 1958.

Kublin, Hyman, 'Japanese Socialists and the Russo–Japanese War', *Journal of Modern History*, Vol. XXII, No. 4, December 1950.

Kublin, Hyman, *Asian Revolutionary: The Life of Sen Katayama*, Princeton, New Jersey: Princeton University Press, 1964.

Lake, Marilyn, 'Mission Impossible: How Men Gave Birth to the Australian Nation – Nationalism, Gender and Other Seminal Acts' *Gender and History*, Vol. 4, No. 3, (Autumn 1992), pp. 305–22.

Large, Stephen S., *The Rise of Labour in Japan: The Yūaikai 1912–1919*, Tokyo: Sophia University Press, 1972.

— 'Revolutionary Worker: Watanabe Masanosuke and the Japanese Communist Party, 1922–1928', *Asian Profile*, Vol. 3, No. 4, August 1975, pp. 371–90.

— 'The Romance of Revolution in Japanese Anarchism and Communism During the Taishō Period', *Modern Asian Studies*, Volume II, No. 3, July 1977.

— *Organized Workers and Socialist Politics in Interwar Japan*, Cambridge: Cambridge University Press, 1981.

Lebra Joyce et al. (eds), *Women in Changing Japan*, Berkeley: University of California Press, 1976.

Lewis, Michael, *Rioters and Citizens: Mass Protest in Imperial Japan*, Berkeley: University of California Press, 1987.

Lloyd, Genevieve, 'Selfhood, War and Masculinity', in Carole Pateman and Elizabeth Gross (eds), *Feminist Challenges: Social and Political Theory*, Sydney: Allen & Unwin, 1986, pp. 63–76.

Mackie, Vera, 'Feminist Politics in Japan', *New Left Review*, January–February 1988.

— 'Motherhood and Pacifism in Japan, 1900–1937', *Hecate*, Vol. 14, No. 2, 1988.

— *Imagining Liberation: Feminism and Socialism in Early Twentieth Century Japan*, Papers in Feminist Cultural Studies No. 1, Women's Research Centre, University of Western Sydney: Nepean, 1995.

— 'Engaging with the State: Socialist Women in Imperial Japan', in Vera Mackie (ed.), *Feminism and the State in Modern Japan*, Melbourne: Japanese Studies Centre, 1995.

— 'Narratives of Struggle: Writing and the Making of Socialist Women in Japan', in Elise Tipton (ed.), *Society and State in Interwar Japan*, London: Routledge, forthcoming.

— '"In a Woman's Body": Gender and Activism in Meiji Japan', in Freda Freiberg and Vera Mackie (eds), *Re-Orienting the Body*, forthcoming.

Marsland, Stephen E., *The Birth of the Japanese Labour Movement: Takano Fusatarō and the Rōdō Kumiai Kiseikai*, Honolulu: University of Hawaii Press, 1989.

Mason, Mary G., 'The Other Voice: Autobiographies of Women Writers', in James Olney (ed.), *Autobiography: Essays Theoretical and Critical*, Princeton, New Jersey: Princeton University Press, 1980.

McLaren, W. W. (ed.), 'Japanese Government Documents', *Transactions of the Asiatic Society of Japan*, Vol. LXII, Part II, 1914.

Mitchell, Jane, 'Women's National Mobilization in Japan 1901–1942', Unpublished Honours thesis, University of Adelaide, 1986.

Mitchell, Richard, *Thought Control in Prewar Japan*, Ithaca: Cornell University Press, 1976.

Mitchell, Richard H., *Censorship in Imperial Japan*, Princeton, New Jersey: Princeton University Press, 1983.

Miyake Yoshiko, 'Doubling Expectations: Motherhood and Women's Factory Work in the 1930s and 1940s', in Gail Lee Bernstein (ed.), *Recreating Japanese Women, 1600–1945*, Berkeley: University of California Press, 1991, pp. 267–95.

Miyamoto, Ken, 'Itō Noe and the Bluestockings', *Japan Interpreter*, Vol. 10, No. 2, Autumn 1975, pp. 190–204.

Mohanty, Chandra Talpade, 'Cartographies of Struggle: Third World Women and the Politics of Feminism', in Chandra Talpade Mohanty et al. (eds),

Third World Women and the Politics of Feminism, Bloomington: Indiana University Press, 1991, pp. 1–47.

Mohanty, Chandra Talpade et al. (eds), *Third World Women and the Politics of Feminism*, Bloomington: Indiana University Press, 1991.

Monnet, Livia, '"In the Beginning Woman was the Sun": Autobiographies of Modern Japanese Women Writers', *Japan Forum*, Vol. 1, No. 1, April 1989, pp. 55–81; and Vol. 1, No. 2, October 1989, pp. 197–233.

Morris-Suzuki, Tessa, *A History of Japanese Economic Thought*, London: Routledge.

Murray, Patricia, 'Ichikawa Fusae and the Lonely Red Carpet', *Japan Interpreter*, Vol. 10, No. 2, (Autumn 1975).

Nagai, Michio, 'Westernisation and Japanisation: The Early Meiji Transformation of Education', in D. Shively (ed.), *Tradition and Modernisation in Japanese Culture*, Princeton, New Jersey: Princeton University Press, 1971, pp. 35–76.

Nead, Lynda, *Myths of Sexuality: Representations of Women in Victorian Britain*, Oxford: Basil Blackwell, 1988.

Noguchi, Takehiko, 'Love and Death in the Early Modern Novel: Japan and America', in Albert M. Craig (ed.), *Japan: A Comparative View*, Cambridge, Massachusetts: Harvard University Press, 1972.

Nolte, Sharon H., 'Women's Rights and Society's Needs: Japan's 1931 Suffrage Bill', *Comparative Studies in Society and History*, 1986, pp. 690–713.

Nolte, Sharon Hamilton. 'Individualism in Taishō Japan', *Journal of Asian Studies*, Vol. XLIII, No. 4, August 1984, pp. 667–84.

Nolte, Sharon H., *Liberalism in Modern Japan: Ishibashi Tanzan and His Teachers, 1905–1960*, Berkeley: University of California Press, 1987.

Notehelfer, F. G., *Kōtoku Shūsui: Portrait of a Japanese Radical*, Cambridge: Cambridge University Press, 1971.

Passin, Herbert, *Society and Education in Japan*, New York: Columbia University Press, 1965.

Pateman, Carole *The Sexual Contract*, Cambridge: Polity Press, 1988.

Pathak, Zathia and Rajan, Rajeswari Sunder, 'Shahbano', in Judith Butler and Joan W. Scott (eds), *Feminists Theorize the Political*, New York: Routledge, 1992, pp. 257–79.

Phelan, Shane, 'Specificity: Beyond Equality and Difference', *Differences: A Journal of Feminist Cultural Studies*, Vol. 3, No. 1, 1991.

Pierson, John D., 'The Early Liberal Thought of Tokutomi Sohō: Some Problems of Western Social Theory in Meiji Japan', *Monumenta Nipponica*, Vol. XXIX, 1974, pp. 199–224.

Pittau, J., *Political Thought in Early Meiji Japan 1868–1889*, Cambridge, Massachusetts: Harvard University Press, 1967.

Pollock, Griselda, 'Feminism/Foucault – Surveillance/Sexuality', in Norman Bryson, Michael Ann Holly and Keith Moxey (eds), *Visual Culture: Images and Interpretations*, Hanover & London: Wesleyan University Press, 1994.

Pyle, K. P., *The New Generation in Meiji Japan: Problems of Cultural Identity 1885–1895*, Stanford: Stanford University Press, 1969.

Rajan, Rajeswari Sunder, *Real and Imagined Women: Gender, Culture and Postcolonialism*, London: Routledge, 1993.

Reich, Pauline and Fukuda, Atsuko, 'Japan's Literary Feminists', *Signs*, Vol. 2, No. 1, (Autumn 1976).

Riley, Denise, '*Am I That Name?*' *Feminism and the Category of Women in History*, London: Macmillan, 1988.

Riley, Denise, 'Left Critiques of the Family' in Cambridge Women's Studies Group (eds), *Women in Society*, London: Virago, 1981.

Robins-Mowry, Dorothy, *The Hidden Sun: Women of Modern Japan*, Boulder, Colorado: Westview Press, 1983.

Rowbotham, Sheila, *Hidden From History*, London: Pluto Press, 1973.

Rowbotham, Sheila, et al., *Beyond the Fragments: Feminism and the Making of Socialism*, London: Merlin Press, 1979.

Satō, Barbara Hamill, 'The *Moga* Sensation: Perceptions of the *Modan Gâru* in Japanese Intellectual Circles During the 1920s' *Gender and History*, Vol. 5, No. 3, Autumn 1993, pp. 363–81.

Scott, James C., *Weapons of the Weak: Everyday Forms of Peasant Resistance*, Newhaven: Yale University Press, 1985.

Scott, Joan Wallach, *Gender and the Politics of History*, New York: Columbia University Press, 1988.

Shapcott, Jennifer, 'The Red Chrysanthemum: Yamakawa Kikue and the Socialist Women's Movement in Pre-War Japan', *Papers on Far Eastern History*, No. 35, March 1987, pp. 1–30.

Shea, G. T., *Leftwing Literature in Japan*, Tokyo: Hōsei University Press, 1964.

Sievers, Sharon L., 'Feminist Criticism in Japanese Politics in the 1880s: The Case of Kishida Toshiko', *Signs*, Vol. 6, No. 4, Summer 1981, pp. 602–16.

Sievers, Sharon L., *Flowers in Salt: The Beginnings of Feminist Consciousness in Meiji Japan*, Stanford: Stanford University Press, 1983.

Silverberg, Miriam, *Changing Song: The Marxist Manifestos of Nakano Shigeharu*, Princeton, New Jersey: Princeton University Press, 1990.

Silverberg, Miriam, 'The Modern Girl as Militant', in Gail Lee Bernstein (ed.), *Recreating Japanese Women, 1600–1945*, Berkeley: University of California Press, 1991, pp. 239–66.

Smith, Sidonie, *A Poetics of Women's Autobiography: Marginality and the Fictions of Self-Representation*, Bloomington: Indiana University Press, 1987.

Smith, T. C., *Native Sources of Japanese Industrialization, 1750–1920*, Berkeley: University of California Press, 1988.

Smith, T. C., *The Agrarian Origins of Modern Japan*, Stanford: Stanford University Press, 1959.

Sowerwine, Charles, *Sisters or Citizens? Women and Socialism in France Since 1876*, Cambridge University Press, 1982.

Stanley, Thomas A., *Ōsugi Sakae: Anarchist in Taishō Japan*, Cambridge, Massachusetts: Harvard University Council on East Asian Studies, 1982.

Stanton, Domna C. (ed.), *The Female Autograph*, Chicago: University of Chicago Press, 1984.

Steedman, Carolyn, 'Women's Biography and Autobiography: Forms of History and Histories of Form', in Helen Carr (ed.), *From My Guy to Sci-Fi: Genre and Women's Writing in the Postmodern World*, London: Pandora, 1989.

Tamanoi, Mariko Asano, 'Songs as Weapons: The Culture and History of *Komori* (Nursemaids) in Modern Japan', *Journal of Asian Studies*, Vol. 50, No. 4, November 1991, pp. 793–817.

Tanaka, Hideo and Smith, Malcolm. *The Japanese Legal System*, Tokyo: Sophia University Press, 1976.

Taylor, Barbara, *Eve and the New Jerusalem*, London: Virago, 1983.

Tickner, Lisa, *The Spectacle of Women: Imagery of the Suffrage Campaign 1907–1914*, London: Chatto & Windus, 1987.

Tilly, Louise A., 'Paths of Proletarianisation: Organization of Production, Sexual

Division of Labour, and Women's Collective Action', *Signs*, Vol. 7, No. 2, 1981; reprinted in Barbara Laslett et al. (eds), *Rethinking the Political: Gender, Resistance and the State*, Chicago: University of Chicago Press, 1995, pp. 127–44.

Tipton, Elise, *Japanese Police State: Tokkō in Interwar Japan*, Sydney: Allen & Unwin, 1990.

Tonomura, Hitomi, 'Women and Inheritance in Japan's Early Warrior Society', *Comparative Studies in Society and History*, 1990, pp. 592–623.

Totten, G. O., *The Social Democratic Movement in Prewar Japan*, New Haven: Yale University Press, 1966.

Tsurumi, E. P., 'Female Textile Workers and the Failure of Early Trade Unionism in Japan', *History Workshop Journal*, No. 18, (Autumn, 1984), pp. 3–27.

Tsurumi, E. P., 'Feminism and Anarchism in Japan: Takamure Itsue, 1894–1964', *Bulletin of Concerned Asian Scholars*, Vol. 17, No. 2, April–June 1985, pp. 2–19.

Tsurumi, E. P., *Factory Girls: Women in the Thread Mills of Meiji Japan*, Princeton, New Jersey: Princeton University Press, 1990.

Ushioda, Sharley Conroy, 'Fukuda Hideko and the Women's World of Meiji Japan', in Hilary Conroy et al. (eds), *Japan in Transition: Thought and Action in the Meiji Era*, Cranbury, New Jersey: Associated University Presses, 1984, pp. 276–93.

Ushioda, Sharley Conroy, 'Women and War in Meiji Japan: the Case of Fukuda Hideko, 1865–1927', *Peace and Change: A Journal of Peace Research*, No. 4, (Fall 1977).

Vavich, Dee Ann, 'The Japanese Women's Movement: Ichikawa Fusae, Pioneer in Women's Suffrage', *Monumenta Nipponica*, Vol. XXII, Nos 3–4, 1967, pp. 402–36.

Vernon, Victoria, *Daughters of the Moon: Wish, Will and Social Constraint in the Fiction of Japanese Women*, Berkeley: Institute of East Asian Studies, University of California Press, 1988.

von Mehren, Arthur Taylor (ed.), *Law in Japan*, Cambridge, Massachusetts: Harvard University Press, 1963.

Wakita, Haruko, 'Marriage and Property in Pre-modern Japan from the Perspective of Women's History', *Journal of Japanese Studies*, (Winter 1984).

Walthall, Anne, *Peasant Uprisings in Japan: A Critical Anthology of Peasant Histories*, Chicago: University of Chicago Press, 1991.

Walthall, Anne, 'Devoted Wives/Unruly Women: Invisible Presence in the History of Japanese Social Protest', in Barbara Laslett et al. (eds), *Rethinking the Political: Gender, Resistance and the State*, Chicago: University of Chicago Press, 1995, pp. 282–312.

Watanabe, Yōzō, 'The Family and the Law: The Individualist Premise and Modern Japanese Family Law', in Arthur Taylor von Mehren (ed.), *Law in Japan*, Cambridge, Massachusetts: Harvard University Press, 1963.

Wilson, Sandra, 'Popular Responses to the Manchurian Crisis', unpublished Doctoral Thesis, Oxford University, 1990.

Yamazaki Tomoko, *Yamada Waka: From Prostitute to Feminist Pioneer*, Tokyo: Kōdansha International, 1985.

Yeo, Stephen, 'A New Life: The Religion of Socialism in Britain, 1883–1896', *History Workshop*, No. 4, (Autumn, 1977), pp. 5–56.

Yuval-Davis, Nira and Anthias, Flora (eds), *Woman: Nation: State*, London: Macmillan, 1989.

Index